# CRIMINAL JUSTICE

NOMOS

# XXVII

# NOMOS

**Lieber-Atherton, Publishers**

**New York University Press**

# NOMOS XXVII

Yearbook of the American Society for Political and Legal Philosophy

# CRIMINAL JUSTICE

Edited by

**J. Roland Pennock,** *Swarthmore College*

and

**John W. Chapman,** *University of Pittsburgh*

New York and London · New York University Press · 1985

*Criminal Justice: Nomos XXVII*
edited by J. Roland Pennock and John W. Chapman
Copyright © 1985 by New York University
Manufactured in the United States of America

Library of Congress Cataloging in Publication Data
Main entry under title:

Criminal justice.

(Nomos ; 27)
Bibliography: p.
Includes index.
1. Criminal law—Philosophy—Congresses. 2. Criminal
law—Congresses. 3. Punishment—Congresses.
I. Pennock, J. Roland (James Roland), 1906–
II. Chapman, John Williams, 1923–     . III. Series.
K5018.A3 1983     345'.001     84-14776
ISBN 0-8147-6588-2 (alk. paper)     342.5001

Clothbound editions of New York University Press books are Smyth-sewn and
printed on permanent and durable acid-free paper.

# CONTENTS

vii

## PART III:   CRIMINAL RESPONSIBILITY IN GOVERNMENT

## PART IV:   THE ECONOMIC THEORY OF CRIMINAL LAW

# CONTRIBUTORS

HUGO ADAM BEDAU
*Philosophy, Tufts University*
ANDREW C. BLANAR
*Legal Studies, University of Pittsburgh*
R. B. BRANDT
*Philosophy, University of Michigan*
JULES L. COLEMAN
*Philosophy, University of Arizona*
MICHAEL DAVIS
*Philosophy, Illinois State University*
ALVIN K. KLEVORICK
*Law, Yale University*
MICHAEL S. MOORE
*Law, University of Southern California*
JEFFRIE G. MURPHY
*Philosophy, Arizona State University*
RICHARD A. POSNER
*Judge, U.S. Court of Appeals for the Seventh Circuit*
LAWRENCE ROSEN
*Anthropology, Princeton University*
STEPHEN J. SCHULHOFER
*Law, University of Pennsylvania*
MARTIN SHAPIRO
*Law, University of California, Berkeley*
CHRISTOPHER D. STONE
*Law, University of Southern California*
DENNIS F. THOMPSON
*Politics, Princeton University*
SUSAN WOLF
*Philosophy, University of Maryland*

# PREFACE

In his book *The Political Tradition of the West,* Frederick Watkins, a former president of the American Society for Political and Legal Philosophy, called attention to the fact that Western civilization, as contrasted with the great ethical civilizations of the East, is an essentially legal civilization. Neither Confucius nor Gandhi had much use for the rule of law, and only recently have the Chinese begun to establish a system of criminal law. But the standing and operative ideals of the West have been freedom under law and justice according to the law. These ideals have metaphysical and religious origins.

The ancient Greeks hit upon the idea that we live in an ordered universe; they conceived this order as both natural and moral. Their conception of justice carried the meaning of the divinely appointed order of the world, and this order was enforced by Zeus. As Hugh Lloyd-Jones points out, "A man who commits an injustice against another man offends Zeus in his capacity as the protector of justice, so that if the victim of such an act appeals to Zeus, he will not go without redress."[1] Crime is an offense against the honor of Zeus.

Christianity took over from the Greeks this crucial belief in a morally ordered universe, and the Christian God became, like Zeus, a God of justice. In his monumental work on the legal significance of the "Papal Revolution" of Gregory the Great, Harold J. Berman demonstrates that behind that revolution was "the belief in a God of justice who operates a lawful universe, punishing and rewarding according to principles of proportion, mercifully mitigated in exceptional cases."[2] In this metaphysical perspective, "The Western law of crimes emerged from a belief that justice in and of itself, justice *an sich,* requires that a violation of a law be paid for by a penalty, and that the penalty should be appropriate to the violation."[3] As in the case of

Zeus, crime was seen as an offense against the Christian God's honor and as such must be vindicated.

Today we find an echo of fundamental Greek and Christian conviction in Hyman Gross's "anti-impunity" justification of criminal punishment. Gross says, "the rules of conduct laid down in the criminal law are a powerful social force upon which society is dependent for its very existence, and there is punishment for violation of these rules in order to prevent the dissipation of their power that would result if they were violated with impunity."[4] In the West criminal justice derives from and preserves the primordial belief in an objective moral order.

This volume is based on papers presented at the twenty-seventh Annual Meeting of the American Society for Political and Legal Philosophy. Our meeting was organized by Owen Fiss of the Yale Law School, and we all owe him our gratitude. It took place in conjunction with the 1983 meeting of the Association of American Law Schools held in Cincinnati. As usual, the editors of NOMOS solicited additional chapters with a view to making the volume more comprehensive with respect to points of view and issues considered.

Breaking with our standing policy, the editors include a paper that had been previously published, "How to Make the Punishment Fit the Crime," by Michael Davis. Without it, retributive theory would have received scant attention. We are grateful to the editor of *Ethics* and to the author for permission to reprint it.

We thank our contributors, and once again our special thanks go to our peerless editorial assistant, Eleanor Greitzer. We also express our thanks to the Managing Editor of New York University Press, Despina Papazoglou, for her patience and helpfulness.

J.W.C.
J.R.P.

NOTES

1. Hugh Lloyd-Jones, *The Justice of Zeus* (Berkeley: University of California Press, 1971), p. 55.
2. Harold J. Berman, *Law and Revolution: The Formation of the Western Legal Tradition* (Cambridge: Harvard University Press, 1983), pp. 529–30.
3. Ibid., p. 194.
4. Hyman Gross, *A Theory of Criminal Justice* (New York: Oxford University Press, 1979), p. 401.

# INTRODUCTION

## J. ROLAND PENNOCK

Books on "justice" usually have relatively little to say about "criminal justice." Indeed, this topic is completely absent from John Rawls's *A Theory of Justice*. NOMOS VI, *Justice*, discussed criminal justice only tangentially, in one chapter. Justice, in the unqualified form, generally, perhaps especially today, suggests distributive justice, or social justice, while criminal justice, almost by definition, is the special concern of lawyers, although of course philosophers have had much to say about the justification of criminal law as a whole and the justification of criminalizing certain acts and of what constitutes appropriate punishment for them. Our Society has devoted only part of one of its sessions to the subject. (See the six chapters of Part II of NOMOS III, *Responsibility*).

Typically and very roughly, those who theorize about criminal justice, and especially about the justification of punishment, may be classified as utilitarians (stressing deterrence, incapacitation, and reform, with varying emphases) and deontologists (whose concerns in this context are with desert and, more specifically, retribution). This issue having been discussed widely in the literature of late, however, the present volume is largely, but by no means exclusively, devoted to other matters. (Issues relating to the concept of retribution are discussed in II.)

Part I opens, as did our meetings, with Michael Moore's paper "The Moral and Metaphysical Sources of the Criminal Law," which becomes also the title of this part. Confining himself to the "general part" of the substantive criminal law, he notes four

1

principles that comprise, or at least are included among, the sources of this branch of the law. They are (1) the principle of accountability, (2) the principle that the persons in question must have had a fair chance to acquaint themselves with the norms of their society, (3) the principle of answerability, and (4) the principles of justification and excuse. Together these principles constitute a set in that they in turn may be justified by some more general principles, such as responsibility or liberty. They themselves neither imply nor depend upon any particular morality. They are in this sense neutral.

After a brief consideration of these moral principles, Moore turns to the second half of his topic, which is his main concern. It is entailed by the moral principles already advanced that persons are rational and autonomous agents. This is revealed in the concepts of action, intention, negligence, causation, compulsions, accountability, and so on. The major part of Moore's chapter is devoted to a careful examination of the concepts of rational and autonomous agency. He defines these terms, shows why they are properly termed "metaphysical," and gives them a partial defense. This defense consists in the attacks of legal realists, or hermeneutic skepticism, and of behavioral skepticism. In general, his arguments against these sources of skepticism do not take the form of contending that no evidence could controvert the metaphysical beliefs in question. Rather, he argues that those beliefs are not challenged by the apparently competing views derived from psychiatry, behaviorism, sociobiology, physiological psychology, and computer science.

The next chapter, although it deals with one of Moore's moral concepts, employs a completely different method. Lawrence Rosen is a cultural anthropologist. His method is comparative and, as might be expected, the comparisons he makes are of strikingly different cultures—in this case Islamic Morocco, medieval Europe, and our own. "The question of the concept of the person," he declares, "is often at the heart of the way in which a legal system handles issues of fact and fault, procedure and remedy."[1] The concept of intentionality must be placed in the context of cultural definitions of personality. He believes that the study of Islamic law and of the development of the concept of personality in medieval Europe will shed light on how ideas about the individual contribute to a gradual shift in legal concepts. He goes on to speculate on how competing views of the self have influenced the formation of the concept of intentionality in contemporary American law. He concludes that English and American law are currently in a state of uncertainty and lack of consensus. More specifically, this legal uncertainty grows out of our psychological uncertainty about how to conceive the self—whether as an "inner self" or as a more socially determined one.

Commenting on Rosen and Moore, Martin Shapiro places them in the broad framework of modern trends in philosophy, while at the same time relating them to more specific legal principles. With respect to the latter, he suggests that the different approaches to intent that Rosen finds as between Moroccan and Western courts do not flow from a less autonomous version of personhood among the Muslims, as Rosen argues; rather, he believes that it is the Western secular view as opposed to the religious approach of the Islamic courts that account for any differences. Rosen errs, Shapiro believes, in looking at the black-letter law of Western countries rather than taking a more realistic view of the judicial process. More broadly, he holds that Rosen's and Moore's differences grow out of Moore's constructivism and Rosen's deconstructivism, the latter bypassing the commonsense approach in favor of the dark, the deep, and the peculiar.

The next four chapters, comprising Part II of this volume, all relate, more or less directly, to the issue of retribution. Hugo Bedau discusses classification-based sentencing and shows, among other things, that such systems indicate the direction in which retributivist theories lead. Classification-based sentencing schemes are one type of determinate sentencing and one such scheme is represented by the 1980 proposals of the Pennsylvania Commission on Sentencing. Bedau devotes his chapter to a close study of these proposals. The "guidelines" for sentencing set forth by these proposals are, on the whole, based on retributive theory. They are followed, however, by a list of post-classification factors that introduce other considerations, the effect of which is to modify retributivism both by considerations of equality and equity and also by those of utility. Only if such a system is put into operation will it be possible to see what it would lead to. It might well turn out to be an improvement both on current law and on what a primarily utilitarian system of sentencing would provide.

The following chapter, by Michael Davis, "How to Make the Punishment Fit the Crime," constitutes a departure from standard NOMOS practice in that it was not written for NOMOS but has been previously published.[2] Recognizing that a main difficulty confronting the retributivist is that of providing principles for determining the nature and severity of the punishment to be meted out, he addresses himself to that problem by proposing and defending a scheme that is in principle practically identical to the system discussed by Bedau—a two-stage system in which the first stage makes use of retributive principles, while the second stage introduces other considerations. His chapter comprises a defense as well as an exposition of this kind of system. Jeffrie Murphy raises an interesting and seldom discussed question about the retributive theory of punishment: not, Do criminals deserve certain punishment? but, Is it right for the state to take it upon itself to mete out such punishment? In Constitutional language, is it a "compelling state interest," and one that could not be satisfied by means that are less burdensome to fundamental rights?

The concluding chapter in this part is Richard Brandt's "A Motivational Theory of Excuses in the Criminal Law." It is not an appraisal of retributive theory, but it sets forth a theory of excuses that, he argues, provides a philosophical foundation for any sound recommendations that might be derived from retributive theory—foundations that he finds lacking in that theory. His argument is that criminal liability requires a "motivational fault" in the agent. Absent such fault, the agent should be exempt from punishment. His theory would bring unity in the law where plurality now reigns. Its substantive results would closely parallel existing law, but would not be identical with it in all cases. Divergences would generally correspond to areas now contested among legal scholars or about which they show some uneasiness. Not suprisingly, his theory bears a marked resemblance to the ethical theory that he has set forth elsewhere. He contends that "legal principles are justified if that *moral system,* which factually informed and rational persons would prefer to any other if they expected to live under it, would call on individuals to obey and require officials to enforce them."[3] Obviously, while the placement of this chapter in this part results from the bearing it has on retributive theory, the main thrust of its argument deals with the theory of excuses.

Part III of this volume deals with the special problem (of great importance in modern society) of criminal responsibility in government. Dennis Thompson provides the lead-off paper for this discussion. Dealing first with the problem of criminal responsibility in complex organizations generally, he argues, contrary to the "structuralist thesis," that we have a strong basis for imputing criminal liability to officials in organizations, while we should be wary of imputing organizational responsibility lest we give organizations too much autonomy and punish where it is unwarranted. Turning to governmental organizations, he argues that their special nature does not shield their officials from even stricter standards of liability. Similarly with other means of sanctioning conduct, such as impeachment. "In fact, concept of trust is a better guide for the responsibility of government officials than is the concept of immunity."[4]

Commenting on Thompson's chapter, Christopher Stone wants to hold governments criminally liable in appropriate cases, without being called a "structuralist," although he will accept this designation if necessary. He believes that the dangers of the structuralist thesis are less serious than Thompson does. He also thinks Thompson's argument is deficient because it fails to develop a theory of government—a theory that would tell us, for instance, whether an entity like Amtrak is "government" or not. He also lists several possible bases for disparate treatment of governmental and nongovernmental agencies that Thompson does not consider.

Susan Wolf concludes this part with a chapter titled "The Legal and Moral Responsibility of Organizations." Making adroit use of the distinctions between causal and moral responsibility and between practical and moral responsibility, she argues that the distinction between the Atomistic and the Organic views of organizations is unable to ground the legal and moral responsibility of organizations. Rather, her analysis leads her to hold that it is appropriate to subject organizations to the civil law, including those parts of it that are infused with moral judgment, but inappropriate to apply criminal law directly to them.

Part IV of the present volume, harking back to the subject of

NOMOS XXIV, *Ethics, Economics, and the Law,* deals with the economic theory of crime. Alvin Klevorick begins by lamenting that the economic theory of crime has failed to penetrate mainstream legal theory in the way that economic analysis has in the case of other branches of the law. He finds two reasons for this: (1) failure of the economic theory to include a requisite political theory and (2) lack of communication between various strands of the economic literature. The implication is that both of these deficiencies should be corrected, but that the first of them falls outside of the realm of economic analysis. A political theory of rights is a minimum requirement.

In a brief reply to Klevorick, Richard Posner contends that the lack of a requisite political theory in no way distinguishes the economic theory of criminal law from the economic theory of torts; yet the latter has entered mainstream legal theory. The real problem, he contends, is simply that theorists have not done enough work in this area. Judges and practitioners can't be expected to do it, argues Judge Posner, therefore the theorists should get busy. They should not await the development of relevant political theory.

Jules Coleman, in criticizing Klevorick, goes in the opposite direction from Posner. He would not have the economic theorists work more or harder with their bag of tools. Rather, it must be recognized, whether or not the economic theorists do so, that what is lacking in the economic theory is something that is not properly economic at all. Thus far he is in agreement with Klevorick. But the element lacking, according to Coleman, is not a political theory; it is a moral theory. More specifically, it is a theory of "desert," which, incidentally, is what distinguishes criminal law from tort law.

Finally, this part, and the volume, concludes with Stephen Schulhofer's reflections on Klevorick's thesis. He finds that Klevorick has confronted "all of us" with a dilemma, one that, if he is right, will require a great deal of rethinking. This dilemma arises from the paradox that economic analysis of the law has produced mutually contradictory reactions in the field of criminal law from those that it has evoked in other parts of the law. The nature of this paradox, along with the bulk of the substance of what the other authors have to say, is now left for the reader to discover.

## NOTES

1. Below, p. 53
2. Michael Davis, "How to Make the Punishment Fit the Crime," *Ethics* 93 (1983) pp. 726–52.
3. Below, p. 169
4. Below, p. 223

# PART I

# THE MORAL AND METAPHYSICAL SOURCES OF THE CRIMINAL LAW

# 1

# THE MORAL AND METAPHYSICAL SOURCES OF THE CRIMINAL LAW

## MICHAEL S. MOORE

INTRODUCTION

My topic calls for clarification: what is meant by "criminal law" and by "source?" The criminal law that is the subject of this paper is, first of all, *substantive* criminal law, not criminal procedure. Secondly, within substantive criminal law, I will discuss only what for decades now has been known as the "general part,"[1] that set of legal doctrines and principles that have relevance to all crimes and which do not concern themselves with the elements of particular crimes. The requirements of *actus reus, mens rea,* and the principle of legality are examples of the doctrines and principles of the general part, as are most of the rest of the standard fare of a first-year law course in substantive criminal law.

Whether a (truly) general part of the substantive criminal law exists is a matter of some controversy. George Fletcher, for example, urges that we operate with three different "patterns of criminality," each with its own characteristics.[2] Mark Kelman's more recent attempt at "deconstruction" is even more extreme in its denial that a coherent, general part to the criminal law exists.[3] Without arguing the point, I think it is demonstrable that neither of these kinds of criticism can show that the traditional view of the matter is mistaken. The case for there being a set of doctrines cutting across all crimes is much stronger than is

11

the corresponding case for there being, say, a general part to property law that cuts across all kinds of property, real as well as personal. Assuming, then, the existence of a general part to the substantive criminal law, my interest is to inquire into its sources.

By "source," I do not mean to designate the legitimating origin of criminal doctrines—the sense in which jurisprudes speak of the "sources of law." Whether criminal law is statutory, common law, customary, etc., is not my question. Neither is this an historical inquiry. By "source" I mean to designate those non-legal ideas that in some sense can be said to underlie our criminal law. The relation between these ideas and the criminal law is a logical one, such that the criminal law can be said to presuppose these other, more general ideas.[4]

I believe the criminal law has two such sources, one moral and one metaphysical. Since the metaphysical basis of the criminal law is the principal topic of this paper, I shall utilize this introduction to say something about the relation of the criminal law to its underlying moral basis. The moral basis of the criminal law is to be found in those moral principles under which fault is properly ascribed to persons for their behavior. These are the moral principles that tell us: (1) when a being is sufficiently accountable for his actions that he may be counted a moral agent; (2) on what occasions moral or legal norms may fairly obligate such agents; (3) when an act is done, a harm is caused, and with which mental states culpability is to be found; and (4) what circumstances amount either to a justification or an excuse for having caused a harm. These four principles are so closely embodied in criminal law that criminal lawyers are apt to forget that they are also moral principles defining culpability and telling us when a person may fairly be blamed for his actions.

These four principles together form a system that I shall here minimally sketch. First, the principles of accountability define the range of beings who are moral agents and thus the proper addressees of our substantive moral norms. As usually construed, these principles exclude animals, corporations, infants, and the insane from being the kinds of agent that are capable of being morally responsible. So construed, moral agency becomes coextensive with personhood, so that all and only persons are moral agents; aggregates of persons (corporations), and members of the human species that lack certain distinctive features of personhood (as the insane and the very young lack rationality) are not moral agents, on this view.

Second, the principles of fairly imposed obligation limit blameworthiness to those moral agents who have had a fair chance to acquaint themselves with the norms of any society. The aliens who come among us, children, and (more controversially) what used to be called psychopaths, who have not had such chance at moral education, are not fairly blameable for the harms they cause.

Third, in our fault ascriptions we apply what might be called a principle of answerability, which requires the simultaneous concurrence of three things: (1) that the individual acted; (2) that he did so intentionally, recklessly, or negligently; and (3) that he either caused some morally bad result, or, if he did not cause it, such result was the object of some further intention of his with which he acted. Excluded by the first of these, the act requirement, are involuntary movements, such as reflex movements, as well as another's use of one's body as an instrumentality. The mental state requirement excludes people who are non-negligently ignorant or mistaken about what it is they are doing by their actions. The causation requirement excludes persons who neither tried to cause some bad result nor in fact did so. If, on the other hand, someone's behavior satisfies all three requirements (and assuming he is a moral agent with a fair chance to become morally educated), then he is prima facie answerable for that behavior.

Such a person is only prima facie answerable, however, and not actually culpable, because of the fourth set of principles relevant here. These are the principles of justification and excuse. If one can show that in the particular circumstances in which one acted, the harm caused or intended was less than the harm prevented, one may be justified in so acting; alternatively, we may be justified in acting if the party who suffers the harm is himself at fault in placing us in a position of peril. The principles of excuse, by way of contrast, don't tell us when it is legitimate to act in ways otherwise prohibited; rather, they tell us when it was sufficiently difficult for an agent to resist causing some harm that he may not fairly be blamed for bringing it about. People who act under the coercion of others, who are placed by nonhuman circumstances in positions requiring very hard choices, and people who act under extreme emotional disturbance, are the kinds of people typically excused under these principles.

These four sets of principles form a system in the sense that they together determine when a being is morally culpable and thus, morally blameworthy. They may themselves be justified by yet more general principles, such as H.L.A. Hart's principle of responsibility or even yet more general principles of liberty.[5] More pertinently here, the four principles by-and-large justify the doctrines that make up the general part of the substantive criminal law.[6] These principles are the source of criminal law doctrines in the sense that they form part of the most coherent justification that can be given of these doctrines.

I do not regard the thesis that our criminal law has such a moral basis to be very problematic. It can only be made to *seem* problematic if one confuses it with much stronger theses about the relationship of criminal law to morality. The thesis I have sketched is not, to begin with, a natural law theory—or at least it needn't be. The connection between law and morals asserted here is only a contingent one: the doctrines of our criminal law turn out to be based on particular moral theory about when a being is morally responsible. Such a connection to morality is not *necessary* for our criminal laws to be laws, as a natural law theory would assert. We could have laws that assign liabilities in ways that have little resemblance to this or any other moral theory, and they would still be laws. As it happens, however, our criminal law does reflect this underlying moral theory about when it is fair to ascribe responsibility to a person.

Secondly, no necessary *or* contingent connection between what it is the criminal law prohibits and what it is that morality prohibits need be asserted. The general part of the criminal law, as we have seen, is "topic-neutral" in the sense that it is not concerned with what is defined as criminal; the general part deals with the conditions under which liability can attach, no matter what acts or harms may be prohibited by the special part of the criminal law. The relevant morality, accordingly, is not that which concerns itself with what are good or bad acts or states of affairs or right or wrong actions, but rather, "topic-neutral" morality, those moral principles that define the conditions under which it is fair to attribute moral responsibility for acts or harms, *no matter what the moral status of the latter.*[7] It is this topic-neutral morality, the moral principles of fault ascription, with which the general part of the criminal laws is to be linked. One can imagine a system with wildly immoral criminal law prohibitions that nonetheless parceled out liability only under those moral conditions of fair fault ascription; for such a system my thesis about the criminal law having a moral basis would be satisfied.

The second set of ideas underlying our criminal law—what I shall call its metaphysical basis—consists of those presuppositions of what persons must be like if the moral system that I have just described can fairly be applied to them. The moral principles that determine when fault is fairly ascribed, I contend, themselves utilize concepts that link morality (and thus the criminal law) to a particular metaphysical view about persons. This is the view that persons are rational and autonomous agents. The concepts that reveal such a view of man are the concepts of action, intention, negligence, causation, compulsion, accountability, and the like—the key concepts in the moral principles of fair fault ascription. These concepts are not only concepts in terms of which moral responsibility is ascribed but are also the concepts in terms of which we understand ourselves as persons. Such concepts, in other words, are not just moral concepts; they are more generally the concepts in terms of which we describe and explain human doings in everyday life and throughout most of the social sciences. Thus, the morality in which the criminal law is embedded is itself built upon a more general metaphysical view of what persons are like.

Since I do not regard the moral thesis, as I have described it, as very problematic, I shall not argue for it here beyond what has already been said. Nor will I seek to give the metaphysical thesis the defense it requires in terms of a detailed consideration of how the principles of fault ascriptions presuppose that persons are rational and autonomous agents, for this I have done elsewhere.[8] Rather, in the body of this paper I seek to do three things: first, to sharpen the metaphysical thesis by defining rationality and autonomy; second, to show why any view of persons in terms of such attributes is properly characterized as "metaphysical;" and third, to give a partial defense of the metaphysical thesis, not by making the positive case for it, but by rebutting several common skepticisms about the metaphysics of minds and persons prevalent in legal circles. I shall close with some remarks about why we should care about the metaphysics of personhood presupposed by both the criminal law and the morality that underlies it.

## THE METAPHYSICS OF PERSONS AS RATIONAL AND AUTONOMOUS AGENTS

### Rationality and Autonomy

The attributes of rationality and autonomy are best analyzed in terms of the idea of an agent acting for reasons. This idea is actually a conjunction of two ideas: that of action, and that of reasons for acting. These two ideas correspond, respectively, to the ideas of autonomy and rationality, and will be considered separately.

*Rationality and Reasons.* Reason-giving explanations of human behavior have two parts and serve two explanatory functions.[9] With regard to the two parts: a full explanation in terms of reasons for action requires, first, a statement specifying the agent's desires (goals, objectives, moral beliefs, purposes, aims, wants, etc.), and second, a statement specifying the agent's factual beliefs about the situation he is in and his ability to achieve, through some particular action, the object of his desires. For example, if someone (X) opens the window in order to chill the room, we will have explained his action by citing explicitly or implicitly:

1. His desire that the room be chilled, and
2. His belief that opening the window will chill the room.

Knowing this desire and belief set of X, we can understand his action in the fundamental way in which we understand all human actions, in terms of the agent's reasons or motives for acting.

This mode of explanation serves two quite distinct functions: reasons for an action both *rationalize* the action and *causally* explain it. A belief/desire set rationalizes an action in the sense that it portrays the action as the rational thing to do, given the agent's beliefs and given his desires. We understand the action in this sense because we can understand that a rational agent would so act, and that had we a similar belief/desire set, we too would so act. We can see the action as a means to something the agent wants. As long as the object of the agent's desire is intelligible to us as something a person in our culture could conceivably want, and so long as the factual beliefs are not themselves irrational, we can empathize with the action, even if we disagree with it morally or esthetically. We empathize because, knowing the belief/desire set, we perceive the activity to be the rational thing for an agent with such beliefs and desires to do.

This aspect of reasons for acting is sometimes confusingly expressed by saying that there is a *logical* connection between the sentences describing the belief/desire set and the sentence describing the action. Yet without supplementation with further premises, there is no logical connection between sentences describing a desire and a belief of an agent and a sentence describing his action. Still, some connection exists between the *content* of the beliefs and of the desires, on the one hand, and the action they explain on the other. The content of X's belief about means will necessarily include the same description of the action to be explained (opening the window) as is given in the conclusion, and the content of this belief will also necessarily include the same description of the end (chilling the room) as is given in the sentence describing X's desire. One may see this easily by schematizing a reason-giving explanation as:

STATEMENT 1. $XD(q)$.
STATEMENT 2. $XB(p{\supset}q)$.
STATEMENT 3. $p$.

Here $XD(q)$ in the example means "X desires that the room be chilled;" $XB(p{\supset}q)$ means "X believes if he opens the window, then the room will be chilled;" and $p$ means "X opens the window."

To specify with any precision what kind of relation must exist between each of the occurrences of $p$ and $q$ in the above schema is surprisingly complex. Deep philosophical difficulties beset the semantics of those sentence fragments describing the content of mental states such as beliefs and desires.[10] Nonetheless, for our purposes it may suffice to say that $p$ and $q$ name the same proposition in each of their occurrences in the expla-

nation schema above, so that the relations required for a be-
lief/desire set to constitute a reason-giving form of explanation
are three: two of propositional identity (p = p in statements 2
and 3, and q = q in statements 1 and 2), and one of material
implication (p⊃q in statement 2).[11] To say that these relations
hold for belief/desire sets that are reasons for actions is but to
say that we presuppose the rationality of the agent who will see
these relations in selecting a means to his desired end. To say
there is a "logical relation" in such patterns of explanation is
really to say that an action is *rationalized* in the fashion just outlined.

The second sense in which we understand an action when we
understand its reason is that we understand which of an agent's
many beliefs and desires actually caused the action. When we
say that X opened the window because of his beliefs and desires, the "because" is necessarily causal. X might have had any
number of belief/desire sets that would equally well rationalize
his actions. He might have desired, for example, to offend his
guests and have believed that an intentional opening of the
window would accomplish that; yet even if he has such a desire,
and even if he intentionally opens the window, it need not be
for the latter reason at all. He may be much too polite for that.
His reason may be simply as stated earlier: to chill the room.
Which reason is his reason for opening the window is a
straightforward causal hypothesis: whichever belief/desire set
caused him to act as he did explains his action. Thus, the ety-
mology of "motive": something that moves us to action.

Having outlined a relatively standard account of reasons for
action, it remains to relate that account to the ideas of practical
reason and practical reasoners. Reasons for acting is a form of
explanation in terms of states that exist at a time in the world,
and which enter into causal relations with themselves and actions. Often confused with this form of *explanation* is the kind
of *logic,* or patterns of valid inferences, that a rational agent
employs as or before he is acting.[12] Logic deals with timeless
propositions (not states or events) and with the logical (not causal)
relations between them. The kind of inference-drawing patterns that deal with action have, since Aristotle, been called
"practical syllogisms" and the kind of reasoning one does who

employs such practical syllogisms Aristotle called "practical reasoning."[13]

Practical reasoning involves the formulation of ends and the selection of means to the attainment of those ends. Practical reasoning thus takes the *content* of one's desires or moral beliefs, and the *content* of one's factual beliefs, to be premises in an argument. The actor worrying about chilling the room might reason:

1. Let the room be chilled.
2. If I open the window, then the room will be chilled. Therefore:
3. I open the window.

Such reasoning is "practical" in that it aims at telling us what to do. In this it is to be distinguished from what Aristotle called theoretical reasoning, which aims at telling us what to believe. The conclusion of a practical syllogism is accordingly a directive to action, not the more typical proposition about how the world is, the conclusion of true logical syllogisms. Moreover, practical syllogisms do not fit any of the patterns of valid inference of standard deductive logic. The conclusion that I should open the window does not follow deductively from the two premises stated.

The relation of practical reasoning to reason-giving explanations should be relatively apparent: the premises of a valid practical argument leading to some directive to action as its conclusion are just the contents of a belief/desire set that could rationalize the action in question. The extent to which an agent must actually reason through a valid practical argument before we are entitled to explain his action as having been done for reasons is somewhat less apparent. It seems very implausible to think that one must *consciously* reason through such practical arguments in order for reason-giving explanations to be appropriate. *Unconscious* reasoning may suffice, but at least this much is essential.[14]

All relevant senses of "rationality" center on the ideas of reason-giving explanations and practical reason. In the most basic sense of "rational," to describe an *act* as rational is to say that the actor had a set of beliefs and desires the contents of which, taken together with an act description, form a valid practical syllogism; in this sense, to say of an *actor* that he is rational is to say that he by-and-large acts on valid practical syllogisms.

The idea of rationality is not exhausted by the basic sense described above. Numerous notions of rationality having to do with practical reasoning are stronger than the simple requirement that an agent act on valid practical syllogisms.[15] Each of these stronger senses relates to one or another of the premises of an agent's practical reasonings. We may, for example, describe an agent's desire as rational and mean by that: that it is an intelligible desire for one in our culture to hold; that the individual desire is consistent (free of formal contradiction in its object) with the full set of the agent's desires; that the individual desire fits within a set of transitively ordered desires; or that the desire is (morally or prudentially) right. Analogously, one may describe a means/end belief as rational, and mean by that: that it is an intelligible belief for one in our culture to hold, given other, widely shared beliefs; that the individual belief is consistent with the full set of the agent's beliefs about the world; that the individual belief fits within a coherent system of beliefs; or that the belief is (factually) true. Each of these stronger requirements of rationality is in places presupposed by the criminal law, but the basic sense of rationality—the acting on valid practical syllogisms, no matter how bizarre the premises—is the sense of rationality generally presupposed throughout the criminal law and its underlying morality.

*Actions and Autonomy.* A basic or simple action is an action one performs by doing no other action.[16] One opens a door by pushing against it; one pushes against it by moving one's arm; but by what further act does one move one's arm? Simple motions of the body that a person brings about are basic acts because we don't do anything else in order to do them. One wants to isolate such simple acts, not because they figure often in everyday life, social science, law, or morals, but because they properly focus the important question about the metaphysics of action: what is the difference between the (simple) *action* of raising one's arm, and the mere *movement* of the body described by saying that the arm went up?[17] That they do differ is shown by the relationship between the following statements:

STATEMENT 1. *X raised his arm.*
STATEMENT 2. *X's arm went up.*

Statement 1 implies statement 2, but statement 2 does not imply statement 1. X's arm may go up because, for example, the wind blows it, someone grabs it, or a reflex occurs. Hence statement 1 and 2 are not equivalent; statement 1 says more than statement 2.

This is demonstrably not true for the "actions" of inanimate objects.[18] Suppose the following is said of some water that was partly elevated in a U-shaped tube:

STATEMENT 3. *The water sought its own level.*

Although the grammatically active mood might suggest that the water performed some action in the same sense that X performed some action in statement 1, this is not the case. Compare statement 3 with the following:

STATEMENT 4. *The water fell to a constant level.*

Not only does statement 3 imply statement 4, but statement 4 implies statement 3. The statements are equivalent; the "actions" of inanimate objects, such as water, do not share some crucial features of *human* action. Simple behaviorism may serve for the "actions" of inanimate objects, but will not do as an account of *human* action.

A long-popular attempt to capture the uniqueness of human action relies on the concept of reasons to do the job. This theory asserts that a bodily movement will be an action if it is caused by some mental state of desire, intention, or volition. John Stuart Mill succinctly stated an early version of this theory, and was echoed in legal theory by John Austin, and more recently, by J.L. Mackie.[19]

The theory that Mill, Austin, and Mackie articulate is in fact but a partial version of the contemporary causal theory of action. The full theory is that a movement is an action if and only if it is caused by a belief/desire set whose contents form a valid practical syllogism. Although Mackie, for example, seems to believe that it is the causation by a *desire* that makes movement an action, as Alvin Goldman has shown, *both* a belief and a desire must cause the movement; further, the belief and desire must be related to one another and to the action they cause in the manner earlier described for reason-giving explanations.[20]

If the Mill/Austin/Mackie/Goldman theory of action were correct, then one could explicate the concept of an action in terms of the concept of reasons: explicability by reasons would be a necessary and sufficient condition for a movement being a basic action. However, an apparently insurmountable problem for any version of the causal theory arises from what are called "deviant causal chains."[21] Suppose someone is behind the wheel of a car and sees her hated enemy step before her. Suppose further that she forms the desire to run over her enemy, and believes that if she shifts her foot from the brake to the accelerator, she will run over her enemy. Suppose further that her foot moves from the brake pedal to the accelerator, and that this movement was caused by her desire and by her belief. Is the causal role of this belief/desire set enough to say that the person *acted* in moving her foot? Before one says yes too readily, consider the following elaboration: the driver's beliefs and desires got her so excited in anticipation of finally being in a position to kill her enemy that her foot slipped off the brake to the accelerator. Our intuitions are plain in such a case that the person's foot movement is *not* an action, despite the causal role of her belief/desire set. If this is so, our idea of an action is not captured by the causal theory even in its most sophisticated modern form.

Consequently, one cannot avoid saying that persons have causal powers over their own bodies. The Mill/Austin/Mackie/Goldman causal theory attempts to eliminate talk of irreducible causal powers of persons in favor of a more Hume-like notion of event or state causation (e.g., by beliefs and desires). Yet the causal theory fails precisely because it leaves out the central idea of human action, that of a *person* bringing about (causing) some new state of affairs.[22]

If a person possesses causal powers not themselves reducible to causation by states of belief and desire, then the concept of a basic action has equal dignity with the concept of reasons in terms of explicating our concept of a person. The argument from deviant causal chains, if it succeeds, establishes just that fact.

We are now in a position to define autonomy: autonomy refers to a person's causal power over the movements of his own body. One of our fundamental ideas about persons is that they are beings who are (to paraphrase Locke) masters of themselves and proprietors of their own bodies, and thus, of the actions or labor of it.[23] That persons have such irreducible causal powers—i.e., that they can perform basic actions—is one of the defining characteristics of personhood, part of our metaphysics about persons.

Nothing in such a concept of autonomy commits one to viewing persons as having "free will." Autonomy commits one to persons having a will, but not to a will that is "free" (in the sense of exempt from the laws of causation). It is true, as I have just argued, that the causal agency of a person cannot be reduced to event or state causation. But this does not mean that a person's acts must be uncaused by those states or events. Indeed, most commonly basic acts are caused by various belief/desire sets, and they remain basic acts nonetheless.

More generally, one might plausibly urge that basic actions are caused by all kinds of factors, not just states of belief and desire. Mental states other than belief/desire sets, such as emotional states, may cause us to perform basic acts. Environmental conditions or conditioning may also operate as causes. Undoubtedly many physiological events in our body cause us to act as we do. None of these forms of determinism, mechanistic or otherwise, is incompatible with persons having irreducible causal powers.[24]

### Rationality and Autonomy as Intentionalistic Metaphysics

The concepts of practical reason and of basic action partly define our commonsense view of persons: persons are rational and autonomous agents, agents who exercise causal powers for reasons. Neither of these basic concepts can be reduced to the other. They jointly form the basic vocabulary in terms of which we understand and evaluate ourselves as persons.

This view of persons is "metaphysical" in the sense that the concepts in terms of which persons are conceived are not themselves (in any straightforward way, at least) reducible to concepts that are yet more basic. Rather, we seem to have a family of concepts applied to persons that are both systematically re-

lated to one another and that are systematically different from
the concepts in terms of which we conceive of the natural world.
Rationality and autonomy apply to persons and are not in any
apparent way reducible to nonpersonal concepts, such as those
used in the natural sciences.

The "philosophical psychology" of the 1950s and '60s sought
in various ways to capture this striking fact about the metaphysics of personhood, following Ryle's proclamation of a "categorical difference" between the vocabulary of persons and the
vocabulary of natural science.[25] The claims were often both overstated and weakly supported. Nonetheless, some systematic
difference that Ryle and others sought to capture with the doctrine of category differences does seem to exist. A more defensible statement of this distinctiveness of "personal" concepts is
in terms of their Intentionality.[26]

Whether Intentionality is the "mark of the mental" is a matter of some debate in the contemporary philosophy of mind.[27]
In any case, it is a distinguishing feature of many mental words,
including those most pertinent here, "belief," "desire," and "action." One can see that these concepts are Intentional by considering the nonsubstitutibility of the nominal referents of their
objects, as illustrated in note 26. Suppose John *desires* the largest room in the inn, or that he *believes* that he is approaching
the largest room in the inn, or that he is *acting* so as to seek the
largest room in the inn. Suppose further that "the largest room
in the inn" refers to what turns out to be the dirtiest room in
the inn. Despite the last supposed identity, one cannot substitute "the dirtiest room in the inn" for "the largest room in the
inn" and still preserve truth about what John desires, believes,
or seeks. This inability to substitute codesignative terms marks
desire, belief, and action as Intentional concepts.

The striking feature of Intentional concepts is their apparent
irreducibility to the non-Intentional concepts of natural science. Our logic and our natural science depend upon the existence of what is called an *extensional* language. An extensional
language is one in which (1) the logical connectives are truth
functional, and (2) codesignative terms may be substituted
without changing the truth value of the overall expression in
which they occur.[28] The first is a basic requirement for the logic
of Frege-Russell-Quine to work. The second is a requirement

of scientific laws, which generalize about *things* irrespective of how those things are described or named.[29] (Imagine, for example, Kepler's laws of planetary motion being true of Venus only under some descriptions, such as "Venus," but not under others, such as "the morning star"—Kepler's laws are true of the thing, Venus, not the thing under a certain description.)

Rationality and autonomy, then are basic in two senses. First, they cannot be reduced to other Intentional concepts, although those other Intentional concepts (such as "intention") can be explicated in terms of them. Second, the entire family of Intentional concepts cannot at present be reduced to our more typical vocabulary of natural science.[30] That persons have causal powers over their bodies, and that they act for reasons, in an essential part of our conception of ourselves. "Metaphysical" is as good a label as any for such basic defining attributes of persons.

### Skepticism About the Metaphysics of Personhood in the Contemporary Theory of Criminal Law

Metaphysics generally has a bad reputation among lawyers. "Metaphysical" is often a pejorative label for a point or argument that is so ethereal, abstract, and without content that it is thought to be an arbitrary posit rather than a discovered truth about the world. Yet we all have a metaphysics, an implicit or explicit view of how the world is constructed. It shows up when we discuss causal relations, when we ascribe properties to objects, indeed, whenever we speak. Our metaphysical beliefs are simply those most general beliefs about what exists and about the qualities and relations between those existent things. Metaphysical beliefs, although more abstract, are not different in kind than scientific or ordinary factual beliefs.

Metaphysics as such is thus not to be written off as "much ado about nothing," as did the logical positivists. Nonetheless, lawyers and legal theorists are often quite unreceptive to a metaphysical description of persons, for three sorts of reasons: (1) criminal theorists, like other legal academicians, are descendants of the legal realist tradition according to which the use of a concept should be guided by the social consequences attached to that use, not by some underlying metaphysics; (2) some criminal theorists have imbibed of the antirealism[31] about

minds (and thus of persons) of the hermeneutic and Wittgen-
steinian tradition in philosophy; and (3) some criminal theorists
have also imbibed of another version of antirealism about minds,
namely, that skepticism about the reality of mental states represented by behaviorism in philosophy and psychology. I shall
discuss each such purported basis for skepticism in turn.

*Legal Realist Skepticism.* Perhaps the easiest route to understanding the skepticism about metaphysics bequeathed to us by
the legal realist tradition is to ask some more general questions
about legal concepts and what it is to seek their meaning. Prima
facie, one might advert to two quite distinct sorts of things in
"giving the meaning" of a legal concept such as "criminal intent" or "person": (1) one might seek to describe the set of *facts*
under which the legal concept is correctly applied; or (2) one
might seek to describe the set of *legal consequences* which attach
to the authoritative use of that concept by a judge.

Consider the concept of ownership. If asked to give the
meaning of the two-place predicate, "X owns y," one might describe the facts under which a person X could correctly be said
to own some thing y, facts such as that X received y as a gift
from his uncle, that X purchased y, that X occupied y for a certain period, and the like. Alternatively, one might mention the
kind of legal consequences that are supposed to flow from it
being authoritatively pronounced of X, that he owns y. Such
consequences include the fact that X may dispose of y by gift,
sale, or devise; that X can be taxed on y; that X may enjoin interference by others in his use and enjoyment of y; and so forth.

The reason for this Janus-faced aspect of legal concepts lies
in what Hohfeld called their "dispositive" function.[32] Legal
concepts such as ownership, malice, intention, or person, are used
both to describe in legal terms the facts in particular situations
and to "dispose" of the issues in cases by prescribing what results a judge should bring about in his application of those concepts. Dispositive legal concepts form the "conceptual cement"
that connects a judge's factual findings to his legal remedies.

It is sometimes thought that this dual function of legal concepts renders them essentially ambiguous. George Fletcher, for
example, finds criminal law theory seriously muddled because
of the "systematic ambiguity" he sees between the descriptive
and the normative uses of concepts such as action or inten-

tion.[33] Yet ambiguity is a semantic category having to do with two senses of a word.[34] "Entertain," for example, is ambiguous in that it can mean thinking about or considering a question or it can mean hospitable and amusing behavior. The two functions served by legal concepts is not a semantic distinction but rather a distinction of *use*. A judge performs two distinct speech acts when he uses a dispositive legal concept such as "intention" or "ownership" in a legal proceeding. His "assertorial" speech act is to describe the facts before him, while his "prescriptive" speech act is to prescribe that certain legal consequences should attach.

These same dual functions appear in our use of language to express moral judgments. To use a moral term, such as "person" or "intention," is often both to *describe* an entity or a state of affairs as being of a certain kind, and to *prescribe* that moral guilt or blame should attach to the entity or event so described. The difference between moral and legal usages is that the moral consequences prescribed are not fixed by conventional rules of such detail as are the legal consequences attached to dispositive legal concepts.

Skepticism about metaphysics is generated for many lawyers by their preoccupation with the consequences of using a concept such as person or intention. This preoccupation leads them to think that such concepts have no descriptive content, that we do and should guide our usage of them not by metaphysical truths about persons but by pragmatic policies having to do with what we want to achieve by use of these concepts in particular contexts. Consider in this regard the concept of an action. If one gives up on articulating the metaphysics of action, one will adopt something like H.L.A Hart's once-held ascriptivist theory of action.[35] According to it, one first decides whether responsibility should be ascribed to some person for some harm, and only then whether the bodily motion causing the harm was his action. If one wishes to ascribe responsibility, his behavior will be described in the Intentional idioms of action; if one wishes to say he is not responsible, the behavior will not be described.

Hart's kind of argument—because one is *ascribing* responsibility one cannot be *describing* some factual state of affairs with a concept such as "action"—has been made for mental states as well as action. John Dewey, for example, argued that motives are characterizations of conduct that are merely "a refinement of the ordinary reactions of praise and blame," so that motive words, such as "greed," "simply [mean] the quality of [an] act as socially observed and disapproved."[36] George Fletcher, analogously, analyzes the concept of intention as having as one of its two meanings, "an intent to act under circumstances (such as failing to enquire about the age of a sexual partner) that render an act properly subject to blame."[37]

This kind of preoccupation with the consequences of saying that someone has performed an action, or done so with a certain intention, motive, or reason, is to be found with regard to each of the concepts in terms of which responsibility is ascribed in law and morals. Judge Andrews, in dissent in *Palsgraf* v. *Long Island Railroad Co.*,[38] speaking no doubt as an accurate representation of the thoughts of many contemporary lawyers, urged that the requirement of proximate cause "is all a question of expediency" and of "practical politics": "What we do mean by the word 'proximate' is that because of convenience, of public policy, of a rough sense of justice, the law arbitrarily declines to trace a series of events beyond a certain point."[39] Stanley Ingber has recently analyzed the excuse of duress as first consisting of the moral judgment that one is not responsible, and only then is the judgment made that the behavior in question was "involuntary."[40] Thomas Szasz and his legal followers are constantly contending that phrases such as "mental illness" have no descriptive meaning; such phrases are merely labels we apply to persons after deciding for one reason or another to degrade them as persons.[41]

The most general strain of this kind of legal thinking has been by the Americal legal realists. They held that in applying a legal term one must look to the legal *consequences* being prescribed by its authoritative use by a judge, and further, that it was an illusion to think that such legal terms had a *meaning* that determined their correct use apart from such consequences. This general view came to be known as functionalism.[42]

Ethical philosophy has also had its share of theorists who urged that ethical utterances were used either to express the speaker's emotions or to prescribe what one ought or ought not to do.[43] These "emotivist" and "prescriptivist" theories in ethics urged that because such expressive or prescriptive functions were served by moral uses of language, descriptive functions could not also be served.

If one adopted such a position about the legal or moral usages of the word "person," one would urge that *anything* could be called a person—it would simply depend on whether one wished to attach the legal or moral consequences of being so labelled to that entity. Consider, for example, the debate about whether corporations (as entities distinct from their shareholders, directors, and officers) are moral or legal persons. One adopting the functionalist analysis of legal concepts of American legal realism will collapse the question of whether corporations *are* moral persons into the question of whether they *should be called* moral persons in light of the consequences attached thereto. Christopher Stone, for example, argues that the question of whether "it is *intelligible* to blame the corporation draws on considerations that it is *useful* to speak in that manner."[44] Similarly in law, if one wishes to know whether a corporation is a legal person, one will inquire into "the likely effect of holding the corporate body legally accountable. One wants to know how making the corporation the law's quarry will affect those both 'outside' the corporation and those who labor 'within,' in terms of their perceptions (most importantly their self-perceptions) and their behavior."[45] Like any good functionalist, Stone relegates the descriptive question of whether corporations are legal persons and thus can intelligibly be held legally accountable as persons, to the scrap heap of intellectual history and (pejoratively) academic pursuits.[46]

My own view is that the legal and moral questions of whether some entity is or is not a person, whether that person performed an action, whether he did so intentionally or with a certain motive, whether that act proximately caused harm, whether the actor acted under threats of another amounting to duress, and whether the actor is mentally ill, are all factual questions. The concepts employed in discussing all such questions are not empty labels for a moral or legal conclusion reached on other grounds, or on no grounds at all; they are concepts having a descriptive and explanatory function, no matter what other expressive, prescriptive, or ascriptive functions they may serve in contexts such as those of responsibility assessment. It accordingly makes sense to seek the meaning of "persons" and its related terms ("action," "reasons") in terms of the facts that must be true if these concepts are to be correctly employed.

I have elsewhere addressed this kind of meaning-theory-generated skepticism about ethical discourse,[47] and will not recapitulate that branch of the argument. About legal utterances, it should be a simpler matter to see that preoccupation with the consequences of *saying*, e.g., that a corporation is or is not a legal person, cannot be exclusive of some concern as to whether corporations *are* legal persons. If our legal concepts had as their only meanings that certain consequences could be achieved by their use, they would be completely vacuous. They could never be used in giving reasons to justify legal results, but only to summarize those results. At the least, therefore, any concepts actually doing any work in legal reasoning must have some descriptive content.[48] This is not to say that such content must always be given by an analysis into, e.g., the metaphysics of what persons really are; it could come from legal conventions, like those that invest "merger" in corporations law with meaning. In the case of such borrowed concepts as personhood, however, it is unlikely in the extreme to think that the meaning is to be found solely in legal conventions. In any case: to rebut the legal realist skeptic it is enough to show that the meaning of legal, ordinary, and moral concepts cannot be found solely in the consequences of authoritative utterance.

*Hermeneutic Skepticism.* Another form of skepticism about the metaphysics of the person stems from a deep skepticism that anything "in the world" is referred to when one talks about actions and mental states (and thus about persons). This doubt is a kind of antirealism about minds and about anything that smacks of "mentalism," including human action. There are different kinds of distrust of the mental. The behaviorist skepticism of private, nonphysical, inferentially validated, internal but nonetheless causally efficacious states of mind, is considered below. Recently, more influential skepticism has stemmed from the Intentionality of mental concepts. The fear here has been that the *objects* of mental states cannot be specified objectively, that the only way such objects are fixed is by a certain interpretive stance adopted by the observer. Given the centrality of Intentional objects to saying what mental states *are*, the skeptical conclusion has been that they are not things at all.

Two recent criminal law theorists illustrate this kind of skepticism about the metaphysics of minds and persons. Hyman Gross has oriented his recent *A Theory of Criminal Justice* around an explicit antirealist position about mind. In considering specific intent, for example, Gross urges that "the intent is part of the act not some state of mind that may have accompanied it."[49] What Gross apparently has in mind here (to speak loosely) is G.E.M. Anscombe's point that many of our descriptions of action are formally descriptions of executed intentions.[50] One can, for example, redescribe a crouching as a hiding, if the purpose with which the crouching was done was to hide. "In doing what he does," Gross would say of such a croucher, "the actor has a purpose that makes the act an act of that kind rather than of another kind . . . But having a purpose as one acts does not mean that one then has a purpose in mind."[51] About purposes themselves, Gross argues that they "are not accounts of mental occurrences or states at all, nor in fact are they accounts of any sort of personal occurrence or state." The reason for this, we are told, "is that an account of motives does not tell us what caused an act to be done, but tells us rather *in what cause* it was done. An account of the motives for an act is not an explanation telling why the act occurred, but rather an explanation of the role of the act in a larger story of the actor's pursuits." Finally, about the crucial criminal law notion of acting *intentionally* (which Gross rightly distinguishes from acting with a further or "specific" intention), Gross similarly urges that "mentalism is objectionable because it purports to give an account of intentional and unintentional acts—and thus of culpability—in terms of the mental affairs of the actor." Again, we are told that acting intentionally involves no reference to "private inner workings" nor to "what is going on in the mysterious region where acts originate." Rather, when we say that an action is done *intentionally* we are merely rebutting someone else's claim that the act was nonstandard ("unintentional") with respect to the actor's control. The actor's control, Gross further urges, is not a mental matter at all.[52]

George Fletcher's recent "rethinking" of criminal law has also led him to an antirealist position about minds (although of a somewhat less trenchant variety than that of Gross). Fletcher also explicitly rejects the "mentalist bias in philosophical psychology,"[53] and urges that we "drop the notions of causation [by mental states] from the metaphysics of acting and willing."[54] In place of the metaphysics defended earlier—of belief/desire sets causing actions—Fletcher would emphasize the observer's role in interpreting behavior as an action done for a certain aim or reason. We must stress "the perception of human acting as a form of intersubjective understanding"[55] if we are to have an adequate theory of action or intention. Such intersubjective understanding is possible only if the observer and the actors share a "form of life." All of this is to deny that intending or acting are states or events that really exist in the world in the way that tables and chairs do; seeing an event as an action, or a state as an intention, on this view, depends entirely on there being a certain interpretive stance which the observer brings to these events in order to so view them.

These skepticisms about mind should be seen as part of a larger tradition that stems in part from the philosophy of the later Wittgenstein,[56] in part from certain work in the philosophy of history,[57] and in part from the influence of the hermeneutic tradition in Continental philosophy.[58] All of these traditions have in common their blurring of any distinction between the mental states that an actor really possesses, on the one hand, and the mental states his behavior is interpreted as expressing because of the observor's interpretive stance, on the other. As G.H. Von Wright puts it, himself influenced by each of these traditions: "Behavior gets its intentional character from being *seen* by the agent himself or by an outside observer in a wider perspective, from being *set* in a context of aims and cognitions."[59]

Various reasons might convince one that such mental states as beliefs and desires do not exist except as some kind of fictional posits in the interpretive stance of an observer. Most pertinent to the skepticism considered here is that skepticism about mental states stemming from one of their long-noticed features, namely, their Intentionality. Because the objects of mental states are essentially linguistic, it might seem inevitable that the necessary linguistic characterization of those objects could come from nowhere else *but* the linguistic efforts of the interpreter. The only seeming alternative would be to think that the *actor* explicitly says to himself the sentence that forms the content of his beliefs and his desires. Yet such silent soliloquies surely can't be the source of such contents, because the observer often rewords the actor's own explicit formulation of his beliefs and desires into the observer's own language and his own idiom. We think this quite legitimate. Hence, the interpretivist skeptic concludes, the *only* way such objects or contents can be formulated is by the observer's "empathetic understanding," his desire to fill out a story so that it makes sense, etc.

If I am right, the basic motivation for believing that ascribing "real" beliefs or desires to an agent makes no sense lies in the difficulties one has in formulating the objects of mental states without observer interpretation.[60] That this is an insufficient motive for being an interpretivist can be seen by repairing to another "essentially linguistic" context, that of reported speech. Suppose an observer reports: "John said that Mary is a hard worker." Such indirect speech, which does not quote the original speaker but paraphrases what he meant, is much like sentences of mental states in that both take propositional objects. In addition, in neither context is the connection between the dependent clause and the overall sentence truth functional. The truth of the overall sentence, "John said that Mary is a hard worker," does not depend on the truth of the enclosed sentence, "Mary is a hard worker." John could have said it without Mary being a hard worker, just as John could have believed that Mary is a hard worker without Mary in fact being a hard worker. Moreover, just because John said that Mary is a hard worker, it is not true that John said that the laziest worker in the office is a hard worker—even if "Mary" and "the laziest worker in the office" both refer to one and the same person. From these three features one may conclude that the object of the "saying that" is essentially linguistic, just as it is for belief, desire, and other mental states.

The truth of the overall sentence, "John said that Mary is a hard worker," is a function of two items: (1) that there was some utterance U by John; and (2) that "Mary is a hard worker" is an *accurate interpretation* of U. Thus an interpretive task *is* bound up in verifying the truth of the sentences of indirect speech. Yet that some interpretation is required for the truth of sentences reporting indirect speech would tempt no one, I should think, to assert that there is no fact of the matter about what the utterance really was.[61] It is true, the observer must characterize (interpret) that utterance—itself a bit of language used by John—but surely the necessity of such interpretation is no argument at all that utterances don't exist except in the observer's "story" or "interpretive stance" or whatever. Utterances are real-world speech acts by real-world people who unproblematically exist.

An interpretivist might well respond that beliefs and desires are unlike utterances in a crucial way. While both beliefs and utterances take linguistic objects that require interpretation, utterances have an established text to be interpreted. For beliefs or desires, he might ask, what is *the* authoritative formulation of their objects that can serve as the text against which all interpretations are to be judged for accuracy? One might urge that "the text" forming the objects of beliefs and desires is to be found in the actor's speech to himself about what he wants and what he believes on certain occasions. But this idea—that we have beliefs or desires only when we have engaged in some such silent soliloquy—is a very inaccurate view of mind. We unproblematically explain behavior by reasons when the actor has engaged in no such explicit recitals of the premises of his practical reasoning.

The "text" for beliefs or desires is to be found in two sources: first, in the abilities of the actor to avow the objects of his beliefs and desires. These abilities do not depend on any silent sayings to oneself, nor need they be readily exercisable by an agent—they may be "repressed." Second, the text may be found in whatever physiological events turn out to be "the language of thought" in the brain.[62] Hence, although finding the text is a more complicated affair for beliefs and desires than for utterances, it is not the case that *no* text exists save that which an external observer brings with him when he seeks to explain the behavior. Because a text exists, the need for interpreting that text—the object of beliefs and desires—no more commits one to the interpretivist tradition than does a similar need commit one to interpretivism about utterances. Some interpretation is involved in formulating the objects of beliefs, of desires, and of utterances; in all cases, however, what was *really* believed, desired, or uttered is a matter of fact.

*Behaviorist Skepticism.* Another antirealist form of skepticism about the metaphysics of persons that has had some influence with criminal law theorists stems from behaviorist psychology. Two kinds of behaviorism are relevant here, methodological behaviorism and logical behaviorism.[63]

Those philosophers and psychologists who are called "methodological behaviorists" simply put mentalistic explanations to the side, urging that mental states are too "private," "internal," "inferred," or in some other way unfit for a (methodologically) proper science of human behavior. Although not classifying himself as a methodological behaviorist, B.F. Skinner is most consistently construed to be skeptical on methodological grounds about the utility of mental concepts.[64] For Skinner, concepts like belief, desire, or willing are to be shunned for a variety of reasons, the most important of which is that such explanations presuppose some kind of "homunculi" who resides "inside" the brain.

Logical (often called "philosophical," or "analytical") behaviorism is not skeptical about the methodological adequacy of mental concepts; rather, this form of behaviorism is reductionist in character, for it asserts that mental words like "belief" or "desire" name either behavior itself or *dispositions* to behave in certain ways—in any case, not inner states that cause behavior. On such an account, to say that X believes that it is raining can be reduced to statements about what X is disposed *to do*, e.g., carry his umbrella, not take long walks, say "it is raining," etc. To explain an action by citing a belief or a desire, accordingly, will not be to name a set of states *causing* the action; rather, it will be to say that X was disposed to do an act of that type, much in the way that to explain the dissolving of a lump of sugar by citing the sugar's solubility will be to say that it was disposed to do that under certain conditions.

Such a reduction is mechanistic because the dispositions to which mental states are reduced are themselves mere theoretical stand-ins ("behavioral constructs") for the real causes of action, environmental stimuli. It is because of our past conditioning that we are disposed, e.g., to avoid painful things; so that to explain that X avoided the fire because he did not want to get burned, is ultimately to say that events in his past caused him to engage in pain-avoidance behavior.

Each of these forms of behaviorism has inclined some judges

and theorists to a kind of skepticism about the mental states of belief, desire, and willing on which the metaphysics of persons is built. One who, for example, is convinced that mental states are too private, internal, or inferred to be the (methodologically) proper basis for psychology, will also believe that these same characteristics prevent mental states from being the touchstone of moral culpability and legal liability. Herbert Fingarette has nicely characterized this latter view: "In essence, the viewpoint in question consists in supposing that in saying these things we are trying to describe certain states as processes within the person's mind or 'inside another's skin.' Being internal, these states or processes are necessarily unobservable by others. Therefore, we ought not to try to judge what in the nature of the case we cannot know."[65] Such a view leads directly to the well-known "objective" theory of mental states, according to which one puts aside any enquiry into whether a defendant actually believed his conduct would cause a certain result, in favor of an enquiry about whether a reasonable person would have foreseen such a result. The objective theory of mind in criminal law is often (but not inevitably) motivated by the same distrust of private, internal mental states that motivates some psychologists to become behaviorists.[66]

Similarly, if one is a logical behaviorist about mental states, one will believe that no one (criminal lawyers included) should be concerned about anything internal or private. Rather, the criminal law will be concerned with a mental concept such as an intention only because it names a *disposition* to engage in behavior of a certain sort; when that behavior is of a prohibited sort, the law cares about the intention only because it cares about dangerous propensities. As Justice Holmes put it, in discussing criminal attempts: "The importance of the intent is not to show that the act was wicked, but to show that is was likely to be followed by hurtful consequences."[67]

If one is either a methodological or a logical behaviorist one will be deeply skeptical about anything that could be called a metaphysics of personhood. The inner states of personal causation (willing) and of causally efficacious beliefs and desires either do not exist (logical behaviorism) or, if they do exist, are too private for use by law or science (methodological behaviorism).

Yet the problem for a behaviorist skeptic is to make plausible either of these forms of behaviorism.

Sometimes methodological behaviorism is only a plea to pursue a particular strategy in building a theory with which to explain human behavior. The strategy might be paraphrased as the injunction, "see if you can explain behavior using only environmental causes and eschewing mental states and neurophysiology." Such an explanatory strategy need be skeptical about minds no more than it is about brains, since it eschews both in favor of causes of other kinds. The truly skeptical forms of methodological behaviorism must go further than this, and prefer behaviorist accounts because of suspicions about competing accounts in terms of mental states, on the ground for instance that mental states are private, internal, or inferred, and thus can only be known by their holder.[68] Yet we infer many things, such as forces, fields, electrons, kinetic energy; from the point of view of phenomenalism, we also infer the existence of physical objects from their appearances. The inference-laden nature of our knowledge about any of these things can hardly be a legitimate ground of skepticism.

Similarly, the privacy of mental states is easily overstated. It is true that we do have privileged access to our own states of mind, that is a privileged (because noninferential) way of knowing what we desire or believe. It is not true, however, that *only* the holder of a state of mind can know its contents.[69] We make legitimate (warranted) inferences about others' states of mind every day, based on behavior and what we know about a culture. Such explanatory inferences by others may supplement or supplant the agent's own beliefs about his mental states. We are not guessing at something that only the agent can know for certain when we make these inferences about others' mental states. Freud taught us as much, if indeed we needed the lesson.

The main thrust of Skinner's skepticism does not stem from these features of mental states, but from the fear earlier identified: mental states lead to the unacceptable positing of a homunculus in the brain, a little man in the machine, whose scientific status is about as high as that of a "possessing demon" or goblin. Skinner's target here is just the metaphysical view of persons earlier described; what must be abolished, Skinner tells us, is "the autonomous man—the inner man, the homunculus, the possessing demon, the man defended by the literature of freedom and dignity."[70]

Skinner's fear is that persons conceived as autonomous agents presents us with an unacceptable dilemma: either we conceive of them as "uncaused causers," in which event no explanation is possible of why such agents do what they do; or, if we give an explanation, it will be in terms of another autonomous agent, and then another, leading to an infinite regress:

> . . . the little man . . . was recently the hero of a tele-
> vision program called "Gateways to the Mind' . . . The
> viewer learned, from animated cartoons, that when a man's
> finger is pricked, electrical impulses resembling flashes of
> lightning run up the afferent nerves and appear on a tele-
> vision screen in the brain. The little man wakes up, sees the
> flashing screen, reaches out, and pulls the lever . . . More
> flashes of lightning go down the nerves to the muscles, which
> then contract, as the finger is pulled away from the threat-
> ening stimulus. The behavior of the homunculus was, of
> course, not explained. An explanation would presumably
> require another film. And it, in turn, another.[71]

Skinner's dilemma is a false one. Our metaphysics of ratio-nality and autonomy does not presuppose an uncaused causer. Autonomy, as I have argued, should be conceived in terms of causal power, and yet the exercises of that power may be (and surely are) themselves caused. Secondly, the explanations possible are *not* limited to the autonomous acts of other little agents, leading to Skinner's feared infinite regress. We currently explain most such autonomous doings by the Intentional states of belief and desire, but there is no reason why those Intentional states may not themselves be explainable by non-Intentional states. That remains to be seen. Only an indefensibly strong (and very implausible) version of the doctrine of category differ-ences we earlier encountered could sustain Skinner on this point.

Skepticism proceeding from logical behaviorism fares no bet-ter than does that proceeding from methodological behavior-ism. Despite its famous proponents, logical behaviorism is vir-tually dead among philosophers, psychologists, artificial intelligence specialists, linguists, and others currently worrying about the nature of mental states such as "belief" and "desire." This is in part due to a variety of philosophical attacks on philosophical behaviorism.[72] The death knell for logical behaviorism had not come from any of these arguments, however (some of them, indeed, are not persuasive), but from other considerations. One is the erosion of the logical positivist theory of meaning underlying philosophical behaviorism. The main temptation to seek to reduce "belief" or "desire" to behavior comes from a logical positivist view about meaning, according to which all nonanalytic expressions must have presently verifiable conditions that can serve as the criteria for the correct use of those expressions. For mental terms such as "belief," the only public evidence we have is the behavior of the person whose belief it is—which leads directly to the reductionist analysis of logical behaviorism. Few persons today would subscribe to such a logical positivist theory of meaning, for reasons that I have detailed elsewhere.[73] Briefly, "belief" can have meaning even if we have no criteria for its application. Beliefs, desires, and other mental states may be real physiological states of the brain, or they may be functional states of the brain that cannot be identified with any types of brain states. This scientific question cannot be foreclosed by enshrining our present indicators of when mental states exist in others (behavior of certain sorts) as if such indicators were analytically necessary or sufficient conditions. It is good evidence that someone is in pain, for example, when he engages in pain-expressing behavior; such evidence however, cannot be said to be an analytically necessary or sufficient *criterion* for being in pain. An individual could learn the pain behavior and not be in pain, or he could be in pain but not engage in the behavior (curare, which paralyzes but does not eliminate the painful feelings, is not an anesthetic). Only in light of our best theory of what sort of state pain is can we answer whether someone is in pain. One cannot foreclose the development of such scientific theories by positing fixed connections (meaning connections) of "pain" to certain kinds of behaviors.

Aside from this erosion of the meaning theory foundations of logical behaviorism, the position can be seen to be untenable simply by examining carefully attempted behaviorist reductions of mental terms like "belief." It is no accident that nowhere in

*The Concept of Mind*[74] does Gilbert Ryle give more than a sketch of what a translation of mental terms into "multi-track" dispositions would look like. The kind of translations Skinner casually throws off from time to time throughout his work are not persuasive even to his admirers, who regard them as loose paraphrases but not reductions.[75] Just as logical positivism's attempted reduction of object language to phenomenal language failed in large part because no adequate translations were ever proposed, so logical behaviorism has foundered in large part because of the reductionists' similar failure to deliver the promised translations.

Neither form of behaviorism can sustain the rejection of the subjective mental states of belief, desire, and willing. If one is going to argue either for the objective theory of mental states or for limiting the legal relevance of intentions to manifesting dangerous propensities, it will have to be on grounds other than those supplied by behaviorists.

More generally, none of the forms of skepticism we have examined should shake the realist intuition that "the state of a man's mind is as much a fact as the state of his digestion."[76] Persons really possess the mental states of belief and desire, really will (cause) the movements of their bodies, and nothing from contemporary legal theory, philosophy, or psychology should convince us otherwise.

## Conclusion

It is easy to parody the view of persons as autonomous and rational agents by showing that it leaves out much of what we know to be true about persons. One such parody is A.P. Herbert's well-known portrait of tort law's reasonable man, about whom Herbert concludes: "All solid virtues are his, save only the peculiar quality by which the affection of other men is won."[77] Such parodies are not challenges to the legal view of persons because they show only that it is incomplete. Many of the most valued attributes of the particular persons each of us care about have nothing to do with autonomy and rationality, in either the fundamental or some richer senses of those words. The very abstract view of persons in terms of autonomy and rationality is of course radically incomplete as a picture of any person we know. In particular, left out is the life of the emotions where, if anywhere, the "affections of other men" are gained. Yet such radical incompleteness of the law's view of a person is no argument that it is wrong. As far as it goes, the law's view of persons could be quite correct even if radically incomplete. It takes a view of mind quite different than that of commonsense psychology to challenge the law's own view of persons, rooted as is the law's view of mind in part of the commonsense psychology.

There is no dearth of such challenges. One we have already touched upon is radical behaviorism's quite different view of persons, which eschews any Intentional conceptualization of persons. More generally, as science progresses in its understanding of the relation between genetic background, environmental influences, the brain and behavior, the law's view of persons will seem increasingly threatened. More—and better— books will urge us to lay aside the Intentional idioms and to move beyond the accompanying moral vocabulary of "freedom and dignity." Advances in genetic research, brain physiology, information theory, and artificial intelligence will increasingly seem to many to be replacements for an Intentional conceptualization of persons. In the face of such apparent challenges it will become ever more important to be clear about what is the metaphysical view of persons presupposed by our moral and legal principles of responsibility assessment. Only with such understanding of personhood can one assess the degree to which this view is actually inconsistent with (and thus threatened by) the competing images of man proposed by the various sciences of human thought and behavior.

My own position is that nothing that science is likely to tell us can shake our metaphysical view of ourselves.[78] I have recently defended such a position with regard to one familiar view of persons long thought to challenge the legal view. In my recent book[79] I examine three seeming challenges to the legal view of persons coming from psychiatry and psychoanalysis. The first is a kind of conceptual imperialism whereby the psychiatric notions of health and illness are urged as substitutes for the ethical notions of goodness and badness. These are the familiar views that identify mental health as human flourishing or which identify any form of social deviance as mental illness. Such views, if accepted, would make meaningless the law's attempt to separate the sick from the bad. For on such views no one is really bad except in the sense that one is sick or ill. On such views the law's division of human beings into accountable or nonaccountable agents makes little sense; given the merger of badness into sickness, *no* human beings are accountable for the bad results they may cause. This view is destructive of the law's idea that a person is a being who has passed some threshold of rationality such that he can fairly be ascribed responsibility. The second challenge stems from the idea that Freud made almost definitive of twentieth-century psychiatry, that of the unconscious. "All of the categories which we employ to describe conscious mental acts, such as ideas, purposes, resolutions and so forth," Freud wrote, could be applied to describe the *unconscious* mental life.[80] "Indeed, of many of these latent states we have to assert that the only point in which they differ from states which are conscious is just in the lack of consciousness of them."[81] This idea, of a kind of shadow mind, the existence and contents of which are unknown to its possessor, could have a radical impact on the legal view of persons, depending upon how the unconscious is conceived. If the unconscious is conceived of in Intentional terms, then it seems that the mental life of man is far richer than the law has supposed, so that nominal accidents may really be (unconsciously) intentional actions for reasons. Alternatively, if the unconscious is conceived of in the nonIntentional vocabulary of the Freudian metapsychologies, it may seem that the supposed rationality and autonomy of persons is an illusion, that really no one is responsible because no one is free from the grip of the seething, irrational currents of his primary process thinking.

The third challenge to the legal view of persons comes from the temptation not only of psychiatrists but of others as well, to fractionate the person into smaller selves. An animistic conception of the unconscious—as a kind of second autonomous and rational self—is one strand of this kind of subdividing of persons. But there are other strands as well. Whenever a theory attributes causal agency and practical reasoning to subpersonal entities, be they called "ego," "id," "censors," "the past," "ancestors," "roles," "other people," or "System Ucs.," one presents the same challenge to the legal view of persons. The challenge is to the legal assumption that one, but only one, rational agent with causal powers (person) resides "in" any human being.

In my recent book I seek to defuse these apparent challenges to law and morality coming from psychiatry. Such a task is possible—for psychiatry, for behaviorism, sociobiology, physiological psychology, and computer science as well—only if one is clear about the metaphysics of personhood presupposed by the law. This essay is intended to serve as such a clarifying first step in a general defense of our most basic views about our nature.

## NOTES

1. See Glanville Williams, *Criminal Law: The General Part*, 2d ed. (London: Stevens and Sons, 1961).

2. George Fletcher, *Rethinking Criminal Law* (Boston: Little, Brown, 1978). Fletcher nevertheless concedes that "the quest for a general part has much to commend it" (p. 393) and proceeds in the second half of his book to articulate that general part in terms of the concepts of wrongdoing and attribution.

3. Mark Kelman, "Interpretive Construction in the Substantive Criminal Law," *Stanford Law Review* 33 (1981): 591–673. Most of Kelman's arguments would, if true, undercut the moral thesis stated below, that a coherent moral theory governs the attribution of fault to individuals.

4. Spelling out with any precision the nature of this logical relation is a notoriously difficult task. The literature in contemporary jurisprudence that speaks of principles "underlying" positive law generally contents itself with a variety of different relations paraded under this label. We seek some relation that is stronger than mere freedom from contradiction between rules and principles, and yet is weaker than strict implication. The same relation is needed by coherence theorists in epistemology.

5. H.L.A. Hart, *Punishment and Responsibility* (Oxford: Oxford University Press, 1968).

6. The "by-and-large" hedge is to take into account the obvious fact that the identity between legal and moral conditions of fault ascription is not perfect—the counterexamples of strict liability statutes, the objective standard of negligence, the partial disallowance of mistake or ignorance of law as an excuse, and the lack of an excuse version of natural necessity, are well know. For a defense of my moral thesis here, despite these discrepancies, see Jerome

Hall, *General Principles of Criminal Law,* 2d ed. (Indianapolis: Bobbs-Merrill, 1960), chaps. V and X.) Such counterexamples cannot destroy the general thesis that these moral principles fit the established doctrines of the criminal law better than any other principles, such as utilitarianism.

7. For an example of the broader moral thesis that I am not defending, see David A.J. Richards, "Human Rights and the Moral Foundations of the Substantive Criminal Law," *Georgia Law Review* 13 (1979): 1395–1446. Richards ignores any distinction between the morality of fair fault ascription and the morality that condemns certain harms or acts. It is this distinction that Hart also overlooks when he criticizes the moral thesis stated in the text. The dependence of criminal liability on moral culpability is not falsified by showing that many criminal norms prohibit conduct that is not orally prohibited. Hart, *Punishment and Responsibility,* p. 37. On this error of Hart's, see Ronald Dworkin, *Taking Rights Seriously* (Cambridge: Harvard University, 1978), p. 9.

8. Michael S. Moore, *Law and Psychiatry: Rethinking the Relationship* (Cambridge: Cambridge University Press, 1984), chap. 2.

9. The account of reasons for action stated herein follows closely the account in Michael S. Moore, "The Nature of Psychoanalytic Explanation," *Psychoanalysis and Contemporary Thought* 3 (1980): 459–543; reprinted in expanded form in L. Laudan, ed., *Mind and Medicine: Explanation and Evaluation in Psychiatry and the Biomedical Sciences, Pittsburgh Series in the Philosophy and History of Science* vol. 8 (Berkeley: University of California Press, 1983).

10. These are the difficulties having to do with the Intentionality of mental states.

11. The problems elided here are, first, that it is unclear whether we have any coherent idea of propositional identity (see P.T. Greach, *Logic Matters* [Berkeley: University of California Press, 1980], p. 170), and second, even if we do, that it guides our individuation of mental states such as those of belief or desire. In addition, the relation of material implication in premise 2 is plainly too strong: an actor need not believe that his action is a sufficient condition of bringing about his desired end; if he believes it is possible (or at least does not believe that it is impossible) that his act will have the desired effect, that is enough for him to be said to have acted with that end as his reason.

12. For a good explication of the distinction, see Brian Fay, "Practical Reasoning, Rationality, and the Explanation of Intentional Action," *Journal of the Theory of Social Behavior* 8 (1977): 77–101.

13. It is not at all clear what Aristotle meant by "practical reasoning"

and "practical syllogisms" in the scattered writings in which he used these phrases. For a defense of the view that he used it in the manner suggested in the text, where the premises of a practical inference are just the contents of a belief/desire set, see Martha Nussbaum, "Practical Syllogisms and Practical Science," in her *Aristotle's De Moto Animalum* (Princeton: Princeton University Press, 1977).

14. On the idea of the unconscious and its relation to explanatory reasons, see Moore, *Law and Psychiatry*, chaps. 7–8.

15. These stronger senses of rationality are explored in Moore, *Law and Pschiatry*, chap. 2.

16. See Arthur Danto, "Basic Action," *Amer. Philos. Quart.* 2 (1965): 141–148; D.F. Pears, "The Appropriate Causation of Intentional Basic Actions," *Critica* 7 (1975): 39–69.

17. Which is the question bequeathed to the contemporary philosophy of action by Ludwig Wittgenstein: "What is left over if I subtract the fact that my arm goes up from the fact that I raise my arm?" Ludwig Wittgenstein, *Philosophical Investigations* (London: Basil Blackwell, 1958), p. 161.

18. For further argument and example, see Richard Taylor, *Action and Purpose* (Englewood Cliffs, N.J.: Prentice Hall, 1965), p. 59.

19. John Stuart Mill, *A System of Logic* (London: Longman Group, 1965), p. 35; John Austin, *Lectures on Jurisprudence* (London: J. Murray, 1869), p. 427, and J.L. Mackie, "The Grounds of Responsibility," in P.M.S. Hacker and J. Raz, eds., *Law, Morality and Society* (Oxford: Oxford University Press, 1977), pp. 175–188. Mackie shifted the Mill-Austin theory slightly to take into account an objection H.L.A. Hart once voiced (Hart, *Punishment and Responsibility*, 90–112). Mackie points out that a causal theorist may reject any notion that an actor must desire *to move his arm* in order for that arm movement to have been an action. It is enough that such movements, "though not themselves desired, . . . were such as would normally fulfill the desire that brought them about and that they came about because they were so associated with its fullfillment" (Mackie, p. 179).

20. Alvin Goldman, *A Theory of Human Action* (Englewood Cliffs, N.J.: Prentice-Hall, 1970).

21. See Roderick Chisholm, "The Descriptive Element in the Concept of Action," *J. of Philos.* 61 (1964): 613–624; for an attempted solution, see C. Peacocke, "Deviant Causal Chains," *Midwest Studies in Philosophy* IV (1979): 123–155. Donald Davidson has reviewed Goldman's and other causal theorists' attempts to provide a causal criterion for actions, and concludes that one must "despair of

spelling out . . . the way in which attitudes must cause actions if they are to rationalize the action." Davidson, *Actions and Events* (New York: Oxford University Press, 1980), p. 79.

22. One might show that the causal power of a person itself depends on the knowledge of the acting subject that he is acting. This is not a causal theory of action (act = movement caused by belief) but rather, an epistemic indicator of when a person acts. I articulate this epistemic criterion in "Responsibility and the Unconscious," *Southern California Law Review* 53 (1980): 1536–1675.

23. John Locke, *Two Treatises of Government* (New York: Hafner Publishing, 1956), p. 134.

24. See generally Moore, *Law and Psychiatry,* chap. 10, for a defense of this "compatibilist" position.

25. Gilbert Ryle, *The Concept of Mind* (London: Hutchinson and Co., 1949). A considerable literature followed Ryle in pursuing the various distinctions that have been thought to constitute this category difference.

26. The word "Intentional" is capitalized to distinguish this characteristic from the more familiar "intention" or "intentional" of ordinary speech. Brentano held that "every mental phenomenon is characterized by what the scholastics of the Middle Ages called the Intentional Inexistence of an object and which we would call . . . the reference to a content, a direction upon an object." Franz Brentano, *Psychologie vom Empirischen Standpunkt* (Leipzig, 1874). A selection of this work is translated in: R. Chisholm, ed., *Realism and the Background of Phenomenology* (Glencoe, Ill.: Free Press, 1960). A more modern characterization of Intentionality is in terms of three criteria: (1) A sentence is Intentional if it uses a name or description in such a way that neither the sentence nor its contradictory implies either that there is or there isn't anything to which the name or expression truly applies. "I hope for a 60-foot sailboat," for example, does not imply that there is a 60-foot sailboat. (2) A sentence is Intentional if it contains a propositional clause whose truth or falsity is not implied by the sentence as a whole, or its contradictory. "I hope that it will rain," for example, does not imply that "it will rain" is true or false. (3) A sentence is Intentional if codesignative names or descriptions cannot be substituted and preserve truth. I may, for example, order the largest room in some inn; even if the largest room is identical with the dirtiest room in the inn, one cannot substitute the second description for the first; I did not order the dirtiest room in the inn. See R. Chisholm, *Perceiving: A Philosophical Study* (Ithaca: Cornell University Press, 1957), pp. 170–171.

27. See William Lycan, "On Intentionality and the Psychological,"

*American Philosophical Quarterly* (1969): 305–312; Dan Dennett, *Content and Consciousness* (London: Routledge and Kegan Paul, 1969), chap. II.

28. For the classic treatment of this, see Willard Van Orman Quine, "Reference and Modality," in his *From a Logical Point of View* (Cambridge: Harvard University Press, 1961), pp. 139–159. To say that a language is Intentional is to say that it is not extensional. See James Cornman, "Intentionality and Intensionality," *Philos. Quart.* 12 (1962): 44–52.

29. See W.V.O. Quine, "The Scope and Language of Science," in his *Ways of Paradox* (New York: Random House, 1966).

30. The "at present" hedge in the text is to avoid taking the Rylean position that one can logically show that no such reductions are possible. See Alan Garfinkel, *Forms of Explanation* (New Haven: Yale University Press, 1980), p. 49, for a discussion of the provisional independence we should grant Intentionalist descriptions. See also Moore, *Law and Psychiatry,* chap. 1.

31. A realist view about minds grants that there really are mental states, that in any taking of inventory of the furniture of the universe mental states must be included just as surely as tables and chairs. Such a philosophical realist about minds is to be distinguished from the ill-named legal realists, who were typically antirealists in their metaphysics.

32. W. Hohfeld, *Fundamental Legal Conceptions* (New Haven: Yale University Press, 1923), pp. 27–31. See also Alf Ross, "Tu-Tu," *Harvard Law Review* 70 (1957): 812–825.

33. Fletcher, *Rethinking Criminal Law,* pp. 396–401. For a similar idea, see Daniel Dennett, "The Conditions of Personhood," in A. Rorty, ed., *The Identities of Persons* (Berkeley: University of California Press, 1976), pp. 175–196, wherein Dennett urges that we have two different concepts of a person, "the moral notion and the metaphysical notion" (p. 176). That different speech acts are being performed with "person" is no argument that the word is ambiguous.

34. For a discussion of genuine cases of ambiguity in legal uses of words, see Michael Moore, "The Semantics of Judging," *Southern California Law Review* 54 (1981): 151–294, especially pp. 181–188.

35. H.L.A. Hart, "The Ascription of Responsibility and Rights," *Proc. Arist. Soc'y* 49 (1949): pp. 171–194. Hart later came to repudiate his ascriptivism.

36. John Dewey, *Human Nature and Conduct* (New York: Holt, Rhinehart and Winston, 1922) pp. 120–121.

37. Fletcher, *Rethinking Criminal Law,* p. 397.

38. 248 N.Y. 339, 162 N.E. 99 (1928).

39. Idem at 354, 162 N.E. at 104.

40. Stanley Ingber, "Book Review," *U.C.L.A. Law Review* 27 (1980): 816–848, at pp. 822–24.

41. For discussion of this argument, and citation to the Szaszian literature, see Moore, *Law and Psychiatry,* chap. 4.

42. Felix Cohen, "Transcendental Nonsense and the Functional Approach," *Columbia Law Review* 35 (1935): 809–849. For an exposition of the dependence of American legal realism upon a functionalist theory of meaning, see Robert Summers, *Instrumentalism and American Legal Theory* (Ithaca: Cornell University Press, 1982), p. 32.

43. For example, C.L. Stevenson, *Ethics and Language* (New Haven: Yale University Press, 1944); R.M. Hare, *The Language of Morals* (Oxford: Oxford University Press, 1952). For a helpful summary of the early forms of emotivism in ethics, see J.O. Urmson, *The Emotive Theory of Ethics* (Oxford: Oxford University Press, 1968).

44. Christopher Stone, "Corporate Accountability in Law and Morals," in J. Houck and O. Williams, eds., *The Judaeo-Christian Vision and the Modern Business Corporation* (Notre Dame: University of Notre Dame Press, 1982).

45. Idem at p. 285.

46. Idem.

47. Michael Moore, "Moral Reality," *Wisconsin Law Review* 1982, pp. 1061–1156.

48. Another way of putting the legal realist's point about meaning is to say that the meaning of legal concepts is wholly "context-dependent," that is, that they depend on what (purpose) one wants to achieve in uttering them. For an attack on this Fullerian version, see Moore, "The Semantics of Judging," pp. 274–277.

49. Hyman Gross, *A Theory of Criminal Justice* (New York: Oxford University Press, 1979), p. 103.

50. See G.E.M. anscombe, *Intention,* 2d ed. (Ithaca, N.Y.: Cornell University Press, 1963).

51. Gross, *Theory of Criminal Justice,* p. 100.

52. All the quotations in this paragraph are from Gross, *Theory of Criminal Justice,* at pp. 109, 98, 91, and 97. The last two sentences refer to pp. 88 and 89.

53. Fletcher, *Rethinking Criminal Law,* p. 437.

54. Fletcher, p. 436.

55. Fletcher, p. 436.

56. Wittgenstein, *Philosophical Investigations.*

57. See Michael Oakshott, *Experience and its Modes* (Cambridge: Cambridge University Press, 1933); William Dray, *Laws and Explanation in History* (Oxford: Oxford University Press, 1957); R.G. Collingwood, *The Idea of History* (Oxford: Oxford University Press, 1946).

For a sympathetic relating of Collingwood to the issues of contemporary action theory, see Rex Martin, *Historical Explanation: Re-enactment and Practical Inference* (Ithaca: Cornell University Press, 1977).

58. For a brief discussion of the *verstehen* tradition in German history and sociology, see G.H. Von Wright, *Explanation and Understanding* (Ithaca, N.Y.: Cornell University Press, 1973), pp. 4–7.

59. Von Wright, *Explanation and Understanding*, p. 115.

60. Donald Davidson (despite his staunch adherence to a causal view of reasons) is led to what he calls "the necessarily holistic character of interpretations of propositional attitudes" by this motivation. See Davidson, *Actions and Events*, pp. 238–9.

61. Davidson, who sees this analogy, believes that to say what the utterance *meant* is to infuse one's own (observer) concepts into the interpretation of the utterance. Yet Davidson would not dispute that a particular act of speech existed at a particular time, even if that act of speech requires interpretation to be understood.

62. Whether there is anything that could be called a "language of the brain" is a hotly contested matter. For an introductory, if skeptical, treatment of the issues involved, see Dan Dennett, "Brian Writing and Mind Reading," in *Brainstorms* (Putney, Vt: Bradford Books, 1978), pp. 39–50. Compare Jerry Fodor, *The Language of Thought* (New York: Thomas Y. Crowell, 1975). Although one might doubt that the relation between language and brain physiology is as simple as the "language of thought" school would suggest, surely some relation exists between language abilities and such physiology.

63. For the separation of methodological from philosophical behaviorism, see Michael Martin, "Interpreting Skinner, *Behaviorism*. 6 (1978): 129–138.

64. Norman Malcolm (with a good deal of textual support) construes Skinner to be a reductionist about mental terms. See Norman Malcolm, "Behaviorism as a Philosophy of Psychology," in T.W. Wann, ed., *Behaviorism and Phenomenology* (Chicago: University of Chicago Press, 1964), pp. 141–154. In her attempt to construe Skinner in such a was as to immunize him from the defects of philosophical behaviorism, Brenda Mapel makes the case for Skinner as a nonreductionist. See Brenda Munsey Mapel, "Philosophical Criticism of Behaviorism: An Analysis," *Behaviorism* 5 (1977): 17–32. Dan Dennett nicely separates Skinner's various arguments against mentalist language, and rightly concludes that Skinner never even saw that he had to take a position on this issue: "It is unfathomable how Skinner can be so sloppy on this score, for reflection should reveal to him, as it will to us, that this vacil-

lation is over an absolutely central point in his argument." Dennett, *Brainstorms*, p. 63.

65. Herbert Fingarette, *The Meaning of Criminal Insanity* (Berkeley and Los Angeles: University of California Press, 1972), p. 82

66. As Jerome Hall points out, the objective theory of mental states need not rest on such antirealist positions about minds: "Holmes did not rest his theory upon that so-called 'skeptical' position. . . . He acknowledged that mental states can be discovered and, in the face of that, he maintained that this knowledge is irrelevant in modern penal law, and properly so! In sum, his theory challenges the ethics of penal law, not its epistemology." Jerome Hall, *General Principles of Criminal Law*, p. 156.

67. Oliver Wendell Holmes, *The Common Law* (Cambridge, Mass.: Harvard University Press, 1963), p. 56

68. Dennett, "Skinner Skinned," in *Brainstorms*, nicely separates these various methodological claims.

69. For a separation of the claims of privileged access from those of incorrigibility, and an attack on the latter, see Moore, "Nature of Psychoanalytic Explanation."

70. B.F. Skinner, *Beyond Freedom and Dignity* (New York: Knopf, 1971), p. 200.

71. Skinner, "Behaviorism at Fifty," in T.W. Wann, ed, *Behaviorism and Phenomenology* (Chicago: University of Chicago Press, 1964), p. 80.

72. These included Norman Malcolm's epistemic arguments, based on the oddness of behavioral translations of first-person psychological reports ("I am in pain" is a statement whose truth is not inferred by the actor from observing his own pain-behavior). See Norman Malcolm, "Behaviorism as a Philosophy of Psychology," in T.N. Wann, ed., *Behaviorism and Phenomenology*. Richard Peters and others also urged that behaviorial reductions could not bridge the "logical gulf" or "categorical difference" between intelligent, rule-following, purposive action on the one hand, and colorless movements and other "dumb" phenomena, on the other. See Peters, *The Concept of Motivation* (London: Routledge and Kegan Paul, 1958). More recently, Quine and others have urged that certain logical peculiarities of mentalistic language—having to do with "belief" and other mental words taking *objects* or contents—preclude any kind of reduction, whether of a behavioral or a neurophysiological kind. For Quine, as for Skinner, this means one should *avoid* "belief," "desire" and other Intentional idioms in formulating a truly scientific (and behaviorist) science of human behavior; one should avoid such idioms precisely because one could *not* reduce them to scientifically respectable (i.e., non-Intentional) speech. See W.V.O. Quine, *Word and Object* (Cambridge, Mass.: M.I.T. Press,

1960). Quine admits that "there is no breaking out of the Intentional vocabulary by explaining its members in other terms" (p. 220).

73. Moore, "The Semantics of Judging," at pp. 208–210.

74. Ryle, *Concept of Mind.*

75. See Mapel, "Philosophical Criticism of Behaviorism."

76. Justice Bowen, in *Edington* v. Fitzmaurice, 29 Ch. Div. 459, 483 (1882).

77. A.P. Herbert, *Uncommon Law,* 7th ed. (1952), pp. 2–3.

78. This is not because our metaphysical beliefs can't be controverted by evidence or changed, but rather, because our metaphysical beliefs about persons are not in fact challenged by the *seemingly* competing views of behaviorist psychology, dynamic psychiatry, and the like.

79. Moore, *Law and Psychiatry.*

80. Sigmund Freud, "The Unconscious," in *Collected Papers,* vol. IV (New York: Basic Books, 1959), pp. 98–136, at p. 101.

81. Freud, "The Unconscious."

# 2

# INTENTIONALITY AND THE CONCEPT OF THE PERSON

## LAWRENCE ROSEN

Social scientists have long accepted as the starting point of their task the analysis of the ways in which the people of a given culture interpret one another's actions and orient their own endeavors accordingly. Such interpretations and their assessment may be given as a matter of common sense in everyday affairs or left to the special consideration of professionals to whom the task of making sense of something on behalf of all may be incorporated into the overall scheme of an acceptable social order. But whatever its particular components—from the most obvious recognition of another's acts to the most arcane account rendered of them—it remains an axiom of modern social science that the modes by which we perceive and act toward others are intimately entwined with—and have systemic repercussions for—a host of social, economic, religious, political, and other aspects of that culture. To raise the question of how another is perceived, or how, in a given society, the very idea of a person is conceptualized, is to tap into one of the central understandings by which a culture is composed and sustained.

The author acknowledges with gratitude the support provided by the John Simon Guggenheim Foundation, the Rockefeller Foundation Study Center at Bellagio, and the John D. and Catherine T. MacArthur Foundation Award. I also greatly appreciate the discussions I have had about this paper with Paul Gehl, Penny Schine Gold, Anthony T. Grafton, R. Kent Greenawalt, Stanley N. Katz, Amelie Rorty, and Abraham L. Udovitch.

As in other realms, the question of the concept of the person is often at the heart of the way in which a legal system handles issues of fact and fault, procedure and remedy. For even if legal specialists have developed methods and ideas concerning the nature of the individual, his personality, his social responsibilities, his command over his own acts, and the nature of his inner state, these legal concepts will be deeply embedded in, and draw much of their sustenance and meaning from, the way the person is conceptualized in the broader realm of society. Indeed, it is both the subject and the thesis of this chapter that in order to understand the development and application of the concept of intentionality in any legal system it is indespensable to place this concept in the larger context of the cultural definition of the person. Specifically, I consider the relationship between the way in which intentionality is attributed in the Islamic law of contemporary Morocco and the way in which the individual is constituted in that culture. Then by drawing a comparison with the development of the idea of the individual as the possessor of a distinct interior state in early medieval Europe I consider how, subtly and often quite indirectly, a change in ideas about the very nature of the individual might contribute to a gradual shift in legal concepts. Finally, I consider some of the ways social scientists have tackled the problem of other minds in other cultures and to speculate on the role that competing views of the self have played in the formation of the concept of intentionality in contemporary American law.

I

To the Western eye the Moroccan concept of the person seems strikingly familiar for its emphasis on the individual as the fundamental social unit and its frequent and explicit reference to an inner state, a frame of mind, an intentional structure that is integral to each individual.[1] Yet elements that may have analogues in one culture may, by their arrangement and interpretation, carry a quite different set of meanings in another. Thus, in the Moroccan case familiar ideas take on a distinctive shape when viewed as an ordered system.[2]

To Moroccans each individual is the embodiment of a constellation of situated traits and ties, a cumulation of features that are made available through the medium of a set of defining concepts and subject to an on-going process of negotiation. Specifically, there are three central ideas, each embraced in a set of critical terms, through which the person is defined and known, concepts that relate to the nature of human nature, the sources of one's attachments and customs, and the essentially negotiable quality of interpersonal obligations.

Human nature is, in the Moroccan view, centered on the relation, indeed the struggle, between two major attributes: *nafs*, or "passion," and *ʿaqel*, "reason." Each individual, it is said, possesses both of these qualities but their distribution, particularly as between men and women, children and adults is seen to vary considerably. Men not only possess a greater capacity to develop reasoning powers than do women but must, for that very reason, be held to higher standards. Children, being all *nafs* and little *ʿaqel*, must be placed under the guidance of wise teachers and made, by habit and repetition, to develop their reasoning powers so they may channel their passions into useful and legitimate pursuits. Passions are not, in and of themselves, evil: "to have *nafs*" is to have "self-respect," but to be "eaten up by one's *nafs*" is to be an "egotist." Study and the acquisition of worldly knowledge will keep sexual passion within bounds: attachment to others who have developed the capacity for reason will increase the socially desirable aspects of acquisitiveness and personal ambition. Thus to characterize others and be characterized in turn in terms of the *nafs-ʿaqel* paradigm is to stress that men and women are responsible for the development of their own knowledge and reasoning powers, that the consequences of an action may be attributable to this inherent quality of passion and reason, and that the standard of behavior to which different kinds of persons may be held is, in part, itself a function of the interaction of one's nature and the situations in which it is developed and enacted.

The emphasis on the interplay of context and nature is similarly represented in another Arabic concept, *asel*. The term itself means "origin," "patrimony," "descent," "strength of character," "authentic," "proper," and "indigenous." As an attribute of personal identity, *asel* summarizes the idea that individuals draw much of their character from the physical and social environment that has contributed to their nurture and sustenance. To say of a man that he "possesses *asel*" is to imply that he has roots in a group and a locale whose characteristic modes of establishing and enacting relationships can give another a sense of the ties it may be possible to form with him. Thus where an American may wish, first, to place another by asking what he *does* (i.e., what occupation he practices) because such information conveys a host of implications for economic, social, and political attitudes, in Morocco the central question is "where are your 'origins'" since it is this information which, initially, conveys a degree of predictability about the sort of ties that are possible with such a man. Summarized in personal names or nicknames, and signaled by everything from the way a turban is tied to the way one sits in the marketplace, the concept of a man's "origins" focuses attention on his relationships and the customs by which they are formed, and feeds directly into the belief that all relationships imply the need for reciprocity. The key word here is the Arabic term *ḥaqq*.

*Ḥaqq* is usually translated as "truth" or "reality" and, as such, is both a name for the Almighty and a characterization of worldly utterances and events. But *ḥaqq* also means "right" and "duty" and thus conveys the idea of obligation, indeed of an attachment born of a contract or covenant, whether explicit or implicit. To Moroccans this is a vital concept, for to them every relationship implies an obligation: whether it is a bond formed by kinship or residence, political affiliation or economic association it is a central assumption of Moroccan life that every action toward another creates an obligation that may be called up later in a similar or varied form. "Truth" and "reality" are therefore the arrangement of obligational bonds among men and between man and God. And the social world is one in which each man must come to know and operate within a realm of ever-shifting bonds of indebtedness.

Through each of these three conceptual domains, as well as many others, common themes can be seen at work. Each incorporates a sense of the interaction between qualities and relationships available in the world of everyday experience and the individual as the entity who draws from this available repertoire in the construction of his or her distinctive patterning of these features. The trick, as it were, is to arrange one's ties in such a way as to secure oneself and one's dependents as best as possible in a world conceived as constantly on the brink of chaos (*fitna*). Two culturally distinctive features—each of which has an important bearing on the concept of intentionality—thus become central to the arrangement of such ties.

In the construction of personal networks Moroccans recognize that the very terms they use to characterize others—as a "cousin," a "fellow tribesman," a "neighbor" and so on—contain, at their very heart, a quality of essential negotiability. That is to say, the referent of such a term is not a specific tie that is fixed in the world and given institutional support by the arrangement of individuals in a series of corporate groups for which the specific acts of an individual would be largely defined by the expectations and sanctions associated with each of the terms used to characterize their ties. Rather, each individual is expected to negotiate with and through these terms in the arrangement of his own affiliations. To call another "cousin" or to say that "we are from the same family (*ʿāʾila*)" is not to depict a settled relationship but to invoke a basis of affiliation whose specific content must be bargained out in the process of forming an interpersonal bond. This means that, just as men must negotiate a price in the marketplace, so, too, the repertoire of relational possibilities upon which they play and through which their obligations will be formed must be negotiated using all the knowledge, associations, and shrewdness one can marshal in the formation of a personal network.

An important concomitant of this quest for negotiated bonds concerns the Moroccan concept of truth. Since the terms that imply some form of obligation remain incompletely defined, open-textured, until, by a process of negotiation, an actual relationship comes to be defined through them, it is not surprising that Moroccans distinguish between the role words play in assaying the ties that are *possible* in any encounter and the role such words play in *fixing* a relationship, in linking such utterances to a series of specific consequences. What is at issue, therefore, is the way in which mere utterances come to possess some attachment to the quality of truth. But whereas a Westerner who makes a statement about his relation to another may expect his utterance to be seen as having some implications of truthfulness—even if it is a bald-faced lie—Moroccans assume that a statement about relationships to others, standing alone, has absolutely no bearing whatsoever on the question of truth or falseness. It is, again, like a price mentioned in the market, which is not "true" in any sense until the parties make it applicable to their circumstance. Similarly, in Moroccan social life, a statement about relationships has no truth value until something more happens, until that utterance receives some validation. This may occur in a variety of ways, including the use of oaths, validation by a reliable witness, stylized modes of conducing the agreement of others, or by convincing others that one's reliant actions were properly based. By delaying the point at which a statement about relationships is seen to trigger expectations and demands for reciprocity, one puts at a distance entangling obligations. By characterizing all unvalidated utterances as having no truth value leeway is granted for the negotiation of one's personal attachments.

Some of the implications of these cultural principles for the Moroccan concept of the person are immediately apparent. To Moroccans the concept of the self is not that of a personally fashioned individual, one who has, by whatever spiritual or psychological means, created an inner self distinctive from all others. Nor is it a concept of the self as *persona,* a mask presented to others that conceals an inner self but which is itself an artifact created by that inner self. Rather, it is a concept of the individual as one who maneuvers within the broad set of relationships, human qualities, and changing circumstances to cumulate for himself a set of publicly recognized and worldly consequent traits and ties. The world is pictured as a place within which individuals forge alliances and affiliations by drawing on relations and concepts that are, at their most fundamental level, fraught with the idea of implicit obligation.

It is a world—and hence a self—in which a man is known by his situated obligations and by the consequences that his actions have on the entire chain of obligations by which he and his society are known. Each individual is not only free to negotiate within and beyond the confines of kinship, locality, and linguistic community the bonds of obligation that will form his own web of indebtedness: the very words he uses—from kinship terms to the concepts of *ḥaqq* and *asel* themselves—are subject to a great deal of bargaining, the specific meaning they will carry in any given situation being the momentary result of a process of bargaining over the applicability and implications of the term employed.

Thus, for Moroccans the person is always a situated actor. He embodies qualities of human nature, attachment to the people and place of his nurture, and association with those to whom he owes and from whom he receives negotiated bonds of obligation. Men do not create themselves, but they can place themselves in contexts—with teachers, partners, kinsmen, or strangers—such that the process of bargained-for relationships that will define their place in the world of men will yield a characterization that tells who, quite literally, they are. Men, says an Arabic proverb, are men through men; only God is God through Himself.

This emphasis on man as a socially situated self whose public person is the socially relevant person is at the heart of the Moroccan concept of intentionality.[3] The word in Arabic for intent is *niya*, which is usually translated as "intent," "purpose," "plan," "volition," or "desire." *Niya* also means "naive" or "sincere," and hence to act "with *niya*" is to act with loyalty and good faith. *Niya* also has deep religious significance. Before each of the daily prayers—and in some Islamic countries, before many other ritual and legal acts—the believer declares, softly or aloud, the *niya*, the statement of intent by which he signifies the meaning and purpose of his act. But intent, in the Moroccan view, is not simply a matter of one's inner state, a secret domain into which God alone can peer and that lies either hidden from or irrelevant to the world of human affairs. Rather, Moroccans believe that overt acts are directly connected to interior states, and that if you know a man's traits and ties, and the contexts in which these are revealed you will also know that person's intentional structure. This attitude, which can be seen at work in the explanation of everyday behavior, is central to, and not sharply differentiated from its application in, the realm of legal decisions.

The question of intent arises in a number of legal contexts: in determining the validity of a religious bequest, in characterizing the nature of certain partnerships and contracts, and in assessing culpability in matters of criminal law. Although specific aspects of an inquiry into intent vary from one legal issue to another, a glance at the example of homicide may help us to understand the general development of the concept of intentionality in Moroccan legal culture.

In almost all parts of the Middle East and North Africa, in the years before Western influence became predominant, the appropriate recompense for killing another was the payment of blood money *(diya)*. Compensation was also the appropriate remedy for injury. The Quran distinguishes between killing with intent *(ʿamd)* and by mistake *(kaṭaʾ)*, and the four main schools of Islamic law that developed in the early Islamic period made further refinements in this distinction. For Islamic jurists, therefore, the question of intent was very important: the amount of compensation due or the permissibility of retaliation *(qiṣāṣ)* was a function of whether the act was deemed intentional. But for scholars and jurists alike intent was not a question of the accused's state of mind as such. Rather, inner state was assumed from overt acts. The intention of killing was presumed whenever an illegal killing followed an act generally regarded as fatal in its result. A great deal of casuistry developed over matters of external evidence, especially the nature of the weapon: for example, that a deadly weapon was used was sufficient to impute an intent to kill. Even when an act was the result of a mistake—thinking the injured man was a wild animal, accidentally suffocating a bed partner by rolling over on him in the night—blood money had to be paid by the offender or his kinsmen. Victorien Loubignac reports that among the Zaer tribe, for example, even if a harm was unintentional the perpetrator had to pay for the upkeep of the guests who visited the injured and for part of the injured man's support if his wounds were especially grave.[4]

The emphasis, then, is squarely on the consequences of an act. External evidence, such as the kind of weapon used, is taken as an index of an interior state, an insight into what the person must have meant. By categorizing types of situations jurists were saying something about a state of mind. The connecting point would appear to be the idea that no one who is not immature, insane, or spiritually possessed would engage in a particular kind of act without intending its usual consequences. Whatever the other advantages of, for example, blood money payments—as a form of social insurance, a limitation on the scope of violence, or a less harsh penalty when situation and intent were ambiguous—drawing a direct correlation between act and intent reaffirmed the link between private choice and public consequence. Intent, in Islamic law, was therefore neither irrelevant nor the subject of more direct religious or psychological inquiry: it was assumed to be a necessary and discernible element of a given act.

This emphasis on discerning intent through situated acts continues to manifest itself in Moroccan adjudication, notwithstanding the use, during the Protectorate and post-Protectorate periods, of European criminal codes. In interviews, judges repeatedly insist that they can tell what a man's intent is and whether he is lying simply by inquiring carefully into his background, relationships, and prior behavior. Similarly, when stories are told in Morocco—rather like those related in the *Thousand and One Nights*—of really clever judges, they often involve the judge disguising himself and entrapping the suspect into committing the same or a similar infraction as that of which he is accused. The clever judge is not, of course, determining whether the man did in fact do what he is accused of: he is seeing if he is a person who will ever do such a thing; he is making an investigation into the accused's character. "If a man is bad," one judge told me, "he cannot hide it. It will show up in the way he acts. If you ask a lot of questions a man cannot keep his thoughts hidden: his intention *[niya]* will be obvious."

Thus the belief that a man's interior state is directly accessible and relevant for legal determinations is clearly embedded in the broader perception of the person in Moroccan culture. Men are formed and known by the contexts—the situations of interlocking bonds of reciprocity—they have forged with one another through the medium of terms and concepts that take on meaning as the relationships created through them take shape. To know a man one needs to know the contexts of his acts. That is why, in the telling of stories or historic accounts, Moroccans find temporal sequence far less revealing about why someone acted as he did than an account of how that individual has acted in a wide variety of situations. Similarly, in the courtroom, evidence is often adduced as to a wide range of an individual's activities and relationships since it is context that reveals action and action that reveals intent. The logic by which intent is attributed in the law is, notwithstanding four decades of French colonial rule and the subsequent adoption of some codes based on European examples, one that is squarely linked to the modes of reasoning and the perception of other minds that inform a wide range of Moroccan cultural life.

## II

From roughly the middle of the eleventh century and throughout most of the twelfth European concepts of the nature and role of the individual underwent a profound alteration, an alteration that stemmed from and affected such diverse realms as religion, literature, law, and political life. It was, in essence, a shift from the view, current in late antiquity, of the individual as deeply embedded in a set of loyalties and conventions that allowed and encouraged little scope for personal initiative and development to a concept of the individual as the possessor of an inner self that is capable of being understood and expressed in relations with God and one's fellow men. From an emphasis on overt acts as the central quality and defining feature of the individual, a person's inner state—his feelings, his motives, his reasoning capacity, and his sense of the moral—came to take precedence. Although the change cannot be attributed to a simple set of causal factors, it is clear that much of the impetus came as a result of changes in the realm of religious thought.[5]

The central embodiment—the archetype and metaphor—of the complete human being in the early Middle Ages was the monk. Not only was the monk the exemplar of other-worldly asceticism, he also lived in an order in which adherence to strict rules, obedience to the dictates of his society, and an unwavering stress on the proper acts of ritual life defined his very existence. Failure to perform requisite acts, rather than inappropriate motives, was central. Even in the world outside the walls of the monasteries, where cities were few and kinship attachments central, where scholarship was at its low ebb and even the introspection of a St. Augustine had been lost to common view, the stress on man as the enactment of his obligations and the lack of concern with an inner state was unmistakable.

By the second half of the eleventh century a significant change was under way. In place of the unquestioned acceptance of monastic routine or a spirituality based on the overt, the attention of theologians and scholars turned more toward the nature of a man's mind and his active engagement in comprehending an inner state separable from his every act. "Stir up your torpid mind," preached the great Benedictine, St. Anselm: "Enter into the chamber of your mind and exclude all else but God and those things which help you in finding Him."[6] In an age when (with the exception of Italy) cities were just beginning to burgeon, when the rediscovery of classical writers added the rigor of logic to the earlier concern with regularized conduct, and when new classes and concepts of social rank were beginning to emerge, this recasting of the fundamental Christian conviction that the sinner may be made over by the Holy Spirit if only he opens himself to Him carried great force. To the most important figure in this development, Bernard of Clarivaux, a man's inner life—his devotion, his love, his humility, and his inward drive for knowledge—could propel him to the acquisition of self-knowledge and thenceforth to knowledge of God. Through an emphasis on the stages of a man's mental growth St. Bernard was able to articulate an educational program firmly ensconced in the monastic setting yet give voice to the centrality in this development of a distinctive inner self.

It was, however, in St. Bernard's great rival Peter Abelard that the concept of an interior self received its furthest extension in this period. To Abelard intention was all: sinfulness was not a function of overt act but of the sinful desire that lay within, and therefore a man might believe he was acting rightly yet be sinful, or vice versa. Men might punish actions, but God looks to the inner self; God remains omnipotent but men must struggle within themselves to achieve a kind of inner conversion. Although St. Bernard was to succeed in repressing Abelard's views,[7] there was, in the view they and many others shared, a common orientation toward self-awareness and the primacy of man's inner self.

These theological reconceptualizations were not without their attachments to the daily routine of Christian religious life and secular politics. The Eucharist, with its stress on Christianity as a community of believers, became less central than those elements of the Mass directed toward the cultivation of individual devotion. The doctrine of contritionism, which argued that repentance was sufficient for absolution, ultimately lost out to the Church's insistence on the role of the priest in granting forgiveness, but it did spark a body of confessional literature in which men and women explored the nature of their inner selves. The Virgin Mary took on new significance. She appeared miraculously to individuals and her direct and private encounters encouraged men in the pursuit of personal devotion. Even Christ, who for a thousand years had been represented in painting and sculpture as dead on the cross, now became a living, suffering figure, an individual whose agony was quite recognizably private and interior no less than redemptive and universal. In politics, we can detect a concomitant shift from consensual decision making within ecclesiastical bodies to a recognition that legitimate authority might reside in individual leaders, a shift that gave further impetus to man's image of himself as a rational creature.

Nowhere is the new sense of self-awareness more fully represented than in the burst of literary activity of the twelfth century. The epic poems that were so popular in preceding centuries had shown men fulfilling their obligations by adhering to the code of aristocratic convention. As the epic form gives way to the development of the romance—whether in tales of chivalrous knights, the satires of a Chrétien de Troyes, or the popular *Miracles of the Virgin*—the affections, experiences, and intentions of the individual knight, lover, or believer are given central place. As Robert Hanning has convincingly demonstrated, the characters in a romance "use their personal wit and ingenuity to shape their encounters with the world outside themselves to their own benefit, self-consciously and in ways that are often morally problematic."[8] The figure in a romance thus comes to view reality from a personal perspective, and by his emphasis on the inner life to shift the very terms by which men apprehend their world. "Chivalric romance, as it emerged in twelfth-century courtly society, offered a literary form in which to work out the implications of individuality, implications which twelfth-century theology and philosophy were beginning to confront, but were not yet able for lack of technical and conceptual vocabulary, fully to describe and categorize."[9] With this emphasis on the inner self also comes a new meaning to time.

In the narrative style of the romance, time exists to allow man
to grow and experience; becoming replaces being. It is not the
passage of great events or ages that marks a man's biography;
what is significant is the way, at critical moments, "the personal
experience of time shapes responses which contribute to self-
definition, and in the long run, impel the individual toward or
away from self-fulfillment."[10] One can understand events,
therefore, only by the cumulation of numerous individual-cen-
tered views, and one can know individual men only by comprehending their discovery of truth through the discovery of
themselves.

The discovery of the individual (to borrow Colin Morris's
characterization of this development) was, as scholars have been
careful to note, neither uniform nor sudden nor without its
contradictions. Its central features involve, as Morris himself
argued, "a concern with self-discovery; an interest in the relations between people, and in the role of the individual within
society; [and] an assessment of people by their inner intentions
rather than by their external acts."[11] These qualities are no less
central to the changes that occur in this period in various aspects of European law.

In the mid-eleventh century both England and the continental countries were, in quite different ways, laboring under formal rules of law that were only gradually becoming subject to
alterations in the concept of the self. In England, the Anglo-
Saxon laws effectively held sway for a half century after the
Conquest, and monetary compensation—with its emphasis on
impersonality and delay—bore strong resemblance to the early
payments of *wer* and *bot*.[12] Although elements of an accused's
state of mind appear in the ninth-century laws of Alfred, the
predominant thrust is toward assessing the consequences of a
man's acts, the question of intent, unsystematically evoked, going
more to the questions of deliberation and mitigating penalties
than to any subtle exploration of a man's inner direction.[13] Indeed, it is precisely the contending, and often contradictory,
images of the person and of the role of the state in monitoring
his conduct that reveal themselves in the conflicting elements of
these early laws. The *Leges Henrici*, compiled in the early decades of the twelfth century, gave greater attention to the issue
of intent, particularly in the famous proposition that "a person

is not to be considered guilty unless he has a guilty intention *(reum non facit nisi mens rea)."*[14] Yet contradictory propositions (e.g., "where one is unwilling, two persons do not come to blows;" "a person who unwittingly commits a wrong shall wittingly make amends"),[15] coupled with the retention of royal mercy to forgive unintended acts, suggest that the tension, on the one hand, between the individual Christian's moral choice and the needs for community harmony, and, on the other, between kin-group cohesion and the role of the state in constraining violence, had not yet achieved that degree of resolution which the developing concept of the person was to aid.

Similarly, on the continent the years leading up to the eleventh century had been marked by an emphasis on customary laws, bearing a certain family resemblance from country to country, that were far more readily comprehended by judge and petitioner alike than were the available Roman compilations. A strong emphasis on the impact of individual actions on community life added support to the elaborate use of compensatory payments based on the nature of the act. As in England, however, neither custom nor procedure implied an absolute rejection of the individuality of an accused. Thus, the ordeal, the pre-eminent fact-finding mechanism of the period, contained elements of the supernatural and the social. The ordeal not only called forth a divine determination of absolute certainty, but, as Peter Brown has argued, served the needs of tightly knit local communities by both slowing down the joinder of differences until tempers could cool and providing a symbolic vehicle for the expression of community consensus.[16] Moreover, as we know from the study of oaths and ordeals in other cultures, the decision as to who should submit to this supernatural sanction is often based on a prior, culturally inscribed assumption about which person—or, more often, which *category* of person—is most likely to know the truth and hence be put to the test. Ordeals were thus consonant with customary law and relatively weak monarchies in their emphasis on the individual as possessing a soul, an obedient heart, and a social place, but not a self that could be explored for its own distinctive intent.

The gradual shift on the continent in theology, literature, and political thought to which we referred earlier shows most clearly in the law through the development of legal education. It was, as Marc Bloch noted, "an age when every man of action had to be something of a lawyer."[17] By the early eleventh century, particularly in Bologna, men were rediscovering Roman law and applying its rules, and more generally its measured approach of reason, to a host of mundane affairs. The emphasis on logic was not unrelated to the approach of Anselm, Abelard, and others, for in both cases men sought the underlying reasons, the logical structure, of a text presented them. Where this led, in the case of religious thinkers, to a developing interest in the particularities of human emotions and thought, and, in the case of the satiric poets, to a heightened sense of the individual as set against the decadent order of church and state, in the hands of the lawyers it yielded a powerful new mentality that legitimized the rational calculation of human affairs. What was to develop into an inquisitorial form of judicial fact-finding resulted, therefore, not simply from the reception of a body of rediscovered law or from the growing realization that ordeals were subject to human manipulation. Rather, the emphasis on man's own capacities for rational fact-finding and judicial organization was inextricably linked to the establishment of a climate of thought in which the very idea that men possessed an inner self capable of discernment, expression, and investigation had become the received assumption of those who were to give such matters judicial implementation.[18]

The story in England is, of course, quite different in its legal forms but, we may conjecture, not unrelated to the developing concept of the person. In the first century after the Conquest the state was concerned with centralizing its control, through a small number of administrators, over a vast realm populated by a conquered people. Homicide, which under Anglo-Saxon law had been punishable when committed in secret, came to include killings that had occurred quite openly but which, in the eyes of the state, could lead to further disorder and for which the penalty of death could, therefore, be imposed if pardon was not granted by the king. It is not clear whether juries in the twelfth century, like those of a later century, regarded simple homicide as inappropriately characterized as murder and thus took into account some aspects of a man's moral and mental state in fashioning a definition of his crime that fit the available punishments.[19] What does appear possible is that as Church doctrine, popular sermons, and the use of some Roman concepts in legal literature converged, a climate of thought slowly developed in which the individual, and not the entire community, came to be seen as the irreducible unit of moral and social life, and hence a climate established within which distinctively English concepts of criminal liability and procedure could develop. As Francis Bowes Sayre wrote, in his analysis of the history of *mens rea,* by the early thirteenth century defenses that took account of a man's inner state—defenses that included insanity, infancy, and compulsion—began to be taken into consideration: "The point is not that morality first began to make its appearance in the law, but that an increasing and now conscious emphasis upon morality necessitated a new insistence upon psychical elements in determining criminality."[20] This morality was, I would suggest, not solely related to internal alterations in legal procedure as such but to the interaction, in the English case, of the twelfth-century stress on self-awareness and the relative autonomy of man's psychic composition, with its evocation by both jury and royal court as a central ingredient in the definition of any given situation. It is perhaps not simply, as James Marshall has suggested, that "when the law of England reached the point at which it distinguished between intended and unintended acts, judges and lawyers were already conditioned by the doctrine of free will:"[21] it is also, perhaps, that the concept of the person as one who could envision himself as a distinct and private soul capable of personal devotion and salvation through his own acts, could serve as a basis for regarding others not solely as components of an interdependent community but as persons whose inner qualities must be taken as an integral part of their overall identity. The twelfth century thus witnessed a fundamental shift in the terms and concepts by which the person was comprehended, a shift that, by its emphasis on the inner self, not only served to establish the individual as the central figure in the social and moral order but changed the very terms and concepts from a focus on external acts to a vocabulary of inner intent by which a host of legal issues could themselves come to be formulated.

## III

When Max Weber chose as the central focus of his sociology the ways in which individuals attach meaning to other's actions and orient their own activities accordingly he was not ascribing to human beings either the characteristics of cultural automata—programed to decipher one another's moves by the dictates of inviolable custom—or the insight of born mind readers—capable of clairvoyant apprehension of another's purpose and direction. Rather, for Weber, the meanings we attribute to other's acts are *socially* situated, *culturally* constructed. Our assessment of others—including any interior state—is a public process, one in which the terms that are used, the symbols employed, and the ends sought possess culturally distinctive qualities. Taken from this angle, motives and intentions are neither wholly private nor independently causal: they are culturally characteristic ascriptions by means of which the situations in which people find themselves and the kinds of people they encounter are made more or less comprehensible.

To shift the quest for motives and intentions from the private to the public, from the causal to the ascriptive, and from the realm of the positive to that of the interpretive is to open up a whole world of issues and ideas. It was in this vein, for example, that C. Wright Mills, in his essay "Situated Actions and Vocabularies of Motive," argued that "rather than fixed elements 'in' an individual, motives are the terms with which interpretation by social actors proceeds."[22] Whenever we attribute motives to others, he argued, we are really trying to define the situation in which we find ourselves. To speak of a situation as one involving "love" or "duty," "kinship obligation" or "malice" is to anticipate and judge the consequences of an act, not simply to assert a prior condition. As Gilbert Ryle put it: "The curious conclusion results that though volitions were called in to explain our appraisals of actions, this explanation if just what they fail to provide. If we had no other antecedent grounds for applying appraisal-concepts to the actions of others, we should have no reason at all for inferring from those actions to the volitions alleged to give rise to them."[23] "Actions," as Stanley Cavell has noted, "unlike envelopes and goldfinches, do not come named for assessment, nor, like apples, ripe for grading:"[24] Through the publicly worked terms by which situation, morality, and social consequences are asserted, a culture may construct, and not simply denominate, the qualities, both external and interior, of the people who make up the society.

It is particularly in the concept of the person that many of the strands by which a society articulates its vision of reality are drawn together.[25] Thus in Morocco, with all the forces of its social relations and cultural categories marshaled to form a vision of the person as a densely situated entity, an amalgam of his or her consequences in a network of obligational bonds personally forged and personally serviced, the idea of intent as directly discernible through overt act partakes of that logic of covenant and negotiation, reciprocity and maneuverability that runs through each domain of Moroccan life. For all its formal qualities, Islamic law couples with this image of the person, partakes of its central themes, and while giving special effect to its implications, is itself an integral part of that articulated vision. So, too, in medieval Europe, where the revolutionary ideas of the twelfth century about man's inner existence not only spread from the realm of theology into other domains but in a sense harmonized many concepts that were even then in flux, the situations in which men were seen to exist were redefined and with them the ways in which reasons were attributed to their acts. Legal concepts of intentionality, which had been the expression of a man's social identity as seen in his social relationships, had reflected the conflicting social and political claims made on a man's actions. But as the idea of the individual as comprising an inner, as well as a relational, self seeped into the logic of administration, literature, private devotion, and political identity the law, too, came not merely to reflect but to articulate the strains, the prospects, and the implications of the new reality.

It is, of course, not only in distant cultures or distant times that an approach to legal concepts of intentionality as part of a culture's larger view of the person may prove useful. Consider, for example, the situation in the common law countries in our own day. We are, I believe, in a time when no single concept of the self holds sway. No uniform vision of how the person is constituted or how individuals ought to be assessed commands unanimous and commonsensical acceptance. Several different, though related, views of the person are at work. There is the romantic vision of the self, which sees the inner self as the measure against which all external affairs are to be known and valued. This romantic self may be seen as given its greatest chance

for development if freed from the oppression of civilization, in-
hibitions, or social conventions or as capable of its own discovery through the possession of a private, even sacred, domain of
its own, but it invariably asserts that individuality is both a moral
good and a necessity of personal existence.[26] Except in its most
deterministic forms, the psychoanalytic vision of the self forms
a version of the romantic conception: it sees the person as an
arena in which biology and experience, impulse and convention carry on a constant struggle. The world outside each psy-
che is viewed from within and is seen to affect or service this
most central realm accordingly. Assessment of others' acts makes
sense only if viewed against the dynamics of the inner self. By
contrast, the concept of the communitarian self, while not denying private thoughts or personal meanings, sees each individual as predominantly a social personality, one whose involvement in society, whose associations and impact, constitute the
central factor in his identity and qualities. From such a vantage
a man's inner state is not as crucial as his effect on and his
treatment by society, his demonstrated commitment to the orderliness of the team, the profession, the community, or the
nation.[27]

Given these contending views of what a person is, it is small
wonder that the law, in its specific concerns with intentionality,
should appear no less uniform. There has been considerable
discussion by courts in England and the United States in recent
years over the appropriate standard to use when inferring intent from a person's acts. The English high court and Parlia-
ment have refused to be bound by the idea that one can infer
either intent or foresight simply from the natural and probable
consequences of a man's acts however much one may use the
full range of evidence to draw a variety of inferences about a
man's state of mind.[28] Similarly, in the United States, the issue
has recently been addressed in the Supreme Court's decision in
Sandstrom v. Montana.[29] In that case, a unanimous Court held
that it was error for the judge in a trial for "deliberate homicide" to instruct the jury that if they found that the accused had
committed the act of killing the law presumes he intended the
ordinary consequences of his act. Such an instruction, the Court
reasoned, has the effect of shifting the burden of proof on the
question of purpose or knowledge from the state to the de-

fendant. The jury might very well take the term *presume* to mean that they had to find a certain mental state when, in fact, it is not the defendant's task to disprove such an inference. Leaving aside that this opinion is clearly consistent with the common law use of burdens of proof and presumptions as mechanisms for establishing the indeterminable as fact, what is striking for our present purposes is that the Court is clearly faced with a society in which no common view of the person exists such that one could, as a matter of common sense, expect to make inferences about another's inner state. As in the United Kingdon, we may all be heirs to a language of intent that has had a significant impact on legal development.[30] But we are not heirs to a sufficiently uniform view of the person—a view that organizes our actions and sustains a commonsense vision of the orderliness of our experience—such that we can, as a matter of law, direct judges and jurors to draw inferences about others' minds that will reflect our common values and beliefs.[31]

That no single conception of the self holds sway in Anglo-American society and law is not inherently good or bad. It does, however, carry certain systemic implications. Our use of a language of intent serves not only to guard against what might be regarded as the oppressive force of society but against assaults on our view of individual autonomy: paradoxically, an emphasis on the inner person helps to ward off intrusions into that interior self. It also means that, as Mills suggested, we contest the characterization of actions because such definitions imply an evaluation of motive and intent. To define the actions of a John Hinckley as sane or insane, is, in part, to contest the very definition of a person in our society. If we focus on the victim and the impact of the act we discount the relevance of the accused's inner state. But if we grant heightened stature to the romantic/psychotherapeutic image of the person as interior self we obtain an explanation, a moral view, and a course of treatment of a significantly different nature. The "objective" standards we may seek in the law can suggest new concepts by which to comprehend our view of legal responsibility but it is unlikely that, in the peculiar domain of attributing states of mind to others, we will, in the law, achieve resolutions when the same considerations remain unsettled in the ordinary perceptions of those who will decide the actual cases.[32]

There are, in sum, few places in the law where our views of others and our need to decide what to do about their behavior come into greater confrontation than in constructing an explanation for others' actions that can be given legal effect. In some cultures and times the very idea that the self incorporates an element of the interior is absent; in others it is subsumed within the meaning of the external; in still others the idea of a separate self is the subject of intense concern. The goal for social and legal scholars is not the cataloguing of such variations nor the sterile quest for which takes greater causal priority, law or culture. It is, at least from the anthropologist's point of view, to see how the concept of the person and its legal articulation mesh with one another and with a host of other concepts in a society and to recognize that the very fact that we raise such questions is integral to the process by which we have come to construct our own conception of ourselves.

## NOTES

1. On the nature of the individual in Islamic thought, see S.D. Goitein, "Individualism and Conformity in Classical Islam," in Amin Banani and Speros Vryonis, Jr., eds., *Individualism and Conformity in Classical Islam* (Wiesbaden: Otto Harrassowitz, 1977), pp. 3–18; and Fazlur Rahman, "The Status of the Individual in Islam," in Charles A. Moore, ed., *The Status of the Individual in East and West* (Honolulu: University of Hawaii Press, 1968), pp. 217–25.
2. On the Moroccan concept of the person and the ethnographic background of this essay, see Clifford Geertz, " 'From the Native's Point of View:' On the Nature of Anthropological Understanding," in Keith H. Basso and Henry A. Selby, eds., *Meaning in Anthropology* (Albuquerque: University of New Mexico Press, 1976), pp. 221–37; Clifford Geertz, Hildred Geertz, and Lawrence Rosen, *Meaning and Order in Moroccan Society* (New York: Cambridge University Press, 1979); and Lawrence Rosen, *Bargaining for Reality: The Construction of Social Relations in a Muslim Community* (Chicago: University of Chicago Press, 1984). For discussions of the relation between culture and legal process in Morocco, see Lawrence Rosen, "Equity and Discretion in a Modern Islamic Legal System," *Law and Society Review* 15, no. 2 (1980–81): 217–45; and Clifford Geertz, *Local Knowledge* (New York: Basic Books, 1983), pp. 167–234.

3. On intent in Islamic law, see generally Louis Milliot, *Introduction à l'Etude du Droit Musulman* (Paris: Recueil Sirey, 1953), pp. 225–35; and Joseph Schacht, *An Introduction to Islamic Law* (Oxford: Oxford University Press, 1964), pp. 116–18.

4. Victorien Loubignac, *Textes Arabes des Zaer* (Paris: Librairie Orientale et Americaine Max Besson, 1952), pp. 273–78. See also Edward Westermarck, "Customs Connected with Homicide in Morocco," *Transactions of the Westermarck Society* 1 (1947): 7–38. On similar blood-money practices in other Islamic countries, see Austin Kennett, *Bedouin Justice* (London: Frank Cass & Co., 1968 [1925]); and Herbert J. Liebesny, *The Law of the Near and Middle East* (Albany: State University of New York Press, 1975), pp. 230–32. Many of the themes present in the Islamic concept of legal intent possess interesting analogues in Jewish law. See, for example, "Homicide" in the *Encyclopedia Judaica* vol. 8, pp. 944–46; and Michael Higger, "Intention in Talmudic Law," in Edward M. Gershfield, ed., *Studies in Jewish Jurisprudence* (New York: Hermon Press, 1971), pp. 235–93.

5. The argument presented here is drawn from the following main sources: Robert L. Benson and Giles Constable, eds., *Renaissance and Renewal in the Twelfth Century* (Cambridge: Harvard University Press, 1982); R. Howard Bloch, *Medieval French Literature and Law* (Berkeley: University of California Press, 1977); Peter Brown, "Society and the Supernatural: A Medieval Change," *Daedalus* 104, no. 2 (Spring 1975): 133–50; Caroline W. Bynum, *Jesus as Mother* (Berkeley: University of California Press, 1980), pp. 82–109; Robert W. Hanning, *The Individual in Twelfth-Century Romance* (New Haven: Yale University Press, 1977); Colin Morris, *The Discovery of the Individual, 1050–1200* (New York: Harper & Row, 1972); Alexander Murray, *Reason and Society in the Middle Ages* (Oxford: Oxford University Press, 1978); Charles M. Radding, "Evolution of Medieval Mentalities: A Cognitive-Structural Approach," *American Historical Review* 83 (1978): 577–97; R.W. Southern, *The Making of the Middle Ages* (New Haven: Yale University Press, 1953); Walter Ullmann, *The Individual and Society in the Middle Ages* (Baltimore: Johns Hopkins Press, 1966); and Karl J. Weintraub, *The Value of the Individual: Self and Circumstance in Autobiography* (Chicago: University of Chicago Press, 1978). I have also found helpful the discussion of Greek concepts of the person in Bruno Snell, *The Discovery of the Mind* (New York: Harper & Row, 1960).

6. Quoted from several of St. Anselm's works in R.W. Southern, *The Making of the Middle Ages*, p. 226.

7. Abelard thus wrote: "Seeing, in a most wonderful manner, what none other sees, He takes no account of actions when He punishes

sin, but the intention only, while we, on the contrary, take no account of the intention which quite escapes us, but punish the action which we see." Quoted in Etienne Gilson, *The Spirit of Medieval Philosophy* (New York: Scribner's, 1940), p. 349. See also the role of Abelard's thought on the developing concept of the individual in Karl J. Weintraub, *The Value of the Individual*, pp. 72–92. For an account of the conflict between St. Bernard and Abelard, see Fredrich Heer, *The Medieval World* (New York: New American Library, 1961), pp. 101–25. On the related concept of conscience, see Timothy C. Potts, *Conscience in Medieval Philosophy* (Cambridge: Cambridge University Press, 1980).

8. Hanning, *The Individual in Twelfth-Century Romance*, p. 12.

9. Hanning, p. 3. The emphasis on individuality is also evident in the fact that whereas earlier authors usually remained anonymous, the names of the authors of chivalric romance are highlighted. Individual distinctiveness also begins to appear in such everyday practices as the development of a personal style of handwriting.

10. Hanning, p. 140.

11. Morris, *The Discovery of the Individual*, p. 158.

12. See the discussion in Theodore F.T. Plucknett, *A Concise History of the Common Law* (Boston: Little, Brown, 1956), pp. 425–26.

13. F.L. Attenborough, ed., *Laws of the Earliest Kings* (Cambridge: Cambridge University Press, 1922), especially the well-known instance of a man carrying a spear over his shoulder, Cap. 36. Compare Albert Levitt, "The Origin of the Doctrine of Mens Rea," *Illinois Law Review* 17 (1922): 117–37, in which he argues that, owing to the influence of St. Augustine, intent was a significant factor in early English law, *with* the more measured argument that "prior to the twelfth century, a criminal intent was not recognized as an indispensable requisite for criminality" made by Francis Bowes Sayre, "Mens Rea," *Harvard Law Review* 45 (1932): 974–1026 at p. 977. The argument by Percy H. Winfield, "The Myth of Absolute Liability," *The Law Quarterly Review* 42 (1926): 37–51, properly acknowledges that there were in this period elements of both absolute liability and a concern for the reasons behind a man's actions, but he fails to recognize that rather than a mass of indecipherable contradictions we can view these rules as statements about situations, a kind of calculus of consequence by which behavior is assessed in situational terms rather than by general rules. Moreover, different powers—church, king, local baron—claimed jurisdiction over these various situations, such that a statement of situation was both a statement about motive and political obligation.

14. L.J. Downer, ed., *Leges Henrici Primi* (Oxford: Clarendon Press, 1972), Section 5,28b. It should be recalled that this provision ap-

plies to perjury, and that as Pollock and Maitland noted: "We receive a shock when we meet with a maxim that has troubled our modern lawyers, namely *Reum non facit nisi mens rea,* in the middle of the *Leges Henrici* among rules which hold a man answerable for all the harm that he does. . . . But the borrowed scrap of St. Augustine speaks only of perjury, and that anyone should ever have thought of charging with perjury one who swore what he believed to be true, this will give us another glimpse into ancient law." Frederick Pollock and Frederic W. Maitland, *The History of English Law,* vol. 2 (Cambridge: Cambridge University Press, 1968), p. 476. See generally, Bloch, *Medieval French Literature and Law,* pp. 28–29.

15. *Leges Henrici Primi,* sections 84,2 and 90,11a respectively.
16. "What we have found in the ordeal is not a body of men acting on specific beliefs about the supernatural; we have found instead specific beliefs held in such a way as to enable a body of men to act." Peter Brown, "Society and the Supernatural," p. 140.
17. Marc Bloch, *Feudal Society,* vol. 1 (Chicago: University of Chicago Press, 1964), p. 107.
18. On the role of church thinkers in the abolition of the ordeals see J.W. Baldwin, "The Intellectual Preparation for the Canon of 1215 against Ordeals," *Speculum* 36 (1961): 613–36, and R.C. van Caenegem, "The Law of Evidence in the Twelfth Century: European Perspectives and Intellectual Background," in *Proceedings of the Second International Congress of Medieval Canon Law* (1965): 297–310. However, both authors draw the boundaries of the intellectual climate affecting changes in the law of evidence too narrowly. Thus Baldwin states: "The revival of theological studies at the beginning of the twelfth century by such writers as Abelard was occupied chiefly with speculative issues, and it was not until the end of the century that theologians turned to more practical affairs" (p. 626). He thus restricts the intellectual roots of the Canon of 1215 to theology and even in that context fails to see the impact that changes in the concept of the person had on both theology and law. Similarly, van Caenegem, in his brief discussion of "changes in intellectual attitude" (pp. 306–310) limits himself to the changes that occurred in the thinking about judicial procedure. It is precisely my argument here that, important as the changes in bureaucratic approaches to criminal procedure were, the intellectual background of this development cannot be limited to the sphere of judicial activity alone—a view that sees the law as working through to more rational procedures solely as a function of its own internal history—but as interdependently associated with shifts in the concept of the person for which the terms, the concepts, and

the initial applications first found development in theology, literature, and social relations. See also Bloch, *Medieval French Literature and Law*, p. 39 ("It was not until later in the twelfth century that jurists influenced by the theological discussions of the intentionality and the mental elements of sin, began to discern diverse degrees of criminal guilt according to individual cases").

19. See Thomas A. Green, "Societal Concepts of Criminal Liability for Homicide in Mediaeval England," *Speculum* 47 (1972): 669–94; and "The Jury and the English Law of Homicide, 1200–1600," *Michigan Law Review* 74 (1976) 413–99.

20. Sayre, "Mens Rea," p. 989.

21. James Marshall, *Intention in Law and Society* (New York: Minerva Press, 1968), p. 21.

22. C. Wright Mills, "Situated Actions and the Vocabulary of Motives," *American Sociological Review* 5 (1940): 904–13 at p. 906.

23. Gilbert Ryle, *The Concept of Mind* (New York: Barnes & Noble, 1949), p. 66.

24. Quoted in Hanna F. Pitkin, *Wittgenstein and Justice* (Berkeley: University of California Press, 1972), p. 166.

25. For an example of this approach and a discussion of its theoretical implications, see Clifford Geertz, "Person, Time, and Conduct in Bali," in his *Interpretation of Cultures* (New York: Basic Books, 1973), pp. 360–411.

26. On the romantic view of the self, see Stephen Greenblatt, *Renaissance Self-Fashioning* (Chicago: University of Chicago Press, 1980). On the transition to the psychoanalytic view, see Lionel Trilling, *Sincerity and Authenticity* (Oxford: Oxford University Press, 1974). See also the argument in Ralph H. Turner, "The Real Self: From Institution to Impulse," *American Journal of Sociology* 81 (1976): 989–1016 concerning the view of the person in social versus volitional terms. For a fascinating example of how one domain of meaning—the concept of the person—couples with another domain— the nature of illness—see Susan Sontag, *Illness as Metaphor* (New York: Vintage Books, 1974).

27. For a recent expression of this perspective see Michael Novak, "Mediating Institutions: The Communitarian Individual in America," *The Public Interest* 68 (1982): 3–20.

28. See *D.P.P.* v. *Smith* (1961) A.C. 290 and *R.* v. *Hyam* (1974) 2 All E.R. 41. For discussions of these English cases, as analyzed in terms relevant for the present discussion, see Anthony Kenny, "Intention and Purpose in the Law," in Robert S. Summers, ed., *Essays in Legal Philosophy* (Berkeley: University of California Press, 1968), pp. 146–63; and his "Intention and *Mens Rea* in Murder," in P.M.S.

Hacker and J. Raz, eds., *Law, Morality and Society* (Oxford: Clarendon Press, 1977), pp. 161–74.

29. 422 U.S. 510, 61 L.Ed. 2d 39 (1979).

30. It could, for example, be argued that inchoate crimes, including attempt and conspiracy, are ones that have come to be couched in terms of intent because, as the result of the developing concept of the romantic self, we have come to stress the person as the crucial ingredient in our characterization of acts, even though one could well conceptualize these issues wholly in terms of social harm and apply canons of strict liability. The standard of intent is intuitively comprehensible to us because our concept of the person has become couched in these terms, whatever its merits as a vehicle for earlier intervention by the state in unlawful conduct. See, in this regard, George P. Fletcher, "The Metamorphosis of Larceny," *Harvard Law Review* 89 (1976): 520–25. See generally Robert L. Misner, "The New Attempt Laws: Unsuspected Threat to the Fourth Amendment," *Stanford Law Review* 33 (1981): 201–230, at pp. 207–13. For a fascinating exploration of how, in the absence of a language of attempt and incitement, the language of intent contributed to the differentiation of inchoate offenses in Judaic law, see Bernard S. Jackson, "Liability for Mere Intention in Early Jewish Law," in his *Essays in Jewish and Comparative Legal History* (Leiden: E.J. Brill, 1975), pp. 202–34.

31. It is, in part, the absence of a common view of the person, therefore, that contributes to disagreements over what would constitute manifestly criminal activity. See, in addition to Fletcher's "The Metamorphosis of Larceny," the debate between Lloyd L. Weinreb, "Manifest Criminality, Criminal Intent, and the 'Metamorphosis of Larceny,'" *Yale Law Journal* 90 (1980): 294–318 at pp. 310–18 and George P. Fletcher, "Manifest Criminality, Criminal Intent, and the Metamorphosis of Lloyd Weinreb," *Yale Law Journal* 90 (1980): 319–48, at pp. 340–48.

32. The idea of competing concepts of the person, as discussed here, also has relevance to many other areas of the law. See, for example, the discussions about property, evidence, and privacy, in, respectively, Margaret Jane Radin, "Property and Personhood," *Stanford Law Review* 34 (1982): 957–1015; H. Richard Uviller, "Evidence of Character to Prove Conduct: Illusion, Illogic, and Injustice in the Courtroom," *University of Pennsylvania Law Review* 130 (1982): 845–91; and Note, "Toward a Constitutional Theory of Individuality: The Privacy Opinions of Justice Douglas," *Yale Law Journal* 87 (1978): 1579–1600.

# 3

# THE DECONSTRUCTION AND RECONSTRUCTION OF INTENT

## MARTIN SHAPIRO

We are presented in the previous chapters with two expositions of the bases of criminal law, one by a lawyer anthropologist, the other by a lawyer philosopher. The anthropologist says that the criminal law must operate from some basic concept of the person, which it draws from the notions of personhood prevalent in a culture, and that Western criminal law is based on a concept of the autonomous individual that entered Western high culture during the medieval period. The philosopher agrees that Western criminal law is based on conceptions of the autonomously acting, means-ends calculating person. Through a survey of criminal law and philosophic materials he shows that these conceptions are the common sense of our intellectual heritage and present an intellectual system sufficiently coherent to render at least the broad outlines of the "general part" of the criminal law coherent.

## ANTHROPOLOGY AND PHILOSOPHY

This happy conjunction of anthropology and philosophy in the constellation of law signals some interesting developments in both disciplines. Professor Moore, practicing as peripatetic synthesizer and critic of the professional philosophy of the last fifty years, tells us in effect that our old-fashioned folkway of

78

thinking about crime, in which X wants to hurt Y and does hurt Y and so ought to be punished, makes sense after all in spite of all the confusing things philosophers and social scientists have been saying. Yes, Virginia, there are bad guys who do bad things and, yes, Virginia, it's OK to punish them. Well, the Moral Majority and most of the cops, except those who have been to graduate school, knew this all along. What's new?

Actually quite a lot of what Professor Moore says is new, at least in the sense of being reconstruction. The well-educated may argue that Western philosophy has been disintegrating just as fast as it has been integrating since the Greeks. To most of us, however, disintegration seemed to have reached a peak of acceleration in the 1930s, '40s and '50s, and certainly the movement to deconstruct everything continues apace. Philosophers of science and action philosophers and ordinary language philosophers and structuralists and new critics and behaviorists and Marxists have been telling us that nothing that we say or do makes sense or means what we think it means; that our world is absurd, mysterious, indeterminant and complexly problematical beyond the wildest dreams of simple folk. Even the young lady from Natchez's simple rule of conduct was called into question by a philosophy that was increasingly in tatters and patches.

In the face of all this deconstruction, a reconstruction has begun in philosophy. Its hallmarks are an appeal to logical discourse in ordinary language aimed at discovering what most of us would agree was right or true or at least more right or more true than something else, and then the construction of a satisfying demonstration of the defensibility of those agreements. Although one of the basic techniques of this movement is appeal to widely shared moral intuitions, we are forbidden to call this movement intuitionism or consensualism. Its other basic technique or claim is that it is perfecting a mode of moral discourse that generates ethical truths that rise above the level of "I like vanilla," or even "we like vanilla," up to the level of all thinking people, who should be persuaded that vanilla really is, if not true and beautiful, at least better than chocolate. Perhaps, without offense, we could label this movement a neo-common sense school of philosophy.

## DECONSTRUCTION AND RECONSTRUCTION

What Professor Moore says is that, in spite of all the stuff that the learned have churned out, it is all right to believe that persons choose to do crimes and then do them; that we don't have to say that the victims did the crime, or that society did the crime, or that nobody did the crime or that nobody knows what crime means or what doing means or that all we mean is that an event has occurred that a majority of us or a class of us have decided we don't like. The philosophers of deconstruction and reconstruction will no doubt do battle for many years over the astonishing proposition that some persons do crimes—and no doubt I have stated it in a form unacceptable even to Professor Moore. Nevertheless, it is comforting to know that at least some learned people will be able to say with some ease that a fellow who picks up his gun and goes down to the liquor store and demands your money or your life has—six chances in ten—committed a crime.

Which of course brings us to the conjunction of philosophy and anthropology. No matter what the new philosophers may claim in terms of "truth," the anthropologist can view their work as the collecting and systematizing of the high culture of a given society—a report of what the culture specialists of a complex society conclude are its belief systems after an extended, critical examination of its stock of ideas. This product of philosophical discourse may be particularly welcome to the anthropologist because of the weaknesses of other methods. In complex societies with large volumes of written materials, it appears to be quite arbitrary to rely on a scattering of individual informants as is done by those studying simpler societies. The alternative typically has been Weberian-style historical sociology, in which the investigator singlehandedly attacks the huge mass of written materials, attempting to draw from them the basic cultural traits of the society. The *verstand* of even the most esteemed of these investigators must always raise suspicions of individualized colorations that are only partially corrected by successive re-interpretations by subsequent scholars.

For a time, social science seemed to offer an alternative in survey research. A scientifically drawn sample of the entire population, or of any particular subset, could simply be asked questions designed to elicit its beliefs; a quantified statement of the basic belief system of the society could then be constructed. It has turned out, however, that while surveys can do very well at revealing transitory public opinion about particular issues or persons, they do not seem to do very well at revealing fundamental beliefs. The basic problem seems to be that survey respondents cannot be made to take seriously fundamental ethical problems. At least within the limits of the kinds of questions and interviewing formats that are feasible economically, survey respondents appear to make rather snap judgments highly conditioned by immediate circumstances. More fundamentally, the beliefs stated do not emerge from a careful working through of the possibly contradictory ideas held by the respondent.

The kind of exercise conducted by Professor Moore, that is, the critical working through of the common sense of the society, makes up for precisely these deficiencies of survey research. Or, to put the matter differently, a couple of dozen informants like Moore might place the anthropological student of complex cultures on a par with those who study simpler cultures through native informants.

## Personality and Criminal Law

Assuming for the moment, at least, that this proposition is true, we might turn to Professor Rosen's hypothesis that the Moslem criminal law of Morocco differs in some ways from Western criminal law because of differing concepts of the person, and more particularly that Western criminal law presupposes an autonomous person whereas Islamic criminal law presupposes an individual who earns his personality by cementing his familial, social, and religious relations with others in his society.

Both these papers deal with intent, one of the central problems of criminal law. A major ambiguity in this area is whether particular legal rules on intent are generated by fundamental philosophic and/or psychological conceptions of intent or whether they are pragmatic adjustments to the practical problem of proving intent at trial. While Professor Rosen does not give us much detail, he suggests that, in establishing criminal intent, a Moroccan court is prepared to hear far more than a Western court about the defendant's web of social relations. Professor Rosen attributes this difference to the differing Islamic and

Western concepts of the person, rather than simply to different pragmatic responses to the proof problem. Yet Professor Moore, fully conscious of the problems of free will, determinism, and causation in Western philosophy, reduces personal autonomy to the irreducible common-sense minimum that when one wills a part of one's body to move and it then moves without some independent, external force being applied to it, one has acted intentionally. For all the Islamic stress on interrelations, I believe that Islam too accepts this minimum definition of personal autonomy.

Professor Moore goes on to show that criminal intent in the West is built up out of this definition of autonomy plus an assumption of means-ends rationality in individuals so that the prototype action runs: because I want X and because moving my arm in manner Y will help me achieve X, I will my arm to move in manner Y. The movement of the arm is then held to be intentional in the absence of an external force. Here again I believe Islam accepts the same prototype of action. I would, therefore, tentatively suggest, pending fuller elaboration by Professor Rosen, that if Islamic courts admit a wider range of evidence on intent than do Western ones, it is not because Islam offers a less autonomous version of personhood than does Western philosophy. Professor Moore has had so to reduce concepts of personal autonomy to get them through the screens of modern Western philosophy that they reach a minimum level that Islam accepts as well. The Sharia too assumes that persons move their bodily parts by will for the purpose of achieving some arrangement of the physical world that they prefer to that which will occur if they don't move their bodily parts. Judges under both Western and Islamic law are instructed to discover those instances in which the defendant's conduct does not correspond to this prototype and relieve him of criminal responsibility in such instances.

## CULTURE AND INTENT

If a Moroccan judge is more prepared to infer intent from the whole corpus of the defendant's previous conduct unrelated to the events at issue than is his Western counterpart, it may be far less because he holds different conceptions of personhood than because of a number of other factors. The West may simply be more solicitous of individuals, seeking to make the prosecutor's job harder. Or, put another way, it may be more anxious to limit the power of government to put bad actors away and so require the government to go further in proving a particular bad act rather than allowing it to rely more on cumulative bad behavior. Alternatively, the judges of closely knit societies might be expected to have more confidence in their abilities to infer intent in one particular incident from the whole pattern of past behavior than judges of anomic societies in which behavior in one context at one time is barely connected to behavior in other spheres at other times. Or, more fundamentally, the process of secularization may have gone much further in Western than in Moroccan courts.

Where criminal law retains strong religious overtones, and where legal and moral or religious obligations are not rigidly distinguished, courts may be more inclined to judge the whole man—to judge the state of the soul rather than the nature of the act. The courts of Morocco are not in the strict sense khadi's courts directly applying the orthodox religious law of Islam, the Sharia. On the other hand, it would be foolish to see them as simply secular arms of a secular government administering a purely secular, national, statutory law. They are Islamic courts administering Islamic law. I would be more inclined to trace differences in the "general part" of criminal law to this striking difference between secular and religious legal traditions than I would to differences in concepts of personhood, particularly if the Western concept of person has to be reduced as far as Professor Moore rather persuasively argues it must be.

If the Islamic judge is prepared to receive more evidence than his Western counterpart on the social roles of the accused, Professor Rosen tells us he is prepared to receive far less bearing directly on the subjective state of mind of the accused. The Moroccan court imputes subjective intent from the outcome of the act. How different is this approach from the Western assumption that a person intends the natural consequences of his acts? As far as I can see, not much different except that the Islamic judge begins not with a generalized person but with a person in his/her particular social setting. Thus, from the same outcome he may infer a different intent on the part of a male head of family than on the part of a young female servant. But I would argue that in reality the same account is taken of roles in Western imputations of intent.

My difficulty in accepting the differences between Western and Islamic judicial thought that Professor Rosen finds so obvious stems from two secondary causes and one primary cause. Let me address the secondary causes first. Professor Rosen gives us no actual cases against which to test his position, and he is actually comparing the realities of what goes on inside the real Moroccan criminal process with the formal rules of evidence of a Western criminal trial.

At the conference at which his paper was initially given, I offered him the following case, noted by Lynn Mather during her study of the Los Angeles Superior Court.[1] A man is found sleeping next to a safe. There is physical evidence of a break-in. There are marks on the safe of an attempted safecracking and the tools are lying next to the safe and the man. There is a large amount of money in the safe. The man is charged with burglary and attempted grand larceny. At the plea bargaining session, the assistant district attorney argued that it was obviously an attempted safecracking, citing not only the physical evidence but the defendant's long criminal record as a safe-cracker and burglar. The public defender argued that the man was not a safe-cracker but an old drunk. Years ago he was a professional burglar, but now he is an alcoholic. He no longer lives the life of a big-time burglar. He has no money and knows no fences. He is a semi-derelict, hanging around street corners. He got drunk and for old times' sake went through the motions of a job, but the few pitiful tools he collected could never have gotten him into that modern safe, and he was so drunk that he fell asleep in the middle of his charade. The D.A. accepted a plea of guilty to a minor trespassing offense.

I would argue that the same treatment of intent occurs here as occurs in Morocco. Basic imputations of intent are made from the physical evidence, but in the light of the social roles that the defendant has created for himself. If the defendant is indeed a professional burglar—a distinct social role in our society—then one inference of intent is drawn from the physical evidence. If he is an old drunk—also a distinct social role in our society—then a different inference is drawn. And what influences the assistant D.A. is not direct evidence of the subjective intent of the defendant, but evidence of the defendant's current life. I believe that Professor Rosen misses these similarities between Western and Moroccan justice because he deals with the real criminal process in Morocco and the black-letter law of the West, and because he does not present us fully developed Moroccan cases that we could compare with Western cases.[2]

## EVIDENCE AND INFERENCE

Professor Rosen's response to this case when I presented it brings us to the primary cause of our disagreement. He simply replied that this case did not sound to him at all like what would have happened in Morocco. I still don't know why it didn't sound the same to him. I realize that professional burglar and old drunk are American urban roles quite different from such Moroccan roles as young male cousin and employee of wealthy head of family. However, they are certainly social roles created by the role player and used along with physical evidence to infer intent.

Within anthropology and comparative studies more generally, there are today two general movements that we might also call constructive and deconstructive, borrowing the categories I applied earlier to philosophy. The ethnographers insist that each culture is different, opaque, mysterious, pervasive, and determinative of individual thought and behavior. The outsider cannot know what a person in the culture is doing until he can "think" in the culture. A culture is not merely a set of constraints but a special and peculiar way of thinking. If it appears to me that neither the Moroccan khadi nor the American D.A. can look into the mind of the accused so that both depend on inferences from who he is and what he has done, I am simply told to go and live in Morocco for ten years and then see if I am still duped by the surface similarities.

The other school of comparativists tends to find that individuals in all cultures act primarily on the basis of self-interested, means-ends calculations designed to improve their material positions in life.[3] Different cultures create different channels and constraints on this "rational" behavior. Nevertheless, anyone can make sense of what someone in another culture is thinking and doing once he understands the alternatives that that culture offers, because all of us everywhere are seeking to be a little better off tomorrow than we were today. From this perspective I see two people both charged with punishing certain intentional acts, both unable to gain direct evidence of intent, and both using the same process of inference on the same physical and social evidence in order to overcome the intent problem and clear their docket. If the real Islamic judge in a real courtroom appears more brusque in moving from what happened to what was intended than the ideal American judge of the evidence text, then I suggest we move from the text to the reality of what goes on at the American plea-bargaining sessions that are our real criminal trials.

In the final analysis, what makes the papers of Professors Moore and Rosen so different is not that they attack the problem of criminal intent from the differing prospectives of philosophy and anthropology, but that one is in the constructivist and the other in the deconstructivist camp. Professor Moore stresses what is both common and commonly available to the instructed intelligence. Professor Rosen stresses the dark, the deep, the peculiar, that which is not commonly available but must be sought in the labyrinth. I forbear to mumble about yin and yang.

## NOTES

1. See Lynn Mather, *Plea Bargaining or Trial* (Lexington, Mass.: Lexington Books, 1979).
2. Thus returning to my earlier instance of the Western doctrine that a person is assumed to intend the natural consequences of his act, it is true that the doctrine is not, as a technical matter, applicable in criminal proceedings, where the prosecution bears the burden of proving subjective intent, but it is certainly the maxim that underlies the judge and jury's thinking about whether the prosecution has met that burden.
3. See Samuel Popkin, *The Rational Peasant* (Berkeley: University of California Press, 1981).

# PART II

# CONCERNING RETRIBUTIVE THEORY

# 4

# CLASSIFICATION-BASED SENTENCING: SOME CONCEPTUAL AND ETHICAL PROBLEMS

## HUGO ADAM BEDAU

For centuries, philosophers have debated principles of punishment generated from two dominant considerations, either the backward-looking concerns of retributive justice or the forward-looking concerns of general welfare. Meanwhile, officials charged with the day-to-day development and administration of criminal justice have had to rely on actual schemes to mete out sentences to convicted offenders, typically based on some unarticulated and eclectic combination of retributive and utilitarian considerations. Legislatures designing and revising a jurisdiction's penal code, prosecutors recommending sentences for convicted offenders, trial judges handing down sentences case by case, administrative officials acting on applications for parole, commutation, and release from punishment, lawyers advising clients liable to sentencing—all such persons have a di-

This chapter is a revision of a paper originally prepared at the request of the Panel on Sentencing Research, Committee on Research on Law Enforcement and the Administration of Justice, Commission on Behavioral and Social Sciences and Education, of the National Research Council, and presented at the Panel's conference on July 27–29, 1981. I am grateful to the Panel members and especially to my commentators, Norval Morris and Andrew von Hirsch, for stimulating criticism, though of course they are in no way responsible for my views.

rect interest and involvement in the practice of punishment. They must also be concerned with the actual system, whatever its moral rationale, enforced by law in terms of which legally authorized punishments are currently being determined.

Conspicuously influencing the discussion and reform of punishment in this country at the present time is the "determinate sentencing" movement,[1] and prominent in that movement is the development of "classification" schemes as a technique of determinate sentencing. The purpose of this essay is to evaluate such schemes from the moral point of view, that is, from a point of view in which ethical considerations (as distinct from economic costs, political feasibility, and administrative efficiency) are paramount. Related considerations that play a considerable role in determining the actual punishments experienced by convicted offenders and that arise from preconviction constraints on the prosecution (e.g., plea bargaining) and from postsentencing powers of the prison administration that lead to revision of court-awarded sentences will be left aside. Important as these issues are in any complete moral evaluation of the system of punishment in our society, they do not shed any light directly on the classification and sentencing system itself.

To grasp the general idea of the nature of classification and its role in sentencing, consider the simple and familiar distinction between *felonies* and *misdemeanors.* Typically, a person convicted of a felony must serve not less than a year in prison, whereas a person convicted of a misdemeanor is liable to punishment of not more than a year in prison. In order to connect these two categories of offense and their respective punishments, at least three intervening steps must be taken: (1) a wide variety of offenses, say, from murder to embezzlement, must be classed together as felonies, and another wide range of offenses, say, from overparking to off-track betting, must be classed together as misdemeanors; (2) the offenses classed together must have roughly the same relative gravity, so that any offense in the felony category is graver than any in the misdemeanor category; (3) punishment, or sentence, or at least the presumptive sentence upon conviction, will be proportionately more severe for an offense in the felony category than for an offense in the misdemeanor category. Crude as the felony/misdemeanor distinction may be, it contains the rudiments of any possible classification scheme; for the nonce it can serve as the backdrop of our discussion.

The point of introducing a classification scheme as part of an overall program of punitive sentencing, as viewed from an ethical perspective, is twofold: (1) to guarantee that only (though perhaps not all) the factors ethically relevant to a sentence are determinative of that sentence, and (2) to guarantee that offenders convicted of the "same" offense get the "same" punishment, while offenders convicted of "different" offenses get "different" punishments. To achieve these results, two things at a minimum will be needed: an adequate normative theory to account for the relevant empirical factors of which the sentence should be a function; and the exclusion of gratuitious discretion from the deliberations that result in sentencing decision, lest these decisions defeat the results of prior classification.[2]

If one is asked to defend (1) and (2) on moral grounds, the natural line to take is that retributive justice is the source of (1) and equal justice is the source of (2). Surely, it is prima facie unjust for any convicted offender's sentence to be influenced by factors theoretically irrelevant to sentencing. Furthermore, whatever the relevant factors are, they must be so identified by reference to morally relevant aspects of the criminal's act. Hence the retributive basis of consideration (1) above. Likewise, it is prima facie unjust for any two convicted offenders to be sentenced to different punishments when no factor relevant to sentencing can be cited as the basis for the difference. Hence (2) with its egalitarianism.[3] In this way, fundamental claims of justice seem to propel us in the direction of creating a classification scheme and making it the dominant factor in sentencing.

There are, however, at least two possible lines of objection to such a strategy, each of which can be couched in moral terms. One objection would be that the introduction of classification has no appreciable effect on justice in sentencing. Since there is no way to achieve just sentencing (so the objection runs), the introduction of classification is simply spinning one's wheels in the sand—or worse. A classification system purportedly based on considerations (1) and (2) above casts a false illusion of justice on the practice of sentencing. I shall ignore this objection as being too cynical to deserve a serious reply. Even if it were correct, one might still hope to reduce the grosser injustices and adopt a classification scheme as a useful, even necessary, tool to that end.

The second objection is that there is a better way than classification to ensure that the claims of justice in sentencing are satisfied. This objection is based on the hypothesis that classification is unnecessary or insufficient to achieve both (1) and (2) above, whereas an identifiable alternative strategy will succeed in these objectives. Any argument attacking classification along the latter lines is likely to derive from a concern to "individualize" sentences and thus punishments, i.e., to enable the sentencer to decide the punishment for each convicted offender on a case-by-case basis, free of the constraints imposed by a classification scheme. Individualization of sentencing in turn is likely to be defended on grounds either of equity or of special deterrence; the claim here would have to be that all schemes of classification defeat, ignore, or prevent individualization and thus both equity and special deterrence.

If there is a reply to this objection, it must be on either of two general grounds. One is that individualization is unfeasible; an unbiased comparison between an orderly classification system and an individualized system gives the palm to the former because of the chaotic features of the latter in actual practice. The other reply is in fact a partial concession, namely, it is possible to design a classification scheme in which the claims of justice as retribution and as equality are modified where appropriate in favor of individualized treatment, in order to satisfy the claims of justice as equity or of utility. As we shall see shortly, the latter reply has much to commend it. Even where classification dominates sentencing, it need not (one might even argue it must not) do so at the expense of ruling out on a priori grounds any opportunity for more individualized sentencing, provided some relevant moral principle is served by such individualized sentencing—indeed, in the ideal case, the very moral principles that underly the classification scheme itself.

## A MODEL CLASSIFICATION AND SENTENCING SYSTEM

For the purposes of the rest of this discussion, the relation of classification to sentencing will be illustrated through a close study of the 1980 proposals of the Pennsylvania Commission on Sentencing.[4]

As our previous account of the felony/misdemeanor distinction showed, basic to the very idea of a classification scheme is the notion that statutory offenses can be distinguished from one another by reference to their moral seriousness or gravity. This fundamental assumption prompts two comments. First, we must assume that we are dealing with an ideal criminal code, complete in the sense that it is neither under- nor over-inclusive of true wrongs designated by the code as offenses. If this is not true, the classification scheme will reflect the error and end up either by recommending for punishment something that should not be punished at all, or by failing to recommend for punishment something worthy of such a response. These are gross errors from a moral point of view, and no doubt exist in most penal codes. But we shall simply assume that they do not arise in the scheme about to be examined. (How we are to tell whether they have arisen raises issues that cannot be discussed here.)[5] Second, an unmistakably retributive basis underlies any attempt to classify offenses by reference to their gravity. How the relative gravity of offenses is to be determined is, of course, crucial to the claims of justice advanced on behalf of the classification scheme and to the sentences based upon it. Although the Pennsylvania Commission on Sentencing did not discuss this matter in its report to the legislature, others have set forth elsewhere the general basis for judgments of the relative gravity of criminal offenses.[6] As the problem is so central to the project of basing sentencing on classification, I shall return to it below.

In order to see the exact relation between classification and sentencing, we need to look closely at the details of the classification scheme itself. Under the Pennsylvania system, an offender's classification after conviction and prior to sentencing is a function of two variables, "offense score" and "offender score." Offense score is itself a function of "offense rank" (on a scale of 1 to 10, in order of ascending gravity) and four other factors of lesser importance. One of these factors (namely, inchoate offense) subtracts one point from offense score; the other three (possession of a deadly weapon, use of such a weapon, infliction of bodily injury) each may add one point to the final score. Since murder necessarily involves bodily injury and is the only crime ranked at 10, no crime can have a final offense score higher than 12. At the other end of the scale, presumably, no offense ranked at 1 can ever be reduced to 0 in virtue of being an inchoate offense. Thus, the offense score varies along a scale of uniform intervals from 1 to 12 and constitutes one dimension of the classification scheme.

The other dimension, offender score, is independent of the offense score. (Actually, the two dimensions are not strictly independent; for discussion see the appendix at the end of this chapter.) This score is constructed on a seven-point scale (0 to 6, in order of ascending gravity), with position on the scale being determined by the offender's prior criminal record. Each prior serious felony conviction adds 1 point, each prior misdemeanor conviction counts as roughly half a felony; any combination of felonies and misdemeanors that sums to more than 6 is automatically reduced to 6.

The result is a two-dimensional table with 72 cells, each cell containing a sentence deemed appropriate for its coordinate offense score and offender score. The penalties distributed through the cellular matrix are typically incarcerative. Thus, where the offender score is 6 and the offense score is 4, the classification scheme yields a prison sentence of 15 to 18 months. Incarceration is mandatory in all but 20 of the 72 cells. In five of these 20, the classification scheme dictates an alternative sentence to incarceration; under the Pennsylvania system, this would be a sentence of probation, a fine, restitution, or some combination thereof. In the other 15, incarceration is optional. In all 20, the offense score must be fairly low, although the offender score may be quite high. Hence, for example, incarceration for up to a year is the most severe sentence for an offender with a long record of only minor offenses. These and other details of the classification scheme are evident in table 1.

Any sentence located by use of the classification scheme, however, is only a guideline to the actual sentence received by any given offender. Indeed, this is part of the nomenclature; the cellular array is called the "Guideline Sentence Chart."[7] Thus the classification scheme functions as a presumptive sentencing recommendation; it sets the sentence the court must mete out except as other considerations enter. The purely presumptive status of the classification scheme is clearly revealed by the role

Table 1  Sentences under the Classification Scheme

| Offense Score | Offender Score | | | | | | |
|---|---|---|---|---|---|---|---|
| | 0 | 1 | 2 | 3 | 4 | 5 | 6 |
| 12 | 78–90[a] | 84–96 | 90–102 | 102–114 | 108–120 | 114–120 | 120 |
| 11 | 60–72 | 66–78 | 72–84 | 84–96 | 90–102 | 96–108 | 102–120 |
| 10 | 48–60 | 54–66 | 60–72 | 72–84 | 78–90 | 90–102 | 90–114 |
| 9 | 36–48 | 42–54 | 48–60 | 54–66 | 60–72 | 66–78 | 72–90 |
| 8 | 24–36 | 30–42 | 36–48 | 42–54 | 48–60 | 54–66 | 60–78 |
| 7 | 8–11½ | 12–17 | 17–22 | 22–27 | 27–37 | 32–42 | 37–52 |
| 6 | 4–7 | 6–9 | 8–11½ | 12–17 | 17–22 | 22–32 | 27–37 |
| 5 | 0–6(*)[b] | 3–6 | 5–8 | 8–11½ | 12–15 | 15–18 | 18–24 |
| 4 | 0–3(*) | 0–6(*) | 0–8(*) | 5–8 | 8–11½ | 12–15 | 15–18 |
| 3 | (*)[c] | 0–1(*) | 0–1(*) | 0–6(*) | 2–6 | 5–8 | 8–11½ |
| 2 | (*) | (*) | 0–1(*) | 0–1(*) | 0–6(*) | 2–6 | 5–8 |
| 1 | (*) | (*) | 0–1(*) | 0–1(*) | 0–3(*) | 0–6(*) | 0–6(*) |

SOURCE: *Pennsylvania Bulletin* 11, no. 4 (January 24, 1981): 466.

[a] The recommended sentence expressed in months of incarceration, i.e., not less than 78 months and not more than 90 months.

[b] The recommended sentence is either a prison term of up to 6 months or an alternative of probation, fine, or restitution.

[c] The recommended sentence is nonincarcerative, i.e., probation, fine, or restitution.

alloted to a number of other (hereafter, *post-classification*) factors:

1. The sentence specified in each cell is typically only a "range," from a minimum to a maximum. This range exhibits considerable variation, from three months to two years. (There is also typically a considerable overlap in the maximum of a given cell and the minimum of the next most severe sentence, in the cell adjacent to the right.) In addition, as already noted, roughly a quarter of all guideline sentences permit choice between modes of punishment. Once the guideline sentencing cell has been fixed, the sentencer must decide whether to impose the minimum, the maximum, or a sentence in between. The guideline merely "recommends total confinement within that range."[8]

2. Any guideline sentence of imprisonment may have an "additional" sentence imposed of fine or restitution or both. For such additions the classification scheme itself offers no guidance; their imposition and degree are entirely at "the discretion of the court."[9]

3. The guideline sentence may be revised by reference to an explicit list of circumstances that either "aggravate" or "mitigate" the offense (henceforth these will be called *aggravators* and *mitigators,* respectively). The aggravators number five (e.g., the offense had multiple victims), the mitigators seven (e.g., the offender was under 21). Thus, where the guideline sentence is 15 to 18 months in prison, and where in addition the sentencer finds certain aggravators, the sentence "may" be shifted one cell to the right (i.e., in the direction of greater severity) to yield a guideline sentence of 18 to 24 months. Were mitigators found instead, the guideline sentence could be reduced by a leftward shift to a sentence of 12 to 15 months. All such shifts are discretionary with the sentencing court.[10]

4. Any sentence under the guidelines may be increased or decreased, but only if, the judgment of the sentencer, "the guideline sentence is clearly unreasonable because of recorded facts specific to the case."[11]

The picture of sentencing that emerges is of a classification scheme that serves as no more than a first approximation to the actual sentence any offender receives. The classification scheme itself is constructed in terms of fairly rigid considerations. The guideline sentence, however, is to be fine-tuned by reference to a set of post-classification modifications. These considerations transform the sentence as initially identified by classification into an actual sentence by means of a series of individualizing considerations, including but not confined to the set of aggravators and mitigators, and the catch-all provision that authorizes the sentencer to modify any guideline sentence whenever all the facts show that such a sentence is "clearly unreasonable." Thus, we have neither a pure classification-based sentencing scheme nor a purely individualized sentencing scheme, but a hybrid of the two.

In light of these features, is it really true that classification dominates sentencing, in the sense of being the most influential single factor? The classification system by itself, in conjunction with the facts sufficient to classify convicted offenders, does not enable an observer to predict with precision what any actual sentence will be; the post-classification factors allow too much freedom for that. The fragment of the sentencing system that is controlled by the classification scheme is sufficiently small and complete by itself that, a priori, one has no way of knowing precisely what effect on sentences actually meted out the initial classification of offenders will have. This is bound to look like a signal defeat for equal justice, and even for retributive justice if the sentencer uses his discretion to rely on nonretributive factors. It may be, of course, that these apparent defeats for equal and retributive justice can be vindicated as triumphs of equitable justice. Presumably, that is the aim of the overall system. In any case, it seems likely that sentences imbued with the spirit and the letter of a guideline sentencing scheme such as that proposed for Pennsylvania would, over time, issue sentences dominated by the classifications given to offenses, rather than by any other factor among the many post-classification considerations that could be brought into play (see below). We are dealing here, of course, with an empirical question, but in the absence of evidence one way or the other there is no reason to be unduly pessimistic over the possibility that a presumptive sentencing system derived from a classification scheme actually would play the dominant role its supporters intend it to have.

## THE ETHICAL PROBLEMS OF SENTENCING

The ethical problems of sentencing as they arise under a system like that discussed here can be divided between those that arise from the classification scheme itself and those that arise from the post-classification factors. Let us turn to the former.

The first concern has to be whether the actual moral gravity of different offenses, ranging from flag desecration to murder, is captured by the ten-point scale on which the offender score relies. Is the spread from least (1) to worst (10) adequately large? Are the intervals themselves of adequate size, or too small or too large? Are the end-points of the scale correctly set? In particular, is the upper bound of the sentencing scale (ten years in prison) neither too severe nor too lenient for the gravest offense (murder)? The problem of spread and range reappears with regard to the offender score as well. Does the seven-point scale developed for this concept adequately express the true gravity of the offender's desert insofar as that is a function of his criminal history?

These questions pose ethical problems because the classification scheme has to answer to two ethical considerations somewhat independent of each other. On the one hand, the scheme is rooted in tacit but unmistakably retributive considerations, in which severity of punishment is supposed to be coordinated with desert in the offender, and desert in the offender determined jointly by the harmfulness of the offense and the fault in the offender (see below). The other consideration is that equality of treatment in sentencing requires that different persons guilty of offenses of the same gravity be put into the same classification, and thus have visited on them (at least as a first approximation) the same sentence. None of these results can be achieved if the calibrations of the classification scheme are inaccurate or arbitrary.

A further problem is whether considerations not introduced into the classification scheme should be introduced there. Thus, to take the simplest case, instead of a two-dimensional guideline, a three-dimensional grid might be envisioned to create a logical space within which guideline sentences might be more fully and adequately defined than at present. Whether any true independent variable can be identified, however, in terms of which a 3-space (much less a 4- or 5-space) could be created is not clear. It may be that every other possible dimension or independent variable for sentencing turns out on closer inspection to be an aspect of the offender and offense variables already identified, or is an irrelevant factor, or is best treated (like the aggravators and mitigators) as a post-classification factor. For example, certain variables are easily identified as affecting sentencing outcomes in the criminal justice system as it really operates in society, such as case-processing or judge-related factors, sex and race of offender and victim, or community variables.[12] However, even if such factors turn out to be relevant to sentencing, in the sense of explaining actual sentencing patterns in a given jurisdiction, it is difficult (except on straightforwardly political or cost/benefit, utilitarian grounds) to see how they could be relevant to justifying differences in sentences and punishments. Accordingly, they are not strong candidates for additional variables in classification or post-classification; despite their importance to social scientists, they can be ignored here.

So long as a classification scheme utilizes two or more dimensions, the question will arise how to coordinate the scales along each dimension and what to put into the resulting cells. In the scheme before us, this reduces to the questions whether (1) each increment in offender score (= previous criminal record) should carry the same, less, or more increase in punitive severity than is carried by each increase in offense rank, and (2) whether these increases in severity should be in increments of uniform size. As inspection of table 1 will show, no one answer is given to question (1) and a negative answer is given to question (2). Choose any cell (other than one on the top or right border, or in the lower left-hand corner of the table) at random and see how the sentence severity increases faster by moving one cell to the right than by moving one cell up. Occasionally, the increase is identical in either direction. But as sentences increase in their severity (i.e., move toward the upper right-hand corner of the table), they typically do so somewhat more rapidly as a function of offense rank than of offender rank. This seems to be a product of wanting left-right differences typically to involve considerable overlap, whereas up-down differences are rarely allowed to overlap. (Instead, the latter occasionally present striking gaps, so that the minimum sentence of a given cell is sometimes well above the maximum of the cell immediately below it.)

Are these asymmetries owing to defective draftsmanship, or

to the inherent limitations of any classification scheme constructed along these general lines? Or do they arise from hidden but systematic differences that are relevant to the assessment of desert, and thus of a guideline sentence? The same questions and uncertainties arise from reflection on the variations in the range of severity within different guideline sentences, i.e., the variation between the minimum and maximum sentence from cell to cell.

Unquestionably, the ethical problem most thoroughly buried by the classification scheme is the fundamental decision it expresses concerning the available modes of punishment and their distribution: mandatory incarceration is to be widely used, and its only alternatives (sometimes optional, otherwise mandatory) are probation, fines, and restitution. It seems clear that purely retributive considerations cannot account for the choice of and among these modes of punishment. What, then, does account for them? Are there ethical principles that categorically rule out all other modes of punishment, in particular, corporal and capital punishments? What ethical principles justify or require incarceration and permit no alternatives except the three proposed?

Three major issues of ethical concern are raised by the post-classification features of the sentencing system. The first is to determine precisely what the moral basis is, and whether it is sound, for introducing any of these post-classification factors as modifications of the guideline sentence. The second is whether the degree of modification introduced is ethically defensible; this is a version of the interval problem in the classification scheme discussed above. The third is whether there are other post-classification factors that ought to be introduced or used to supplement or supplant those already proposed, either because they have a better claim for this role given the ethical considerations justifying post-classification modifications of a guideline sentence or because they rest on better and stronger ethical grounds than do the modifiers already proposed.

Of these three questions, the most troublesome is the first. Given the division of the sentencing system into two phases, some ground must be identified for the lexical order (*pace* Rawls) that requires the sentencer always to count offense score and offender score ahead of other relevant factors, which are assigned to a secondary role in the post-classification phase of sentencing.

Regardless of how the foregoing questions are answered, there is or ought to be the nagging worry over whether the discretion left in the hands of the sentencer to be exercised during the post-classification phase of sentencing will in practice defeat the retributive and egalitarian aims that underlie the creation of the classification scheme in the first place. The ethical issue parallel to this empirical worry is whether any adequate moral principle justifies introducing such extensive discretion and the possibilities of unpredictability and abuse of power that it creates.

## SOLVING THE PROBLEMS OF CLASSIFICATION

Since the hypothesized foundation in justice of the classification scheme is retribution, it is necessary that the scale of gravity in the ranking of offenses proposed by the scheme reflect the gravity of the crime. Thus, for example, we need some assurance that corruption of minors really is no more and no less (or is not justifiably treated in the scheme as more or less) grave than the unlawful sale of explosives, because under the Pennsylvania scheme both crimes are ranked at 3; and that each of these offenses is neither more nor less than half as grave as filming sexual acts of a minor under 16 (ranked at 6), and three times as grave as falsely registering domestic animals (ranked as 1).[13]

For reasons that have been discussed elsewhere,[14] it is more than doubtful whether there is any theoretically sound, nonarbitrary way to rate the gravity of offenses in a classification scheme. To be sure, such objections can be obviated if we ignore at the start any attempt to make the classification scheme reflect the desert of the offender, i.e., abandon the effort to make the sentencing system into a genuine desert-based scheme. If we are content to make sentencing, and in particular classification, into a purely harm-based scheme, then there may well be nonarbitrary and theoretically acceptable ways to construct a scale of the sort needed for that purpose, as research over the past generation has shown.[15] There may even be a moral rationale for such a scale; since it would have to be a rationale based on perceived relative social costs of the various criminal harms inflicted by the classified crimes accordingly ranked, the rationale would appear to be mainly if not wholly utilitarian.

The classification scheme under discussion, however, has been assumed to be fundamentally retributive, and so its penalty schedule must be based on two basic retributive principles: (1) the severity of the punishment must be proportional to the gravity of the offense, and (2) the gravity of the offense must be a function of fault in the offender and harm caused the victim.[16] Both of these principles are directly reflected in the classification scheme, and in particular the latter principle (2). As we have seen, that scheme attempts to provide for a guideline sentence that is a direct function of only two variables, one that measures the relative wrongness of the offense (roughly, in terms of the harm caused the victim) and another that measures the relative fault of the offender (roughly, in terms of the degree to which the offender is a hardened recidivist).

If we assume that the moral point of view requires us to accept some form of retributive theory of punishment (an issue discussed elsewhere),[17] and that no nonretributive theory can incorporate principles (1) and (2), then a classification scheme based on such principles is unquestionably superior to any sentencing system that ignores them. But it remains unclear how one is to show that the classification scheme under discussion is the only, or the best, interpretation of principles (1) and (2), rather than merely one from among an infinite number of possible interpretations that would vary from this one in either or both of two directions, namely, by increasing (decreasing) the internal spread of the guideline sentences or by increasing (decreasing) either or both the minimum and maximum sentences of the entire scheme. To put this point another way, there seems to be no way in principle for two retributivists, who agree completely in their ordinal judgments of offense ranking (e.g., rape is a graver crime than robbery), of offender fault (e.g., a two-time recidivist deserves a more severe punishment than a first offender), and of penalty ranking (e.g., ten years in prison is more severe than five years), to resolve a dispute over which of two cardinal judgments of deserved punishment (the first-time rapist deserves five years in prison vs. ten years in prison) is correct. The possibility that either judgment is correct, because correctness is determined entirely by the prior choice of a sentencing scheme in which each individual judgment is generated, falls short of the implicit rigor in the notion of "just deserts."

Inability to resolve such a dispute, which is tantamount to the inability to make a nonarbitrary choice among many interpretations of principles (1) and (2), does not show that the classification scheme under discussion is unjustified on retributive grounds. Such a conclusion would follow only if the scheme were manifestly inconsistent with principles (1) and (2), and there is no evidence that it is. Rather, it is to argue that the scheme is not known to be justified solely on retributive grounds relative to any alternative classification scheme drawn up on the same first principles. Succinctly, it shows us that *retributive principles of punishment under-determine the classification scheme* and therefore any sentencing system involving classification.

For this reason, it is impossible to regard the classification scheme here proposed, or, for that matter, any alternative scheme that might be preferred, as a reflection of the offender's "just deserts"—unless each offender's "just deserts" are vague and arbitrary because they depend in each case on which among an infinite number of possible interpretations is given to principles (1) and (2).

Could we say, at least, that the guideline sentence scheme and the sentences it generates are not unjustified, in the sense that although they are arbitrary vis-à-vis alternative classification schemes, taken in themselves they are not unjust? It might be argued that we could say this if we could show that these classifications are cases of pure procedural justice (as in fair gambling), where although we have no independent idea of what the actual sentence ought to look like—any of an infinite range of possibilities is as defensible as any other—we do at least know that whatever sentence is reached is just, or not unjust, because it is the result of a series of steps that employ a just or fair procedure[18]—in our case, principles (1) and (2).

In the present instance, even this result goes beyond what can be shown because the assumptions that govern the classification scheme go well beyond what can be claimed as no more than principles of fair procedure. For example, central to the classification scheme is the shift from mandatory nonincarcerative sentences through optionally incarcerative sentences to mandatory incarcerative sentences, as the offender and offense scores

increase in magnitude. But no purely procedural consideration, as defined solely through principles (1) and (2), generate
this shift. This is but one of many crucial features of the classification scheme that rests on some substantive (nonproce-
dural) moral intuition or principle. Thus we cannot characterize the classification scheme as just, or not unjust, because it is
the product of pure procedural justice.

The final important ethical issue raised by the classification
scheme concerns the way in which imprisonment is given priority over probation, fines, and restitution, while no place whatever is alloted to corporal or capital punishments. On what moral
grounds is loss of liberty to be given pride of place in a morally
defensible sentencing system?

No doubt some would defend it as the least restrictive mode
of punishment consistent with the general welfare (for which
read public safety, or general deterrence). Others might defend it in the same way but shift the emphasis to incapacitation
and special deterrence.[19] On either of these rationales, prevention of harm to the innocent is the aim, an aim easily justified
on any of several different moral principles. But a different argument is also worth considering, one that should appeal to the
egalitarian if not to the retributivist. Loss of liberty is a mode
of penalty that everyone can pay; like loss of life or limb, and
unlike loss of money or reputation and the provision of services
or goods of value (the necessary feature of any restitution),
everyone has his or her own liberty to lose. On the Benthamite
(but not for that reason uniquely utilitarian) principle that each
is to count for one and none for more than one, we can decide
to treat one person's liberty as valuable as another's (despite some
empirical reasons for doubting such equality). We can take a
further step in this direction and assume that each unit of one
person's liberty (e.g., each month of a prison sentence) is worth
as much to that person as is every other such unit of another's
liberty (no doubt also empirically false, in many cases). These
assumptions are fundamental to egalitarian justice, and they
dictate priority for any mode of punishment that will satisfy
them.

The orchestration of probation, fines, restitution, and incarceration raises further problems. That the offenders who deserve the least punishment should get it in the form of proba-

tion, as the classification scheme provides, seems hardly to need discussion; it is readily justified given the other assumptions already at out disposal. The cases of fines and restitution are quite different; they present us for the first time with *victim-oriented* punishments. In contrast to incarceration, which confers a benefit on the victim or society only in special cases (namely, where the costs of the burden of punishment are outweighed by the losses avoided through incapacitating the offender), fines directly benefit society and restitution directly benefits either the victim or society or both (depending on the form the restitution takes). Some have argued that restitution can be justified in terms of retributive considerations.[20] This is distinctly a minority view. Whether similar or other difficulties attend the defense of fines on retributive grounds is not clear.[21] What is clear is that general principles of social justice warrant imposing costs on guilty offenders in an effort to replace or compensate for losses incurred when offenders victimize the innocent. The entire practice of punishment rests fundamentally on this consideration, and it therefore seems especially appropriate that, where possible, certain modes of punishment should be preferred over other modes because they have this feature as well. Whether there is as well a cost/benefit defense of fines and restitution is not so obvious. It will depend entirely on whether the costs of collection and administration of such penalties, plus the costs of the crime itself, are outweighed by the benefits conferred on the victim and society, given the costs and benefits of alternative sanctions. Claims on behalf of restitution as an alternative to prison and probation rarely consider whether it satisfies cost/benefit considerations,[22] and so the unbiased observer must doubt whether this factor can be counted in its favor.

This brings us to the considerations, if any, that properly exclude the use of corporal or capital punishments. Whether a purely retributive sentencing system could consistently repudiate such modes of punishment is doubtful. Traditionally, of course, when retribution in punishment was understood to require modeling the punishment on the crime—roughly, *lex talionis*—corporal and capital punishments were the very paradigm of retribution. Recently, however, several writers have argued that general principles of retribution (such as those cited above) do not require the use of such punishments.[23] Some have even claimed that these principles prohibit such modes of punishment.[24] It remains unclear, therefore, whether the silent exclusion by the classification scheme of corporal and capital punishments is evidence of the tacit presence of principles of justice in punishment that depart from whatever is sufficient to yield sentences based on retributive "just deserts" to the offender. It is also clear, as I have argued elsewhere, that purely utilitarian considerations cannot suffice to exclude categorically all recourse to capital punishments;[25] it seems likely that the same is true of corporal punishments.

Exclusion of corporal and capital punishments from the penalty schedule is probably based on one or the other of two different lines of tacit reasoning. One relies upon some single basic moral principle relevant to punishment, such as is to be found in the Bill of Rights (Eighth Amendment) prohibition against "cruel and unusual punishments" or in Article 7 of the International Covenant on Civil and Political Rights that prohibits "inhuman or degrading punishment." The other (explained in greater detail elsewhere)[26] relies on several different moral principles, no single one of which is decisive in itself, in conjunction with general facts about society and human conduct, and yields a balance of reasons against any use of such penalties as flogging or death.

## SOLVING THE POST-CLASSIFICATION PROBLEMS

The post-classification aspects of the sentencing system under examination here primarily involve the introduction of two theoretically independent types of modifications of the guideline sentence: (1) modifications that result from using aggravators and mitigators, and (2) modifications that arise from unspecified factors on which the sentencer relies when the guideline sentence is rejected in a given case as "clearly unreasonable" (henceforth the *reasonableness* criterion). What is the moral basis in terms of which each of these types of factors can be justifiably introduced to modify a guideline sentence? Let us examine each in turn.

Regarding the aggravators and mitigators, a rationale needs to be provided to explain why such factors should be handled as variables to modify the guideline sentence, rather than either excluded from consideration altogether or included directly into the classification scheme itself. There are, perhaps, two quite different answers to this question. One concerns the priority of previous criminal record over any other general consideration in the construction of a desert-based classification scheme. The argument here is that previous criminal record, better than anything else, shows the moral character of the offender relevant to his or her culpability in a given crime: the more previous convictions the worse the offender's character, and therefore the more deserving of severer punishment is the offender.[27] This argument has been criticized primarily on the ground that it allegedly reveals a departure from desert-based considerations in favor of special deterrence with its underlying utilitarian (and antiretributivist) assumptions.[28] Desirable though it is in principle to resolve this dispute, it is not necessary to do so here. It is enough to note that, if there is a coherent retributive argument in favor of confining the classification scheme to a structure dominated by the offender's prior criminal record rather than to any other aggravating factor in the offense or the offender, it must be some version of the argument proposed above.

The other and less important argument points to an important empirical difference between the sentencing-relevant variables that define the classification scheme in contrast to those employed as aggravators and mitigators. The two variables used to construct the classification scheme can be known with complete certainty to be present in *every* case that calls for sentencing; not so with the several factors that can be used to aggravate or mitigate the severity of the guideline sentence. Many of these will not be present in any case, and few cases will involve several of these factors. This alone guarantees their secondary importance. Their relative infrequency of application permits them to be treated separately and independently at a later stage of the sentencing process. The general idea here is as old and as fundamental as Aristotle's contrast between equitable and legal justice. Equal justice is best regarded as a function of universally applicable factors suitably expressed in a general rule (the classification scheme); equitable justice can be counted on to incorporate relevant but infrequent individuating considerations (the aggravators and mitigators).[29]

The argument so far provides a reasonably secure basis for the two-stage sentencing system, in which the second stage is governed by a set of explicit aggravators and mitigators that are used to fine-tune the offender's sentence beyond what can be provided by the classification scheme itself. We may now turn to the problems of justifying on retributive grounds the particular set of aggravators and mitigators in question (as well as the weight to be attached to each), which is to say the logic of their combination in modifying a guideline sentence.

The Pennsylvania scheme is unusually sensitive to confining the aggravators and mitigators to factors that express desert-relevant considerations. To illustrate, the more victims involved in a given crime, ceteris paribus, the more harm is done; accordingly, the guideline sentence is aggravated if the offense involves more than one victim.[30] Similarly, the offender's fault is less than otherwise, ceteris paribus, if the victim provoked the offense; accordingly, such provocation is a mitigating factor.[31] Other factors often found in schemes of aggravation and mitigation (e.g., the victim was a police officer), which doubtfully have a retributive rationale (but which are nonetheless popular), play no role in the Pennsylvania system.

As to the weight of these factors and their internal logic, however, the Pennsylvania system is anything but rigid and predictable. In theory, the simplest scheme would be to have each aggravator and mitigator count the same, so that in any given case, e.g., involving three aggravators and two mitigators, simple arithmetic would yield a modification of the guideline sentence, in this example, by the net amount of one aggravator. This is not how the Pennsylvania system works. There, the sentencer is told only to "consider their respective impact" when one or more of each type of factor is present in a given case; if such a factor is present "the court may in its discretion" modify the guideline sentence accordingly.[32] Only the most confident trust in the sentencer's ability to weigh accurately and judge equitably justifies such a vague instruction. Whether such trust is misplaced or not is an empirical question not easy to answer.

In regard to the reasonableness criterion, there is no doubt some implicit principle that underlies its introduction, but precisely which principle it is impossible to say. There are several candidates, ranging from retributive-based concerns to individualized punishments (a principle that clearly plays a role elsewhere in the overall sentencing system) to political expediency and the preservation of arbitrary judicial power. The best reason to introduce such a criterion must be that no matter what rule-structured sentencing scheme might be designed, there will often (though, of course, not in every case) be unforeseeable circumstances that must be taken into account if the actual sentence meted out is to be just to the offender. The general point might be argued in this way: consider two sentencing schemes exactly alike except that one has and the other lacks the reasonableness criterion. Assume that each scheme is built on the same rules and that these rules are as just as they can be. Even so, there is still no way to guarantee that a case will not arise in which the very considerations that gave rise to the rules themselves will not also give rise to an exception to them. Yet under the latter scheme (the one lacking a reasonableness criterion) there will be no way to accommodate such an exception. This entails that a justifiable exception to the rules cannot be made, and that the individual must accept a sentence that, in justice, ought to be modified. Thus, a scheme with the reasonableness criterion would be preferred by rational and disinterested persons because it introduces from the start a device by means of which the rules can be left intact (which would be desired, since by hypothesis these rules are the best that justice in legislation can devise) without having to ignore the occasional justifiable exception.

To be weighed against these rather abstract moral considerations, in terms of which the moral basis for the post-classification features of the sentencing system have been defended, are the ethical aspects of the actual consequences to which these features lead. For example, it is obviously possible that the reasonableness criterion can be abused in the name of any of several prejudicial and unjust considerations, thereby destroying whatever is just in the classification scheme itself. The convicted offender's future dangerousness—unquestionably one of the most popular aggravating factors in the criminal justice system as it actually operates at present[33]—looms silently as the unacknowledged consideration that might ("reasonably?") be taken into account in increasing the severity (e.g., duration) of a sentence of incarceration. The omission of this factor from the explicit list of aggravators is but one more sign that the sentencing system under discussion has primarily a basis in retribution. Yet its omission from the explicit list of aggravators does not suffice to eliminate it from the sentencer's consideration. Nothing explicitly prohibits the sentencer from attempting to take it into account after the guideline sentence and each of the explicit aggravators has been considered. Future dangerousness, however, is a factor that a purely retributive theory of punishment cannot accommodate at all. Rather, it is the most obvious factor to be taken into account only where special deterrence plays a prominent role, as it will in most utilitarian approaches to punishment.[34]

Once the doors are opened to sentencing discretion, as they are through the reasonableness criterion, are the offender's future dangerousness or other nonretributive factors likely to play a role in the actual sentences meted out? Presumably, those who defend the entire system on grounds of retributive justice will hope otherwise and be alert to these unsettling possibilities. It might be appropriate to introduce constraints on exercise of the reasonableness criterion with an aim to channeling still further any exercise of discretion. No such constraints are part of the Pennsylvania system as proposed, however. On the other hand, eliminating discretion entirely can be defended on grounds of justice only if assurance can be given that any abuses to which its exercise leads outweigh the good that it permits through the operation of relevant equitable considerations, or exceed the good unobtained and the harm incurred by employment of a more rigid, discretionless sentencing system. It is unlikely that such assurances can be given.[35]

## CONCLUSION

The attempt to base punitive sentencing by the criminal courts on a two-stage system, the first stage of which depends on a fairly rigid classification scheme by means of which presumptive sentences are the result of assessments of the offender's desert (itself measured in terms of the harm caused by the offense and the offender's fault), is an important step in the direction of constructing a rational moral system of punishment. Such a system is best understood as an attempt to rest punishments on grounds of retributive justice, with due regard both for equality among similarly situated offenders and for equitable individualization of sanctions in each case. Accordingly, vague sentences and opportunities for unbridled sentencing discretion are at a minimum. They are not, however, reduced to zero. The classification scheme contains some room for maneuver as the sentencer searches for the best sentence in each case. When we turn to the second stage of the system, however, the balance may seem to begin to tip the other way. While it would be an exaggeration to say that the post-classification aspects of the system unravel what the classification scheme has woven, it is true that discretionary considerations are generally more conspicuous and more prominent in the conception of the system, even if they prove in practice not to be manifest or troublesome in every case.

The designer of a sentencing system, imbued with exclusively retributivist principles, cannot, of course, hope to produce an entire system of punishment. His materials are too meager. The decision made by the Pennsylvania system against corporal and capital punishments, and in favor of incarceration, is one of several that cannot be explained on purely retributive grounds. This is not to say that it cannot be justified, however. There is no reason to believe that justice in punishment is confined to the set of considerations that constitute a reasonable retributivism.[36] More to the point are doubts whether considerations of utility, cost/benefit, and efficiency (not to mention political expediency) creep back into the overall sentencing system to such an extent that the antecedent retributive concerns are not in the end so watered down and compromised that little is left of them. No doubt it is possible to imagine retributive-based sentencing schemes that differ from the Pennsylvania proposal in being more faithful to the requirements of the original inspiration; it is doubtful, however, whether any have been recently enacted into law.[37] On a spectrum of possible sentencing systems, ranging from the primarily utilitarian to the primarily retributive, the system we have examined here falls well to the right of center, but by no means at the extremity. Even so, this sentencing system constitutes a model system in terms of which retributivists can see written in some detail where their first principles (in conjunction with some other plausible principles) would lead if given statutory effect. What would be the result in actual prac-

tice cannot be foreseen. For that, experimentation under law is
indispensible. It is not unreasonable to hope that such a system,
imperfect though it may be, may nevertheless be a definite improvement both on that we have under current law in most jurisdictions and on what any purely or primarily utilitarian-based
sentencing scheme would provide.

## APPENDIX

The independence of the "offender" score from the "offense" score is somewhat more doubtful than first appears. One
might argue that although the two variables appear to be defined (or definable) strictly independent of each other, there are
built into the concept of the offense score aspects of criminality
that ought to be treated as owing not to the *harm done in the
offense,* as an objective feature of the criminal act, but to the
*culpability of the offender.* The Offense Rank List used by the
Pennsylvania Commission on Sentencing includes some 240
criminal offenses, three dozen drug-related offenses, and a further dozen motor vehicle offenses.[38] To varying degrees, each
of these offenses is defined by statutes that refer to the *mens rea*
of the offender. *Negligence* and *recklessness* as minimally culpable
mental states are expressly used in the definition of some offenses. *Maliciousness* and *willfulness* (or *purposefulness*) as maxi-
mally culpable mental states, although not mentioned explicitly
in the short title of the offenses as cited in the Offense Rank
List, implicitly figure either in the full language of the statute
defining the offense or in the evidence needed to sustain a conviction under the statute, or both. Along with *intentionality* and
*deliberateness,* these mental states indicate varying degrees of
culpability and thus properly fall on the offender's side of the
offense/offender distinction. Yet they are not explicitly given such
a role in the classification scheme—and quite rightly; as things
stand, this would be tantamount to counting these factors twice,
first in securing the criminal conviction and second in apportioning the degree of punishment. Thus, the concept of offense score as used in the classification scheme is not truly confined to harmful aspects of the criminal act; the concept of
offender score does not include degree of culpability for the
criminal act. (Whether it would be possible and desirable to re-

define these concepts in the directions indicated goes beyond the scope of this discussion.) For the defender of "just deserts" in sentencing, however, there is a somewhat awkward consequence, because as things stand fault seems to enter not once but twice as a factor in determining presumptive sentences. First, it enters tacitly as part of the concept of Offense Rank, with the result (as we have seen above) that this concept is not purely a measure of harm caused by the offense. Yet fault enters also in terms of the concept of Offender Score. No doubt an offender's desert is some function of his fault and the harm his criminal act causes. But is there any reason to believe that whereas harm can be calculated along one dimension, fault needs to be counted along two? Or should one conclude, as have some critics of classification schemes in which prior criminal record plays a prominent role, that recidivism is really not a proper way to measure fault at all?

## NOTES

1. See David B. Griswold, and Michael D. Wiatrowski, "The Emergence of Determinate Sentencing," *Federal Probation* 47:2 (June 1983): 28–35; Andrew von Hirsch and Kathleen Hanrahan, "Determinate Penalty Systems in America: An Overview," *Crime and Delinquency* 27:3 (July 1981): 289–316; Gray Cavender, "The Philosophy of Justifications of Determinate Sentencing," *American Journal of Jurisprudence* 26 (1981): 159–177; National Institute of Law Enforcement and Criminal Justice, *Determinate Sentencing: Reform or Regression?* (Washington, D.C.: U.S. Department of Justice, 1978); Michael S. Serrill, "Determinate Sentencing: History, Theory, Debate," *Corrections Magazine* 3:3 (September 1977): 3–15.

2. There is another reason underlying some sentencing classification schemes: to make future sentencing decisions approximate as closely as possible to past sentencing decisions. See, e.g., Leslie T. Wilkins et al., *Sentencing Guidelines: Structuring Judicial Discretion* (Washington, D.C.: National Institute of Law Enforcement and Criminal Justice, 1978). This approach has been rightly criticized for failing to reflect any ethical concerns beyond what amounts to very weak conformity to principle (1) in the text. See Andrew von Hirsch, "Constructing Guidelines for Sentencing: The Critical Choices for the Minnesota Sentencing Guidelines Commission," *Hamline Law Review* 5:2 (June 1982): 164–215, at pp. 171–174.

3. This version of the connection between equality and justice is consistent with but does not entail the very relaxed connection proposed by Norval Morris, namely that sentencing should impose "equality of punishment unless there are substantial utilitarian reasons to the contrary." Norval Morris, "Punishment, Desert and Rehabilitation," in Hyman Gross and Andrew von Hirsch, eds., *Sentencing* (New York: Oxford University Press, 1981), pp. 257–271, at p. 267. In the sentencing system to be discussed in the text, as will be evident, "utilitarian reasons" enter only at two points. One is deep in the background of the whole system: namely, it is useful to threaten punishment in order to increase the level of general public compliance with just laws. The other appears in the effort to specify details of sentencing on a case-by-case basis in light of particular facts about the offender and the offense.

4. The Pennsylvania Commission on Sentencing, "The Courts: Title 204—Judicial System General Provisions: Part VIII. Criminal Sentencing," *Pennsylvania Bulletin* 11:4, part II, (January 24, 1981): 463–476. The proposed sentencing system was expected to go into effect on July 24, 1981; however, in April, the Pennsylvania legislature refused to adopt the Commission's recommendations. For discussion, see Susan E. Martin, "The Politics of Sentencing Reform: Sentencing Guidelines in Pennsylvania and Minnesota," in Alfred Blumstein, Jacqueline Choen, Susan E. Martin, and Michael H. Tonry, eds., *Reasearch on Sentencing: The Search for Reform* (Washington, D.C.: National Academy Press, 1983), vol. 2, pp. 265–304.

5. Underreach of the criminal law is rarely the problem that overreach is. For discussion of the latter, see Edwin M. Schur and H.A. Bedau, *Victimless Crimes: Two Sides of a Controversy* (Englewood Cliffs, N.J.: Prentice-Hall, 1974); and David A.J. Richards, *Sex, Drugs, Death and the Law: An Essay on Human Rights and Overcriminalization* (Totowa, N.J.: Rowman and Littlefield, 1982).

6. Notably, by Thorsten Sellin and Marvin E. Wolfgang, *The Measurement of Delinquency* (New York: John Wiley, 1964). See also note 15 below. For an attempt to rely on the Sellin-Wolfgang analysis as the basis of a professedly retributive sentencing system, see Andrew von Hirsch, *Doing Justice: The Choice of Punishments* (New York: Hill and Wang, 1976), pp. 77–83. Such an analysis does not work, unfortunately, for this purpose, as I have explained elsewhere; see H.A. Bedau, "Retribution and the Theory of Punishment," *The Journal of Philosophy* 75:11 (November 1978): 601–620, at pp. 613–615.

7. Pennsylvania Commission, "The Courts: Title 204," p. 465 (§303.3 (h)); cf. pp. 463–464 ("sentencing guidelines").

8. Ibid. (§303.3 (b)).

9. Ibid. (§303.3 (f)); cf. §303.5(c) (2).

10. Ibid. (§303.4 (a)).

11. Ibid. (§303.4 (a)).

12. See Blumstein et al., *Research on Sentencing*, vol. 1, pp. 69–125.

13. Pennsylvania Commission, "The Courts: Title 204," pp. 468–476 (§303.9).

14. See Bedau, "Retribution and the Theory of Punishment," pp. 611–615; also Edmund Pincoffs, "Are Questions of Desert Decidable?" in J.B. Cederblom and William L. Blizek, eds., *Justice and Punishment* (Cambridge, Mass.: Ballinger, 1977), pp. 75–88. For a recent attempt to get around this problem without actually solving it, see Michael Davis, "How To Make the Punishment Fit the Crime," *Ethics* 93:4 (July 1983): 726–752.

15. See Sellin and Wolfgang, *Measurement of Deliquency*. This research has been subject to extensive review, summarized in Charles F. Wellford, et al., "Symposium on the Measurement of Delinquency," *Journal of Criminal Law & Criminology* 66:2 (June 1975): 173–221. The results from more recent research can be gauged from V. Lee Hamilton and Steve Rytina, "Social Consensus on Norms of Justice: Should Punishment Fit the Crime?" *American Journal of Sociology* 85:5 (March 1980): 1117–1144; Maynard L. Erickson and Jack P Gibbs, "On the Perceived Severity of Legal Penalities," *Journal of Criminal Law & Criminology* 70:1 (Spring 1979): 102–116; and Leslie Sebba, "Some Explorations in the Scaling of Penalties," *Journal of Research in Crime and Delinquency* 15:2 (July 1978): 247–265.

16. See von Hirsch, *Doing Justice,* and his subsequent discussion, "Desert and Previous Convictions in Sentencing," *Minnesota Law Review* 65:4 (April 1981): 591–634. Principles (1) and (2) in the text do not suffice to constitute a retributive theory of punishment. What would suffice I have discussed elsewhere; see Bedau, "Retribution and the Theory of Punishment."

17. See H.A. Bedau, "Concessions to Retribution in Punishment," in Cederblom and Blizek, *Justice and Punishment*, pp. 51–73. For the most recent account of just punishment in terms of retribution, see Robert Nozick, *Philosophical Explanations* (Cambridge, Mass.: Harvard University Press, 1981), pp. 363–397.

18. John Rawls, *A Theory of Justice* (Cambridge, Mass.: Harvard University Press, 1971), §14.

19. See e.g., Norval Morris, *The Future of Imprisonment* (Chicago, Ill.: University of Chicago Press, 1974), pp. xi–xii, 58–83. Morris cites "defined social purposes" (p. 59) and "socially justified deterrent purposes" (p. 60) on behalf of incarceration, but it is ambiguous

whether this is meant to be a defense of imprisonment as (1) a mode of punishment, in preference to other modes, or as (2) the best punishment in a particular case, or as both (1) and (2). See also note 34 below.

20. J.P. Day, "Retributive Punishment," *Mind* 87:348 (October 1978): 498–516. Day writes " . . . I submit the following definition: 'a retributive political punishment' means 'a restitution or a compensation [to the victim from the offender] . . . for a crime' " (p. 503). It has also been argued that the biblical view of *lex talionis* inextricably weaves together retributive and restitutionary ideas; see David Daube, *Studies in Biblical Law* (Cambridge: Cambridge University Press, 1947), pp. 102–153.

21. Nevertheless, this is not the ground on which they are currently defended. The Pennsylvania Commission, "The Courts: Title 204," at p. 465 (§303.3 (f) (1)) defends the imposition of fines over and above incarceration whenever "the court is of the opinion that a fine is especially adapted to deterrence of the crime involved or to the correction of the defendant. . . ." In his recent general discussion of the punitive use of fines, Ernest van den Haag, *Punishing Criminals: Concerning a Very Old and Painful Question* (New York, N.Y.: Hill and Wang, 1975), merely observes that fines can be made as "punitive" as other modes of severe punishment (pp. 229–240).

22. Cost-effectiveness is typically ignored altogether by writers who favor offender restitution; see e.g., Stephen Schafer, *Compensation and Restitution to Victims of Crime (Montclair, N.J.*: Patterson Smith, 1970), pp. 117–135, Joe Hudson and Steven Chesney, "Research on Restitution: A Review and Assessment," in Burt Galaway and Joe Hudson, eds., *Offender Restitution in Theory and Action* (Lexington, Mass.: D.C. Heath, 1978), pp. 131–148. When an occasional writer speaks of restitution as "a low-cost . . . approach" to corrections, it is done without any serious consideration of its cost-effectiveness; see James H. Bridges, John T. Gandy, and James D. Jorgensen, "The Case for Creative Restitutions in Corrections," *Federal Probation* 43 (September 1979): 28–35, at p. 29.

23. See, e.g., Igor Primorac, "On Capital Punishment," *Israel Law Review* 17:2 (April 1982): 133–150; Jeffrie G. Murphy, "Cruel and Unusual Punishments," in his *Retribution, Justice, and Therapy* (Boston, Mass.: D. Riedel, 1979), pp. 223–249; David A.J. Richards, *The Moral Criticism of Law* (Belmont, Calif.: Dickenson, 1977), pp. 235–262; H.A. Bedau, "A Social Philosopher Looks at Capital Punishment," *American Journal of Psychiatry* 123:11 (May 1967): 1361–1370, at pp. 1364–1366. A number of other writers have defended a generally retributive theory of punishment without any mention of or support for the death penalty, e.g., von Hirsch, *Doing*

*Justice.* For a defense of the death penalty on retributive and denunciatory grounds, see Walter Berns, *For Capital Punishment: Crime and the Morality of the Death Penalty* (New York, N.Y.: Basic Books, 1979).

24. Robert A. Pugsley, "A Retributivist Argument Against Capital Punishment," *Hofstra Law Review* 9:5 (Summer 1981): 1501–1523.

25. H.A. Bedau, "Bentham's Utilitarian Critique of the Death Penalty," *Journal of Criminal Law & Criminology* 74 (Fall 1983): 1001–1034.

26. H.A. Bedau, "Capital Punishment," in Tom Regan, ed., *Matters of Life and Death* (New York: Random House, 1980), pp. 148–182, especially pp. 179–180, and H.A. Bedau, "The Death Penalty: Social Policy and Social Justice," *Arizona State Law Journal* 1977:4, 767–795, especially pp. 791–795.

27. See von Hirsch, "Desert and Previous Convictions in Sentencing."

28. Nigel Walker, *Punishment, Danger and Stigma: The Morality of Criminal Justice* (Totowa, N.J.: Barnes & Noble, 1980), pp. 125–128; and Blumstein et al., *Research on Sentencing*, vol. 1, pp. 171–172.

29. Aristotle, *Nichomachean Ethics*, v. 10.

30. Pennsylvania Commission, "The Courts: Title 204," p. 467 (§303.4(c) (5)).

31. Ibid. (§303.4(d) (1).

32. Ibid. (§303.4(b)).

33. This is most conspicuously true where future dangerousness is a factor the sentencer must use in choosing between death or imprisonment after a conviction of capital murder, as under current Texas law. See George E. Dix, "Administration of the Texas Death Penalty Statues: Constitutional Infirmities Related to the Prediction of Dangerousness," *Texas Law Review* 55:8 (November 1977): 1343-1414.

34. See especially Andrew von Hirsch, "Utilitarian Sentencing Resuscitated: The American Bar Association's Second Report on Criminal Sentencing," *Rutgers Law Review* 33:3 (Spring 1981): 772–789. Contemporary nonretributivists divide on the role to be given to predicted future dangerousness in the sentencing of convicted offenders. Nigel Walker, for example, a professed "eclectic," regards such predictions as a legitimate basis for differential sentencing and especially for delaying release from incarceration; see Walker, *Punishment, Danger and Stigma*, pp. 88–113. Norval Morris, however, somewhat more of a utilitarian than Walker, regards it as "an unjust basis" for imposing or prolonging punitive incarceration; see Morris, *Future of Imprisonment*, pp. xi, 59, 62–73, 76, 91–92. See also, however, note 19 above. Ernest van den Haag, after wringing his hands over the unreliability of predictions of

future violence, endorses them as a morally proper basis for the decision to incarcerate; see van den Haag, *Punishing Criminals*, pp. 241–250.

35. Some sceptics of retribution-based sentencing systems have suggested that the chief result of such systems, if enacted into law, will be an overall increase in severity of sentences, which should be deplored by all sensible persons, since our society already has "the longest average prison sentences in the western world and an extraordinarily high per capita rate of imprisonment . . ." in John C. Coffee, Jr., "The Repressed Issues of Sentencing: Accountability, Predictability, and Equality in the Era of the Sentencing Commission," *The Georgetown Law Journal* 66:4 (April 1978): 975–1107, at p. 1079. It is all the more worth noting that the chief advocate of "just deserts" in current sentencing declares his hope that his favored approach will achieve a significant "moderation in punishment levels." Andrew von Hirsch, "Recent Trends in American Criminal Sentencing Theory," *Maryland Law Review* 42:1 (1983): 6–36, at p. 29. Who has the better of the argument at present seems impossible to say.

36. This view is held by most, if not all, of the writers cited in the notes above, in particular, Morris, Richards, van den Haag, von Hirsch, and Walker. My own views are spelled out in an unpublished paper on the justification of punishment.

37. See von Hirsch, "Constructing Guidelines for Sentencing," and "Recent Trends in American Criminal Sentencing Theory," and von Hirsch and Hanrahan, "Determinate Penalty Systems in America."

38. Pennsylvania Commission, "The Courts: Title 204," pp. 468–476 (§303.9).

# 5

# HOW TO MAKE THE PUNISHMENT FIT THE CRIME

## MICHAEL DAVIS

Though the retributive theory of punishment has recently enjoyed a startling revival,[1] there seems to remain one decisive objection to it. The objection has been stated: "The retributivist's difficulty is that he wants the crime itself to indicate the amount of punishment, which it cannot do unless we first assume a scale of crimes and penalties. But on what principles is the scale to be constructed, and how are new offences to be fitted into it? These difficulties admit of no solution unless we agree to examine the consequences to be expected from penalties of different degrees of severity: i.e., unless we adopt a utilitarian approach."[2] The objection is to retributivism both as a theory of what a judge should do (act-retributivism) and as a theory of what the legislature should do (rule-retributivism). But the ob-

Republished (slightly revised) from *Ethics* 93, no. 4 (July 1983): 726–752, with the kind permission of the author and The University of Chicago Press. © 1983 by The University of Chicago. All rights reserved.

Part of an earlier version of this paper was read before the Philosophy Colloquium of Illinois State University, January 26, 1979, and before the Philosophy Club of the University of Chicago, April 13, 1979. I should like to thank those present for their comments and criticisms. I should also like to thank Richard Epstein for his helpful editorial advice on two later drafts, and my old criminal law professor, Yale Kamisar, for long ago asking all the right questions (and, fortunately, giving all the wrong answers).

jection strikes hardest at retributivism as a theory of legislation. The judge at least has the statutory maximum (and perhaps minimum) to limit his discretion, the legislative intent to guide him. The legislature has only the principles of punishment (and perhaps certain constitutional restraints). The objection does not deny that there are nonutilitarian principles by which to scale crimes: shock, injury to victim, similarity to crimes already on the books, and so on. The objection is that each of these principles is incomplete, counterintuititive in important applications, and anyway always less satisfactory than a utilitarian principle. The objection is that, without a utilitarian scale of crimes and penalties, retributivism is at best vacuous.

I believe this objection misunderstands the relation between retributivism and consequences, between utilitarianism and consequences, and between theories of punishment and the world.

By "retributivism" I mean any theory of punishment claiming at least (1) that the only acceptable reason for punishing a person is that he has committed a crime, (2) that the only acceptable reason for punishing him with such-and-such severity is that the punishment fits the crime, and (3) that the fit between punishment and crime is independent of the actual or probable consequences of the particular punishment or the particular statutory penalty.[3] When contrasting retributivism with utilitarianism, I mean by "utilitarianism" not the general ethical theory but merely any theory of punishment making the fit between punishment and crime depend upon the actual or probable consequences of the particular punishment or statutory penalty. I do not intend anything I say here to affect the debate between (ethical) utilitarianism and competing ethical theories. Indeed, I hope to convince even the devoutest act-utilitarian that there is good reason not to make direct appeal to utility when imposing a punishment or enacting a penalty.

I shall argue that there is a retributive principle for setting statutory penalties, that the principle should sometimes yield statutory penalties different from those a utilitarian principle would yield, that the retributivist penalty appears morally preferable where it differs from the utilitarian, and that the retributivist penalty is the one more likely to be chosen in practice.

Because the setting of statutory penalties is supposed to be the major difficulty for retributivism, I shall say little about what judges do until the final section of the paper. I do not intend my silence to suggest that judges should behave in a way much different from the way I argue legislatures should. I just do not think the distinction between act-retributivism and rule-retributivism important.[4]

Because "punishment," "justification," and certain other crucial terms have been used with importantly different meanings of late, I shall begin my discussion by going over what should be familiar ground. It will, I think, be worth our while, since even here we will now and then leave the familiar path: I shall be concerned to point out how the problem of making the punishment fit the crime changes once we take seriously the place of punishment within the criminal law. The change, though no greater than that from "man" to "person" is nevertheless the hook upon which everything else hangs.

## I. PUNISHMENT AND THE CRIMINAL LAW

What is punishment? It is an evil satisfying these six conditions:

1. There is a body of rules capable of guiding action ("primary rules");

2. There are beings ("persons") capable of following these rules or not as they choose, capable of choosing on the basis of reasons, and capable of treating the prospect of suffering a specified evil as a reason against doing an act (to be weighed with other reasons for and against);

3. There is a procedure ("authority") for inflicting types of evil ("penalties") upon a person if he does not follow the rules;

4. There are ("secondary") rules connecting failure to follow primary rules ("crimes" or "offences") with certain penalties;

5. Both the primary and secondary rules are supposed to be known to the persons subject to them (in general, at least); and

6. Imposition of the penalty is (in general, at least) justified by the person's not having followed the appropriate rule when he could have.[5]

The criminal law provides the central cases of punishment. A theory of punishment must come to terms with the criminal law or fail. What goes on in clubs, corporations, universities, and other associations of persons is relevant only insofar as close to the criminal law. What parents do with their children, owners with their pets, or the wind with the countryside, is at best peripheral.

There are many means of social control that need not take into account the personhood of its subjects: for example, terror, incapacitation, or conditioning. What distinguishes the criminal law from these is that the criminal law presupposes people who *(1)* can follow rules or not as they choose and *(2)* can be persuaded to follow the rules by the distant prospect of set penalty. The criminal law would have no use where people were not more or less rational, where, that is, people did not adjust their acts to take into account possible consequences far off, uncertain, and limited. The insane, the feebleminded, the immature properly do not come under the criminal law. They are brought into court only to be sent elsewhere.[6] The criminal law does not, however, require a society of crafty deliberators or practical Newtons. The criminal law requires only that, somehow or other, people will generally adjust their acts to take the penalties into account (or, for other reasons, stay clear of wrongdoing).[7]

Punishment (so understood) cannot be conceived apart from the criminal law (or some analogue). To ask the justification of punishment as an institution is then to ask the justification of the criminal law as a whole. To ask that is, however, to ask for one of two justifications. "The criminal law" may refer either to the criminal law in general (*the* criminal law) or to this or that system of criminal law (the criminal law we live under). To ask the justification of the first is to ask why a rational person should prefer a system of criminal law, given a choice between a fair representative of the criminal law and a fair representative of any alternative method of social control. To ask the justification of a particular system of criminal law is, in contrast, only to ask why a rational person should prefer that system over any alternative system of criminal law. (For the purpose of justification, a method of social control or system of criminal law is an alternative to another only insofar as the two are possible but incompatible methods of ordering the same affairs of the same persons.) What I shall now argue is that neither the justification of the criminal law in general nor the justification of a particular system of criminal law entails a utilitarian principle for setting penalties (a principle, that is, which would make the choice of penalty depend upon the actual or probable consequences of having a particular penalty on the books).

## II. Justifying The Criminal Law in General

There is surprisingly little disagreement about what justifies the criminal law in general. A rational person would (it is agreed) prefer the criminal law to any alternative method of social control because the criminal law serves the interests of rational persons better than does any alternative. Only the criminal law can order certain important social relations so as to allow rational persons to plan and act, without ordering society so completely that there is little at once worth planning and free from the defeating interference of authority.[8] Though it may seem obvious that the criminal law thus strikes the best balance between protecting persons and respecting them, we must consider why that is so to see that the general justification of the criminal law entails no utilitarian principle for setting penalties. We may treat what follows as if it were an (ethical) utilitarian argument. But it would be wise to notice that the argument is not necessarily utilitarian. We shall not have to say whether the benefits justifying the criminal law accrue to society as a whole or to everyone individually. Thus, we shall not have to decide between utilitarian and "contract" theorists. We shall also not have to say whether the benefits justifying the criminal law are merely contingent facts about this world or conceptual truths about rational persons (and all the possible worlds where they may be found). Thus, we shall also not have to decide between ordinary consequentialists and those who found ethics upon a priori truths.

The criminal law maintains order by laying down rules, threatening punishment if the rules are not obeyed, and carrying out the threat often enough to keep the threat alive. The criminal law need not establish social tranquility. It does enough if it holds the commotion of life below a roar. The primary rules

need not forbid all conflict between persons or even all undesirable activity. The rules need only forbid the more substantial
harms and regulate major conflict. The threatened punishments need not be so frightful that no rational person would
risk them. The punishments need only be frightful enough to
make crime relatively rare. It does not matter whether the punishments accomplish this by assuring those who wish to obey the
rules that others will not take advantage of that obedience, or
by frightening off most of those who might otherwise commit
crimes, or by satisfying the resentment of those who might otherwise take revenge, or by instilling a horror of the forbidden
acts, or by keeping most criminals where they cannot commit
crimes, or by some combination of these or other means. What
does matter is that the criminal law maintains at least a modi-
cum of order.

Every law takes with one hand while it gives with the other.
The criminal law can nevertheless preserve for persons a sphere
of action free from the interference of authority (as well as from
the interference of other persons) in at least four distinct ways.
First, so long as the primary rules are not too many or too broad,
the criminal law justifies interference with persons only in a
limited and predictable way, that is, only for disobeying a rule
the person could have obeyed. Second, so long as the procedure of the criminal law is reasonably designed for its purpose,
the criminal law will rarely interfere with a person except when
he has in fact disobeyed a rule. Third, when someone has disobeyed a rule, the criminal law justifies only that interference
to which the *act* corresponds, the statutory penalty. The criminal cannot be punished for what he is, only for what he has done.
The penalty cannot be freely tailored after the act so that, had
the criminal known in advance what the penalty would be, he
would never have committed the crime. The punishment is a
foreordained response to the crime.[9] And last, because penalties are foreordained (and so long as they are not too frightful),
the potential criminal can treat each penalty as the price of the
corresponding forbidden act. The criminal law might not long
survive if everyone treated penalties that way all the time. But
there is much to be gained if people do treat them that way
sometimes. All human rules fail of sense now and then. A law
made to be disobeyed (occasionally) serves our interests better

than one which, threatening penalties too frightful to risk, pretends to be the work of a god.[10]

This is the criminal law we are to compare with other methods of social control. Its superiority is considerable, so considerable that it remains preferable though penalties are set in any number of radically different ways. Even drawing statutory penalties from a hat would not undo that superiority as we just described it (provided, of course, penalties in the hat were neither trivial nor too severe). But, if the justification of *the* criminal law does not exclude (on the basis of actual or probable consequences) such a silly method of setting penalties as drawing from a hat, it cannot require a principle linking particular penalties to particular consequences. The justification is too strong to rely upon the consequences of choosing penalties according to any particular principle (though not so strong as to survive choosing penalties by any principle whatever). Hence, there is nothing in the justification of criminal law in general to entail a utilitarian principle for setting penalties.

## III. Justifying Particular Systems of Criminal Law

The justification of a particular system of criminal law may seem to lead directly to a utilitarian principle for setting penalties, even if the justification of the criminal law in general does not. To justify a particular system of criminal law should in part mean justifying it against systems very much like it and so (it may seem) against those differing from it only by a single penalty. We may, for example, throw open the statute book, notice that the penalty for kidnapping is one to five years imprisonment, and ask why the maximum penalty is not death. To ask that question is, it seems, to compare two systems differing only in the penalty for kidnapping, to suppose there is good reason to prefer one penalty over the other (as indeed there is), and to ask what that reason might be. What might it be? Surely (it will be said) the only reason one could offer would be the overall advantage (actual or probable) of living under one system rather than the other. It seems then that the justification of a particular system of criminal law entails appeal to a principle of setting penalties and that the principle appealed to will be utilitarian.

Legislatures do choose between penalties; we do argue about whether this or that choice is justified. There is no doubt about that. The question is whether justification must be in terms of the actual or probable consequences of slightly different systems of criminal law. The answer is that it cannot be. Consider how strange a justification in such terms is. We would compare two complete systems differing only in a single penalty. We may perhaps imagine them on a counter, side by side, ticking like clocks. But where are we to get two such systems? Systems of criminal law are not (like clocks and beakers) available through laboratory services. We cannot even come close to laying two such systems side by side. If we compare two contemporary systems, we must compare systems differing at least in personnel, history, and surrounding society, even if we can find two systems with the same procedures and statutes. And we are not likely to get two systems with procedures or statutes with more than a family resemblance. If instead we compare two successive states of one system of criminal law, we have the same problem. The successive states will differ in personnel (death caring little for our inquiry), history (the change of penalty being potentially as important as what the penalty is changed from or to), and surrounding society (fashion, business cycles, war, and so on caring as little for our inquiry as death does). Even the other statutes and procedures cannot be counted on to remain fixed during the comparison. The life of the law is no more to be pent up than life in general. Above that picture of legal systems ticking away side by side towers a vanity of intellect so enormous it deserves a name. I would suggest "the fallacy of omnipotent science" (the fallacy being to suppose that whatever experiment we can imagine—however indistinctly—is within the power of science).

It might seem that I am unfair. After all (it will be said) we do not have to lay systems side by side. We can compare them less fancifully. We can use statistical procedures to isolate the crucial variables, follow the effects of those variables in different systems, and so compare penalties. Or we could construct a mathematical model of the particular system of criminal law, hypothesize various penalties, and in each case deduce the consequences just as a physicist would do if he wanted to know the effect on pressure that heating a fixed volume of gas to such-

and-such temperature would have. Or, at least, we can perform "thought experiments."

Same fallacy. Some day we may be able to do such wonders (though section IV casts doubt even on that). Certainly we cannot do them today. Who knows what the consequences would be if, say, Illinois adopted death as the maximum penalty for kidnapping? Would there be fewer kidnappings, more, or the same number as now? Would there be any sentences of death? Would Illinois be better off, worse off, or much the same as now overall? We can guess, of course. But we cannot do more. There is no mathematical model of society from which to make deductions about the actual or probable consequences of such a penalty. There will be none tomorrow, or the next day. And without some model, we cannot even perform thought experiments. Nor can we hope the statisticians will help. They do not have the data they would need. They do not know what procedures to use. And perhaps given the data and procedures they would face a problem of such magnitude they would still not be able to get significant results. Their computers, time, and other resources are finite. Much that is possible is far from practical.

If we cannot now find out what would be the actual or probable consequences of making such a dramatic change in the penalties of a single state, what are we to make of the claim that we are to decide *every* penalty by considering the consequences? What are we to do when the choice is between two and three years imprisonment? The trouble with the utilitarian principle of setting penalties is not so much that it leads us astray as that it leads us not at all.

Still (someone might respond), the utilitarian theory provides an ideal toward which we can strive guided by other means until science can come to our aid. We must reject that response. Under the circumstances in which penalties are in fact chosen, we would not know whether we approached or fell from the ideal. We simply cannot do what utilitarianism tells us to do, only nervously shift from foot to foot.

Nor will it do to respond that we *must* be able to make such comparisons because we make them all the time. The question is what we do when we justify one penalty against another. What I have argued so far is that we cannot justify one penalty against another by comparing two systems of criminal law differing only in one penalty or (what is supposed to come to the same thing) by comparing directly the actual or probable consequences of adopting each penalty. I admit we do talk about the "consequences" of this or that penalty (especially about whether the penalty will "deter"). I only deny that such talk has anything to do with the actual or probable consequences of the penalty. How can that be?

## IV. INSIDE THE CRIMINAL LAW

Before I answer that question, I should like to draw an analogy between scientific theories and systems of criminal law. The analogy will, I hope, make what I say about deciding penalties less disturbing and so more convincing.

It is commonly held that a scientific theory consists both of claims that can be tested (more or less) directly ("experimental laws") and of claims that can be tested only by testing the theory as a whole ("theoretical laws"). Both kinds of law are, of course, "empirical" and "contingent," but the proof of one is quite different from the proof of the other. Experimental laws, though deducible from the theory as a whole and important in its defense, can survive the theory's overthrow. They ultimately rest upon experiment, not deduction. While claims *for* the theory, they are (more or less directly) claims *about* the world. Theoretical laws cannot likewise survive a theory's overthrow. They draw their content from the theory as a whole. Every change in the theory changes them, too. A name may move from theory to theory but the connection between entities referred to is familial, not personal. While theoretical laws are claims *within* a theory, they are not quite claims about anything. They are vehicles for reaching the world, not points of interest in it, abstractions, not tangible objects. Consider, for example, that part of Bohr's theory of the atom stating that electrons have an electrical charge of $e$ ($4.77 \times 10^{-10}$ electrostatic units). It contains both an experimental and a theoretical claim. The experimental claim is that $e$ is the minimal electric charge. That claim can be confirmed by any number of experiments without any commitment to Bohr's theory as a whole. That claim is about the world. The theoretical claim is that there are electrons. That claim has one meaning within Bohr's theory (a particle with such-and-such properties) and other meanings in succeeding theories (a particle or wave packet with somewhat different properties). Bohr's claim that there are electrons cannot be confirmed apart from his theory of the atom because the claim draws its meaning from that theory. The claim is only a claim within the theory, standing or falling with the theory as a whole.[11]

A system of criminal law is like a scientific theory in this way: certain claims about a system are, like experimental laws, capable of proof independent of the system as a whole. Others are not. For example: the claim that, if at least one kidnapper in ten is put to death, the rate of kidnapping will not exceed one per 10,000 persons in the jurisdiction, is an "experimental law." The claim can be understood without supposing any particular system of criminal law, can be confirmed in any number of jurisdictions (if it can be confirmed in any), and may be true even of a system which is hardly a system at all. In contrast, the claim that the death penalty is the most effective deterrent of kidnapping is, though superficially like the other claim, a "theoretical law." The claim does not itself say anything about the rate of crime if death is put into the kidnapping statute. "Deterrent" does not have any relation to actual or probable crime without assumptions about the rationality of criminals, the efficiency of police, the likelihood that the penalty will not itself make the crime glamorous, and so on. Similarly, "death penalty" does not itself mean that anyone will fear for his life, be put to death, or anything else. Reaching a claim about the actual or probable consequences of making a certain crime capital requires consideration of the full machinery of a particular system of criminal law. The claim that death is the most effective deterrent of kidnapping is a claim *within* a particular system, a deduction from its presuppositions, a vehicle by which the system reaches the world. That claim, unlike the first, stands or falls with the particular system of criminal law. By itself, it can neither stand nor fall.

This analogy makes the inquiry discussed in the last section seem more dubious. Even an omnipotent social scientist could not freely change penalties in a system of criminal law while holding all else constant. The presuppositions of the criminal law generate certain principles of punishment. Those princi-

ples guide the operation of the system as a whole and decisively
settle all sorts of particular questions. One can easily change the
words of a statute (well, relatively easily, since even such a change
would require much political power, acumen, or luck). But one
cannot control what happens thereafter. A certain statutory
penalty may be declared unconstitutional while one much like
it would not be; it may be nullified by a jury or prosecutor where
one much like it would not be; and so on. For some penalties,
there is only a grave of paper unless the whole system is re-
made to suit. An omnipotent social scientist cannot study penalties apart from particular systems of criminal law, cannot directly compare the actual or probable consequences of penal
provisions of different systems, and cannot freely change penalties within a particular system without making one system into
another. So, even an omnipotent social scientist is not likely to
learn much from the study of statutory penalties. For those interested in the actual or probable consequences of living under
a particular system of criminal law, what is important is the system as a whole. The penalties themselves are nothing.[12]

Now, back to that question at the end of section III: I can
admit that we talk about the "consequences" of this or that penalty while denying that such talk has anything directly to do with
the actual or probable consequences of the penalty because I
believe such talk goes on *within* the criminal law. The claims involved are "theoretical" and therefore to be defended by appeal to the presuppositions of the particular system of criminal
law, not by direct appeal to the world (which is to say, not by
direct appeal to the actual or probable consequences of particular penalties). The dispute which is the topic of this paper would
have been impossible if both utilitarians and retributivists did
not suppose that claims of deterrence (and other "consequences") were "experimental laws." The utilitarians are right
to claim that the "consequences" of a penalty should be considered in deciding what penalty to adopt. They are wrong only
in supposing that "consequences" has here the same meaning
as it has in (ethical) utilitarianism generally. Having justified the
criminal law as a system, they are no longer free to argue as if
it were not a system. Similarly, the retributivists are right to claim
that the actual or probable consequences have nothing to do with
deciding particular statutory penalties. They are wrong only in

supposing that their claim rules out considerations of deterrence and other theoretical "consequences." They too have not understood how much justifying the criminal law as a system entails. The criminal law has the richness and power of a physicist's theory.

## V. Seven Easy Steps to a Fitting Penalty

The time has come to offer an alternative to the utilitarian procedure for setting penalties. In this section, I shall state the alternative, explain its relationship to the presuppositions of the criminal law, and explain what makes it retributive rather than utilitarian. The alternative may be stated in seven steps:

> 1. Prepare a list of penalties consisting of those evils (a) which no rational person would risk except for some substantial benefit and (b) which may be inflicted through the procedures of the criminal law.
> 2. Strike from the list all inhumane penalties.
> 3. Type the remaining penalties, rank them within each type, and then combine rankings into a scale.
> 4. List all crimes.
> 5. Type the crimes, rank them within each type, and then combine rankings into a scale.
> 6. Connect the greatest penalty with the greatest crime, the least penalty with the least crime, and the rest accordingly.
> 7. Thereafter: type and grade new penalties as in step 2 and new crimes as in step 4, and then proceed as above.[13]

### Step 1

The criminal law, as noted in section I, presupposes persons who can follow rules or not as they choose and can be persuaded to follow rules by the distant prospect of set penalties. The list of penalties should therefore consist just of what no rational person subject to the particular system of criminal law in question would risk except for some substantial benefit. Nothing less would be persuasive. The list may vary somewhat from society to society. For example, in a society of honor a single slap across the face publicly administered by the common hangman may be a penalty only death could exceed in severity; while, to us, such a penalty seems lighter than a five-dollar fine (and so, amounts to no penalty at all).

The list of penalties should not contain any evil commonly believed beyond the power of the criminal law to inflict. Eternity in hell, for example, though once the greatest penalty in Christendom, would not be appropriate in the criminal code of Illinois. Who would believe Illinois to have such power? The list of penalties should also not contain anything the procedures of the criminal law are commonly believed unwilling to inflict. Exile to the moon, for example, though today a penalty within the power of some governments, is still one no government would be willing to pay for. Hence, it too would make an empty threat.

The list will, I think, usually include death, loss of liberty (e.g., by imprisonment or supervision), pain (e.g., by flogging or hard labor), loss of property (e.g., by fine or forfeiture), and mutilation (e.g., by branding or amputation).

### Step 2

An inhumane ("cruel and unusual") penalty is one the criminal law would sometimes inflict if available. The penalty is, nevertheless, to be struck from the list because most members of the society object to it on principle (and independent of its utility within the criminal law). ("Most" is defined by the political constitution of the society.) We may be willing to use inhumane penalties on some people. We may believe inhumane penalties to be effective deterrents. What we object to is their general use. We find such use morally shocking. We prefer to take the risk of operating our legal system without such penalties.[14] (Flogging and mutilation would, e.g., be struck from the list in this society as inhumane.)

### Step 3

Penalties need to be put in an order the potential criminal can appreciate. That is the point of step 3.

1. Dividing penalties by type is grouping them so that each group contains all those penalties, and only those penalties, differing from one another only by degree. For example: fines (that is, taking money or its equivalent in property) constitute a single type of penalty. Fines differ from one another only in the

amount taken. A "fine" of a day in prison or of an arm is, however, a penalty of a different type. Such a "fine" is not simply a greater taking. It is a different taking. No rational person would prefer to risk a greater fine rather than a lesser (all else equal); so, fines differ only in degree. But some rational persons (though surely not all) may prefer to risk a day in prison rather than a fine of this or that amount while others may prefer a fine of this or that amount rather than a day in prison; so, fines differ from imprisonment in type. Where a penalty is of mixed type—thirty lashes of the whip and $500 fine, one year in prison and two years supervision thereafter, or the like—it should be treated as a type different from those of which it is mixed.

2. Once divided by type, the penalties of a type should be ranked from least to greatest. The least penalty is the one any rational person would risk if (all else equal) he had to choose between risking it and risking any other penalty of that type; the next least is the one any rational person would risk if he had to choose between risking it and risking any other type except the least; and so on up to the greatest. Where a type of penalty has a huge number of degrees, these should be reduced to a manageable few. That may be done either by selecting certain round numbers (e.g., ten dollars, fifty dollars, and so on) or by grouping the penalties into ranges (e.g., one to ten dollars, eleven to fifty dollars, and so on), or by some combination of these.

3. Once penalties are typed and ranked in this way, they can be combined into an ordinal scale. The scale may branch like a tree (each branch being a type of penalty), be an interweave of vines (each vine being a type of penalty), or be otherwise messily multiplex. Such complexities, though often inconvenient (and best avoided), are not important here. (So long as we are concerned with more than one type of penalty, there is no interesting unilinear system of preference all rational persons must share.) What is important is that there be a single direction to the ordering (least penalty of one type nearest least penalty of other types) and general (if rough) agreement about where to start and end a type (e.g., fines to begin before prison time and end at one year in prison). Of course, no penalty should ever be preferable to one *below*.

*Step 4*

The list of crimes should contain any act the legislature forbids on pain of penalty. A crime may be an act itself morally objectionable, one objectionable for some other reason, or even an act the legislature just madly chose to object to. The procedure for setting penalties works independently of the wisdom of the legislature in establishing crimes (except that the unwisdom of the legislature may reappear in step 5 as a lack of "seriousness").

*Step 5*

The crimes, like the penalties, must be in some order.

1. Dividing crimes by *type* is grouping them by "intent" (i.e., by what a rational person would ordinarily aim at if he did the act, whatever else he might aim at). The minimal aim of both theft and blackmail is getting another's property. These crimes are, then, both of one type. The aim of murder, mayhem, or vandalism is not ordinarily gain. So, none of these crimes is of the same type as theft or blackmail. We group crimes by intent because we set penalties so that the potential criminal will have reason to choose the lesser crime rather than the greater when he chooses his crime. Intent tells us what the criminal will be choosing between. Whether a criminal's aim is revenge or gain, he will *not* ordinarily choose between a type of theft and a type of murder. There are, of course, exceptions (the gunman who chooses between robbing a bank and contracting to kill, the revenge seeker who wonders whether his intended victim loves money more than life, and so on). The criminal law is not concerned with such exceptions ("mere motive"). But, when an exception becomes common, there is reason to define a new crime, the peculiar aim of individuals being grouped as a new intent (e.g., "use of a weapon for unlawful gain" or "taking vengeance").

2. Once divided by type, the crimes of each type should be ranked from least to greatest. The least crime is the one a rational person would prefer to risk (all else equal) given a choice between risking it and risking any other of that type; the next least is the one a rational person would prefer to risk given a choice between it and any other of that type except the least;

and so on.[15] The ranking of crimes need be no finer than the ranking of penalties, and the more diverse the society, the less fine it is likely to be. We may distinguish between, say, grand and petty theft, simple and aggravated theft, and so on, because such distinctions do mark significant differences in what we (as rational persons) fear. But, because we (as rational persons) need not agree on every detail (e.g., on whether a theft of fifty dollars is to be feared significantly more than a theft of five dollars), the distinctions of rank (e.g., between kinds of theft) cannot be very fine. And, in fact, they are likely to be quite crude. Illinois, for example, recognizes only five "classes" of felony (plus capital crimes) and three "classes" of misdemeanor.

The existence of a particular ranking for a particular society is, of course, a contingent fact. But the existence of some ranking or other shared by all rational persons in a society is virtually guaranteed by the need of every society to agree on a few things just to exist and the possibility of making the ranking of crimes crude enough to mirror that minimum agreement. If one doubts the existence of such agreement for *this* society, he has only to go to a statute book and ask himself whether the rankings generally mirror his fears (and whether—all else equal—a person who ranked crimes much differently would be rational). For example: does he not (all else equal) fear grand theft more than petty theft? Would it (all else equal) be rational to fear them equally, much less to fear petty theft more than grand theft?

This method may put several seemingly different crimes—for example, burglary and blackmail—in the same rank. That does not mean there is no difference between them, only that there is no general reason (given the society in question and the abstractness necessary for legislation) for rational persons to prefer to risk one rather than the other. Which is preferable: to lose one's property by burglary or blackmail? Well, it depends, doesn't it?

3. Once crimes are typed and ranked, they can be combined into an ordinal scale. What I said of the scale of penalties applies equally to the scale of crimes. The scale may well resemble a New York subway map. What is important is that, for each crime (but the most serious), we prefer to have it occur rather than any ranked immediately above. Thus, if we have the two lines (i) first-degree murder, second-degree murder, man-

slaughter (where there is intent to kill but suitable provocation) and (ii) aggravated kidnapping, simple kidnapping, unlawful restraint, first-degree murder should be closer to aggravated kidnapping than to unlawful restraint and unlawful restraint nearer to manslaughter than to murder. The two lines need cross only where the kidnapping is so aggravated that it amounts to murder (e.g., where the victim dies because of the bad treatment he receives from the kidnappers even though they did not intend his death).

*Step 6*

Connecting the two scales is more or less mechanical. The least penalty should, of course, be assigned to the least crime; the greatest penalty, to the greatest crime. The lines connecting scales should never cross. Crossing lines would mean giving the potential criminal a reason to choose the crime we would rather he not choose should he be choosing between that one and some we ranked lower. The number of lines meeting at any single crime or penalty should be kept as few as possible. To have many lines meet at one crime is to make unclear what penalty the criminal may expect if he chooses to do the crime and so to tell him less about how we rank that crime relative to others than we could tell him. To have too many lines meet at one penalty is to tell the criminal we do not care which of those crimes he chooses when we do care.

Where several penalties are ranked together (say, ten lashes, thirty days in jail, and fine of $300), there may be local reasons for assigning only one to a particular crime (e.g., lashes to assault, jail to false imprisonment, or fine to petty theft). There may also be local reasons for putting all three into each statute, leaving to the judge the decision about who gets what. There may even be local reasons for not using certain penalties for certain crimes. "Local reasons" may include the likely educational effect of suffering what one has made others suffer, the satisfaction of resentment likely from such exact mirroring of the wrong (i.e., the penalty's "expressiveness"), the unpopularity of certain penalties with certain social classes, and so on. While such reasons *are* utilitarian, they do not concern the scale of penalties or the proportion between penalty and crime, only the choice among penalties ranked equally severe.[16]

*Step 7*

Neither appearance of new penalties nor the commoner appearance of new crimes should present any new problem for the procedure outlined here. A new penalty will either belong to an old type or constitute a new type. If of an old type, ranking the penalty will be a matter for clerks. If a new penalty, fitting it into the scale will require only the same crude agreement required to make up the scale in the first place: "Most rational persons would prefer to risk this rather than that." A new crime will also either belong to an old type or constitute a new one. If of an old type ("Larceny by computer is just larceny by trick"), ranking the crime will be easy enough. If, however, the crime is of a new type ("No, larceny by computer is the only crime where the minimal aim is both fun and profit"), then we must compare it with various crimes more or less analogous and already on the books, asking which we would prefer to risk, just as we did to establish the scale initially.

The procedure outlined here may appear clumsy compared to Bentham's mathematics or the equally nice proposals of twentieth-century utilitarians. I make no apology, believing the clumsiness to recognize a certain indeterminancy in what is rational. The procedure may, however, also appear to differ from the utilitarian in no other way. It will be worth a minute to notice how much it does differ.

To scale crimes, the procedure outlined here takes into account the preferences of rational persons in the society to which the system of criminal law applies. No doubt those preferences promiscuously reflect the actual consequences of particular crimes and may themselves affect the probability of such consequences. But a utilitarian principle would take such consequences into account directly and systematically. The procedure outlined here does not. If the two procedures yielded identical scales, it would be fortuitous. Similarly, to scale penalties, the procedure outlined here takes into account the preferences of the potential criminal. The potential criminal (like his brother abstraction economic man) is not someone you will meet in an alley or discover prying open your window. He is there, of course. But he is there in each of us, more or less. A utilitarian procedure would take into account the preferences not of *the* potential criminal but of all those potential criminals we hope never to meet in an alley or at our window. The procedure outlined here needs no sociology, only such knowledge as everyone has, no statistics or experiments, only the procedures of a political constitution. A utilitarian procedure would need a mature sociology to be at all reliable. The procedure outlined here works without information about the actual or probable consequences of the particular penalties. A utilitarian procedure would not (however much trouble it would have obtaining such information). Since the procedure outlined here sets penalties without directly taking into account the actual or probable consequences of particular penalties, it is the retributive principle promised at the beginning of this paper.

## VI. MORAL DESERT

The procedure outlined here is also retributive in the most orthodox sense of apportioning punishment according to the criminal's (act-related) "illicit pleasure," "wickedness," and "moral desert."[17] The procedure assigns the severest penalties (i.e., the penalties the potential criminal most prefers not to risk) to the most serious crimes (i.e., the crimes rational persons most prefer not to risk); the lighter penalties, to the less serious crimes. Such an assignment makes the punishment a function of the special wrong a criminal does simply by committing the crime. What wrong is that? The criminal's act may be morally wrong, law or no law. But, even if his act would be morally indifferent were there no law, the obedience of others makes his disobedience a taking of unfair advantage (all else equal). Others, though they too would like to take such liberties as he has, did not.[18] He has something they do not. The unfair advantage is the "illicit pleasure" in every crime, whether jaywalking or murder, prostitution or stealing. What the criminal deserves (for this act) is a punishment proportioned to that advantage (and to that advantage alone). But how (it may be asked) are we to measure that advantage?

We are not accustomed to think of crimes as objects of commerce. The idea of window-shopping for a crime seems wildly unrealistic when it does not seem just back-slappingly funny. We would rather people concentrate on obeying the law. Still, we can gain a better appreciation of the special wickedness of a particular crime by thinking of crimes as things to be bought and sold. Imagine a market in which the government sells licenses permitting the holder to break a specified law once (a sort of absolute pardon in advance).[19] The number of such licenses would have to be limited just as we now limit hunting and fishing licenses. The principle of limitation would be the same. Licensed acts (together with unavoidable poaching) should not deplete social order below the desired minimum.

How would prices be set? Let us suppose the licenses to be sold at public auction. Since the criminal law forbids only those acts some people would otherwise do, there should be no crime so great or so small that someone would not commit it if he could do so cheaply enough. Here would be the chance. Different licenses would, of course, fetch different prices. But there would be a pattern. Public auction (or any other open market) would tend to make the price of a license rise with the seriousness of the crime (and so approximate the procedure outlined in section V). There are three reasons for that: first, the quantity of licenses would have to decrease as the seriousness of the crime licensed increased. (The more serious the crime, the fewer the social order can tolerate, all else equal.) Second, the demand for licenses is likely to increase with the seriousness of the crime. (If that seems unlikely given moral constraints on potential buyers, ask yourself whether you would prefer to have a license to steal or a license to jaywalk.) And last (and most important), the seriousness of a crime would itself put a floor under the market price. The more people prefer not to risk something, the more they would pay a licensee not to use his license. The license would always be worth at least what they would pay.

We are now ready to measure unfair advantage: the criminal's (act-related) "wickedness" varies with the value of the unfair advantage he takes of those who obey the law (even though they are tempted to do otherwise). They are the society he wrongs by his crime. What he "owes" them is the price of his advantage. The price cannot be the cost of the property taken, bones broken, or lives lost. Such costs measure the private injury he has done, the damages he should pay or the restitution he should make his victims, not the value of the license he has

taken simply by doing the crime.[20] What then does he "owe?"
The obvious answer is the penalty provided by law. The price
of the crime is the penalty the criminal law has set for the crime,
the criminal law operating as a system of administered prices.
Even that price, may, however, not be what he should "owe"
(what he "owes" morally speaking, his "moral desert"). The administered price is not necessarily a fair price. A penalty is a
fair price only if it corresponds to what a license to do that crime
would fetch on the open market (the outcome of a fair procedure). The correspondence is not equality but homology, a relative correspondence. There is, after all, no decisive reason that
the society should choose this or that minimum of social order;
nor is there any privileged rule for converting dollars into years
in prison, lashes of the whip, or the like.

So, a criminal has cause to complain if he is subject to a penalty not corresponding to the fair price of the license he has
taken. The cause of complaint is the same whether the noncor-
respondence is the work of judge or statute. The cause is unfairness, that is, his not being treated like (his not being charged
the same "price" as) those who have acted with equal license.
What he deserves for his act is a penalty corresponding to the
license he took. What he got was something else. To say that a
criminal "owes" a certain penalty for his act is a metaphor but
to say that the penalty is what he deserves (for his act) is only
the literal truth.

Now, someone may think of the following objection: whether
the penalty does correspond to the fair price of a license or not,
"the criminal brought the punishment upon himself." He committed the crime knowing the penalty (or, at least, the criminal
law must suppose such knowledge—as explained in section I).
Surely, he has no cause for complaint whatever the statutory
penalty. The objection would, I think, hold if criminal penalties
were set by open market. Proving knowledge of the penalty in
an open market would prove the punishment fair (fair because
the procedure is fair). But the criminal law is like a system of
administered prices, not like an open market. Other safeguards
must replace the safeguards of the open market if we are not
to risk treating the criminal worse than he deserves (for his act).
(We do not punish for bad business judgment, foolishness, or
whatever else might have led him to "buy" an overpriced li-

cense.) Proving that the criminal "contracted" a certain penalty cannot, therefore, prove the penalty fair. To prove the penalty fair is, on the contrary, to prove the penalty to correspond to the open-market price (to be fair because it corresponds to the outcome of a fair procedure). To prove that is to prove the penalty to correspond to the seriousness of the crime (as the auction analogy shows). And to prove that is to prove the penalty to correspond to the outcome of the procedure outlined in section V. Therefore, what in all fairness the criminal deserves (for his act) is a punishment corresponding to the outcome of the procedure outlined in section V. Anything else would be out of proportion to the crime. The procedure outlined in section V thus fulfills the traditional retributivist function of apportioning punishment to (act-related) moral desert.

This argument provides a second justification for the procedure of section V. The first justification was that the procedure was derived from the presuppositions of the criminal law. Whatever justified the criminal law justified the procedure too. The second justification connects the procedure directly with moral desert. The procedure is justified because the penalties it generates are fair and because it would be unfair to adopt a procedure generating penalties different from those generated by it. Like the first justification, this second is dependent upon justification of the criminal law. Where we cannot justify application of the criminal law (e.g., to the insane), there will be no justifiable punishment and so both no proper punishment under the procedure of section V and no one morally deserving of punishment.

## VII. THE RETRIBUTIVE PROCEDURE IN PRACTICE: *WEEMS* v. *U.S.*

The discussion has necessarily been quite abstract so far. I dare not leave it that way. The abstractest theory must stand up in practice or fall. A theory that cannot guide action is only a scarecrow of theory. The retributive theory described above does, I believe, give a helpful guide to action even where utilitarianism does not.

This section offers an example of punishment disproportionate to the crime, demonstrates that the retributive procedure

easily picks out the disproportion, and then considers what a
utilitarian theory would have to say. The example comes from
the law courts. I have chosen it for three reasons. First, a law
case reminds us of the relation a theory of punishment has to
the practice of punishment (the decisions actually to be guided,
the information actually to be had at the moment of decision,
and the consequences differing theories would actually have).
The use of such a case forbids floating philosophically from this
world to that ideal world where everything is more convenient.
Second, judicial decisions are careful judgments persons of
learning and experience actually made when faced with living
detail and forced to decide what justice requires. They give valuable insight concerning what our own considered judgment
might be. Third, the case chosen is itself a classic, a clear example of punishment not itself inhumane but still so out of
proportion that it shocks. Had I made up such a case, it might
have been dismissed as too contrived for it to matter what a
theory had to say about it. But, coming straight from practice
(and, indeed, having an important position to return to), it cannot be dismissed. The theory that cannot say something sensible about it plainly has not stood up where it most ought to.
Such a case, though by itself not a refutation of utilitarianism,
does at least pose a problem any utilitarian theory of punishment should resolve. But, combined with a satisfactory retributive theory (as I believe it here is), such a case constitutes
something approaching a crucial experiment. If a utilitarian
theory is no good here, what good is it?

The case, *Weems* v. *United States*, was decided by the U.S. Supreme Court in 1909 and remains the leading American case
on the question of proportion between punishment and crime.
Weems, a disbursing officer employed by the U.S. government
in the Philippines, had falsified a cash book of the Captain of
the Board of Manila by entering as paid out the small sums of
208 and 408 pesos, as wages to certain employees of the Light
House Service. He was convicted of falsifying ("perverting") that
public document "corruptly and with intent . . . to deceive and
defraud the United States Government. . . ."[21] The statute
under which he was charged, though dating back to Spanish
times, had been reenacted under authority of Congress. The
statute set a maximum and a minimum penalty. Weems re-

ceived a sentence falling midway between. He was "[to serve] . . . fifteen years of *Cadena*, together with the accessories of section 56 of the Penal Code, and to pay a fine of four thousand pesetas. . . ."[22] The terms *"Cadena"* and "accessories" require explanation: "[Those sentenced to *Cadena*] shall labor for the benefit of the state. They shall always carry a chain at the ankle, hanging from the wrists; they shall be employed at hard and painful labor, and shall receive no assistance whatsoever from without the institution."[23] The "accessories" are (1) civil interdiction, (2) subjection to surveillance during life, and (3) perpetual absolute disqualification. These penalties are defined as follows:

> Art. 42. Civil interdiction shall deprive the person punished as long as he suffers it, of the rights of parental authority, guardianship of person or property, participation in the family council, marital authority, the administration of property, and the right to dispose of his own property by acts *inter vivos*. Those cases are excepted in which the law explicitly limits its effects.
>
> Art. 43. Subjection to the surveillance of the authorities imposes the following obligations on the person punished.
>
> 1. That of fixing his domicile and giving notice thereof to the authority immediately in charge of his surveillance, not being allowed to change it without the knowledge and permission of said authority in writing.
>
> 2. To observe the rules of inspection prescribed.
>
> 3. To adopt some trade, art, industry, or profession, should he not have known means of subsistence of his own.[24]

The penalty of perpetual absolute disqualification is "the deprivation of office, even though it be held by popular election, the deprivation of the right to vote or to be elected to public office, the disqualification to acquire honors, etc., and the loss of retirement pay, etc."[25]

The punishment is shocking, isn't it? But why? The sentence is not "cruel and unusual" in the sense of inhumane. Taking the penalties one by one, there was nothing remarkable about them in 1909; and, except for the chain (and the permanence of the surveillance), there is still nothing remarkable about them today. If the sentence is "cruel and unusual," it is only because fifteen years in prison (and 4,000 pesetas fine) is too much. But the punishment is certainly not too much for any crime. We would have no qualms about imposing such a penalty for, say, murder. It would, after all, be less severe than life imprisonment or death. So, if the sentence is "cruel and unusual" at all, it is so only because it is too much for trying to embezzle 616 pesos by falsifying a public record. But why should the penalty be too much for that?

The retributive procedure outlined above would have us answer that question by comparing the falsification of public records with crimes of the same type to see whether the severity of the penalty corresponds to the seriousness of the crime. That, in fact, is the procedure the majority of the Court adopted.[26] Here is part of what they uncovered:

> There are degrees of homicide that are not punished so severely, nor are the following crimes: . . . forgery of bonds and other instruments for the purpose of defrauding the United States, robbery, larceny and other crimes. . . . If we turn to the legislation of the Philippine Commission we find . . . that forgery of or counterfeiting the obligations or securities of the United States or of the Philippine Islands shall be punished by a fine of not more than ten thousand pesos and by imprisonment of not more than fifteen years. In other words, the highest punishment possible for a crime which may cause the loss of thousands of dollars, and to prevent which the duty of the State should be as eager as to prevent the perversion of truth in a public document, is not greater than that which may be imposed for falsifying a single item of a public account.[27]

The court has no trouble drawing the obvious conclusion: " . . . [This] contrast shows more than different exercises of legislative judgment. It is greater than that. It condemns the sentences in this case as cruel and unusual. It exhibits a difference between unrestrained power and that which is exercised under the spirit of constitutional limitations formed to establish justice."[28] Because even the minimum penalty for falsifying official documents was twelve years of *Cadena,* the Court declared the statutory penalty unconstitutional and set Weems free.[29] "It is," the Court held, "a precept of justice that punishment for crime should be graduated and proportioned to offense."[30]

Of the six justices participating in the case, two dissented. Their dissent (written by Justice White, Justice Holmes merely joining) is instructive. The dissent sounds utilitarian, yet its concern is not proportion in punishment as such but the propriety of letting courts decide such matters.

> [If] it be that the lawmaker in defining and punishing crime is imperatively restrained by constitutional provisions to apportion punishment by a consideration alone of the abstract heinousness of the offenses punished, it must result that the power is so circumscribed as to be impossible of execution, or at all events is so restricted as to exclude the possibility of taking into account in defining and punishing crime all those considerations concerning the condition of society, the tendency to commit the particular crime, the difficulty of detecting the same, the necessity for resorting to stern measures of repression, and various other subjects which have at all times been deemed essential to be weighed in defining and punishing crime.[31]

There is an ambiguity in this passage. What *might* be thought wrong with "abstract heinousness" (seriousness) as a standard of proportion is that it fails to take into account the rational concerns of a particular society. Stealing a horse is abstractly no worse than stealing money. Yet, in an unpopulated country where horses are the only means of transport, stealing a horse may be much the same as firing a gun at someone well within range. The dissent would certainly be right to counsel against abstracting crime from the conditions of the society where the crime is committed. But seriousness is not abstract in that sense. (See step 5 in section V.) If all that worried the dissent were such abstraction from the rational concerns of society, the conclusion to draw is that the case should be sent back to the Philippine courts for rehearing on the question of special conditions justifying the special penalty. The dissent does not draw that conclusion. What it concludes is that no court should delve into questions of proportion. Why?

An unstated premise must be lurking in the shadows. Ordinarily, there is nothing in judicial supervision of abuse to make the exercise of a legislative power "impossible." For the dissent, what is wrong with "heinousness" as a standard of proportion is not its abstractness but its indefiniteness. The standard would (they fear) give the courts a free hand to invade the legislative power. Why? A good utilitarian should not believe that. Utilitarians have traditionally been the ones to argue that "heinousness" is not an arbitrary term but a shorthand for just those "considerations concerning the condition of society" that the dissent wishes to have the legislature take into account.[32] If "heinousness" is no harder to prove than any other fact, why not let courts delve into such facts? The law knows how to grant presumptions in favor of a decision-maker, distribute burdens of proof, and otherwise protect the legislative or executive power from meddling—without closing off review where discretion has clearly been abused. The majority were not willing to act until convinced that they had before them more than mere "different exercises of legislative judgment." Why are the minority not willing to do the same?

Apparently, the dissent does not believe "heinousness" to be just another fact. They should as utilitarians, but they do not. Behind the concern about who should decide questions of proportion is, it seems, the fear that there is no standard by which to decide; the fear that, if judges can enter into such decisions at all, there is no rational limit to what they can review; the fear that the question before the Court is really whose arbitrary judgment should define crimes and punishments. While the majority had no difficulty deciding what seems a clear case to us as well, the minority cannot understand why it is clear and so tremble at the cases to come. Their utilitarianism blinds them to the difference between obvious injustice and ordinary legislative discretion. Why should that be? Both White and Holmes are practical men who know what judges and legislators can do. They must realize that neither judge nor legislator can in practice find out what necessarily must be found out to defend any conclusions about "heinousness" as *they* understand it. And so, they conclude that to give the power to decide "heinousness" (as they understand it) is to give power by its nature arbitrary. The power to find abuse of such a power is simply the power to usurp power. Here is confirmation of the conclusions drawn in sections III and IV. What seems to be wrong with utilitarianism is not so much that it leads us astray as that it leads us not at all. If it seems to utilitarians that I have been unfair, let them explain how this case (or one like it) should have been decided given the information actually available to the courts and legislatures in 1909 (or the information available today). They must, I believe, either adopt the method outlined in section V or take up the position Holmes and White retreated to. They will not, I believe, be able to provide a utilitarian decision of this case.

## VIII. JUDGES, RETRIBUTION, AND CLEMENCY

By now it is evident why I consider the distinction between act-retributivism and rule-retributivism unimportant. Act-retributivism is the fallback position for theorists who would like to claim more. If what I have argued here is sound, there is no need to fall back. What may not be so evident yet is that, if there is any weakness in the defenses of retributivism, it is in the old stronghold, sentencing. The legislature works deep inside the great machine of criminal law; the judge, out where that machine cuts into the world. The legislature has only to follow the procedure described in section V to do all it can or should; but the judge must and does do more. He looks to the person as well as to the act, to reformation as well as to punishment, to mercy as well as to justice. It is his business to know when to sentence with the fullest severity and when to suspend a sentence entirely, when to put a criminal on probation instead of sending him to prison, when to let the new sentence be served concurrently with others instead of afterward. The judge often seems to do less than justice. I do not, however, consider such judicial gentleness either evidence against my claims for retributivism or mere "rummaging about in the serpent-windings of utilitarianism." I do consider that gentleness something deserving at least brief explanation. I shall now give it.

We must conceive of sentencing as proceeding in two quite different stages. The first stage is retributive. Once a person is found guilty of a crime, the judge types and ranks the crime according to the procedures of section V, exercising discretion the legislature has left him to continue the work of refinement they did not dare to complete in advance. Typing should be trivial. A single statute ordinarily deals with only a single type of crime. Ranking is not much harder. The judge imagines (or, more likely, remembers) the least someone could do to violate the statute, what someone might do in addition to make the violation more serious, and how serious the violation must be before being the worst possible under that statute. (The extremes should, of course, be representative rather than bizarre.) The judge then places the actual crime in the appropriate rank (perhaps one of a half-dozen or so). Here is the place for him to consider all mitigating circumstances (duress, provocation, necessity, and so on) and aggravating circumstances (exploitation of a position of trust, extreme brutality, helplessness of victim, and so on). The judge next takes the difference (to give an exact name to a rough process) between the maximum and minimum sentences permissible under the statute, divides the difference into as many ranks as he has ranks of crime, and chooses the sentence corresponding to the rank of the particular crime. The judge has now done all that justice requires. He has found the penalty to fit the crime. He cannot justify a sentence more severe than that by any other consideration. For example, for him to sentence in the following way would be unjust: "The statutory maximum is ten years. I have decided that the crime deserves five years. But, because so many people are committing this crime these days [or because the criminal is such a bad person], I am going to sentence him to the maximum—five years for what he did and five years for what others might do [or for what he is]."

The second stage in sentencing is not retributive. It cannot be because all retributive considerations are taken into account in the first stage. The act has told us all it can. The second stage stands to retribution as promise-breaking stands to promising. The second stage concerns exceptions, not the general case. Here is the place for considerations of personal character, family situation, hope of reform, overcrowding of prisons, and so on. The theory of this stage is properly a part of the same theory of clemency covering decisions not to arrest or not to prosecute; commutations, pardons, and amnesties; and paroles, furloughs, good-time remissions, and similar reductions in severity of deserved punishment. While the theory of clemency is well beyond the scope of this paper, I must make three observations to avoid misunderstanding of what I have already said.

First, the principles of judicial clemency (like those of clemency in general) cannot allow clemency to be too common, predictable, or generous. The criminal law is possible without clemency but not without deterrence. Where clemency becomes the rule, there is no deterrence; the method of social control is no longer criminal law; and so, that principle of clemency is not the principle of exceptions familiar to the criminal law.

Second, the principle of judicial clemency should not be direct appeal to utility. Judges, though in no position to gauge accurately the general disutility of this or that act of clemency, are only too well placed to recognize its utility to the prisoner. A judge who always aimed directly at the greatest good of the greatest number would probably do more harm than good. A judge may, of course, consider the consequences of various sentences, but such consideration will be quite selective.[33]

Third, judicial clemency is not necessarily unjust (though like acts do not lead to like sentences). The criminal who receives clemency has nothing to complain of (except what anyone has to complain of when given better than he earned). The criminal who has committed the same crime as another but not received clemency may also have nothing to complain of. The principles of clemency should be principles all rational persons in the society would prefer if they had to choose between those principles and none at all. A grant of clemency according to such principles is nothing one can rationally complain of on principle (however much one may think another principle of clemency better or wish he too had received clemency under this one). Punishment is what a rational person deserves for his act; clemency, what he deserves for other reasons (perhaps only because of some official's arbitrary grace). There is no injustice so long as each criminal receives what he deserves.[34]

## NOTES

1. See, e.g., Herbert Morris, "Persons and Punishment," *Monist* 52 (1968): 475–501; Jeffrie G. Murphy, "Marxism and Retribution," *Philosophy and Public Affairs* 2 (1973): 217–43; Alan Wertheimer,

"Should Punishment Fit the Crime?" *Social Theory and Practice* 3 (1975): 403–23.

2. S.I. Benn and R.S. Peters, *The Principles of Political Thought* (New York: Free Press, 1965), p. 219 (originally published in 1959 under the title of *Social Principles and the Democratic State*). The same objection is more fully made in Stanley I. Benn, "An Approach to the Problem of Punishment," *Philosophy* 33 (1958): 334–37. Hugo Adam Bedau has recently repeated the objection in "Retribution and the Theory of Punishment," *Journal of Philosophy* 75 (1978): 601–22.

3. Compare Edmund L. Pincoffs. *The Rationale of Legal Punishment* (New York: Humanities Press, 1966), pp. 2–16. I have much changed the wording of Pincoffs' "claim iii" to bring out the inconsistency between what Benn argues in the above quotation and what I argue. I nonetheless believe that the principle I defend below is one of "desert" in something like the traditional retributivist's sense. I explain why I believe that in section VI below.

4. I do not, I might add, think the distinction entirely pointless. As I shall explain in section VIII below, judges do (I believe) behave in ways importantly different from the way legislatures behave. That difference is not, however, so much a function of the act-rule distinction (though it is in part a function of that) as it is a function of which of two stages of sentencing the judge is in. The first stage follows (I shall argue) the same principles of punishment the legislature follows; while the second follows principles of clemency ("forgiveness" in Morris's sense), something the legislature cannot possible do. The act-rule distinction invites us (though it does not require us) to conflate those two stages. But, more of that later.

5. Compare Benn and Peters, p. 202; Morris, pp. 447–80. All differences between this definition and the one Benn borrows from Flew are, I believe, simply explication of what the argument makes clear is there all along. The definition ignores the specific problems posed by vicarious criminal liability, collective criminal liability, "crimes of status," retroactive laws, secret laws, and such other troublesome rarities.

6. See my "Guilty but Insane?" *Social Theory and Practice* 10 (1984): 1–23.

7. Compare E. Van den Haag, "On Deterrence and the Death Penalty," *Ethics* 78 (1967–68): 280–89: Steven Goldberg, "On Capital Punishment," *Ethics* 85 (1974–75): 75–79. To say that the criminal law presupposes knowledge of penalties is not to say either that knowledge of the penalty is an element of any crime or that many people actually know the penalties when they contemplate crimes. Quite the contrary. To say that the criminal law *pre*supposes

knowledge of penalties is to say that the criminal law proceeds as if particular criminals have such knowledge *whatever the facts may be.* The "criminal" who proves himself *incapable* of such knowledge will, of course, be judged incompetent and excused from criminal justice. The criminal who proves the penalty could not have been known to *anyone* (e.g., because the statute was never published) should be excused on a technicality. But the criminal who proves only his own ignorance of the penalty will be convicted even more easily than one who proves himself ignorant of the primary rule he violated. Indeed, he will be convicted as easily as the criminal who proves himself an expert in the law. "Ignorance of the law is no excuse." The discovery that most criminals were in fact ignorant of the penalty when they broke the law would be interesting as a piece of sociology but strictly irrelevant as a point of law. How can that be? Must not the criminal law heed the facts? Not always. Outside a theory, particular facts do not have much to say. Just as a scientific theory may ignore anomalies, so the criminal law may ignore some discoveries inconsistent with its presuppositions. And, just as a theory will stand so long as it handles the phenomena with which it deals better than does any alternative, so the presuppositions of the criminal law need not be rejected so long as the criminal law seems preferable to any alternative method of social control. Even the criminal himself may (as Morris has reminded us) prefer to be treated as a rational agent rather than as the unfortunate fool he may in fact be.

8. See, e.g., Morris, pp. 477–478; H.L.A. Hart, *Punishment and Responsibility: Essays in the Philosophy of Law* (New York: Oxford University Press, 1968), esp. pp. 28–53; Rolf E. Sartorius, *Individual Conduct and Social Norms* (Encino, Calif.: Dickenson Publishing Co., 1975), esp. pp. 106–9.

9. Thus, this analysis of criminal law identifies the use of indeterminate sentences as foreign to the criminal law, a practice tending to reduce the benefits the criminal law provides rational persons by letting them know the consequences of their acts. (By "indeterminate sentence" I mean a sentence where the maximum is either undefined or so uniformly high as to leave the parole board virtually full discretion.) Reform theory—with its preference for indeterminate sentences—is, on this analysis, not so much a theory *of* punishment as a theory of *alternatives to* punishment.

10. I am not here talking about excusing conditions. What I have in mind are cases where we would say, "Yes, I would have done just what you did had I been in your place; but the law cannot recognize such cases as an exception." Civil disobedience is perhaps the sort of case that comes most readily to mind, but such oddities as

*Regina* v. *Dudley and Stephens* (Q.B.D. 1884) are closer to the paradigm. Such cases are fit subjects for clemency as explained in section VIII.

11. I have relied on Ernest Nagel, *The Structure of Science* (New York: Harcourt, Brace, & World, 1961), esp. pp. 82–85, for what I say of scientific theory.

12. Compare John Rawls, "Two Concepts of Rules," *Philosophical Review* 64 (1955): 3–32. Rawls's distinction between the concept of rule as "summary" and rule as "practice" is different from the distinction between claims within the system and claims for the system. His distinction is important for his celebrated contrast between justifying a practice and justifying actions falling under a practice. My distinction concerns two ways a claim (but not the same claim) may be proved. Such a claim may be used either in justifying a practice (e.g., having this statute) or in justifying an act under a practice (e.g., imposing this sentence under the statute or enacting this statute under a particular system of criminal law). Yet, whatever the differences, the two distinctions seem to lead to the same conclusion: "[Where] there is a practice, it is the practice itself that must be the subject of the utilitarian principle" (Rawls, p. 30). The utilitarian principle cannot reach particular sentences (or, though Rawls concludes the opposite, particular statutory penalties).

13. This procedure was suggested by J.D. Mabbot, "Punishment," *Mind* 48 (1939): 152–67, p. 162. Benn's attack upon the possibility of a retributive scale is his answer to Mabbot's suggestion. See Benn and Peters, p. 218. The present paper may be thought of as the response Mabbot should have made to that attack.

14. For a somewhat fuller discussion of what makes a penalty inhumane, see my "Death, Deterrence, and the Method of Common Sense," *Social Theory and Practice* 7 (1981): 145–77.

15. What is feared is not a state of affairs as such (e.g., death or loss of property) but an act (e.g., being intentionally killed or being intentionally deprived of one's property for gain). Murder is not the same type of crime as, say, involuntary manslaughter (since the murderer intends death while the perpetrator of manslaughter does not). Now, certain acts (such as blinding) are crimes not everyone can suffer. Others (such as treason or mutilation of a corpse) are crimes no one can suffer. Such crimes should, of course, still be ranked with those everyone can suffer. So, we must suppose each person ranking crimes to consider how much he fears each crime being committed against himself *or* someone (or something) for whom he cares. If someone cared little or nothing for anyone or anything but himself, he would rank many crimes lower than the

rest of us would. For the same reason, changes in our concern for others (e.g., infants, dogs, the insane, trees) may have an important effect upon what we punish and how much we punish it. For a fuller discussion of the part fear plays in the ranking of crimes, see my "Statory Penalties: What Does Rape Deserve?", *Law and Philosophy*, 3 (1984): 61–110, esp. 81–85.

16. Compare the discussion of "characteristicalness" in Jeremy Bentham, *The Principles of Morals and Legislation* (New York: Hafner Publishing, 1948), pp. 192–93.

17. I do not omit "moral blameworthiness" by accident. Blameworthiness is not, like the terms of my litany, associated with the "moral accounting" of retribution (except at the stage of clemency). Compare William Kneale, *The Responsibility of Criminals* (Oxford: Oxford University Press, 1967), pp. 25–30. This pamphlet is reprinted in full (except for the dedicatory opening paragraph) in James Rachels, *Moral Problems* (New York: Harper & Row, 1971), pp. 161–87.

18. Notice that the claim here is not that everyone—except the criminal in question—has restrained himself from committing the crime in question. There are crimes few of us find tempting enough to require restraint lest we commit them; and perhaps no crime tempts everyone. Few men—and even fewer women—are tempted to commit rape. The rich seldom have any interest in armed robbery. The poor are likely to be equally uninterested in committing stock fraud. And so on. The claim here is only that some of those who did not break the law in question would have done the forbidden act but for the law (or penalty) and that it is these over whom the criminal would gain unfair advantage if he were not punished for breaking the law in question. There will ordinarily be such people because a law failing to restrain anyone (either because everyone with the urge to break the law does or because no one—except this one criminal—has any urge to break it) is either ineffective or pointless (and so not likely to be a law at all). But what if there were a law one, only one, person had any urge to break? How would he take unfair advantage of anyone by breaking *that* law? A hard question. But there is, I think, a plausible answer consistent with what I have already said. The criminal still benefits from the restraint of others who might break other laws from which he benefits (just as *they* benefit from his keeping laws he would rather not keep). The woman who has no urge to rape may yet have an urge to castrate. The unfairness here would depend upon a more complicated practice than before (upon a system of laws rather than a single law); but there is no other difference. Still (it might now be asked), what if the criminal in question

is the only one with any urge to break any law whatever? What if he is a man among angels? While I am not sure this last question deserves an answer, it certainly has one: Yes, according to the retributive theory, this criminal would *not* deserve punishment; and, it seems to me, the theory is right:

> "It was wrong to do this," said the angel.
> "You should live like a flower,
> Holding malice like a puppy,
> Waging war like a lambkin."
>
> "Not so," quoth the man
> Who had no fear of spirits;
> "It is only wrong for angels
> Who can live like the flowers,
> Holding malice like the puppies.
> Waging war like the lambkins."
>
> Stephen Crane

19. Strictly, this analogy applies only to completed crimes. Attempts would have to be licensed with only partial or conditional pardons and so a license to attempt would always be worth less than a license to do the full act. You would be pardoned only if you did not succeed. The market analogy seems to explain what retributivists and utilitarians alike have found perplexing, i.e., why we should punish failures less severely than successes. Compare Lawrence Becker, "Criminal Attempt and the Theory of the Law of Crimes," *Philosophy and Public Affairs* 3 (1974): 262–94.

20. For the opposite (and, I think, mistaken), view, see J.P. Day, "Retributive Punishment," *Mind* 87 (1978): 498–516.

21. *Weems* v. *United States,* 217 U.S. (1909), pp. 357–58.

22. Ibid., p. 358.

23. Ibid., p. 364.

24. Ibid.

25. Ibid., pp. 364–65.

26. For a different interpretation of *Weems,* see Herbert Packer, "Making the Punishment Fit the Crime," *Harvard Law Review* 77 (1964): 1071–1082, esp. 1075.

27. *Weems* v. *U.S.,* pp. 380–81.

28. Ibid., p. 381.

29. Ibid., p. 382.

30. Ibid., p. 367.

31. Ibid., pp. 387–88.

32. Compare Bentham on "mischievous acts," pp. 152–77.

33. For a fuller discussion of why principles of clemency should not

be direct appeals to utility, see Alan Wertheimer, "Deterrence and Retribution," *Ethics* 86 (1975–76): 181–99. This point about clemency is evidently not obvious. Benn expressly claims that judges *should* sentence according to their judgment of the utility of each sentence (Benn and Peters, pp. 222–26). My remarks should not be interpreted as denying the special sort of act-utilitarianism Sartorius argues for. All I want to deny is the possibility of any act-utilitarianism not building in complex factual assumption equivalent to a ban on direct appeal to utility for clemency.

34. For a different view, see Michael Clark, "The Moral Graduation of Punishment," *Philosophical Quarterly* 21 (1971): 132–40. Clark has, I think, confused the two stages I distinguish. For a fuller discussion of the importance of the distinction to understanding justice in sentencing, see my "Sentencing: Must Justice Be Even-handed?" *Law and Philosophy* 1 (1982): 77–117.

# 6

# RETRIBUTIVISM AND THE STATE'S INTEREST IN PUNISHMENT

## JEFFRIE G. MURPHY

The purpose of this brief discussion piece is not to state and defend any thesis but is rather simply to raise a puzzle for the retributive theory of punishment—a puzzle that has received insufficient attention in the literature on the philosophy of punishment.

Most philosophical discussions about the retributive theory of punishment (including most of my own) have focused on the question of whether the goals aimed at by retributive punishment (e.g., an apportioning of suffering to moral desert) are—contrary to some utilitarian bad press—proper moral goals, goals that describe a morally acceptable or even a morally desirable state of affairs. Thus defenses of retributivism often take the form of arguing that much of the moral outlook that we value—i.e., one that contains respect for persons and their rights—might not survive if we fail to take seriously the concepts of moral responsibility, desert, and some notion of the suffering that is proper or appropriate to those concepts. Such concerns have been central not simply in my own work but in the important work of such writers as Herbert Morris and Herbert Fingarette.[1] Because of the uphill fight involved in defending the moral legitimacy of retributivist goals, a question of what is at least of equal importance has been almost totally neglected—namely, the question of whether the retributivist goals, however morally admirable they may be, are *legitimate state goals,* goals that it is the state's proper business to pursue. It is surely logically consistent to regard a goal as morally important and also argue that the state has no business promoting that goal. For example, it is characteristic of the liberal tradition to maintain that the promotion of personal virtue is a morally important goal but (because of fears of state indoctrination, etc.) that the goal is best pursued by private means (e.g., within the family) and not by the state. One thing that must be remembered—but is often forgotten by philosophers of law—is that the philosophy of law is a part of social and political philosophy and not merely of moral philosophy. Thus, in addition to considering the intrinsic moral merits or demerits of a legal practice (e.g., punishment), philosophers of law must also see such practices in terms of the general problems of social and political philosophy, particularly the problem of the nature and justification of the state and its coercive power. When considered in these terms, I shall suggest, the retributive theory of punishment faces very serious problems indeed.

First, a bit of background. Criminal punishment is the application of state coercive power in its most brutal form. The core punishments of the criminal law (deprivation of liberty or life) represent gravely serious assaults on the fundamental rights of persons, stigmatize and humiliate those persons, and typically cause them great personal unhappiness. Even when punishments are not actually inflicted on a particular individual, the possibility that they might be inflicted may be sufficient to generate enough fear in that individual to cause him to refrain from acting in ways he otherwise would have found desirable—a coercive curtailment of his liberty. Because of this radically intrusive nature of criminal punishment, it is natural that persons committed to the values of individual rights and a free society would, on both moral and political grounds, accept a system of punishment only with great reluctance. Adapting constitutional language from a somewhat different context, one might seek to discover if criminal punishment, as a mechanism that encumbers the fundamental rights of persons, is indeed the least restrictive means that could be employed to accomplish whatever *compelling* goals or interests the state seeks to accomplish through punishment.[2] (If one truly values the rights of persons, then

surely one will want to demand that the state not threaten these
rights in the pursuit of goals that are of trivial or even controversial social importance.) A thorough examination of this issue
would, of course, require careful consideration of what it means
to say of one alternative that it is indeed more restrictive or in-
tusive than another and, even more importantly, would require
an articulate and defensible account of what makes a state goal
compelling. Lovers of liberty should, of course, be willing to take
at least this amount of trouble.

One start toward an analysis of the concept of a compelling
state interest might be found in some of the devices of traditional social and political philosophy—particularly the general
idea of a social contract setting for rational social and political
choice. If a group of persons living in competitive proximity to
each other did not have a state or government, what good reasons might they have for forming a state or government and
accepting the resulting lack of liberty that this would entail—
i.e., what reasons would they find "compelling" in reluctantly
making such a decision? The obvious initial answer (one that
gives comfort to deterrence theories of punishment) is *self-protection*—protection of these persons from outside threats (national defense) and from inside threats from the violent and
abusive persons in their midst (police power). Using Robert
Nozick's metaphor, we might also consider the matter in this
way: if we think of the state as an agency that we might *hire* (at
a cost in both money and liberty) to do a certain job for us, what
kind of job would be worth the price? Again, *protection* seems to
be the answer.[3] At least this one goal—definitive of even a minimal state—will surely strike rational persons as compelling, as
clearly sufficient (if used only when necessary) to justify the resulting curtailments of liberty.

Where does retributivism fit into such a story? The retributive theory of punishment, speaking very generally, is a theory
of punishment that seeks to justify punishment, not in terms of
social utility, but in terms of a particular cluster of moral concepts: rights, desert, merit, moral responsibility, and justice.
(Different versions of retributivism differ in which of these
concepts they take as primary and the analysis they give for these
concepts.) Thus the retributivist seeks, not primarily for the socially useful punishment, but for the *just* punishment, the pun-

ishment that the criminal (given his wrongdoing) deserves or merits, the punishment that the society has a right to inflict and the criminal a right to demand. Only a theory of punishment built on these values, so a common argument goes, will respect persons as individuals of special worth—a worth that is compromised if we feel free simply to use them (as utilitarian deterrence theory appears willing to use them) for the social good.[4]

But, of course, only a very weak form of retributivism is required to avoid the horrendous consequences often feared from utilitarian deterrence theory—namely, that the concept of *desert* function, not as a goal or aim of punishment, but simply as a side-constraint on the permissible means that may be employed in the pursuit of whatever goals are properly pursued by the practice of punishment. This form of retributivism (once nicely labeled by the late J.L. Mackie at a conference as "negative retributivism") simply imposes the requirement that, in the pursuit of such goals as deterrence, the criminal never be treated more severely than he deserves.

Anyone familiar with the writings of such classical retributivists as Kant and Hegel will, of course, realize that their theories involve considerably more than the negative or side constraint respect for desert outlined above. These retributivists (and their contemporary followers) are mainly concerned to defend a much stronger claim, a view that Mackie called "positive retributivism:"[5] the retributively just or deserved punishment is not merely a limit on the pursuit of utilitarian deterrence but is itself the general justifying aim of punishment. The very point of having a practice of punishment is to guarantee that criminals will get their just deserts—even in cases where this would be clearly disutilitarian.[6]

But what does it mean to say that a person *deserves* a certain level of suffering as punishment? One model, drawn from our theological traditions of God's final judgment of all sinners, is this: each person should bear a level of suffering that is in exact proportion to his or her own level of iniquity. Whatever one may think of the moral or theological merits of this principle, it seems highly implausible as a justification for legal (as opposed to cosmic or divine) punishment. As argued above, legal punishment must be justified in terms of a compelling state interest, and it is hard to see any state interest at all in bringing about this (perhaps ultimately desirable)[7] state of affairs. There are many states of affairs that might be thought desirable yet not worth forming a state or government to achieve. If we lived in the absence of law and government, it is easy to see why we might think that it is in our rational interest to form a government for protection against external and internal violence (the basis for utilitarian deterrence theory). But is it likely that rational beings would form a government and accept all the resulting limitations on freedom simply to bring about a proper apportionment (whatever the means) of evil and suffering? The very suggestion seems preposterous. It is silly (and perhaps impious) to make God's ultimate justice the model for the state's legal justice; thus any attempt to identify "criminal" with "sinner" should be avoided.[8]

Thus, if the general justifying aim of state or legal punishment is to make sure that criminals are given their "just deserts," we need a more plausible theory of "just deserts"—a theory that will at least make it clear why the state has a compelling interest in such matters. Kant's theory of just deserts rests upon a debt metaphor and what has been called a principle of "reciprocity" or "moral balance." This line of thought, given a contemporary defense by Herbert Morris and others, including myself, goes as follows.[9] Think of a legal system as a system that confers the substantial benefits of the "rule of law" on a group of citizens only because the vast majority of citizens give its rules voluntary compliance. Even in cases where a loyal citizen desires the benefits that would flow from breaking the law, that citizen will forego those benefits and accept the burden of self-restraint in order to keep the system, the rule of law, functioning in a healthy way. The citizen will see that the system would collapse if all citizens felt free to shirk self-restraint and violate its rules whenever they felt like it. The loyal citizen expects others to bear this burden of self-restraint necessary to keep the system going (to obey the laws when they would prefer not to). Thus it is only fair—required by the "principle of fair play"—that the loyal citizen do his part when his turn comes in this beneficial system of reciprocal restraint. This "fair play" model of legal allegiance generates the following model of criminality: the criminal is a parasite or freerider on a mutually beneficial scheme of social cooperation (or, at least, reciprocal restraint)—

an individual who would seek to enjoy the benefits of living under our rule of law without being willing to make the necessary sacrifice (obedience, self-restraint) required. He must thus suffer punishment as a "debt" he owes to his fellow citizens, for, if he is not punished, he will be allowed to profit from his own wrongdoing (something that is clearly unjust) and will thus be allowed to take an unfair advantage of those citizens who have been loyal and obedient, and who have borne the necessary burdens of self-restraint. (The "profit" here is simply the freedom from the burden of self-restraint.) The state interest in punishment, then, is this: to prevent, in this context, one citizen's taking an unfair advantage of the majority of his fellow citizens. It is in this sense that the criminal deserves to suffer punishment.

There are serious (perhaps fatal) problems with this attempted retributivist justification for punishment,[10] but is does seem to be the sort of justification that *could* work. Unlike the model of retribution as a secular equivalent of God's cosmic justice, it is at least not unthinkable that this version of retributivism could link punishment to a state interest: the prevention of one citizen's profiting from his own wrongdoing and thereby taking an unfair advantage of those citizens who are law-abiding.

But even this has problems. Even if this version of retributivism could be worked out and defended, it still seems that it could be at most one state aim in punishing, but surely not the dominant (or most compelling) one. If we were forming a government and deciding to live under a rule of law, our primary concern would surely not be with the question of how to deal with persons who have already violated our rights but with the question of how to prevent persons from violating our rights in the first place.[11] Thus it would seem that deterrence will always be the dominant general justifying aim of punishment, with retribution—even on a sophisticated theory of retribution—being at most a side constraint and a secondary aim.

It might be helpful to distinguish, not merely negative and positive retributivism, but also two forms of positive retributivism: strong positive retributivism and weak positive retributivism. Weak positive retributivism is the view that retributive or desert values function, not merely as side constraints, but also as secondary parts of the general justifying aim of punishment. (Desert values are good reasons in support of punishment.) Strong positive retributivism is the view that retributive or desert values function, not merely as side constraints and not merely as good secondary reasons, but as the dominant and primary justifying reasons for punishment. (Desert values are sufficient reasons in support of punishment.) Kant, Hegel, and other classical retributivists have supported strong positive retributivism. My suggestion in this essay has been that their claims have perhaps been too ambitious—that weak positive retributivism is the most that one might reasonably even hope to defend. In constitutional terms, the pursuit of retributive values might represent a permissible or even rational state interest. It might be difficult to demonstrate, however, that the pursuit of such values could be a compelling state interest—the only kind of interest sufficient to justify the encumberances of fundamental rights involved in the practice of punishment.[12]

## NOTES

1. See Herbert Morris, "Persons and Punishment," *The Monist* 52, no. 4 (October 1968), and Herbert Fingarette, "Punishment and Suffering," *Proceedings of the American Philosophical Association* (1977). See also my *Retribution, Justice, and Therapy* (Dordrecht: D. Reidel, 1979). The closest I come to seeing punishment as a problem in *political* philosophy is in the essay "Marxism and Retribution" contained in that collection. My most recent exploration of the problems of punishment (from which a part of this essay is adapted and expanded) occurs in *The Philosophy of Law: An Introduction to Jurisprudence,* by Jeffrie G. Murphy and Jules L. Coleman, forthcoming in 1984 from Rowman and Allanheld, Totowa, N.J., 1984.

2. Standards of judicial review have been given their most complex articulation in the area of equal protection analysis. The normal standard of review is sometimes called the "rational basis" test: state action will pass review if it serves a purpose that could be regarded as rational. (This is clearly a weak standard, since some good reason can probably be found for all but the most silly state actions.) When fundamental rights are encumbered or when special burdens are placed on members of "suspect classifications" (e.g., racial minorities), "strict judicial scrutiny" is triggered. This involves the "compelling state interest/least restrictive alternative" test:

state action will pass review only if the encumberance of the right is justified by a compelling (not merely rational or legitimate) state interest and if the encumberance is actually necessary to accomplish that interest. This is clearly a very tough test to pass. For a good general discussion of these matters, see John E. Nowak, et al., *Constitutional Law,* 2d ed., (St. Paul: West Publishing, 1983), pp. 590 ff.

3. In his *Anarchy, State, and Utopia* (New York: Basic Books, 1974), Robert Nozick explores the interesting suggestion that the state should be viewed as a "dominant protective agency."

4. There is a sense, of course, in which at least some criminals have simply used others as means to their ends. Does this then mean that they have waived their right not to be so used themselves?

5. For Kant's powerful statement and defense of his version of the retributive theory of punishment, see his *Metaphysical Elements of Justice,* trans. John Ladd (Indianapolis: Bobbs-Merrill, 1965), pp. 99–108.

6. Kant, in *Metaphysical Elements of Justice,* argues that justice requires that all convicted murderers be put to death even by a society that is in the process of disbanding itself. This could hardly have any utilitarian deterrence value for that society.

7. Kant's "moral proof" for the existence of God places such weight on the importance of giving each person his or her just deserts that, realizing that this is usually not possible in this world, Kant feels that we might postulate the existence of God and an afterlife in order to satisfy our moral desire that it get done sometime. See Lewis White Beck, *A Commentary on Kant's Critique of Practical Reason* (Chicago: University of Chicago Press, 1960), pp. 271 ff.

8. Imagine how intrusive of privacy and autonomy a state would have to be if it set out to identify all moral iniquity and punish accordingly.

9. The following argument draws heavily on the so-called "principle of fairness or fair play" defended by John Rawls and H.L.A. Hart and criticized effectively by Robert Nozick. See H.L.A. Hart, "Are There Any Natural Rights?" *Philosophical Review* 64 (1955): 175–191, John Rawls, *A Theory of Justice* (Cambridge, Mass.: Harvard University Press, 1971), section 18, and Robert Nozick, *Anarchy, State, and Utopia* (New York: Basic Books, 1974), pp. 90 ff.

10. For a discussion of these problems, see Murphy and Coleman, *Philosophy of Law,* chap. 3, no. 25.

11. But is not all punishment after the fact? Of course. But the utilitarian deterrence view advocates using such punishment for *future* good. Note that a sophisticated utilitarian theory of punishment does not have to see punishment as justified solely to secure fu-

ture general happiness. It can also advocate other future values—
e.g., rights maximization. For more on this and its problems, see
Murphy and Coleman, *Philosophy of Law,* chaps. 2 and 3.

12. If the state has a legitimate (but not compelling) interest in attempting to ensure that one citizen does not profit by his or her
wrongdoing and thereby take an unfair advantage of others, there
are ways less intrusive or restrictive than punishment that the state
might employ to seek this end—e.g., a system of compensation.
My purpose here, of course, has not been to show that the state's
interest in pursuing such values is not compelling. I have rather
been concerned to show that it is not obvious that this interest is
compelling and thus that the burden of proof is on those who believe that it is to demonstrate its compelling nature. If this interest
is not compelling and if the state pursues it anyway in justifying
the punishment of someone in excess of what would be demanded
to serve utilitarian deterrence values, then perhaps a case could be
made that such punishment would be cruel and unusual in one of
the senses of "excessive" used in the Eighth Amendment—namely,
a punishment that does not stand in reasonable proportion to a
compelling state aim. For a further discussion of this (one with
which I am now not totally happy), see the chapter "Cruel and
Unusual Punishments" in my *Retribution, Justice, and Therapy.*

# 7

# A MOTIVATIONAL THEORY OF EXCUSES IN THE CRIMINAL LAW

## R.B. BRANDT

The central contention of the following paper is that criminal liability requires a *motivational fault* in the agent. More fully, persons who have unjustifiably broken valid law should be exempt from punishment unless their behavior is a result of some defect of standing motivation (one might say "character" instead)—"should be" in the sense that the exemption is required by any reasonably adequate general theory of criminal justice.

I shall suppose that we need four concepts in the criminal law. First, the law prohibits certain types of action (call an instance of one, "actus reus") such as arson, larceny, rape, assault. The traditional view is that these forms of behavior are forbidden because they are thought to be normally harmful, or threatening, or bad in themselves. Of course, some kinds of behavior the law forbids or has forbidden are not harmful, or threatening, or bad, in fact; but let us pass this. Call this forbidden behavior, this violation of "primary" (Hart) legal norms, "unlawful."

Second, in particular circumstances an instance of one of these forbidden types of action may not be, or at least is reasonably believed by the agent not to be, harmful, or bad, on the whole, from the point of view of society; on the contrary, it may be or at least is reasonably believed to be preferable to other options open to the agent. In this case the law permits an exception.

165

Thus whereas arson is forbidden by the law, an agent will not be punished if he sets fire to a house in order to prevent a general conflagration. Call behavior which is unlawful but falls into this special class, "justified unlawful action."

Third, an act may be unlawful but *not* justified in this sense, but nevertheless may not manifest any defective motivation of the agent. Thus, if a person commits a rape, we can normally infer that he has no strong aversion to using violence for obtaining sexual gratification, or to producing fear and shock in his victim, or to forcing a woman to have intimate relations which she does not want, and to infringing the prohibitions of the law. (We might add that the person does not have a strong aversion to the risk of incurring severe legal penalties, but I think we should not include lack of such self-interested aversion among the "defects" of motivation; it would make no difference to the argument if we did.) But sometimes such an inference is blocked. A person who has raped may have honestly believed that he had the woman's consent. In this case a circumstance may or does block the normal inference to substandard motivation; the action in this situation is compatible with the agent having an adequate standard level of motivation in all respects. Now, say of such a case that the behavior is "excused," and the relevant circumstance that blocks the inference we can call "an excuse." So accidents and mistakes of fact are excuses.

Fourth, there is behavior that is unlawful, unjustified, and not excused in this sense, but nevertheless thought not properly punished. For instance, behavior of infants or persons suffering from some forms of insanity. (But unlawful, unjustified behavior arising from a delusion may be excused, as involving mistake of fact.) Say that such behavior is "not responsible." Thus we need four terms: "unlawful," "unjustified," (behavior which is unlawful and unjustified may be called "legally wrongful"), "unexcused" and "responsible." An unlawful unjustified act is done with mens rea only if responsible and not excused; at least I propose we talk this way, giving a clear meaning to "mens rea."

It should be noticed that the foregoing conceptual framework deliberately diverges from familiar legal categories in some ways. First, the "actus reus", or unlawful conduct, is defined so as *not* to require such mental elements as purposefulness, recklessness, and the like, although in order to be conduct at all, it must be different, for instance, from sleepwalking; that is, it must be guided by *some* beliefs and desires. Thus absence of the mental elements is included among excuses. In this and also in the matter of how to explain "justification" I am happy to have the support of Glanville Williams[1]; he notes that the inclusion of mental elements in the definition of an offense raises problems about the liability of accessories. I also note that Herbert Packer pointed out[2] that the Model Penal Code's procedure is clearer and simpler in some ways, but that it is more perspicuous to identify the kinds of overt behavior the law aims to prevent, and then to list the various mental elements that serve to exempt violators from punishment. In this respect my term "excuse" is more inclusive than it is for such writers as George Fletcher. But on the other hand, my use of excuse is in other respects narrower than is usual. Whereas infancy and insanity are often viewed as excuses, I propose not to call them so because they differ from other excuses in important ways, which the following discussion will make clear. I am not, of course, suggesting that infancy or insanity should not exempt from punishment; but the reasons are different. I am calling sanity and noninfancy conditions of "responsibility"—and the list could be expanded. Whether we define mens rea so as to imply both absence of excuse in my sense, and responsibility, or only the former, is a semantic issue to which little importance should be attached. In earlier times, excuse was not even distinguished from justification; this failure to distinguish was a manifest confusion.

The main contention of this chapter departs both from tradition and the Model Penal Code. The motivation theory does have something in common with an earlier period of the law when, for example, Bracton said that "desire and purpose" distinguish "evil-doing,"[3] and "desire to injure" was a part of the definition of arson, and a child of eight was hanged for arson because of "malice and revenge" in him.[4] The law at that time seems to have overlooked that a person's motivation in acting involves not only desires for certain outcomes but also *aversions* to being motivated not to do certain things, and overlooked the central importance of the latter. But the law has moved from identifying the mental element of a crime from something about motivation, to *intent*. There are different intentions comprising the mental element for the various offenses, so that F.B. Sayre, at the conclusion of his historical study, opined that it is futile at present to seek "any single precise meaning" for mens rea.[5] (Of course, that is exactly what I am proposing to do.) The Model Penal Code groups together several unrelated "general principles of liability", namely, that the agent has acted "purposely, knowingly, recklessly, or negligently, as the law may require", but then, in the same Article, lists various specific defenses, including ignorance or mistake of fact or law, involuntary intoxication, duress, entrapment, etc., and separates all this from a section on justification and a further section on responsibility (insanity and infancy). If any general principle underlies the various excuses listed in the Code, it is not made clear; perhaps the motivation theory is wrong, but at least it puts forward a general principle to be assessed. Incidentally, the movement of the law from motive to intent may be more verbal than real, since a person's intent reflects his motivation; this "movement," unless I am mistaken, reflects an overly simplified psychology. But I agree that the motivation theory is a departure from mainstream thinking and therefore has to be defended.

In the course of my argument I explain why certain circumstances (for example, duress, accident, mistake of fact) excuse an action according to the motivation theory, and point out that these circumstances in fact exempt from punishment according to current law. But I am not suggesting that *because* my definition implies that certain circumstances, which are standardly regarded as excusing by the courts, do excuse is a *confirmation* of my proposal. Sociology of the law, or explanatory history of the law, aims to explain actual laws and court decisions ideally in the same way as astronomy explains eclipses; such theoretical frameworks *are* refuted by disconformity with the actual laws and decisions. Not so the theory I shall provide. In any case the conformity is inexact: the theory to be proposed does not follow the law's view that, roughly, nonculpable ignorance of the law is no excuse, or that mens rea considerations may be ignored in connection with the offenses of bigamy or statutory rape, or that a strict felony-murder rule is justified. (Since many lawyers are uncomfortable with the law at these points, perhaps an element of fiction is present in talk of "the law.") I wish to say, however, that the rough conformity of actual law to the proposed general principle is enough to give plausibility to the view that the principle is in some sense implicit in the law; I also point out that where principle and law in principle are discrepant, there is reason to doubt that the law is justified.

## WHAT KIND OF THEORY DO WE WANT?

I am urging the general position that legally wrongful acts ought to be subject to legal punishment only if they are at least partially caused by a defective state of the agent's (long-term) motivation. But how is one to support such a contention?

A full explanation and defense of an answer to this question would be too large a project to be undertaken here; what will be possible is only to outline a view, a parallel to which for the closely related field of ethics the writer has defended in detail elsehwere.[6] What we may say briefly is that we are looking for *justified* legal principles about excuses. But what is it for a legal principle to be "justified," and how do we identify one that is? I make use here of a proposal defended elsewhere for ethical principles: a legal system is justified if and only if all factually informed and rational[7] adults would choose or prefer it to be obeyed and enforced in the society, with its institutions, if they expected to live in it. Or, what may be very nearly the same thing, legal principles are justified if that *moral system,* which factually informed and rational persons would prefer to any other if they expected to live under it, would call on individuals to obey and require officials to enforce them. I hope and anticipate that most readers will be favorably disposed toward this conception of justified principle; I think most if not all persons will be more favorably disposed toward a legal principle or system if they think it is justified in this sense—or better justified than alternatives.[8]

Among the "institutions" of a society like ours is the political system: with legislative and excutive branches roughly democratically chosen, with a Constitution, a Supreme Court, and a division of powers among the three branches of government (not to mention all the pressure groups such as unions, the Moral Majority, etc.). It might be that all rational persons would want any legal system, adopted and supported by this political organization, to enjoy a defeasible presumption of authority—a presumption that might be defeated by a clear showing that some feature of the system must be expected to work contrary to the long-range welfare of people in general.

Can we say anything about what kind of legal/moral system informed rational persons would prefer for a society in which they expected to live? I believe the answer is that they would prefer a legal/moral system the currency of which in the society would maximize general benefit—general happiness, if you like. In other words, a rule-utilitarian system. This chapter is not the place for any extensive argument for this answer. It is admittedly controversial today, and unpopular in some quarters. Among those with whom it is unpopular are neo-retributivists about the criminal law. These writers, however, seldom or never work out a theory of their alleged moral knowledge; nor does the retributive theory ever get a precise statement. Those who lean toward the more traditional utilitarian view need not worry for fear they are out of date.[9] For the present purposes I feel free to suppose that utilitarianism is sufficiently plausible today.[10] to make it worthwhile to develop the implications of a utilitarian theory of the criminal law, as I shall do in the final section of this chapter.

What we are specifically concerned with here is those legal principles that rational persons would want as principles governing exemption from punishment when a legally wrongful act has been committed. The motivation theory of excuses is such a possibility: that a legally wrongful act ought to be subject to punishment only if the act manifested a defect of motivation. (Of course, a person who has acted wrongfully should also be exempt from punishment if he is insane, an infant, etc.)

The motivational theory, as stated, is a restricted principle; it states only what is a necessary condition for being punished at all. It could be expanded, in combination with a principle of proportionality, into the thesis that the severity of punishment for a given crime should be proportional to the gravity of the defect displayed by the criminal act. Retributivists might approve this, unless they think that the punishment inflicted must somehow equal the evil done. Thus, if a worse defect of motivation is shown by intentional homicide than by reckless homicide, one might infer that the punishment for murder should be more severe than for manslaughter. Of course, the "gravity" of a defect is not obvious, except for some cases: willingness to kill is manifestly worse than willingness to *risk* a killing. Mostly our thoughts about relative defects of motivation seem to go with our thoughts about how objectionable is the type of act that typically manifests it. We do have opinions on such matters, shown by how relatively severe a punishment we think acceptable, and also by our thoughts about which kinds of benefit will justify; thus we think and the law holds that use of a lethal weapon is justified to defend one's own life (or that of wife or children), but not to prevent a theft, much less to prevent trespass on one's land. The Supreme Court evidently thinks that murder is more heinous than rape.

However this may be, it is certain that suppositions about the character (= system of motivations)[11] of a defendant play a considerable role both in actual sentences to imprisonment and in normative statements in the Model Penal Code about the principles that should govern sentences.

We should note that some writers think that the dangerousness of a person, as revealed by his criminal act, does and should play a large role in the criminal law. How dangerous a person is, of course, is closely related to the particular defect of motivation shown by his criminal behavior; information about a person's standing motivation is an important guide to prediction of future behavior.

## WHY THE MOTIVATIONAL THEORY?

Why should we think that an agent ought to be exempt from punishment for a wrongful act if a defect of motivation is not among the causal conditions of the act? We shall go into this more deeply in the final section, when we survey the rationale of legal punishment as a whole, but certain considerations merit attention at this point. We can at least call on the authority of ancient tradition if we think that an act is liable to punishment only if it springs from an "evil heart" or "vicious will." According to Sayre, about 1600 the "malice" required for a charge of murder involved "general malevolence or cold-blooded desire to injure."[12] As Sayre puts it,[13] the moral blameworthiness of a criminal deed (and mens rea required this) was "necessarily based upon a free mind voluntarily choosing evil rather than good." This view, if we include the talk about a "free" mind choosing evil, appears to be burdened with a heavy load of questionable metaphysics. We get the picture of a mind, free in the sense of causally undetermined, opting for what is evil rather than what is good. This picture must be modified to some extent if the conception is to deserve a serious hearing today. The first thing we have to do is construe free choice in the ordinary sense, such as when a person says, "You married me of your own free will", meaning in the absence of coercion (it was not a shotgun wedding) and perhaps after an opportunity to deliberate on the options and their probable consequences, and to take the option one most wanted to take, everything considered. This is far from free choice in the sense of causal indeterminism, and is compatible with a science of motivational psychology (a science about lawfulness in action, or causation in action). Suppose, then, we take free choice to mean uncoerced action determined by the desires and aversions of the agent and his conception of the options open to him and their probable consequences. Then we can construe an evil will in terms of the (objectionable) desires or aversions of the agent, from which his actions spring, in part. So we might mean by an evil will the presence of desires to do harm to someone, and the like, or, more importantly, indifference to the prospect of harming others or running the risk of so doing. If we do this, we can regard human agents as causal systems, of which desires/aversions are an important part. If we make this change, and go along with tradition in identifying mens rea with an evil will, then we can claim the support of tradition in holding that mens rea, the mental element necessary for liability to punishment, at least in large part concerns the motivation of the agent, as a consequence of which he chose to do what he did, in the situation as he saw it. Indifference to the welfare of others, then, may be a major part of what it is to have an evil will.

Recent writings, however, emphasize that the mental element of a crime has to do with intention, whether something was done knowingly or purposefully. In the case of *Regina* v. *Cunningham* (Court of Criminal Appeal, 41 Crm. App. 155, 1957), the court proposed that to show that a defendant acted "maliciously," it suffices to show that he "foresaw" that what he did might injure. This seems a departure from a motivational conception of mens rea. But it is not; the psychology of motivation appears to have been widely misunderstood. If we turn to psychological theory, we find that what a person does at a given moment is a function of at least five variables: (1) his beliefs (possibly partly unconscious) about the options open to him; (2) his beliefs about the situation he is in; (3) his beliefs about consequences that might occur if he takes any one of these options and how strong they are (how likely he thinks the consequences would be); (4) the vividness of his representation of these matters at the time; and (5) his desires and aversions for these consequences (taking each action as being a consequence of itself, so that an aversion just to doing something of a certain sort is included). The theory asserts that a person will have a *tendency* to perform an action he thinks open to him, according as it promises to have consequences he wants with how great a probability; the person will actually perform that act which he has the strongest tendency to perform, as fixed by the desires/aversions associated with the anticipated consequences, their influence diminished by the anticipated improbability of a consequence occurring if he performs the act. Some writers put this by saying that people act roughly so as to maximize their expected utility—"utility" being defined in terms of their desires/aversions at the time."

A surprising fact then emerges: the motivation and belief are entangled in the production of an action in a way seemingly overlooked by some writers on the law. Suppose we say Jane is guilty of a crime because she tampered with the brakes of her husband's car, expecting it would bring about his death. Our legal scholar says Jane has mens rea because she knowingly acted so as to bring about a death. (Presumably Jane brought about her husband's death not because she wanted this for itself, but because his death would enable her to collect his insurance and elope with someone else.) Now, when we take psychological theory into account it is clear that what is responsible for Jane's tampering with the brakes and thereby producing her husband's death is not merely her wanting the insurance money along with knowing that tampering with the brakes in order to get it would bring about his death; what is responsible is her relative indifference to bringing about her husband's death. Our legal scholar could as well have said that Jane is guilty of a crime because she tampered with the brakes, relatively indifferent to the prospect that so doing will bring the death. But for that indifference, her action would not have occurred. So it is clear that while the Model Penal Code makes the normal mental condition of criminality that the agent purposefully or knowingly or recklessly do a forbidden thing, it could as well be said that the normal condition of criminal action is *failure to be motivated to avoid* a foreseen forbidden consequence or to be indifferent to a substantial risk that it occur. Thus talk about intention or foresight is misleading; the intentions we have are a function of our desires/aversions, and what a person foresaw is evidence about what he was indifferent to. What is novel in the motivation theory, as compared with the ordinary view, is simply the looking at another side of the picture.

If we speak of "defects of motivation," the question arises which kind of defect we have in mind. Would some moral defect, like lack of generosity or sympathy, or sadism, be enough? (If we answer affirmatively, a judge might have to draw on the positive morality of his day to identify a defect, or, if he happens to be a scholar in the history of philosophy, he might speculate as to "true" defects.) A more plausible view would be to identify as defects those stated or implied by the prohibitions (in statutes or precedents) of a given legal system; so, if the law forbids intercourse with a girl less than ten years of age, absence of an adequate aversion to intercourse with a child, or at least absence of an adequate aversion to obedience to the relevant prohibition of the law, would count as a defect. Sometimes the law specifies that a crime of a certain sort is committed only if the agent intended something, for example, if he enters a building for the purpose of committing some crime; the defect then is not only that of being unaverse to entering a building not one's own, but also that of being unaverse to the prospect of committing some other wrongful act. So our list of defects is essentially taken from the law. Of course, the law may be bad law, in which case the "defects" will not really be defects from any point of view other than that of bad law. The law is always subject to improvement from the standpoint of reflective morality.

When we speak of a "defect" of motivation, we need to specify some degree of strength. A person might have some degree of aversion to killing another, or breaking the law generally, but go ahead anyway because the prospective victim stood in his way.

How much motivation is adequate? It need not be of infinite strength, enough to overcome every possible contrary motivation; to use terminology some favor, it must only be enough to resist contrary motivations that a person of ordinary firmness would resist. So the aversion to cooperating in an armed robbery should be greater than any desire to do what might win the affections of a lady, but it need not be enough to overcome an aversion to having a bullet in one's head, instantly, if one refuses to go along (excuse of duress). One finds some of these comparisons spelled out in cases in which it is debated whether an offense is "justified." One will also get a rough ordering of the expected strength of aversions for various offenses, by looking at the severity with which the corresponding offense is punished. (This correspondence is, however, certainly rough: in *Rummel* v. *Estelle* the Supreme Court upheld Texas statutes that inflicted life imprisonment of a person whose three non-violent felonies, for example, a forged check, involved a total of $240.)

If the motivational theory of mens rea is correct, in holding that an unlawful and unjustified act is subject to punishment only if it manifests a defect of motivation, then an excuse must be some showing, in the face of knowledge that the accused acted illegally and without justification, that the action was compatible with there being no defect of motivation—the normal inference from act to motivation is blocked. If we hold that this theory of excuses is essentially embodied in the law, we expect to find that the recognized excuses (and, mutatis mutandis, at least some mitigations) are of this kind.

It may be thought that obviously a legal excuse is no such thing, for, if it were, judges would be required to dabble in speculations about motivation in order to apply the law. (Of course, according to the motivational theory, a judge is not required to sum up the virtues and vices of a person and decide whether on the whole he is a virtuous man, or at least up to average. Also, he is not required to decide whether a given action would be morally blameworthy—manifest a moral defect—if it were not contrary to law.) But judges in fact necessarily do make some judgments about motivation. (And judgments about the intent or beliefs of the accused need be no less speculative.) If we follow the Model Penal Code, a judge, in order to decide that a voluntary act was performed at all, must conclude that the bodily movement was not a result of a convulsion, made during sleep or unconsciousness or as a result of hypnotic suggestion, but rather that it was "a product of the effort or determination of the actor, either conscious or habitual" (Art. 2.01).[14] The conclusion clearly requires inference beyond observable bodily behavior. Moreover, according to the Code, in order to decide that an act meets the general conditions of criminal culpability, it must be shown that either (1) the "conscious object" of the agent was to behave in a certain way or produce a certain effect, or (2) that the agent was "aware of" or "practically certain" of all material elements of the offense, or (3) that the agent consciously disregarded a substantial and unjustifiable risk "such that its disregard involves a gross deviation from the standard of conduct that a law-abiding person would observe in the actor's situation," or (4) he acts as if he were disregarding a risk, but is unaware of the risk although his failure to be aware of it is itself a "gross deviation from the standard of care that a reasonable person would observe in the actor's situation" (Art. 2.02 (2)). With the possible exception of (2), if this is not speculation about motivation, what would be?

The motivational theory of excuses requires only that someone decide whether a certain feature of the case rules out an inference to a defect of motivation, given the other facts surrounding what the defendant did.

It may be objected that the theory implies that, when illegal behavior is unexcused, there can be inference from behavior to defect of motivation, whereas no such inference is ever possible. But this is absurd. Once we assume, as we must, that action is a function roughly of the beliefs and desires/aversions of the agent, we are in a good position to reconstruct the motivation, and we do so all the time. If a person does not interrupt a friendly game of tennis to make inquiries when a child falls off a bicycle in the next court and is screaming and covered with blood, and no one else is around to render succor, we infer that he is defective in sympathy or empathy. Of course a further story might provide a justification or excuse. And the inference does require commonsense familiarity with how people ordinarily behave in certain circumstances, and why they do the things they do. But we do know these things.[15]

## THE MOTIVATION THEORY AND RECOGNIZED EXCUSES

The motivation theory will appear more plausible if it is clear that the standard excuses recognized are excuses in my sense. I have suggested earlier that this fact does not strictly confirm the theory; but it does show the theory is in touch with the realities of the law. Let us therefore survey the major excuses, and see how well they fit the motivation theory.

*Accidents.* An accident occurs when some untoward event occurs because a causal process has unforeseeably gone awry: a bullet richochets and kills a bystander; a child darts out from between parked cars in front of a motorist; a cable breaks. (The event is not accidental if negligence is involved, for example, if the driver could have stopped had he not been talking with a passenger or waving to a friend.) In such cases, when an event occurs that the law prohibits, the agent is legally excused. The motivation theory implies this conclusion, for in such cases (negligence aside) no inference to a defect of motivation is possible. In some special circumstances, however, the agent is not legally excused. For instance, if a person is committing a felony, and accidentally discharges a weapon, killing someone, he is not excused, since the context of the attempted felony provides "presumption" that the death was caused "recklessly under circumstances manifesting extreme indifference to the value of human life" (Model Penal Code 210.2 (1)(b)). The "presumption," of course, need not correspond with the facts, but the explanation offered by the Code fits the motivation theory, in that the total event is said to "manifest extreme indifference to the value of human life"—certainly a defect of motivation of high degree.[16]

*Mistake of fact.* The motivational theory affirms that an agent is not liable to punishment for a wrongful act (unjustified breach of the law) if the breach was not at least partly caused by a standing defect of his motivation. So, is a woman guilty of a crime if she kills her husband, shooting through a closed door, in the honest belief that she is firing at someone attempting to break into her bedroom to rape her? What would be the defect of motivation? The law does not condemn willingness to use a lethal weapon to protect one's self from being raped. So, in the circumstances, there is no reason to suppose her action was caused by defective motivation, and, according to the theory, she must be excused. That is also the conclusion of the law. (See the Model Penal Code, 2.04, 233.1(1) and 212.4(1)(a).) It can be, however, again as the law affirms, that, given a person's mistaken belief, his action shows some other defect of motivation different from that which would have been shown had he not entertained a mistaken belief, and then he can be guilty of a lesser crime.[17]

It may be objected that the motivational theory does not reflect the law since, according to the motivational theory, an honest mistake of fact could block inference to a defect of motivation, whereas at least the common law tradition requires that the mistake be reasonable, and in some cases (bigamy, statutory rape, abduction, attacking an officer of the law), a mistake of fact is no defense, reasonable or not. (The motivational theory will concede that the reasonableness of a belief is important evidence for whether the belief was actually held.) A view, closer to the motivational theory (Texas statute, see *Green* v. *State*)[18] requires that the belief arise from want of proper care, which of course implies a defect of motivation, but possibly a minor defect. Contemporary legal opinion, however, appears to have moved into substantial agreement with the motivational theory, requiring only actual belief rather than reasonable belief, for serious crimes.

*Mistake of law.* The motivation theory appears to be in conflict with the practice of courts on the question whether mistake of law is an excuse. On the whole, at least in theory, courts have held that mistakes as to criminal law (as distinct, for instance, from property law) are no excuse. For example, a native of Baghdad committed an unlawful "unnatural offence" on board an East Indian ship anchored in an English harbor. The act was no crime in his native country; he did not know that it was in England; and he presumably did not think the action immoral. But his conviction was upheld. How could this be, if liability to punishment requires a defect of motivation? It would be unreasonable to suppose that he should have inquired as to the legality of the act in England; thus there was no evidence of defect of diligence in inquiring into the law, so no lack of respect for the law of England. It may be that in the England of the time (1836), it was thought manifest that "unnatural offences" were immoral and that the man should have been put on notice thereby that the law might well prohibit them;[19] or it may have been thought that absence of an aversion to sodomy was itself a defect of motivation. Public opinion today, however, is probably better summarized in an opinion of the Iowa Supreme Court, in part as follows: "Respect for law, which is the most cogent force in prompting orderly conduct in a civilized community, is weakened, if men are punished for acts which according to the general consensus of opinion they were justified in believing to be morally right and in accordance with law."[20] Nevertheless, a line of distinguished jurists has offered arguments to the effect that allowing ignorance of the law as an excuse would be impracticable and undermine the efficacy of the law. Even an opinion of the U.S. Supreme Court,[21] delivered by Justice Douglas, while overturning a conviction of infringing a California law that the defendent could not have known about, stated that "We do not go with Blackstone in saying that ' a vicious will' is necessary to constitute a crime, for conduct without regard to the intent of the doer is often sufficient. There is wide latitude in the lawmakers to declare an offense and to exclude elements of knowledge and diligence from its definition." The Court managed to distinguish the case at hand on the ground that it was "conduct that is wholly passive—mere failure to register. It is unlike the commission of acts, or the failure to act under circumstances that should alert the doer to the consequences of his deed." The Court found that in this type of situation a conviction violated the constitutional requirement of due process. Oliver Wendell Holmes argued at length that the tests of criminality are external behavior, except for cases of infancy and insanity.[22]

I believe we must concede that some decisions of the courts in denying ignorance of the criminal law as an excuse tend to show that the motivation theory is not entirely in accord with judicial practice. On the other hand, the justification of this practice is open to serious question. The dictum even of the Supreme Court does not justify it. The arguments offered by legal writers, in defense of the practice (for example, that allowing the excuse would be unacceptably burdensome for the courts, that it would encourage ignorance of the law and stand in the way of efficacy of the law in preventing objectionable forms of conduct, or in effect that it would make the law identical with whatever the defendant thinks it is) seem without merit. If what the courts had to decide, in the terms of the Iowa decision, were whether the defendant was "justified in believing his conduct to be morally right and in accordance with the law," the burden on the court would not be too heavy. Nobody would convince a jury that he thinks unjustified murder is morally right and also in accordance with the law. And a person will hardly be justified in thinking his conduct in accordance with the law, unless he has diligently made inquiries, when he is aware at least that there are or may well be differences of moral opinion about an action, so that he is put on notice that the law may contain a relevant provision. It is true that if the Iowa principle were followed, a defendant must be excused when he infringes some unadvertised regulation about which moral considerations give no warning. But such a practice would not undermine the law, especially if it were understood to apply only in the case of serious charges involving possible imprisonment. Here we should go at least part way with Professor Hart when he writes that ". . . we should restrict even punishment designed as 'preventive' to those who at the time of their offence had the capacity and a fair opportunity or chance to obey the law: and we should do this out of considerations of fairness or justice to those whom we punish."[23] We need go only part way with Hart in that we should, I think, replace his phrase about "capacity and a fair opportunity to obey" with an expression about defect of motivation, and replace his reference to reasons of "fairness or justice" by one to long-range utilitarian considerations, as we shall see below.

It should be noticed that the motivation theory does not imply that all ignorance of law should constitute an excuse, but only that kind of ignorance, or ignorance in such circumstances, as to make clear that the defendant's conduct did not spring from a defect of motivation.

*Voluntary intoxication.* The law understands "intoxication" to refer to a state brought on by drugs as well as alcohol; it will do no harm to confine ourselves to the case of alcohol. Let us suppose, then, that a person has become drunk and commits an offense, and that the offense and circumstances are such that, had he been sober, his conduct would undoubtedly have manifested a defect of motivation. Now the law says, in effect, that even if, in his state of intoxication, one cannot assume a defect of motivation, he is nevertheless liable to punishment (barring crimes the definition of which includes "specific intent"), unless he took the alcohol for medical reasons, or does not know (and need not know, morally or legally) that the amount ingested would cause intoxication (see Model Penal Code, 2.08). Is this what the motivation theory implies?

Evidently we must distinguish two acts, what the agent did after he was already drunk, and his acts (one or more) of drinking a quantity of alcohol. Drinking is not a crime, and unless one thinks it morally wrong the taking of a drink does not permit inference, by itself, of a defect of motivation. However, on the basis of past experience of his own reaction to alcohol, or by inductive generalization from the reactions of others, the agent might well have reason to believe that in drinking what he did, he was running a risk—which an ordinary law-abiding person would not run—of becoming drunk and committing an offense in that condition (for example, driving his car). In that case, his initial act showed some defect of motivation: indifference to taking this risk. He might even know he is running a substantial risk of acting violently. In that case we can say that his subsequent offense arose out of this initial defect of motivation, but only indirectly. The offense for which he is culpable is running the risk. If a person runs the risk of acting violently and kills someone, he might well be charged with manslaughter—his behavior could be classified as reckless. However this may be, a person who has demonstrably run a serious risk will have done something that, if one adopts the modified Wootton-like view of punishment defended by H.L.A. Hart and Joel Feinberg, justifies his being placed at the disposal of the system for dealing with criminal offenders. New York State has a statute forbidding reckless endangerment.

The motivation theory, then, is out of line with the law when the law refuses to count voluntary drunkenness as any kind of excuse (except for the case of specific intentions). But then, in this the law is inconsistent: on the one hand it declares that an act must be voluntary (controlled by beliefs and desires), in order to be criminal, and then in effect affirms that acts not so controlled (a drunken act) may be fully liable. The motivation theory has implications identical with those the law ought to have. There is another way of viewing the total situation that might reconcile the law and the motivation theory. Suppose it is agreed that what the law should punish is reckless endangerment (by taking a drink in circumstances such that the agent should know he is taking a risk). The law might wish to deter such reckless-ness by suitable punishment, but the problems of detection make this impracticable. However, the law might say that, in this sit-uation, the sensible thing to do is to punish quite severely those who cause real damage; this is a kind of selective punishment (like punishing every tenth person), and it would serve the pur-pose of deterring from reckless endangerment, if the law is known. If lawmakers do view matters in this light, it would be helpful if the fact were well publicized.

I am not familiar with any full phenomenology of drunken-ness; it could well be that behavior when drunk (depending somewhat on how drunk the person is) could reveal, or be caused by, standing defective motivations.[24] The motivation theory need not object to punishment in some such circumstances.

*Duress.* My theory gives a clear account, superior in simplicity and plausibility, of why and when duress is an excuse. The the-ory, we recall, holds that wrongful behavior is liable to punish-ment only if it manifests a defective level of motivation. But how strong must be the motivation to avoid a certain offense, or to act in a law-abiding fashion? It depends on the offense. For in-stance, aversion to killing one's wife is expected to be strong enough to outweigh a desire to be free to elope with one's sec-retary. But aversion to breaking some laws is not expected to be able to compete with certain other motives, such as a pre-sent, immediate threat of death or serious bodily injury either to one's self or others close to one. So the Model Penal Code (2.09) states that if a person is threatened with unlawful force "which a person of reasonable firmness in his situation" would be unable to resist, there is a valid defense. The standard of motivation expected by the law falls short of the requirement of proving one's self a hero, more dedicated to avoiding illegal acts than persons of reasonable firmness. What a person may do, then, depends both on the unlawful act he is coerced to perform, and also on the nature of the threat.

Matters are more complex if the defendant was responsible

for being in his dilemma: if, for instance, he voluntarily joined a group that he knew might later threaten him if he refused to perform violent acts. In that case the situation must be viewed from a longer time-span, as in the case of unlawful behavior when drunk, and the whole situation may lead to an inference of defective motivation at the time of joining, so that inferences comparable to those in the case of drunkenness are authorized.

*Provocation.* Provocation is not an exculpating excuse in the law, but only a mitigating one, reducing a charge of murder to one of manslaughter. But its legal status is sufficiently similar to that of intoxicated behavior to merit dicussion.

A rather plausible (perhaps unrepresentatively progressive) principle, stated in *Maher* v. *People* (10 Mich. 1962), is that there is legal provocation if "reason should, at the time of the act, be disturbed or obscured by passion to an extent which might render ordinary men, of fair average disposition, liable to act rashly, without due deliberation or reflection, and from passion, rather than judgement." This is somewhat similar to the Model Penal Code rule (210.3 (1)(b)) that a homicide is only manslaughter when "a homicide which would otherwise be murder is committed under the influence of extreme mental or emotional disturbance for which there is reasonable explanation or excuse. The reasonableness of such explanation or excuse shall be determined from the viewpoint of a person in the actor's situation under the circumstances as he believes them to be."

Strong emotional disturbance is known to primitivize thinking (much as does alcohol). A state of anger notoriously enhances one's aggressive tendencies, and reduces one's empathetic or sympathetic concern about injuring its target. So the law has traditionally looked sympathetically at homicide brought on by discovering one's spouse in the act of adultery, or by a violent blow. Why? Herbert Wechsler and Jerome Michael opined[25] that the reason is that the fact of anger blocks inference to a deficiency in the agent's character (standing level of motivation, in my terms); the more an ordinary man, of "fair average disposition," would incline to do the same, the less reason there is to think that the agent falls short, in his normal standing motivation, of a satisfactory level of moral/legal motivation. Not just any strong emotion will do this job: as the Model Penal Code puts it, there must be a "reasonable explanation or excuse," traditionally the objectionable conduct of the victim, presumably because anger not understandable to the average person would be a manifestation of irascibility, which is itself a defect of motivation of a sort.

The law on this topic has puzzling features. Why does provocation not exculpate, and merely mitigate, if the provocation shows that the motivation of the accused is not demonstrably less acceptable than that of the reasonable man? Perhaps the law is best read as suggesting that the standing motivation of the provoked man is not so very far from that of the ordinary man (but surely he is a difficult person with a hot temper!), and hence, combined with a theory of proportionality, that his punishment should be less.

In general, the legally mitigating effect of provocation fits in reasonably well with a motivational theory of excuses (mitigations).[26]

We should notice that the law governing the punishment of attempts fits nicely with what the motivational theory implies. If a man announces to a woman that he is going to rape her, and is in a position to do so, and then abandons his venture, the law takes a very different view of his behavior if his abandoning it is brought about by the unexpected appearance of a policeman, as compared with his saying to her, "No, I simply cannot do a thing of this sort. Please forgive me." Manifestly the latter behavior shows a level of motivation much nearer to what the law expects than does the former.

Somewhat the same might be said of the law in jurisdictions where a crime is punished less severely if the defendant has a low level of intelligence. The intellectual defect leaves open the possibility that the character—motivation—of the agent is not below, or not far below, what the law expects.

*Insanity.* I shall consider two questions about the insanity defense: first, whether it adds anything to the excuses already considered, for example, mistake of fact or law; and second, if it does, whether this defense may be viewed as an excuse in the sense explained above, as a consideration blocking inference from a person's unlawful behavior to a defect of motivation. We may follow the Model Legal Code (4.01(1)) definition of the defense: that a person is exempt from punishment for legally wrongful (unlawful, unjustified) conduct "if at the time of such conduct as a result of mental disease or defect he lacks substantial capacity either to appreciate the criminality [wrongfulness] of his conduct or to conform his conduct to the requirements of law." It is added that "mental disease or defect" does not include abnormality manifested only by repeated antisocial conduct.

We may assume that we are considering only "voluntary" acts within the meaning of the Model Penal Code (2.01), limited to bodily movement that is "a product of the effort or determination of the actor, either conscious or habitual," and thus excluding convulsions, automatisms, movements during sleep or unconsciousness, or resulting from hypnosis. Our questions are not easy to answer because "mental disease or defect" can take many forms, or be manifest in many ways.

One widespread form of insanity is the occurrence of delusions or distortions of judgment, so as (to use terms of the older M'Naghten rule) "not to know the nature and quality" of one's act. Suppose, to take an example that appears to be a favorite of law professors, a man strangles his wife in the honest belief that he is squeezing a lemon. In this case the agent is acting on the basis of a mistake of fact; if the facts were as he believes them to be, his conduct is perfectly lawful. So this kind of "insane" behavior is already covered under "mistake of fact," and no additional insanity defense is needed. The same goes for all behavior that would be lawful or justified if the agent's delusional beliefs were true.[27]

The older M'Naghten rule distinguishes something else from such factual mistake, namely, "if he did not know he was doing what was wrong," echoed by the Model Penal Code as "if he lacked substantial capacity . . . to appreciate the criminality [wrongfulness (moral?)] of his conduct." In both cases it is stipulated that the ignorance must be the product of mental disease or defect. This conception is puzzling. Perhaps the agent is deficient in capacity to visualize the impact of what he does on others. Presumably, if this were intended, the defense would seem to recognize a showing that the inability is a result of some other defect, like brain damage, since some studies have shown prison populations to be relatively deficient in a capacity for visualization. Some interpreters of the law construe the moral knowledge or appreciation to include emotional appreciation.

But then such interpretation might classify most criminal conduct as insane, if we construe, as apparently we must, thinking that an act is wrong or appreciating its wrongness, as essentially not cognitive but a matter of attitudes—essentially aversion to an act, disposition to feel guilty about performing it, and disapproving of others who do. But if that is what is true, then that kind of insanity consists precisely in failure to have adequate moral/legal motivation. And it is puzzling how that could serve as an excuse; adequate moral/legal motivation (or, in other words, character) is exactly what the law expects of people; behavior that must be explained by absence of adequate motivation is precisely unexcused. Another possible interpretation of these passages is that it is suggested that a person's conceptual scheme is so primitive that his concepts of the criminal/morally wrong are too undeveloped to serve as the basis for motivation to avoid criminal forms of behavior. But this is speculation: the meaning of the legal conceptions does not seem clear enough for an answer to our two questions.

The Model Penal Code also, as noted, exempts from punishment if, as a result of mental disease, an agent "lacks substantial capacity . . . to conform his conduct to the requirements of law." This could be a cognitive defect but not a mistake of fact or law, if we follow Sir James Stephen in his account: "The man who does not control himself is guided by the motives which immediately press upon his attention. If this is so, the power of self-control must mean a power to attend to distant motives and general principles of conduct, and to connect them rationally with the particular act under consideration, and a disease of the brain which so weakens the sufferer's powers as to prevent him from attending or referring to such considerations . . . deprives him of the power of self-control."[28] If one attempts to apply this interpretation, one faces the difficulty of discriminating between incapacity deriving from a "disease of the brain" and that incapacity common, more or less, to us all, or at least to many criminals.

More frequently, however, the incapacity of an agent to conform his conduct to the law is explained in a different way. Courts have recognized an "irresistible impulse" to do something, for example, steal, as relieving from responsibility. What seems to be meant is that the desire to steal was so strong that it would overcome even a satisfactory level of moral/legal motivation. If so, there could be no inference from the criminal act to defective motivation, and this insanity defense could be incorporated as an instance of the motivational theory of excuses, rather like duress. But perhaps this is not what is meant by an irresistible impulse, for in cases of kleptomania it is known that the desire is not a normal desire: it is for things that apparently do the agent no good, and can hardly be a source of satisfaction.[29] But the psychological literature on kleptomania is minute, and it may be that any sensible theory of it would require a different account.

Other types of case apparently fall within this "inability to conform" conception of legal insanity. For instance, a man who suffered brain damage and who mutilated himself and killed others in sudden fits of rage.[30] Or a woman, in what was diagnosed as a psychosis brought on partly by repeated ingestion of drugs, who repeatedly stabbed her mother with no apparent motive.[31] One might say that the psychiatrist's account does block an inference to defective moral/legal motivation. But one is left puzzled about the possible state of the defendants' moral/legal motivation. One can hardly say that the evidence raises no doubt that the motivation system is normal/adequate, in the way no doubt is raised when we learn that criminal behavior arose from a nonculpable mistake of fact. I suggest that this kind of insanity defense not be viewed as an excuse.

## THE BASIS OF THE MOTIVATION THEORY: THE GENERAL THEORY OF PUNISHMENT

What sort of justification can be given for the motivational theory, that persons who have unjustifiably broken valid law should be exempt from punishment unless their behavior is a result of some defect of standing motivation (one might say "character" instead)?

One way to answer this question would be to affirm a certain form of the retributive theory of punishment, and point out that the motivation theory follows from it. That is, one might subscribe to that form of retributivism which holds that a person should suffer punishment for lawbreaking to a degree corresponding with his moral blameworthiness, or at least that he forfeit his right not to be used for purposes of deterrence, and to the extent of his blameworthiness. This theory entails the motivation theory if, as I think "X is morally blameworthy for doing A" should be explained roughly as "X did A, and he would not have done A but for a defect of standing motivation (character), and as a result it is fitting for persons to disapprove of X on account of his doing A." Thus, this retributive theory implies that a person should be punished for an act only if it showed a defect of motivation. The retributive theory of course goes beyond the motivation theory in implying a principle of proportionality: of quantity of punishment and degree of blameworthiness.

It seems likely that few philosophers (but perhaps relatively more legal theorists) take the retributive theory very seriously at the present time, despite the popularity of some kind of intuitionism in some circles. Some writers, who would draw back from asserting the retributive principle as just a basic moral principle known intuitively, have tried to derive some forms of it from different principles of justice which they find congenial, but their views are open to serious criticism.[32] In any case, the retributive theory at best gives only an ordinal theory: it tells us that X should be punished more for A than Y should be for doing B, but gives no clue exactly how much either one should be punished. The utilitarian theory has the virtue of yielding, in principle, some quantitative guide.

It seems worthwhile, then, for this and more general reasons suggested earlier, to examine what a utilitarian theory would imply with respect to the motivational theory of exemption from punishment.

We may recall that utilitarianism is a theory roughly that the whole system of social institutions should be appraised for its impact on well-being or happiness. The system of criminal justice is one of these institutions. One important cause of unhappiness, of course, is harmful behavior, and hence one of the aims of an optimal system of institutions, according to the utilitarian, will be to minimize harmful behavior, to the extent that so doing does not impair realization of more important goals. Among the other features of a society that affect happiness are such things as freedom to plan one's own life and implement the relevant decisions, the preservation of personal privacy, a considerable

degree of social and economic equality, knowledge and its uti-
lization in personal planning, and so on. The sytem of criminal
justice is an institution especially aimed to reduce harmful or
antisocial behavior, but, according to the utilitarian, it is open
to criticism if it accomplishes this special aim at too great a cost,
for example, loss of freedom and privacy; some loss in preventing harmful behavior must be accepted if avoiding it would
cost more in loss of other benefits. Of course, certain other institutions should aim, among other things, at preventing antisocial behavior: the economic system by removing incentives to
crime and the crime-fostering conditions of the ghetto; the educational system; the church; the system of medical care for the
mentally defective or ill; and positive morality if we want to call
that an "institution." In view of these points, it is clear that the
system of criminal justice must operate under some constraints.
In order to avoid intolerable intrusion, or undue interference
with freedom of planning, the system cannot give everyone
psychological tests to determine whether, to maximize the general safety, he or she should be in custody; a person must be
left alone unless he or she actually does something contrary to
law—rather like allowing a dog one bite before its dangerousness is scrutinized. So a person cannot be held criminally liable
unless there is an actus reus—a proved unlawful act.

What can the system of criminal justice do, within these constraints, to achieve its primary function of reducing harmful or
antisocial behavior? I mention three things.

1. Partly it can be educational; it in effect announces, in a
forceful way because the announcement is accompanied by a
threat, which forms of behavior the society (or its representatives) considers harmful to the extent of being socially intolerable.

2. It can operate as a deterrent to harmful behavior. We
should be clear just what can be expected of the system in this
respect. Most people have well-interiorized moral standards, and
hence, to a large extent, will conform their conduct to the law
in any case. But if there were no parking meters, even very decent people would be inclined to take more than their share of
that scarce commodity of parking space; and if the Internal
Revenue Service never prosecuted, it is doubtful whether so
many even generally decent people would pay their share of

taxes. So while, for most people, the deterrent threat of the law is unnecessary for most kinds of harmful behavior (most people would not consider murder, quite apart from the law), a threat of punishment is beneficial, for some types of case, to help the average person behave properly. This is not to say that severe penalties (long prison terms) are needed for the average person; the reader need only ask himself for what conceivable gain he would risk being arrested, tried, having his shortcomings spread in the newspaper, being fined or imprisoned for six months, or even just being put on probation. The writer can think of few gains worth such a risk; and one need not escalate the risk to that of twenty years in prison in order already to have maximized deterrence. On the other hand, many people are not deterred by the law, even with the relative severity of its threats in the United States.

Why? For one thing, people with little or no income have little incentive to stay out of jail, where they receive three square meals a day; they may think they are better off in than out. Again, some do not read a newspaper and know little about the threats of law, or perhaps they have never learned to evaluate prospective behaviors in terms of consequences and costs. The law also needs help from morality: if an agent's group does not proscribe violence or crimes of passion, or even idealizes power in a system of organized crime, the targeted deterrence is in for problems.

3. The system of criminal justice can operate to prevent repeaters. Of course, if a person is imprisoned and kept out of circulation, there is no danger of further criminal behavior (at least, outside the prison). Moreover, no one will doubt that a substantial fine for running a traffic light will, at least for some weeks, render the convicted motorist more cautious about obeying traffic signals. Is lengthy imprisonment effective as far as future behavior of the criminal is concerned? Not unless it gets at the causes of the original misbehavior. It would seem that the prison system should aim to return inmates to normal life as soon as is compatible with public safety—and that means such things as treatment for drug addiction, jub training, assistance in finding a job on leaving a prison, and so on.

With these general background considerations in mind, we can now understand the justification of exempting persons from punishment when they have committed an unjustified offense by an action not caused, even in part, by a defective system of legal/moral motivation.

The utilitarian's general answer, of course, and I suggest it is the right answer, is that the motivation theory of exemptions will maximize benefits. Let me summarize the reasoning.

1. If a person has broken the law but with no defect of motivation, no benefit is gained from punishing him, as far as his own future behavior is concerned. To allow him to circulate in society is no more dangerous than in the case of those who have not broken the law. It may be that punishment will attach an additional negative affect to the idea of doing that on account of which he was convicted, but if his level of motivation is already satisfactory, so far as is known, to build up more negative affect is pointless. So the person (and presumably his family) is penalized without any benefit, at least as far as his future impact on society is concerned. Of course, a system of excuses different from the motivation theory (like the present one which emphasizes lack of intention, knowledge, recklessness, or negligence as an excuse) may have much the same effect, but the point of identifying excused behavior for these reasons must be that the indirect effect is that people already adequately motivated are excused. But the motivation theory gets to the central point directly, and points the way to a desirable reform of law, by way of abolishing strict liability conjoined with serious penalties, as well as various irrational anomalies in the law such as, possibly, the felony-murder rule.

2. What is the alternative to the motivation theory, or something essentially identical with it? One possibility is a system of strict liability: a person convicted of unjustifiably breaking the law (or perhaps just breaking the law, justified or not) would be given a specified sentence, depending on the offense (or at least turned over to the detention system for treatment, as Lady Wootton would have it). Such a system could well be a nightmare, intolerable from the point of view of the average law-abiding citizen. What would life be like if one must anticipate a year in prison for accidentally running down a child, with no fault whatsoever on one's own part? The nightmare would be less bad if Lady Wootton's version were adopted, but even so the life of anyone unlucky enough to break the law by accident,

or because of nonculpable mistake of fact, would be grossly damaged.

3. That punishment for excused crimes is pointless because not needed, and that the impact of a pure strict-liability system would be disastrous, might not be totally convincing, if it were not that exempting adequately motivated persons from punishment does not diminish the deterrent impact of the system of criminal justice. The issue is important, since the reason for legal punishment, according to most writers, is the deterrent effect of threat of punishment on potential wrongdoers. Many writers think that in fact the incorporation of excuses in a system of criminal law does diminish the deterrent effect of the system, and therefore hold that the consistent utilitarian would be opposed to a legal system with excuses.

If it were true that a strict liability system would be a more effective deterrent, that would be a utilitarian point in its favor—but only one, to be weighed against the preceding ones just mentioned. But why should it be thought that allowing excuses diminishes deterrence? As far as I know, no comparative studies show that excuses increase the crime rate. So we must simply think the matter through in a commonsense way. Let us ask: what class of crimes would be deterred by a strict liability system but not by a system with excuses (roughly as the motivation theory advocates)? Not those committed by persons who do not know the law, so we must limit the effects to persons relatively informed on the system of criminal justice. Suppose we think of an informed rational person, who for some reason wants his wife out of the way and is deliberating whether to make an attempt on her life. How will the fact of the system of excuses affect his thinking? Perhaps he can manage to have a bullet ricochet? Perhaps he can convince a jury that he mistook his wife for a burglar, or that he was acting under hypnotic suggestion, or that someone threatened to kill him if he didn't, or that the episode was the result of a delusion, of schizophrenia? I think the rational prospective murderer will do better to spend his time thinking how to commit the crime so that the jury will not be convinced that he actually did it. So how much deterrence will be lost, for rational informed persons, from knowledge of the system of excuses? The rational person will see that it is going to be very difficult for him to escape punishment by the excuse route. I think we may agree that people may be encouraged to commit crimes by knowledge that persons who commit crimes are mostly not punished. Perhaps they know that most murderers are never brought to justice. How many of these escape via the excuse route? Perhaps two percent? Will this two percent have a detectible effect on deterrence, given the general situation? Suppose we think, as may be true, that the deterrent effect of the criminal law comes through vicariously attaching negative affect, by conditioning, to the thought of a given offense. Is there any reason to think this conditioning process will be significantly affected by the knowledge that a very small proportion of persons escape punishment by the excuse route?

Nevertheless, various writers at present, as far as I can see without support from either observation or psychological theory, airily assume that we know that allowing excuses must reduce deterrence. Not that these writers advocate that excuses be abolished in view of the alleged impact on the deterrent force of the system. Quite the contrary. What they want to do is pin on utilitarians a commitment to strict liability in the law, because they do, of course, in principle favor a system that on the whole will maximize utility. In fact, these critics fail to show that a strict liability system would actually increase the deterrent effect of the law. Even if it did, the foregoing two reasons, especially the second, are weighty; in view of them, one could hardly advocate a strict liability system on utilitarian grounds even if such a system were somewhat superior in efficacy of deterrence. Thus a utilitarian system of punishment will necessarily exempt from punishment those who have acted wrongly but in so doing manifest no defect of motivation or character.

My conclusion is that a rational and informed person, if he were to be given a choice among possible systems of criminal justice for the society in which he expected to live, would opt for a system exempting from punishment those persons who have committed an unjustified unlawful act, but did not thereby manifest any defect of standing motivation, or character. But I do not suggest that a person would feel happy about the total situation, even if the system of criminal justice were made as humane as possible, compatibly with a reasonable degree of protection of society from harmful actions. This is because of the great inequalities in our society, not only economically, but in intelligence, health, energy, and the type of family in which a person is reared. Many persons with a high level of intelligence and the good fortune of upbringing in a good family and a good education are never put in a position where they are strongly motivated to disobey the law. With others the opposite is the case. Even a humane system of excuses, one that punishes a person for a crime only when it is "his fault," does not remove the unjustified inequality in the lottery that bestows good things on some and bad things on others. It is true that we should say to ourselves, "There but for the grace of God go I." I suggest we all have an obligation to work toward the amelioration or removal of these inequalities, but that is not the job of the criminal law. What justifies the criminal law is that it is the best compromise among unhappy alternatives, for the world as it now is. On the one hand, life would be intolerable if no criminal law existed and no one was deterred from doing as he pleased by the threat of punishment; on the other hand, with the system, many have to suffer who would not have had to suffer had the lottery of life not put them where they are. So the criminal law has to remain an uneasy compromise, attempting to accommodate both the need to protect society from harm, and the obligation to avoid imposing suffering on those who have broken the law. A system that exempts from punishment offenders who are not "at fault"—defective in moral/legal motivation—is an advance toward humanity without significant loss in protection of society.[33]

## NOTES

1. Glanville Williams, "The Theory of Excuses," *Criminal Law Review* (1982): 734 ff. As will be clear in what follows, however, I do not accept his definition of "excuse," p. 735.
2. Herbert Packer, *The Limits of the Criminal Sanction* (Palo Alto: Stanford University Press, 1968), chap. 6. Packer points out rightly that mens rea is also relevant to mitigation. See the discussion of provocation below.
3. *De Legibus,* 136b.
4. Francis Sayre, "Mens Rea," *Harvard Law Review* 45 (1932): 974–1026, at p. 1010.
5. Ibid., p. 1023.

6. *A Theory of the Good and the Right* (Oxford: Clarendon Press, 1979); and "The Explanation of Moral Language," forthcoming.

7. See the writer's "The Concept of Rational Action," and ten other essays by various authors, on the general topic of rational decision, in the September 1983 issue of *Social Theory and Practice*.

8. It is logically possible that not all rational persons would prefer one and the same set of legal principles for a society in which they expected to live, and in that case we should have to adopt a more person-relative conception of "justified" such as, "If I were fully rational, *I* would choose or prefer this set of legal principles to be obeyed and enforced in that society, with its institutions, if I expected to live in it." For our purposes we can ignore this complication, which will hardly arise for the problem with which we are concerned. Another possible complication is that the moral system that all rational adults would prefer for a society in which they expected to live might condemn the very laws that they would want obeyed and enforced in that society. I ignore this logically possible complication.

9. For a criticism of some recent retributive theories, see R.W. Burgh, "Do the Guilty Deserve Punishment?" *Journal of Philosophy* 79 (1982): 193–210; and D.F. Thompson, "Retribution and the Distribution of Punishment," *Philosophical Quarterly* 16 (1966): 59–63. For Kant, see D.E. Scheid, "Kant's Retributivism," *Ethics* 93 (1983): 262–82.

10. For support of this view see John Harsayni, "Morality and the Theory of Rational Behavior," *Social Research* (1977): 623–56, and his *Essays on Ethics, Social Behavior, and Scientific Explanation* (Dordrecht: Reidel, 1976). See also Brandt, *Theory of the Good and the Right,* chaps. 11, 14, and 15.

11. See R.B. Brandt, "Traits of Character: a Conceptual Analysis," *American Philosophical Quarterly* 7 (1970), especially p. 34. Contrast Feinberg, *Doing and Deserving* (Princeton, N.J.: Princeton University Press, 1970). pp. 126–7, 190–1.

12. Sayre, "Mens Rea," p. 997. The present writer has argued that to say an act is morally blameworthy is to affirm that the act would not have occurred but for a defect of character (motivation). See "Blameworthiness and Obligation" in A.I. Melden, ed., *Essays in Moral Philosophy* (Seattle, Wash.: University of Washington Press, 1958); and *Ethical Theory* (Englewood Cliffs, N.J.: Prentice-Hall, 1959), chap. 18. For the connection bewteen character and motivation, see note 11 above.

Professor Fletcher appears to be mistaken when he says "The only way to work out a theory of excuses is to insist that the excuse represents a limited, temporal distortion of the actor's character." See George Fletcher, *Rethinking Criminal Law* (Boston: Little Brown,

1978), p. 802. Assuming we identify character with standing motivation, there is no such thing as a "limited, temporal distortion" of it. Anger might seem an example, but if a person acts from extreme reasonable anger (provocation), we think his character is all right—that is, his standing aversions—it is only that the temporary angry desire to hurt was stronger. In the case of mistake of fact, or duress, there is no defect of character (motivation) at all. (See Brandt, "Traits of Character.") Fletcher remarks, however, that "an inference from the wrongful act to the agent's character is essential to a retributive theory of punishment" (p. 800). Further ". . . if someone violates a legal prohibition under an unavoidable mistake about the legality of his conduct, we cannot infer anything about his respect for law and the rights of others. The same breakdown in the reasoning from conduct to character occurs in cases of insanity. . . ."

It should be noted that moral blameworthiness, as a commonsense term, is no better off than mens rea. I have argued (see "Blameworthiness and Obligation") that it is useful to define it in a certain way, but in fact the term is hardly in active use at all by ordinary speakers (non-lawyers, or more likely, non–law-professors), and the most obvious candidate, "deserves to be blamed," raises more questions than it answers. What is it to blame someone for something? To reproach him face to face? To criticize him behind his back? To affirm that some defect in him is a cause of his act? ("The engine's performance must be blamed on the plugs.") Evidently the meaning of this term does not lie on the surface.

13. Sayre, "Mens Rea," p. 1004.

14. Actually, a judgment is required about a causal relation to beliefs and desires. See A.I. Goldman, *A Theory of Human Action* (Englewood Cliffs, N.J.: Prentice-Hall, 1970), p. 72. Scholars of the criminal law should be familiar with this book.

15. For a view similar in many ways to the motivation theory of excuses, see Michael D. Bayles, "Character, Purpose, and Criminal Responsibility," *Law and Philosophy* (1982): 5–20, especially pp. 9 ff. Bayles attributes a form of the theory to Hume. One might object that a man may be guilty of manslaughter if he kills his brother who has a terminal cancer, is in pain, wishes to die, but cannot find a physician with the courage to give a lethal dose. How is this possible, if criminality requires some defect of motivation? In fact, most people do not think the man a criminal, and are not surprised or shocked if he receives probation or a nominal sentence, perhaps just a fine. The judge is in a dilemma: he cannot himself regard the man as a criminal whom the law ought to punish, but he does not wish to encourage other people to make de-

cisions about the lives of others, possibly in a less discriminating way. Much the same may be said about conscientious objectors to many laws.

16. For a useful discussion of the history and logic of the status of accidents, see George Fletcher, *Rethinking Criminal Law,* pp. 276 ff. and 487 ff.

17. This remark supposes that the defect of motivation is to function not merely as a condition for nonexemption from punishment altogether, but as a clue to the permissible degree of punishment, as it does in those theories that hold that the severity of punishment should be proportional to the blameworthiness of the agent. If this view is rejected, as it would be by the writer, for a largely treatment view of criminal justice, once guilt (some offense + mens rea) is established, then degrees of defect would be of little functional importance. The role of considerations of deterrence will be discussed in the following section.

18. 153 Tex. Crim. 442, 221 S.W. 2nd 612, 1949. See citation in P.W. Low, J.C. Jeffries, Jr., and R.J. Bonnie, *Criminal Law* (New York: Foundation Press, 1982), p. 264.

19. The case was *Rex* v. *Esop,* 173 Eng. Rep. 203 (Cent. Crim. Ct. 1836).

20. *State* v. *O'Neil,* 147 Iowa 513, 126 N.W. 454 (1910).

21. *Lambert* v. *California,* 1957, 335 U.S. 225.

22. See *The Common Law,* chap. 2.

23. Review in *Yale Law Journal* 74 (1965): 1325 ff.

24. See the learned and helpful discussion in Herbert Fingarette and Ann F. Haas, *Mental Disabilities and Criminal Responsibility* (Berkeley, Calif: University of California Press, 1979), chaps. 6, 9, 11, and 12.

25. Herbert Wechsler and Jerome Michael, "A Rationale of the Law of Homicide II," *Columbia Law Review* 37 (1937).

26. I omit discussion of entrapment. It seems impossible to give a coherent account of it as an excuse, since the very seductions to crime that are a defense when they are provided by the police, do not serve as a defense when provided by private parties. (The law does suggest the motivation theory, however, when it speaks of entrapment as providing inducements to crime "by persons other than those who are ready to commit it." Does "ready to" refer to a substandard level of aversion to the offense or to lawbreaking in general?) Maybe what is behind it is the idea that we are all likely to commit a crime if we are tempted often enough, or severely enough, and it may be the victim's bad luck, not his less-than-adequate character, if he is seduced by the police. Or perhaps it is that we do not think the law-enforcement agencies ought to be in the business of tempting people to break the law. J. Feinberg, in *Doing*

*and Deserving,* pp. 191 and 213 ff. gives helpful suggestions. I am indebted to L.M. Seidman's paper, "The Supreme Court, Entrapment, and Our Criminal Justice Dilemma," *Supreme Court Review* (1981): 111–55.

27. See Heathcote W. Wales, "An Analysis of the Proposal to 'Abolish' the Insanity Defense in S.1: Squeezing a Lemon," *Univ. of Pennsylvania Law Rev.* (1976): 687–712.

28. *A History of the Criminal Law of England* II (1883), p. 170.

29. *State* v. *McCullough,* 114 Iowa Supreme Court, 532 (1901). See the interesting discussion in Joel Feinberg, *Doing and Deserving,* pp. 281–88.

30. *People* v. *Robles,* 1970, 2 Cal. 3d 205.

31. *People* v. *Kelly,* Supreme Court of Calif., 1973, 10 Cal. 3d. 575, 111 Cal. Rptr. 171, 516 P. 2d 875.

32. For a critical review see R.W. Burgh, "Do the Guilty Deserve Punishment?", *Journal of Philosophy* 79 (1982) 193–210.

33. I have learned a great deal from the comments of various individuals who kindly read and responded to an earlier draft of the present paper: William K. Frankena, Bruce Frier, J. Roland Pennock, Adrian M.S. Piper, Louis Michael Seidman, Heathcote Wales, and Peter Westen. Needless to say, they are not responsible for the errors that may remain. I am also indebted to Peter Tague, whose course on substantive criminal law I audited while a visiting professor at the Georgetown University Law Center, and to conversations about the topic of the present paper with Patricia D. White and Silas Wasserstrom.

# PART III

# CRIMINAL RESPONSIBILITY IN GOVERNMENT

# 8

# CRIMINAL RESPONSIBILITY IN GOVERNMENT

## DENNIS F. THOMPSON

The criminal law serves better to punish the crimes of citizens than the crimes of government against citizens. One reason no doubt is practical: governments manage the means of punishment. But a more fundamental reason is theoretical: governmental crime does not appear to satisfy the conditions that justify the use of the criminal sanction. In origin and rationale, the criminal law is directed against offenses committed by individuals acting as ordinary citizens. Governmental crime often lacks either an individual criminal or a citizen criminal, or both. Such crime may in this way be structural and official. It is structural when it is more the product of organizational practices than of deliberate decision by individuals. It is official when it can be imputed only to individuals or organizations acting within the scope of office or other legitimate authority.

These two differences between governmental crime and ordinary crime give rise to the theoretical problems that I examine here. The first difference creates a problem of moral responsibility: how can we justify punishing individuals or organizations for structural crime in the apparent absence of the "guilty mind" the criminal law morally requires? This problem plagues the use of the criminal law to control any kind of

For advice in writing this paper, I am grateful to Joe Carens, Mike Comiskey, Jameson Doig, Amy Gutmann, and Walter Murphy.

complex organization, corporations as well as governments. The second difference points to a problem of political responsibility: how can we justify punishing individuals or organizations acting in their official capacity as agents of a democratic government? This problem especially affects the use of the criminal law against governments because they are permitted to adopt methods (such as violence) that would be illegal if used by private parties, and because they are authorized to act, with discretion, on behalf of all citizens. I shall argue that neither the problem of moral responsibility nor the problem of political responsibility stands in the way of using the criminal sanction against public officials, but that both reveal a need for broader notions of personal responsibility and public office, and both undermine the idea of organizational responsibility for crimes of government.

My argument is compatible with a wide range of theories of punishment. It makes only two assumptions about the nature of justifiable punishment.[1] First, I assume that a legitimate practice of punishment must grant certain rights to persons who are subject to its sanctions; it would not, for example, punish anyone who had not voluntarily committed an offense. Second, I assume that punishment characteristically has an expressive function, signifying social attitudes of resentment and judgments of reprobation. No doubt a pure deterrence theory of punishment could not accept these assumptions, but more sophisticated theories, including other utilitarian ones, seek to accommodate them.

## The Problem of Moral Responsibility

Since the problem of moral responsibility in government derives from characteristics that governments share with other complex organizations, we should consider the problem in the context of organizations in general. In the law it is the corporation that has provoked the most serious examination of the problem. Several writers in recent years have pointed out the existence of structural crime in corporations, and noted that the criminal law in its standard form does not cope well with this kind of crime.[2] These observations themselves are consistent with many different theories of responsibility, including the view to be defended here. Certainly any search to discover the causes of such crime, and any reforms to prevent its recurrence, cannot focus exclusively on individuals. But the existence of structural crime is often alleged to have more far-reaching implications. It is taken to dictate a particular solution—what I shall call the structuralist thesis—to the general problem of responsibility in complex organizations.[3]

Proponents of the structuralist thesis make two distinct claims. First, they deny that individuals can be held criminally responsible for many crimes of organizations. Second, they affirm that organizations can be held criminally responsible. These two claims must be distinguished because, though the first often leads to the second, the second may be maintained alone. We may assert, for example, that both individuals and corporations are liable for different types of crimes or even for the same crime.[4] (Less plausibly, we might hold only the first claim, in effect implying that no agent can be held responsible at all for many organizational crimes.)

### Personal Responsibility in Organizations

Consider, then, the claim that we cannot legitimately ascribe personal responsibility for crimes of organizations. Criminal liability, like moral responsibility, requires that an individual charged with an offense had the ability and knowledge to act otherwise than he did. The requirement of a guilty mind for many crimes consists of either the "intention to do the immediate act or bring about the consequences or (in some crimes) recklessness as to such act or consequence."[5] The structuralists who reject personal responsibility for organizational crime presumably do not mean that we can never legitimately charge individuals with crime in an organization. Illegal conduct that is plainly outside of the scope of an office or position in the organization poses no serious theoretical problem. An official who takes a bribe or extorts money from a client, in the absence of any authorization or encouragement by the organization, is surely guilty of a crime as an individual.

The difference between personal and official crime is not always clear, but it is perhaps best captured by the distinction in French administrative law between a *faute personnelle,* for which an individual alone is blamed, and a *faute de service,* for which the organization is also culpable. The former reveals "a man with his [personal] weakness, his passions, his imprudence," whereas the latter manifests an "impersonal" official who, like anyone in the position, is "more or less subject to error."[6] The distinction is not primarily one of motives (acting for one's own ends or for the organization's purposes), since most illegal conduct in organizations probably embodies many different motives at the same time.[7] Official crime is better conceived as conduct authorized or supported by the organization, either formally through instructions and procedures or informally through the norms and practices of the organization.

But not all official crime in this sense creates a problem of responsibility. That an official was merely following orders will not usually protect him from criminal liability, even when he had reason to believe that the order came from the highest officials in the organization.[8] In defense against a conspiracy charge involving the break-in at the office of Daniel Ellsberg's psychiatrist, John Ehrlichman pleaded that he reasonably believed that the President had authorized the entry. The federal district court held that even if the President had done so, Ehrlichman would still be liable for failing to recognize that the break-in violated the law.[9] Nor does the problem of responsibility arise simply because many individuals take part in a crime. The ways the criminal law distinguishes among degrees of participation, including various roles in conspiracies and other inchoate crimes, may be interpreted as more or less conforming to the principles of moral responsibility.[10] Even in cases of collective omissions—as when all the officers in an organization fail in a duty to prevent a harm that any one of them alone could have prevented—the common law generally agrees with morality in holding each of them responsible.[11] If the structuralist thesis is to have any plausibility, its concerns about responsibility must be stated more specifically.

The problem that seems to worry the structuralists springs from two characteristics of organizations—specialization and routinization. Because of the first, individuals who have knowledge of a crime (usually lower-level officials) may not have the ability to do anything about it, and the individuals who have the ability (higher-level officials) do not have knowledge of it. The division of organizational labor thus becomes a division of moral agency: any particular role allows an individual to satisfy only one of the conditions necessary for moral and legal responsibility. Police officers, for example, may observe their colleagues taking bribes but fail to report them out of fear of retaliation, or in the belief that their supervisors will do nothing about the corruption.[12] Subordinates believe, often correctly, that their superiors do not want to know about illegal behavior in the organization.[13] In such cases, prosecuting only those officials who most obviously satisfy the conditions of responsibility will serve neither to prevent the corruption nor to provide fair punishment. As long as we insist on personal responsibility, it seems that we can bring no more than weak charges against those who fail to report crime, and no charges at all against the superiors who know nothing about it.

Routinization also poses an obstacle to ascribing personal responsibility for organizational crime. Contrary to anyone's intentions, practices and norms of an organization may contribute to criminal activity. A practice originally intended to serve respectable purposes may come to promote criminal projects. The city of "Rainfall West" adopted stringent health and safety standards for restaurants and cabarets, presumably better to protect the health and safety of citizens. But the standards were so stringent that almost no business could satisfy them; as a result, city inspectors, police, and prosecutors enjoyed enormous discretion in deciding which businesses to charge with violations. These circumstances invited the selective prosecution, extortion, and bribery that occurred.[14] In other instances, no one consciously establishes the practices; routines simply develop piecemeal over the years, often as part of the informal culture of an organization.[15] Organizational routines appear to take on a life of their own and to play a greater role in creating crime than do decisions of any individuals. It would not make sense, according to the structuralist view, to impute responsibility to any individual in these circumstances, certainly not criminal responsibility.

Even in these kinds of cases, however, the structuralist claim does not seem warranted. The mistake the structuralists make is to take an overly static view of organizational behavior, looking at only one crime at a time. If we adopt a more historical perspective, routinization and specialization can actually aid the ascription of personal responsibility. Because organizations develop routines, their mistakes recur in predictable ways; their designs may not be dark but their crimes are reiterated. The patterns of pathology known to theorists of organizations can be, and often are, as well known to those who work in organizations. Higher officials may not be aware of specific crimes in their organization, but they know, or should know, that certain structural conditions (such as discretion in enforcing overly strict standards) give rise to organizational corruption. Individuals who could be expected to know about these conditions and take steps to correct them could be morally blameworthy and in some cases properly subject to criminal sanctions. At the least, we could require officials to inform legislators that the conditions may be contributing to corruption.

Where the conditions cannot be diagnosed in advance and where higher-level officals must rely heavily on lower-level officials to report and check corruption, we still need not despair of assigning responsibility to individuals. Here specialization can be an ally of personal responsibility. The law can require that organizations establish offices specifically charged with discovering and preventing crime in the organization and protecting officials who report criminal activity in the organization. Inspectors general, merit systems protection boards, ombudsmen, parliamentary commissioners, and vulnerability assessment task forces already go some way toward establishing institutions that could hold specific individuals responsible for failure to prevent organizational crime, and virtually all individuals in the organization responsible for at least reporting such crime.[16] Failure to maintain and protect institutions that help expose crime could itself be a crime. In these various ways, the very characteristics of organizations that make it difficult to hold individuals criminally responsible for isolated crime make it possible to hold them responsible for reiterated crime.

But a problem remains. The personal responsibility that we can accommodate in this way falls short of the standard of mens rea that the criminal law usually requires. If we make officials liable for crime they should have known about, regardless of whether they actually knew about it, we in effect establish negligence as a principal basis for criminal culpability in organizational crime. Although virtually every Western legal system punishes negligence, most confine the practice to offenses involving serious and direct physical harm, and even so it has been the object of persistent criticism by jurists and scholars.[17] When we punish negligence, it is said, we violate a fundamental moral principle of the criminal law—that persons should not be punished unless they have "made a conscious choice to do something [they] knew to be wrong."[18] On this view, the boundary of criminal liability might extend to recklessness (a conscious disregard of risk) but would stop short of negligence (an unreasonable failure to be aware of a risk).[19]

The objection in this form is too broad, however. The moral principle that underlies criminal liability does not imply that persons must have had in their mind at the time of the act the desire for, or awareness of, the harm prohibited by the law. Rather, as H.L.A. Hart has shown, the principle requires that the act must have been voluntary in the sense that the person could have done otherwise.[20] "What is crucial is that those whom we punish should have had, when they acted, the normal capacities, physical and mental, for doing what the law requires and abstaining from what it forbids, and a fair opportunity to exercise these capacities."[21] We may punish negligence if we can show that a reasonable person would have taken the precautions that the accused failed to take, and that the accused had the capacities to take those precautions. Following this approach, we would draw the boundary of criminal responsibility between negligence (which still respects moral responsibility) and strict liability (which disregards it, punishing a prohibited act regardless of efforts the accused made or could have made to avoid committing it).

That negligence may be justifiable grounds for punishing some crimes does not show that it is an acceptable basis for punishing organizational crime. The revised versions of the U.S Criminal Code, even though proposing liability for a failure in supervision that contributes to the occurrence of an offense, adopt a standard of recklessness ("willful default") rather than negligence.[22] Most commentators who endorse the idea of criminal negligence limit its application to "gross" rather than "ordinary" deviations from a reasonable standard of care, and organizational crime frequently results from negligence that seems quite ordinary.[23] The section chief in the Bureau of Mines who fails to assign inspectors to a company with an uneven record of compliance, or the FDA official who ignores an internal memorandum that warns of dangers in a drug about to be approved, hardly seems guilty of "a failure to exercise even that care which a careless person would use."[24]

There are nevertheless several reasons for adopting the stricter standard of negligence in judging organizational crime. First, a view that justifies punishing negligence directs our attention beyond the current state of mind of an alleged criminal and the immediate occasion of an alleged crime to the prior circumstances that led to the negligence. In this way, the view expresses a concept of responsibility that more satisfactorily represents human relationships in a moral community. We would not conceive of officials confronting citizens as isolated individuals coming together at discrete moments, sharing only an awareness that they should not intentionally harm one another. Instead, we regard them as persons having characters shaped over time in association with each other, sharing an understanding that officials owe citizens a more stringent and constant concern. In such a community, citizens would judge officials according to standards of care that the community has evolved, and in light of the past efforts that each has made to satisfy those standards. Organizations provide the order and continuity necessary to sustain such standards. For practical reasons, the criminal law may confine its attention to the immediate context of a crime, but its underlying conception of moral responsibility, at least when applied to organizational life, would be understood as having greater temporal extension.

A second reason that negligence in organizations may deserve the criminal sanction derives from the nature of the harm that this negligence can cause. The degree of care demanded by a standard of conduct traditionally has been set in proportion to the apparent risk; arguably, that risk may be higher in organizations.[25] The magnitude and persistence of the harm from even a single act of negligence in a large organization is usually greater than from the acts of individuals on their own. The greater risk comes from not only the effects of size but also from those of function. In the common law of official nonfeasance, for example, public officials whose duties include the "public peace, health or safety" may be criminally liable for negligence for which other officials would not be indictable at all.[26] Because of the tendency of organizational negligence to produce greater harm, we may be justified in attaching more serious penalties to less serious departures from standards. Although the departure may be ordinary, the potential harm may be gross.

A related reason for imposing stricter standards in organizations is that officials are more likely to underestimate the harm that their negligence may cause. The division of labor and the remoteness of results combine to create a psychological (and perhaps moral) distance that may make efforts to take precautions seem less important than they are.[27] To compensate for this discounting effect, the law may have to attach more severe sanctions to some kinds of negligence than would be warranted either solely by the harm produced in any particular instance or by the harm produced by this type of negligence in general. It is sometimes claimed that intentional harms are more serious than negligent harms because we can usually expect the former to be repeated unless we try to prevent them.[28] Whatever the merits of this distinction in individual conduct, it does not hold in organized activity where persistent harm is at least as likely to be caused negligently as intentionally. The careless bureaucrat is more common than the malicious one.

Finally, the idea of consent justifies imposing the stricter standards of negligence on officials who violate them in any particular instance. In organizations we have a stronger basis for claiming that negligent conduct is voluntary. First, the standards that an individual is supposed to observe can be made more explicit and better known in organized than in unorganized activity. Second, the decision that an individual makes to hold office in an organization can be more plausibly taken to signify acceptance of those standards. How far these considerations warrant our regarding an act of negligence as voluntary depends on how strongly the organization and the law support the standards. It also depends on how readily officials can take steps in advance to prevent organizational crime or to avoid participating in it.

When we cannot reasonably expect any official to take such steps, we may wish to condemn only continuing participation in crime. But even here, the law may require some positive action on the part of the participants at the point when they should recognize that they have become implicated in a pattern of criminal activity. In some cases, they may be required to report the activity to appropriate officials or even to persons outside the organization, and in other cases to resign from office and publicly denounce the activity. While we would hardly want to demand that officials resign whenever they should foresee any risk of involvement in crime, we can surely expect that they resign when they see a pattern of crime in which they are likely to play a part and which they cannot otherwise avoid. Even Talleyrand, one of the most brazen apologists for holding on to power, recognized as much. While rationalizing his own decision to remain in office when ordered to commit a crime, he nevertheless conceded that an official would have to resign if the crime were not isolated.[29] The moral responsibility of office, moreover, does not wholly terminate upon resignation. We may wish to insist that former officials make some effort at least to bring the negligence of their former colleagues to public attention. There is a moral life—and perhaps there should be legal liability—after resignation.

Despite the complications to which any standard of negligence would have to attend, we may conclude that we have stronger reasons for attaching criminal penalties to the violation of standards in organizational than in ordinary life. If these reasons were better appreciated, citizens and officials might come to view negligence in office more harshly than they do now, and prosecution and conviction of such negligence might become more practicable. In any case, these reasons provide theoretical grounds for imputing criminal liability to officials in organizations, and to this extent undermine the structuralist claim that individuals cannot be held personally responsible for organizational crime.

### Organizational Responsibility

The second structuralist claim makes organizations themselves the target of the criminal sanction.[30] While organizations cannot be imprisoned, they can be fined and sentenced to probation, and they can suffer the stigma of a criminal conviction. Some versions of the claim would hold an organization responsible even when none of its members are at fault, but most would charge the organization, under the doctrine of respondeat superior, only when an individual acting on its behalf commits an offense.[31] The latter view thus still has to rely on a notion of individual responsibility in order to establish organizational guilt.

A principal argument for organizational responsibility alleges that it provides a more efficient deterrent than individual responsibility. An organization is in the best position to discover and discipline the misconduct of its own officials, and will do so efficiently if the law threatens the organization with sufficiently stiff penalties. Critics have pointed out that a fine large enough to deter corporations would usually exceed their ability to pay, and would therefore serve as no deterrent at all when the risk of discovery is low and the expected gain is high.[32] Also, the higher the penalty is, the greater the internal pressures are to conceal the illegal conduct from officials who might be able to do something about it. These criticisms cast doubt on the efficacy of this strategy of organizational responsibility, but they are not decisive. We lack the empirical evidence that would show the effects of different schedules of penalties on the frequency and kind of organizational crime. The question of the moral status of organizational responsibility therefore becomes critical. Three objections to holding organizations morally responsible deserve to be considered.

First, it is argued that an organization by its nature cannot be a moral agent in the sense required by the criminal law because organizations lack minds. The notion of a "mental state has no meaning when applied to a corporate defendant since an organization possesses no mental state."[33] Partly for this reason, in virtually all civil law countries the general rule is that corporations are not criminally liable.[34] Organizations certainly do not have minds in the same sense that persons do, and the efforts to show that corporations have characteristics that resemble aspects of the mental states of individuals (such as a decision-making structure and a capacity for long-range planning) do not dispose of the objection.[35] These efforts produce at best only partial analogies. The intention of an organizational mind exists only by virtue of conventions stipulating that the statements and actions of individuals in certain positions will count as expressing the purposes of the organization.

But that organizations do not literally have minds of their own does not entail that they may not be morally blameworthy. The law requires mens rea for persons because they have minds, but from this requirement it does not follow that mens rea is necessary for punishing entities that do not have minds. Since the "minds" of organizations differ so fundamentally from the minds of persons, we should expect the criteria for ascribing organizational responsibility also to differ. The criteria are likely to refer partly to the states of mind of individuals (for example, the principal officers of a corporation and the policies they avow). But there is no reason to suppose that the criteria can be reduced to statements referring only to individuals, and therefore no reason to deny that an organization can be held liable as a collectivity, independently of any responsibility that we may also wish to impute to its members.[36] When we blame Hooker Chemical for dumping hazardous chemical waste at Love Canal or the Niagara Falls Board of Education for permitting a school to be built on the site, we are partly condemning past and present officials of the corporation and the board.[37] But we are doing more than that. We are also criticizing the practices of the organizations—the internal and external patterns of relationships—that persist even as the identities of the individuals who participate in them change.

That we may morally criticize organizations, however, does not imply that we should criminally punish them. A second objection to organizational responsibility maintains that the effects of punishing organizations are unfair.[38] The unfairness results not from the direct punishment of an organization that may not be a moral agent, but from the indirect punishment of individuals associated with the organization who may not be morally responsible. When the law fines a corporation, many persons suffer who could have done nothing to prevent the crime—among them, shareholders, employees, and consumers. To be sure, some of these persons may have benefited from the crime. But it is important to preserve in the law the moral difference between benefiting from a wrong and contributing to it by an act or omission. It is one thing to make the beneficiaries of misconduct pay the costs of damages when the costs must fall somewhere, but it is quite another to impose punitive damages and the stigma of punishment on persons who had neither the knowledge of the crime nor the capacity to do anything about it.

The validity of the objection from unfairness plainly depends on the kind of punishment the law prescribes. The objection is most cogent when the law imposes a fine or penalty that impairs the performance of a organization and spreads the costs of the impairment indiscriminately among all connected with the organization. The objection is less persuasive if the law directs the sanction more specifically toward the source of the criminal activity, as in the proposals for corporate probation or the equity fine.[39] But no matter how precisely targeted the sanction, the stigma of conviction falls in some measure on everyone associated with the organization. If the sanction does not in some sense convey the idea that the organization was a bad one of which to be a member, the sanction seems no more than a civil penalty. But if the sanction carries the moral force of punishment, it should respect the moral constraints of justifiable punishment. Punishing the organization is likely to spread the blame beyond the responsibility and is to that extent without moral justification.

A third objection to organizational responsibility concerns its implications for organizational autonomy. We can begin to see the dangers in punishing organizations when we notice the prerogatives some writers are ready to confer on corporations they regard as fit to assume full moral responsibility for violating the law. If in this respect corporations "are like persons," one philosopher suggests, "then, they should also have the rights that people have" and therefore, he implies, they do not have to be so closely "watched and regulated."[40] We need not accept the implication that would grant to corporations full personhood with all its attendant rights. But we should recognize that a practice of holding organizations responsible has implications for organizations that could be punished as well as for those that actually are. The practice implies that all organizations (at least those with the status of moral agents) deserve to have their autonomy respected on terms similar to those enjoyed by citizens. Seeking a warrant to punish delinquent corporations, the advocates of corporate responsibility may end up granting all corporations a moral license to resist other forms of social control.

Just because we punish corporations, we do not of course have to grant them all the rights we accord persons. The problem is that as subjects of punishment, rather than of only civil penalty, corporations have a stronger moral basis than they should have on which to press claims for autonomy. The legal rights of a corporation (as distinct from the rights of its members) should rest mainly on social utility, and therefore may be overridden when they conflict with the legitimate claims of a majority of citizens.[41] The rights of persons have an independent moral basis and cannot be so directly set aside.[42] This and other important differences between corporations and individuals are obscured by the assumption that both similarly deserve to be held morally and criminally responsible. Such an assumption leads courts and commentators automatically to extend to corporations a wide range of personal rights (especially in criminal procedure)—without insisting that these rights be justified on a basis different from the rights of individuals.[43]

Because organizational responsibility may distribute punishment beyond moral responsibility and because it may entail excessive organizational autonomy, we should be wary of it. We should rely instead on personal responsibility to provide the foundation for the punishment of crimes in organizations.

## The Problem of Political Responsibility

Although governments are organizations, they are a special kind of organization: they and their agents claim various forms of immunity from the law. I wish to argue that their special status does not shield governmental officials from the personal liability that individuals in other kinds of organizations incur. On the contrary, governmental officials may have to meet even stricter standards of responsibility. Similarly, the objections to imposing criminal sanctions on organizations apply even more strongly to imposing them on governmental organizations—not because governments enjoy any special immunities, but because they must accept special duties. Insofar as officials and organizations outside government share the characteristics of those in government, these conclusions apply to them as well. Where we draw the boundary between government and nongovernment (or between public and private institutions) does not critically affect the argument. What matters is that we do not permit claims of immunity to stand in the way of our ascribing criminal responsibility to governmental officials, or to provide the basis for our not ascribing it to governmental organizations.

The rationale for the immunity of governmental organizations differs somewhat from that for the immunity of officials, but both appeal to the same characteristic of government—its sovereignty in the making and enforcing of law. Justice Holmes set forth the classic judicial statement of the rationale: "There can be no legal right as against the authority that makes the law on which the right depends."[44] As his chief authority for this principle, Holmes cited chapter 26 of *Leviathan,* where Hobbes maintains that "the sovereign . . . is not subject to the civil laws."[45] Since in Hobbes's preferred commonwealth the sovereign is a monarch against whom citizens have no effective rights, democrats could hardly embrace the doctrine of sovereign immunity on these terms.

But there is a more nearly democratic version of the doctrine, in which the sovereign consists of a majority of citizens.[46] Public ministers acting on behalf of this majority enjoy the privileges of sovereign office, which include immunity from certain laws. The sovereign majority may prescribe standards for the proper exercise of ministerial authority, and establish penalties for its abuse. But the scope and enforcement of these standards are inherently limited. Some actions that would obviously be crimes if committed by citizens are not always so when performed by officials. Because the circumstances that would justify such actions by officials cannot be specified in detail in advance, officials must have considerable discretion to act on behalf of the sovereign.

Furthermore, to permit any independent authority to punish what it regards as an abuse of this discretion would be to allow it to substitute its judgment for that of the officials directly acting for the democratic sovereign. The sovereign itself could authorize such punishment, but a sensible sovereign will not do so because of the danger of "overdeterrence."[47] The mere general threat of the punishment and the conflicts it can produce among the sovereign's representatives may discourage even conscientious officials from vigorously carrying out the duties of their office, and may dissuade worthy persons from accepting appointment to public office. Therefore, the democratic version of the immunity doctrine would subject governmental agencies and their officials to criminal sanctions only in the most flagrant cases of personal crime, where wrongdoing takes place completely beyond the scope of office. For all other misconduct, only the sanctions of the political process—elections, administrative discipline, legislative oversight, impeachment—would be applied.

The notion of sovereign immunity has left its mark, sometimes in subtle ways, on many different practices in modern democracy. Although explicit discussion of a doctrine of sovereign immunity today usually appears in the civil rather than the criminal law, judges often state the doctrine so broadly that it would, if taken seriously, protect officials from criminal as well as civil liability. In *Nixon* v. *Fitzgerald*, the opinion of the Court, according to the dissenters, places the President above the law, reviving the doctrine that the king can do no wrong: "Taken at face value, the Court's position that . . . the president is absolutely immune should mean that he is immune not only from damages actions but also from suits for injunctive relief, criminal prosecutions and, indeed, from any kind of judicial process."[48] Members of Congress enjoy immunity under the "Speech and Debate" clause that on recent interpretations shields them from prosecution even for some crimes (such as bribery) that are clearly beyond the scope of their office.[49] While executive and administrative officials cannot so easily escape prosecution for such gross personal crimes, they rarely face charges for official crimes.[50]

Even treating officials exactly as citizens can have the effect of conferring immunity in those activities in which only officials engage. The most pervasive manifestation of this kind of immunity is the absence of any provisions in the law to prohibit many of the harms that officials and agencies cause—those that result, for example, from supervisory negligence in the control of corruption, the inspection of mines, or the certification of dangerous drugs. The common law of official misconduct is infrequently invoked, and the criminal law hardly takes notice of the special duties of public office. The sections of the U.S. Criminal Code dealing with public officials refer almost exclusively to bribery, conflict of interest, and fraud.[51]

Although we may wish to preserve some of the practices of immunity on other grounds, we should not rely on the rationale of sovereign immunity even in its most nearly democratic form. That rationale is seriously flawed in several respects. It may be true, as Hobbes and Holmes imply, that the idea of the criminal responsibility of a government as a whole is unintelligible except in an international system. We would have to imagine the government holding itself responsible, simultaneously punishing and being punished. We can, however, view the government not as an indivisible entity, but as composed of various parts (executive and judicial branches, or local and state jurisdictions). From this perspective the criminal responsibility of government simply means that one part of the government pronounces judgment and imposes sanctions on another part (agencies as well as officials). If a democratic constitution assigns these duties to prosecutors and courts, they act in the name of the democratic sovereign no less than the officials whose conduct they judge. As long as the criminal laws and the constitutional arrangements remain open to review through the democratic process, we cannot plausibly argue that the idea of democratic government itself calls for any kind of criminal immunity for anyone.

The argument that the possibility of prosecution for misconduct will "overdeter" officials and agencies depends largely on empirical assumptions that have not been supported with any substantial evidence. Officials and their judicial defenders have repeatedly invoked the same argument in favor of civil immunity, but they never demonstrate the actual effects that such liability might have on the legitimate activities of officials (for example, by comparing jurisdictions that grant greater and lesser degrees of immunity).[52] What little evidence exists tells against civil immunity, at least in its unqualified forms, and one would suppose that the inhibiting effects of civil actions would be at least as extensive as those of criminal charges since so many more people can bring civil suits.[53] Tough penalties for misconduct may discourage some people from accepting public office, but they may also encourage more worthy people to accept office by making public service a more honorable calling. Evidence does not support, for example, the common belief that the stringent disclosure and conflict-of-interest provisions of the Ethics in

Government Act have impeded the recruitment of political executives. The Act may in fact serve to protect honest officials from false charges, and help keep them in public office.[54]

Finally, political sanctions are not adequate to the task that advocates of immunity assign them. The basic problem is that a political judgment may fasten on almost any feature of the whole performance or character of an official or an organization. The clever official can usually point to other achievements which, if they do not outweigh his crime, will at least divert the attention of his judges. When the assembly of the Roman people asked Scipio to "render his accounts," he talked instead of his great military victory and led the people to the Capitol to thank the gods. Bentham remarks that "had I lived at that time, most probably I should have gone up with the rest to the Capitol, but I should always have attained a little curiosity with respect to the accounts."[55] Present-day politicians do not need to distract voters with military victories. Even without immunity and even after conviction, officials can evade political punishment. Convicted of accepting a bribe while mayor of Union City, New Jersey, William Musto pleaded that his crime was "victimless," that his wrongdoing was trivial compared to the corruption in other cities, and that he had already suffered enough from the publicity. The judge was not persuaded, but enough voters evidently were; they re-elected him decisively.[56] However permissively we may interpret the right of citizens to elect anyone they choose, we should not suppose that the criminal sanction and the political sanction serve precisely the same purposes.

Neither are quasi-judicial procedures such as impeachment an adequate substitute for criminal prosecution. Even when successful, they only remove the official from office and (sometimes) bar him from holding office in the future; they do not impose any further punishment. Impeachable offenses, furthermore, are not identical to crimes.[57] Also, disciplinary proceedings against permanent officials are notoriously ineffective in punishing misconduct, partly because accused officials have so many procedural protections. Indeed, the possibility of a criminal charge may often be required to set in motion an adverse action against an official.[58]

*Personal Responsibility in Government*

Instead of looking to Hobbes for the foundation of official responsibility, we should attend to Locke. Neither Hobbes nor Locke conceives of the relation between citizens and the government as a contract, which would imply a reciprocal recognition of rights. Hobbes does not, because he wants to deny that citizens have any effective rights against the sovereign. Locke does not, because he wishes to deny that rulers have rights against citizens. For Locke, the relationship between citizens and the executive, and between citizens and the legislature, resembles a fiduciary trust.[59] Locke in effect transfers the concept of trust from private law to public law, merging the trustor and the beneficiary into one party (the citizen body). The government as trustee incurs a unilateral obligation to citizens to act for their good. The concept implies that citizens can at any time change the terms of the trust or revoke the power that confers the trust.[60] If we adopt the concept of trust as the basis for the responsibility of public officials, we are not likely to be tempted by the claims of governmental immunity. Although for practical reasons we may decide (democratically) to grant some protection to certain offices or certain functions, we would not accept a theoretical principle that confers on public office any independent rights or privileges.

The idea of trust also has a more far-reaching implication: it calls for a more exacting conception of public office. As Justice Cardozo wrote: "Many forms of conduct permissible in a workaday world for those acting at arm's length are forbidden to those bound by fiduciary ties. A trustee is held to something stricter than the morals of the market place. Not honesty alone, but the punctilio of an honor the most sensitive, is then the standard of behavior."[61] Public office, conceived as a trust, thus imposes higher standards of conduct than does citizenship. Actions that may be permissible or civilly wrong when performed by private citizens could be criminally wrong when done by public officials.

This conception would in part rejuvenate the common law offense of official misconduct. In the seminal English case, an official accountant, charged with neglecting and refusing to disclose an item that should have been in government accounts, pleaded that his conduct rendered him liable only for a "civil injury, not for a public offense."[62] Lord Mansfield concluded to the contrary: "if a man accepts an office of trust and confidence, concerning the public . . . he is answerable to the King for his execution of that office; and he can only answer to the King in criminal prosecution, for the King cannot otherwise punish his misbehavior, in acting contrary to the duty of office."[63]

The notion of office as a trust has reappeared in American law in recent years under the unlikely aegis of the federal mail fraud statute.[64] Three state governors, charged with schemes to defraud the public, have been convicted on principles relating to a breach of fiduciary trust.[65] These cases suggest that such a breach can occur even if the scheme defrauds no one of any money or property and even if it enriches no one and was not intended to do so. It is sufficient if in specificable ways the scheme defrauds citizens of their "right to . . . disinterested and honest government."[66] In the case of Governor Mandel of Maryland, "concealment of material information" about political favors he did for his friends seemed to be enough for conviction.[67]

Commentators have objected to this use of the concept of trust.[68] They argue that, by turning aspirational standards into criminal prohibitions, this application of the concept threatens to discourage "robust" political activity. It could do so, first, because incumbents can exploit its vague standards to harass challengers and other political opponents. Second, the standard may have a chilling effect on political participation and "interfere with the delicate process of coalition formation," which requires the "striking of deals."[69]

These concerns about overcriminalizing the political process cannot be lightly dismissed. But whether the expansion of the legal liability of officials would inhibit legitimate political activity surely depends on what standards of trust we establish for various public offices, and how precisely we formulate them. It may well be that we should carry out any expansion only through explicit legislation rather than judicial interpretation, currently the most common method. And we certainly should not seek to support all, or even most, of our moral judgments about politics with the force of the criminal sanction. But from punishing the conduct exemplified in the cases of the corrupt governors—which involved secretly giving favors of office to friends—it is a long way to prohibiting all political deals and all political patronage. Even if the implication of this line of decisions is to turn the mail fraud statute into a "truth-in-government" act, as one critic fears,[70] that result could help citizens know better what kind of "robust" politics is going on so that they can decide what kind of deals and favors they want to tolerate.

If we move toward stricter standards of responsibility for public officials, we should consider at least two general kinds of misconduct. First, in accord with my previous comments about negligence, we would penalize the failure to take reasonable steps to discover and prevent conduct that is already designated criminal. Officials would be liable for supervisory negligence if they hold offices that explicitly require oversight of the specific activity in which the crime occurs. Such oversight need not be the exclusive concern of one office, but could also be part of the duties of general supervision. This approach would extend to governmental officials a modified form of a doctrine some courts have already applied to corporate officials. Officials who stand in a "responsible relationship" to a crime are liable even if they did not participate in it.[71] What this relationship actually requires remains unclear, and presumably would differ for corporations and governments. But determination of responsible relationships in governmental organizations is precisely the kind of task that democratic theory assigns to legislatures, and they are well situated, if any institution is, to fix these relationships in ways that allow for the proper measure of administrative discretion and subsequent judicial review. Legislatures are also in the best position to ensure that greater supervisory liability would not encourage overly cautious, rule-bound administration. They could fashion a package of sanctions that would balance penalties for negligence and rewards for excellence in administration.

A second kind of misconduct may be conceived as official obstruction of the democratic process. Here the concern would be not primarily the protection of procedures in the legal or electoral processes, which are already covered by numerous criminal laws, but the promotion of broader features of the political process such as openness and access. A prime instance of such obstruction would be an official's failure to disclose important

information to the public or to designated authorities. Conceal-
ing the true state of a city's financial condition, for example,
might very well be made a crime even in the absence of any act
of perjury. It is perhaps not surprising in our society that failing to disclose certain information to investors in the financial
marketplace has long been illegal, but refusing to reveal information to citizens in the political arena has rarely been penalized.[72] There is, of course, a need to protect classified information that officials keep secret for legitimate reasons, but there
is equally a need to publicize information that officials conceal
mainly for personal or partisan motives. The law pays more attention to the former than to the latter. The U.S. Criminal Code
contains many sections that meticulously proscribe unauthor-
ized disclosure of information but virtually none that requires
disclosure.[73]

A related kind of obstruction of democracy occurs when officials prevent citizens from reporting information or expressing their views to government agencies. Such intimidation may
take more subtle forms than the law now normally proscribes.
After Cora Walker reported that New York City housing inspectors solicited a bribe as a condition of granting her a certif-
icate of occupancy for her new rooming house, the Superinten-
dent of Housing immediately filed criminal charges against her
for renting rooms without the proper permit. Although she
eventually won on appeal, nothing happened to the superin-
tendent or other officials who initiated the criminal proceedings against her.[74] Further, officials may improperly discourage
not only citizens but also other officials from coming forward
with important information. Because the *Fitzgerald* cases posed
the issue of the civil liability of officials, the court and the liti-
gants focused on the harm that Fitzgerald suffered in losing his
government job and having his constitutional rights violated.[75]
They gave less attention to the most disturbing consequence of
the episode—the inhibiting effect on future officials who, like
Fitzgerald, would expose the mistakes and misconduct of other
officials. To deter and punish such intimidation, the criminal
sanction is in principle (though not always in practice) better
suited than the civil suit.

Another form that obstruction of the democratic process can
take is the encouragement of violations of properly enacted

government regulations. When the Administrator of the Environmental Protection Agency in 1982 promised a small oil refinery it would not be penalized if it violated federal lead standards, she evidently violated no law herself.[76] While the democratic process should grant administrators considerable discretion, it surely does not authorize them selectively to encourage citizens to ignore legitimate regulations (even if administrators plan to change the regulations in the future). These and other instances of official misconduct constitute candidates for offenses under an expansive approach to the criminal responsibility of public officials. That approach, as we have seen, is better guided by a concept of trust than by a concept of immunity.

### Organizational Responsibility in Government

That officials should be held criminally liable for some governmental crime does not necessarily imply that governmental organizations should be. Although I have rejected the general arguments for immunity that would shield both the officials and the organizations of government, I have not yet considered some claims that would specifically protect governmental organizations.

Both the Model Penal Code and the National Commission's Study Draft of a new Federal Criminal Code explicitly exempt governmental entities from criminal liability, but their rationale for the exemption is obscure. The Code's commentator says merely that "corporate liability is generally pointless in such cases."[77] The only reason the Commission's staff offers is that public agencies receive closer scrutiny than do private corporations—a doubtful distinction, which may in any case be overwhelmed, as the staff implies, by the similarities between the conditions of criminal activity in public and private organizations.[78]

There have been few domestic cases in which a governmental organization has been a criminal defendant, and apparently only one in which a court has seriously examined the theoretical issues that such status raises. In *Cain* v. *Doyle,* the Australian High Court overturned the conviction of a government factory manager charged with being an accessory in a crime allegedly committed by the government.[79] Although other considerations played a part, three of the five justices suggested that they would not convict the Crown of a criminal offense (at least in the absence of explicit statutory permission to do so). Apart from some technical points of Australian law, the chief arguments appealed to the "absurdity of supposing that the Executive Government . . . is to be brought before magistrates to receive punishment, a punishment which the Executive may enforce or remit."[80] This claim in part relies on the Hobbesian point I have already rejected, but it also invokes the practical paradox of punishing the authority that controls the means of punishment and the power of pardon. This "absurdity" may seem more difficult to avoid in the absence of a system of separation of powers, but even in its absence, only one justice considered the problem to be insurmountable. As one of the dissenters pointed out, the legislature could authorize the funds to pay the fine, and the courts could direct that at least a portion of the fine be paid to the aggrieved parties.[81]

The most substantial objections to organizational responsibility in government are variations on two of the objections I previously raised against organizational responsibility in general. First, the problem of the dispersion of punishment is even more serious in government than in other organizations. Not only does the punishment fall on citizens who, like shareholders or employees of corporations, had nothing to do with the crime and may not be able to do anything about similar crimes in the future, but it also often falls most heavily on those citizens who have the least opportunity to do anything about such crimes. To assess a fine or punitive damages against the budget of a derelict government agency, as some reformers have proposed,[82] would be almost to guarantee that the agency's clients with the least political clout would find their governmental benefits reduced the most. Some would perhaps not regret this consequence in the case of certain agencies (e.g., the Department of Defense), but we should disapprove of it in the case of others (e.g., Health and Human Services).

The sanction of probation that some legal reformers would impose on corporations seems inappropriate for governmental organizations.[83] Here we might reasonably object that the judiciary would be usurping functions that the legislature or citizens more generally should exercise. Judicial oversight, even the increasingly common use of "special masters," may be warranted in some instances. But if the structures and procedures of a whole agency are the source of persistent crime, the agency is likely to require massive reorganization and continual review. Such extensive intervention should fall within the province of a legislature, which can consider what changes are appropriate in light of the needs of other governmental agencies and policies. Furthermore, if the legislature takes temporary control of an agency in this way, the stigma of a criminal conviction would probably lose most of its significance (since the agency would have become a different organization in critical respects).[84] To the extent that the stigma has any force, it could unfairly discredit officials in the agency who are working to improve it, and discourage others who are considering whether to join it. The social harm could be greater from these effects on government than on a corporation since a discredited governmental agency may be the only provider of certain essential services for citizens.

If the practice of punishment implies a respect for the rights of all agents potentially subject to its sanctions, then we should be even more hesitant about accepting the practice for governmental than for other kinds of organizations. As we noticed earlier, there are dangers in granting any organization the kind of autonomy we recognize in persons. But nongovernmental organizations can sometimes claim independent rights against government insofar as the organizations express the rights of particular individuals or groups in society. Democratic theory, at least in its liberal versions, assumes that individuals and groups do not have to justify their autonomy by showing that every activity they pursue positively contributes to the good of the whole society. Any autonomy that governmental organizations enjoy, however, must be justified on precisely those grounds. An agency may legitimately claim rights against the rest of the government only when citizens, through the democratic process, determine that these rights would ultimately serve collective purposes. As long as we wish to treat governmental organizations as solely means to our common ends, we should deny them the status of moral agency, and therefore exclude them from the practice of punishment. This exclusion does not imply that we should not impose sanctions on the organizations of government. Indeed, in grave cases of reiterated crime, we may need to have recourse to the analogue of capital punishment—the elimination of the agency. But this and similar sanctions are not, or should not be understood as, punishment: they are political policies, and need neither respect the same moral constraints nor express the same moral force as the practice of punishment. To suppose otherwise would be to misapprehend the moral and political foundations of criminal responsibility.

## THE LIMITS OF CRIMINAL RESPONSIBILITY

We have seen that the practice of punishing public officials (though not public organizations) can help sustain moral responsibility and democratic accountability. But we should also recognize that the practice has some significant limitations. The most obvious ones arise from the practical problems of enforcement and deterrence.[85] Governmental crimes often leave few traces since the victims (sometimes all citizens) do not realize they have been harmed. Prosecution may be under the control of officials who do not wish the crimes to come to light. High-level officials can track the progress of investigation and secretly subvert it. Juries are often hesitant to convict, and judges reluctant to impose stiff sentences on, respectable-looking defendants who plead that they were only doing their duty. To some extent, these problems can be overcome by institutional reforms (e.g., authorizing special prosecutors) and by changes in public attitudes (e.g., recognizing the seriousness of negligence in public office). But all these problems concern the capacity of the criminal process to achieve its aims on its own terms. More fundamental are its limitations in serving other purposes of morality and democracy.

First of all, many of the wrongs that governments inflict upon the world are by their nature usually beyond the reach of the criminal sanction. Some of these wrongs are not appropriately deemed criminal either because none of the decisions that produce them is in itself wrong, or because no decisions produce them at all. I have argued that on a proper understanding of responsibility in public office, fewer wrongs fit these descriptions than is usually assumed, but no doubt some still do. The most obvious are those that lie beyond the capacity of any government to correct. Governments help perpetuate the social and economic structures that contribute to disease and famine, but though governments and their officials can sometimes ameliorate this suffering and sometimes exacerbate it, they rarely can change the underlying structures in any period of time that could even in principle fall within the scope of any criminal judgment, however broadly conceived. Other wrongs are the product of identifiable decisions but cannot be crimes because society disagrees deeply about how serious they are, or about whether they are wrong at all. An act perhaps does not have to be "universally disapproved of" by all members of society, as Durkheim maintained,[86] but it cannot be widely approved of by a substantial portion of the society. Many practices that we may wish to regard as criminal must remain the objects of only moral and political condemnation. The injustice of the distribution of wealth in modern societies may be partly attributable to policies of governments and decisions of officials, but its perpetrators are not yet criminals. Finally, some wrongs that are almost universally considered crimes may not be punishable. In the absence of an international system of criminal justice, high officials who commit war crimes are likely to be able to escape criminal sanctions.

A second set of limitations concerns compensatory justice. The criminal conviction of officials does not help the immediate victims of governmental crime; a civil suit for damages is supposed to serve this aim.[87] Citizens may initiate civil actions themselves, and may do so without having to show that the harms are intentional and without having to go through the cumbersome procedures of a criminal trial. The aggrieved citizen will still encounter a (more explicit) doctrine of sovereign and official immunity.[88] But the doctrine does not, or at least should not, have the same implications in the civil as in criminal process. In fact, in an optimal system, the immunities conferred in one process would be just the reverse of those granted in the other: officials (though criminally liable) would be civilly immune, and government (though criminally immune) would be civilly liable. The interrelationships among these forms of immunity and their effects on deterrance and justice are too complex to consider here, but the basic reasons that the civil and criminal process should treat governments and officials differently can be mentioned. Civil sanctions fall more effectively and justly on government (all taxpayers) than do criminal sanctions, but are more likely to "overdeter" individual officials than are properly designed criminal sanctions. An adequate scheme of civil liability for government almost certainly will have to rely on an expanded system of criminal sanctions, but for the purpose of deterring officials rather than satisfying victims.

Perhaps we should not expect the criminal process to ensure that justice is done for innocent citizens, but we should expect it to see that justice is done to guilty officials. An important reason for bringing public officials to trial has traditionally been to demonstrate that all persons—citizens and officials alike—are equal before the law. In the debates preceding the execution of Louis XVI, the Girondin leaders argued forcefully against proscription and for prosecution under the law: "because every man is a citizen, every man can also be a criminal; because no man is without peers, no man is exempt from judgment."[89] One could still argue today that, despite great inequalities in resources, officials are more likely, in the courtroom than in other arenas, to receive the same treatment that citizens receive. Public officials, to be sure, are more visible and perhaps more vulnerable to politically motivated charges. The "political trial" has a long (and not wholly unworthy) history in modern government.[90] But most democracies have given judicial institutions sufficient independence to protect against the most blatantly political prosecutions of officials (if not of citizens). Whatever we may think of the FBI's techniques in the ABSCAM investigation of members of Congress, we cannot deny that the convicted legislators received at least as much impartial judicial review of their claims of unfair treatment as citizens would have enjoyed in similar circumstances.[91]

Former officials, however, seldom suffer as much as ordinary citizens from the subsequent effects of a criminal conviction. Most of the Watergate criminals, especially those who served in the higher offices, have found respectable positions in the private sector.[92] Some have realized substantial profits from lectures and books about their experiences, and some have gained nomination to public office again.[93] Frank Wills, the alert night watchman who started the chain of events that led to the Watergate convictions, has not since found a steady job.[94]

It is often said that the disgrace of conviction is greater for a public official. But if this is so, it should be thought of as merely compensating for the undeserved prestige the official enjoyed while his criminal activity remained undiscovered. Many officials, moreover, elude the disgrace at least in the circles that matter to them. Charged with failing to testify "fully, completely and accurately" before a Senate Committee, CIA Director Richard Helms pleaded nolo contendere (itself a device corporate and government officials commonly use to avoid the stigma of conviction).[95] Helms implied that he would wear this conviction as a "badge of honor." "I don't feel disgraced at all," he said, "I think if I had done anything else, I would have been disgraced."[96] Helms believed that he had acted out of loyalty to the CIA and the agents he led. It is hard enough to cause the full force of punishment to fall on officials who commit personal crimes in government; it is still more difficult to make it felt by officials who commit crimes of state with the approval of professional colleagues.

Neither does the practice of punishment contribute to the democratic process as much as one might hope. The trial of a public official can dramatically focus public attention on crimes of government. It can, upon occasion, stimulate broader reforms that may help citizens hold officials more accountable in the future. Watergate and other investigations of the early 1970s spurred efforts to strengthen control over the FBI and CIA and to toughen the standards governing the financial dealings of federal executives and legislators in office as well as in campaigns.[97] But criminal investigations and prosecutions rarely give rise to such vigorous movements of reform. The exposure to which political authority in the United States was subjected in this period, according to one account, was "unique in modern history, aside from investigations by revolutionary regimes of their predecessors."[98] In any case, the criminal trial itself must fix its attention on particular individuals even when they are charged with structural crimes. Although prosecutors and witnesses may incidentally expose patterns of misconduct, they must confine themselves primarily to the offenses of individuals, and to facts that can survive the stringent standards of criminal procedure.

In their efforts to hold officials accountable citizens should care as much about honoring faithful officials as condemning felonious ones. Although legal reformers at least since Beccaria have criticized society's obsession with punishment and its neglect of reward, our formal institutions remain better suited to denunciation than commendation. Yet the sanction of reward offers several benefits that punishment does not. Bentham noticed that reward serves better to produce "acts of the positive stamp" and is more likely to be self-enforcing (because candidates have an incentive to bring forward the necessary evidence).[99] Most significantly, a system of reward, as Rousseau suggested, can give "more consideration to persons than to isolated deeds" and can therefore honor "sustained and regular conduct . . . the faithful discharge of the duties of one's station, . . . in sum deeds that flow from a man's character and principles."[100] Perhaps robust institutions of reward, such as the Rosière de Salency that Rousseau and Bentham had in mind, are possible only in small, homogenous communities.[101] But something like the broader assessment of character and career that such institutions provide is essential in the democratic process. The institutions of punishment not only fail to serve this function, but because of their pre-eminent position in the processes of public judgment, they may also prevent other institutions from serving it.

The criminal process is not so inhospitable to democratic participation as is sometimes supposed. It is, after all, the home of the quintessential democratic institution—the jury. There also may be ways of encouraging citizens to take part in the earlier stages of a criminal proceeding. Some political scientists have suggested that recipients of governmental benefits (such as medical care and welfare) could organize so that they could discover and report corruption in the administration of these programs.[102] Criminal proceedings, nevertheless, remain a process in which the government usually must initiate the formal charges, few citizens can actively participate, and no one may officially discuss many of the significant implications of the crime in question.

None of these limitations of the use of the criminal sanction in government shows that it is in itself unjustified, only that it is insufficient as a method of realizing moral responsibility and democratic accountability of public officials.[103] How significant a place we should assign it in the pursuit of these goals depends in large measure on how we evaluate its merits compared to those of civil, administrative, and political sanctions. One of its most valuable roles may turn out to be as a sanction of last resort for standards that are not only established but also usually enforced through other institutions and by citizens more generally. The Office of Government Ethics, for example, reviews and clears the financial disclosure reports that high-level officials in the executive branch file to comply with conflict-of-interest rules set by Congress. According to a former Director of the Office, this process "amounts to prospective enforcement of criminal laws by requiring nominees [for public office] to take precautionary steps to stay out of harm's way."[104] Here, as in many other circumstances, the practice of punishing public officials functions best if no official needs to be punished. Furthermore, we can hardly expect individual officials, even under the threat of punishment, to combat crime on their own. They must be able to count on the support of colleagues and citizens who share their concern for the integrity of public office, and they must be able to rely on institutions that protect and promote cooperative activity toward this end.

Despite these limitations, criminal responsibility remains an important resource for judging and controlling democratic governments. Through the practice of punishing public officials, a democratic community seeks not only to deter official misconduct, but also to define its collective sense of the standards of public office. The denunciation that punishment expresses is the most solemn statement of what a betrayal of those standards means to the community. We may not always be able to discover the officials who deserve such denunciation, but we should not suppose that the principles of moral responsibility or political democracy stand in the way of bringing them to justice. Neither the organizational complexity nor the sovereign status of democratic governments precludes our holding officials personally responsible for crimes of government.

## NOTES

1. The assumptions, respectively, follow H.L.A. Hart, *Punishment and Responsibility* (Oxford: Oxford University Press, 1968), pp. 1–27;

and Joel Feinberg, *Doing and Deserving* (Princeton: Princeton University Press, 1970), pp. 95–118.

2. The best discussion is Christopher D. Stone, *Where the Law Ends: The Social Control of Corporate Behavior* (New York: Harper & Row, 1975).

3. E.g., "Developments in the Law—Corporate Crime," *Harv. L. Rev.* 92 (1979): 1227–1375 at pp. 1241–43; note, "Structural Crime and Institutional Rehabilitation," *Yale L.J.* 89 (1979): 353–75 at pp. 357–60; Peter French, "The Corporation as Moral Person," *American Philosophical Quarterly* (1979): 207–15; David T. Ozar, "The Moral Responsibility of Corporations," in Thomas Donaldson and Patricia H. Werhane, eds., *Ethical Issues in Business* (Englewood Cliffs, N.J.: Prentice Hall, 1979), pp. 294–300; and Thomas Donaldson, *Corporations and Morality* (Englewood Cliffs: Prentice-Hall, 1982), pp. 18–34. In "The Place of Enterprise Liability in the Control of Corporate Conduct," *Yale L.J.* 90 (1980): 1–77, Christopher Stone defends aspects of the structuralist thesis (at pp. 28–55) but also emphasizes an approach that would punish violations of "standards" (pp. 36–45). This latter approach seems consistent with the notion of personal responsibility as I develop it here. For philosophical defenses of more general forms of the structuralist thesis, see John Ladd, "Morality and the Ideal of Rationality in Formal Organizations," *Monist* 54 (1970): 488–516; and W.H. Walsh, "Pride, Shame and Responsibility," *Philosophical Quarterly* 20 (1970): 1–13. An example of a sociological approach is Albert J. Reiss, Jr., "Organizational Deviance," in M. David Ermann and Richard J. Lundmann, eds., *Corporate and Governmental Deviance* (New York: Oxford University Press, 1978), esp. pp. 33–35.

4. See, e.g., John C. Coffee, Jr., " 'No Soul to Damn: No Body to Kick': An Unscandalized Inquiry into the Problem of Corporate Punishment," *Mich. L. R.* 79 (1981): 386–459.

5. Glanville Williams, *Criminal Law* (London: Stevens & Sons, 1961), p. 31. Also, cf. Hart, *Punishment and Responsibility*, pp. 19–22, 143–46, 193–95; George P. Fletcher, *Rethinking Criminal Law* (Boston: Little, Brown, 1978), pp. 439–49; and Hyman Gross, *A Theory of Criminal Justice* (New York: Oxford University Press, 1979), pp. 22–23, 155–56, 167–69.

6. Edouard L.J. Laferrière, *Traité de la jurisdiction administrative . . .* (Paris: Berger Levrault, 1887) p. 648. A survey of interpretations of the distinction is in H. Street, *Governmental Liability* (Cambridge: Cambridge University Press, 1953), pp. 58–62.

7. Cf. Edward C. Banfield, "Corruption as a Feature of Governmental Organization," *Journal of Law and Economics* 18 (1975): 587–605 at pp. 587–88.

8. "Developments in the Law," at p. 1259, n. 80.

9. *U.S.* v. *Ehrlichman,* 376 F. Supp. 29 (1974) at 35. For a critical discussion of the rationale of the court decisions reversing the conviction of the individuals who carried out Ehrlichman's orders, see Fletcher, *Rethinking Criminal Law,* pp. 756–58.

10. Williams, *Criminal Law,* pp. 346–427; and Gross, *Theory of Criminal Justice,* pp. 160–61, 423–36.

11. Paul Finn, "Official Misconduct," *Crim. L. J.* 2 (1978): 307–25 at p. 315.

12. Testimony to the Knapp Commission investigating police corruption in New York City showed that officials at each level of the hierarchy up to the Mayor's assistant ignored or minimized reports of corruption for a long time before acting on them. New York City Commission to Investigate Allegations of Police Corruption, *Commission Report,* December 26, 1972 (New York: George Braziller, 1973), pp. 5–7, 210–13.

13. A survey of some 8,000 federal employees indicated that 53 percent of those who observed corruption did not report it because they believed nothing would be done. See U.S. Merit Systems Protection Board, *Whistleblowing and the Federal Employee* (Washington: G.P.O., 1981), pp. 27–31.

14. William J. Chambliss, "Vice, Corruption, Bureaucracy and Power," in Jack Douglas and John Johnson, eds., *Official Deviance* (New York: Lippincott, 1977), pp. 306–29 at pp. 316–25.

15. For an example, see Peter M. Blau, *The Dynamics of Bureaucracy,* rev. ed. (Chicago: University of Chicago Press, 1963), pp. 187–93.

16. Inspectors General Act (1978), 92 *Stat.* 1101 (Public Law 95–452); Civil Service Reform Act (1978) 92 *Stat.* 1111 (Public Law 95-454); Bernard Schwartz and H.W.R. Wade, *Legal Control of Government* (Oxford: Clarendon Press, 1972), pp. 64–75; U.S. Department of Labor, Office of the Inspector General, *Semiannual Report of the Inspector-General* (March 31, 1981), pp. 28–29, 35–36, 72, 94; and Jameson W. Doig et al., "Deterring Illegal Behavior in Complex Organizations," *Criminal Justice Ethics* 1 (1984): 27–56 at p. 33. On the difficulties of the use of the common law offense of misprison, see Williams, *Criminal Law,* pp. 422–27.

17. George P. Fletcher, "The Theory of Criminal Negligence: A Comparative Analysis," *U. Penn. L. R.* 119 (1971): 401–38 at pp. 401–2.

18. Note, "Negligence and the General Problem of Criminal Responsibility," *Yale L.J.* 81 (1972): 949–79 at p. 979.

19. See *Model Penal Code,* sec. 2.02 in *Uniform Laws Annotated* (St. Paul, Minn.: West Publishing, 1974), pp. 464–67.

20. Hart, *Punishment and Responsibility,* pp. 136–57.

21. Hart, *Punishment and Responsibility*, p. 152. Also see Gross, *Theory of Criminal Justice*, pp. 419–23. For criticism of Hart's view, see Richard A. Wasserstrom, "H.L.A. Hart and the Doctrines of *Mens Rea* and Criminal Responsibility," *U. Chi. L. R.* 35 (1967): 92–126 at pp. 102–4.

22. U.S. National Commission on Reform of Federal Criminal Laws, *Working Papers*, July 1970 (Washington: G.P.O., 1970), vol. I, pp. 166, 186–7. But cf. *U.S.* v. *Park* 421 U.S. 658 (1975).

23. Hart, *Punishment and Responsibility*, pp. 148–49; note, "Negligence . . ." p. 979; and Model Penal Code, sec. 2.02.

24. The definition of "gross" negligence is from William Prosser, *Handbook of the Law of Torts*, 4th ed. (St. Paul, Minn.: West, 1971), p. 183. The examples are discussed in Jethro K. Lieberman, *How the Government Breaks the Law* (New York: Stein & Day, 1972), pp. 194–95.

25. Prosser, *Handbook of the Law of Torts*, p. 180.

26. Finn, "Official Misconduct," at p. 317.

27. On "moral distance," see John Harris, *Violence and Responsibility* (London: Routledge & Kegan Paul, 1980), pp. 94–98.

28. Anthony Kenny, "Intention and Purpose in the Law," in R.S. Summers, ed., *Essays in Legal Philosophy* (Oxford: Blackwell, 1970), p. 158.

29. *Memoires of the Prince de Talleyrand* (New York: Putnam, 1891), vol. III, pp. 216–17.

30. French, "Corporation as Moral Person," at p. 207; Donaldson, *Corporations and Morality*, at pp. 30, 124–6; Stone, "Place of Enterprise Liability," at p. 31, but cf. 21–28; "Developments in the Law," at pp. 1247–48. The so-called "Chicago School" favors corporate sanctions on efficiency grounds: see Gary Becker, "Crime and Punishment," *Journal of Political Economy* 76 (1968): 169; and Richard Posner, *Economic Analysis of Law*, 2d ed. (Boston: Little, Brown, 1977), pp. 165–67.

31. U.S. federal courts have held that any employee may make a corporation liable, but most state law, the Model Penal Code, and British law usually require the involvement of a high-level official. See U.S. Senate, Judiciary Committee, *Criminal Code Reform Act of 1977*, 95th Cong., 1st Sess. (Washington: G.P.O., 1977), pp. 74–8; Commission on Reform, *Working Papers*, pp. 176–81 and W. Friedman, *Law in a Changing Society*, 2d ed. (New York: Columbia University Press, 1972), pp. 207–10.

32. Coffee, " 'No Soul to Damn,' " at pp. 390, 407–8; and Coffee, "Corporate Crime and Punishment," *Am. C. L. Rev.* 17 (1980): 419–76.

33. "Developments in the Law," at p. 1241; Commission on Reform,

*Working Papers,* pp. 184–5; Williams, *Criminal Law,* at pp. 856–57; and Kathleen F. Brickey, "Corporate Criminal Accountability," *Wash. U. L. Q.* 60 (1982): 393–423 at pp. 393–94.

34. Gerhard O.W. Mueller, "Mens Rea and the Corporation," *U. Pitt. L. Rev.* 19 (1957): 21–50 at pp. 28–35.

35. Cf. Donaldson, *Corporations and Morality,* at pp. 125–26.

36. Cf. French, "Corporation as Moral Person;" Feinberg, *Doing and Deserving,* at pp. 222–51; and D.E. Cooper, "Collective Responsibility," *Philosophy* 43 (1968): 258–68.

37. U.S. House, Committee on Interstate and Foreign Commerce, Subcommittee on Oversight and Investigations, *Hazardous Waste Disposal,* September, 1979, 96th Cong., 1st sess. (Washington: G.P.O., 1979), pp. 18 ff.

38. Stone, "Place of Enterprise Liability," pp. 26–27; and Coffee, " 'No Soul to Damn,' " pp. 401–2.

39. Note, "Structural Crime," at p. 364; and Coffee, " 'No Soul to Damn,' " at pp. 413–24, 448–57.

40. Donaldson, *Corporations and Morality,* at pp. 18, 26, 209.

41. Cf. Robert Dahl, *Dilemmas of Pluralist Democracy* (New Haven & London: Yale University Press, 1982), pp. 194–202.

42. For recent views of the distinction between utility and rights, see Ronald Dworkin, *Taking Rights Seriously* (Cambridge, Mass.: Harvard University Press, 1978), pp. 184–205; T.M. Scanlon, "Rights, Goals, and Fairness," in Stuart Hampshire et al., *Private and Public Morality* (Cambridge: Cambridge University Press, 1978), pp. 93–111; and J. Roland Pennock and John W. Chapman, eds., *Ethics, Economics, and The Law: Nomos XXIV* (New York: New York University Press, 1982), part II, pp. 107–215.

43. Howard M. Friedman, "Some Reflections on the Corporation as Criminal Defendant," *Notre Dame Lawyer* 55 (1979): 173–202 at pp. 188–201. More generally, see Arthur S. Miller, *The Modern Corporate State* (Westport, Conn.: Greenwood Press, 1976). The best recent judicial discussion of the first amendment rights of corporations is: *First National Bank of Boston* v. *Bellotti,* 55 L Ed 2d 707 (1978).

44. *Kawananakoa* v. *Polybank,* 205 U.S. 834 at 836 (1907). This was a civil case involving a controversy over a foreclosure of a mortgage on a property, part of which had been conveyed to the territory of Hawaii, which claimed immunity from suit.

45. *Leviathan,* M. Oakshott, ed. (Oxford: Blackwell, 1946), p. 173, and generally chap. XXVI, pp. 172–89. Holmes also cited Jean Bodin's defense of absolute sovereignty, found in *Six Books of the Commonwealth,* M.J. Tooley, trans. (New York: Barnes & Noble, 1967), chap. 8: "One may be subject to laws made by another, but it is

impossible to bind oneself . . ." (p. 28). For good measure, Holmes throws in two more absolutists—Sir John Eliot (1592–1632) and Baldus [presumably Baldo degli Ubaldi] (1327?–1400).

46. *Leviathan* at p. 121, and generally chap. XIX, pp. 121–29.

47. On the problem of overdeterrence from *civil* liability, see Ronald Cass, "Damage Suits Against Public Officers," *U. Penn. L. Rev.* 129 (1981): 1110–1188 at pp. 1153–60.

48. *Nixon* v. *Fitzgerald*, 50 *LW* 4797 at 4806, 4810 (1982).

49. Congressional Quarterly, *Congressional Ethics*, 2nd ed. (Washington: Congressional Quarterly, 1980), pp. 169–75.

50. Association of the Bar of the City of New York, Committee on Federal Legislation, *Remedies for Deprivation of Constitutional Rights by Federal Officers and Employees* (New York: Association of the Bar, 1979), p. 28; and Cass, "Damage Suits Against Public Officers," at p. 1167.

51. Cf. *U.S. Code,* Title 18, chaps. 11, 29, 93.

52. Virtually all of the recent literature on civil liability warning of the danger of overdeterrence relies on analytic arguments (such as economic models) that are not subjected to empirical test (see, e.g., Cass. "Damage Suits;" also cf. note 88 below).

53. Joanne Witts, "Federal Executive Immunity From Civil Liability in Damages," *Col. L. Rev.* 77 (1974): 625–48 at p. 643.

54. J. Jackson Walter, "The Ethics in Government Act, Conflict of Interest Laws and Presidential Recruiting," *Public Administration Review* 41 (1981): 659–65 at pp. 663–65.

55. Jeremy Bentham, *The Rationale of Reward* (London: Robert Heward, 1830), p. 59n.

56. *U.S.* v. *Musto,* U.S. District Court for New Jersey, No. 81–144, May 10, 1982, 707–42 [court transcript]. Musto eventually lost both his Senate seat and the mayorship under a state statute that requires officials convicted of a crime to forfeit their office, though his wife was elected to serve on the city commission in his place, and his former legislative aid won his Senate seat.

57. Raoul Berger, *Impeachment: The Constitutional Problems* (Cambridge, Mass.: Harvard University Press, 1973), pp. 59–61, 63.

58. Institute for Social Research, *Organizational Assessments of the Effects of Civil Service Reform,* Second Year Report for U.S. Office of Personnel Management (Ann Arbor: University of Michigan, Institute for Social Research, 1981), pp. 22–23.

59. John Locke, *Two Treatises of Government,* Peter Laslett, ed. (New York: Cambridge University Press, 1960), secs. 135–6, 139, 142, 153, 156, 160 ff. Although recent scholars have neglected the idea of trusteeship in their interpretations of Locke, earlier commentators recognized its significance. See C.E. Vaughan, *Studies in the*

*History of Political Philosophy* . . . (Manchester: University of Manchester Press, 1939), pp. 143–57; and J.W. Gough, *John Locke's Political Philosophy* (Oxford: Clarendon Press, 1950), pp. 136–71. The concept of trust did not necessarily entail a trustee theory of representation. In fact, those eighteenth-century writers who regarded M.P.s as delegates were more likely to use the idea of an "equitable trust" than were those who viewed them as trustees (Gough at p. 166).

60. Locke himself rejects the latter implication, holding that the executive's trust can be revoked only if the trustee violates terms of the trust. Ibid. at secs. 100, 149, 156, 164; but see sec. 153.

61. *Meinhard v. Salmon,* 249 N.Y. 458 at 464, 164 N.E. 545 at 546 (1928).

62. *R. v. Bembridge,* 22 State Tr. 1 (1783). See Finn, "Official Misconduct," pp. 308–9.

63. Finn, "Official Misconduct," pp. 155–56.

64. John C. Coffee, "From Tort to Crime: Some Reflections on the Criminalization of Fiduciary Breeches and The Problematic Line between Law and Ethics," *Am. Crim. L. Rev.* 19 (1981): 117–72; D.V. Morano, "The Mail Fraud Statute," *John Marshall L. Rev.* 14 (1980): 45–87; and W. Robert Gray, "The Intangible Rights Doctrine and Political-Corruption Prosecutions Under the Federal Mail Fraud Statute," *U. Chi. L. Rev.* 47 (1980): 562–87.

65. *U.S. v. Isaacs,* 493 F. 2d 1124 (7th Cir.), *cert. denied,* 417 U.S. 976 (1974) [Otto Kerner, Illinois]; and *U.S. v. Mandel,* 591 F. 2d 1347 (4th Cir.), *cert. denied* 100 S.C+ 1647 (1980) [Marvin Mandel, Maryland]. Governor Blanton of Tennessee was convicted of mail fraud and other charges in June of 1981 (see the *New York Times,* June 10, 1981). Federal bribery statutes could not be applied to the state officials in these cases.

66. *U.S. v. Mandel* at 1359–60.

67. Ibid.

68. Coffee, "From Tort to Crime," pp. 132, 141, 142–48; Morano, "Mail Fraud Statute," p. 45–87; and Gray, "Intangible Rights Doctrine," pp. 566, 587.

69. Coffee, "From Tort to Crime," p. 144.

70. Coffee, "From Tort to Crime," p. 143.

71. See *U.S. v. Dotterweich,* 320 U.S. 277 (1943); and *U.S. v. Park,* 421 U.S. 658 (1975). See the analysis by Doig et al., "Deterring Illegal Behavior," pp. 41–42.

72. Cf. rule on "manipulative and deceptive devices" issued by the Securities and Exchange Commission in accord with the Securities and Exchange Act of 1934 (17 *C.F.R.* 240.10b-5). The Freedom of Information Act does not penalize officials who fail to release requested information: see *J. U.S.C.,* sec. 552.

73. See, e.g., U.S. Code, secs. 1902–8.

74. Note, "Constitutional Law—Equal Protection—Defendant Permitted to Prove Discriminatory Enforcement . . ." *Harv. L. Rev.* 78 (1965): 884–87.

75. *Nixon* v. *Fitzgerald* at 4798–99; and *Harlow and Butterfield* v. *Fitzgerald*, 50 LW 4815 at 4819 (1982).

76. U.S. Environmental Protection Agency, Office of Inspector General, Office of Investigations, Report of Investigation, *Thriftway Company* (File #1-82-045, April 5, 1982). My request, under the Freedom of Information Act, for a copy of this report was denied on the grounds that "the production of such records would interfere with enforcement proceedings" (letter to author from Richard M. Campbell, Assistant Inspector General, E.P.A., July 19, 1982). I obtained a copy from another source.

77. American Law Institute, *Model Penal Code,* Proposed official Draft, July 30, 1962 (Philadelphia, American Law Institute, 1962), sec. 2.07, Comment, p. 38.

78. Commission on Reform, *Working Papers,* p. 165.

79. *Cain* v. *Doyle,* 72 Commonwealth Law Reports 409 (1946). W. Friedman in *Law in a Changing Society,* pp. 210–12, gives the case a somewhat different interpretation by emphasizing that only one justice dismissed in principle the idea that the Crown can be liable for a criminal offense.

80. *Cain* v. *Doyle* at 424.

81. Ibid. at 433–34.

82. U.S. Senate, Committee on Judiciary, Subcommittee on Citizen's and Shareholder's Rights and Remedies and Subcommittee on Administrative Practice and Procedure, *Joint Hearing on the Federal Tort Claims Act,* 95th Cong., 2nd sess., 1978, p. 358.

83. Coffee, " 'No Soul to Damn,' " pp. 448–57; and note, "Structural Crime and Institutional Rehabilitation," pp. 364–74.

84. On the importance of the stigma of conviction in organizational crime, see Association of the Bar, *Remedies for Deprivation,* pp. 20–21; and Friedman, *Law in a Changing Society,* p. 211.

85. See, e.g., Watergate Special Prosecution Force, "Policy and Procedure in Investigation and Prosecution of Government Officials," 12 *Crim. L. Bulletin* 12 (1976):26–57; and U.S. House, Committee on the Judiciary, *New Directions for Federal Involvement in Crime Control* (Washington: G.P.O, 1977), pp. 62–67.

86. Emile Durkheim, *The Division of Labor in Society* (Glencoe, Ill.: Free Press, 1964), pp. 68–132.

87. A principled distinction between crime and tort, difficult enough to draw for ordinary offenses, becomes even more problematic for governmental crime. Most serious wrongs by officials could very

well be seen as offenses against the whole society, and offenses that should be prosecuted by the government and deterred by penalties—traditionally some of the distinguishing characteristics of crimes. For a thoughtful recent analysis of the distinction, see Richard A. Epstein, "Crime and Tort: Old Wine in New Bottles," in Randy Barnett and John Hagel III, eds., *Assessing the Criminal* (Cambridge, Mass.: Ballinger, 1977), pp. 231–57.

88. See Jerry L. Mashaw, "Civil Liability of Government Officers," *Law and Contemporary Problems* 42 (1978): 8–34; Jeremy McBride, "Damages as a Remedy for Unlawful Administrative Action," *Cambridge L. J.* 38 (1979): 323–45; Cass, "Damage Suits Against Public Officers," pp. 1110–1188; and Peter H. Schuck, "Suing Our Servants," *Sup. Ct. Rev.* 1980 (1981): 281–368.

89. Michael Walzer, *Regicide and Revolution* (Cambridge, England: Cambridge University Press, 1974), p. 77.

90. Otto Kirchheimer, *Political Justice* (Princeton: Princeton University Press, 1961), pp. 3–118, 419–31.

91. See, e.g., U.S. Senate, Select Committee on Ethics, *Investigation of Senator Harrison A. Williams, Jr.,* September 3, 1981 (Washington: G.P.O., 1981). More generally, see *Congressional Ethics,* pp. 5–13.

92. Paul L. Montgomery, "10 Years Later, Watergate Figures Recall Turning Point in Their Lives," *New York Times* (June 17, 1982).

93. E.g., President Reagan nominated Maurice Stans to a position on the board of the Overseas Private Investment Corporation. Although acquitted of obstructing justice, Stans pleaded guilty to five misdemeanor charges of campaign contribution violations in the 1972 Nixon campaign. See *New York Times* (December 10, 1981).

94. Montgomery, "10 Years Later."

95. Thomas Powers, *The Man Who Kept the Secrets: Richard Helms and the CIA* (New York: Simon & Shuster, 1979), pp. 382–95. On the use of nolo contendere, see Marshall Clinard et al., *Illegal Corporate Behavior* (Washington: Dept. of Justice, National Institute of Law Enforcement and Criminal Justice), pp. 207–8.

96. Powers, *Man Who Kept the Secrets,* p. 391.

97. Samuel P. Huntington, *American Politics: The Promise of Disharmony* (Cambridge, Mass.: Harvard University Press, 1981), pp. 141–42, 188–89; Sherman Lewis, *Reform and the Citizen* (North Scituate, Mass.: Duxbury Press, 1980), pp. 274–75; Bruce Jennings, "The Institutionalization of Ethics in the U.S. Senate," special supplement, *Hastings Center Report* 11 (1981): 5–9; and John T. Elliff, *The Reform of FBI Intelligence Operations* (Princeton: Princeton University Press, 1979), pp. 3–13.

98. Huntington, *American Politics,* p. 189.

99. Bentham, *The Rationale of Reward,* pp. 21, 43.

240                                                    DENNIS F. THOMPSON

100. Jean Jacques Rousseau, *Gouvernement de Pologne*, chap. XIII, in *Political Writings of Jean Jacques Rousseau*, C.E. Vaughan, ed., vol. II (Oxford: Blackwell, 1962), p. 498n (my translation).

101. See Daniel Mornet, *Les origines intellectuelles de la Révolution Francaise, 1715–1787* (Paris: Collins, 1933), p. 263. More generally, see William J. Goode, *The Celebration of Heroes* (Berkeley: University of California Press, 1978), pp. 151–80, 313, 394.

102. Doig et al., "Deterring Illegal Behavior," p. 35.

103. Criminal sanctions are only one kind of sanction that could enforce our judgments of the moral responsibility of officials; on the general problem of making such judgments, see Dennis F. Thompson, "Moral Responsibility of Public Officials," *American Political Science Review* 74 (1980): 905–16.

104. Walter, "The Ethics in Government Act," p. 662.

# 9

## A COMMENT ON "CRIMINAL RESPONSIBILITY IN GOVERNMENT"

### CHRISTOPHER D. STONE

Some amount of misconduct in government is inevitable. To deal with it, we have devices ranging from political housecleaning—abetted by the "disinfectant glare of publicity"—to civil damage suits, impeachment, and actions in *quo warranto*. The issue Dennis Thompson raises is, what is the place, in this panoply of control techniques, for the law of crimes? Under what circumstances, if any, is it appropriate to turn criminal investigations and sanctions inward against the government's own officers? And under what circumstances, if any, is it appropriate to prosecute a governmental entity? Thompson suggests that these questions have been generally slighted in the literature, and that we may be undercriminalizing government wrongdoing less from thought-through principle than from habit.

Thompson's approach is to identify two general grounds on which our apparent reluctance to invoke criminal responsibility in government might lie, which I will call the General Bureaucratic Considerations and the Special Governmental Considerations. The first involve reservations that might be derived from the fact that much of governmental wrongdoing occurs in a bureaucratic setting. We are not dealing, typically, with the paradigm of the common-law crime, the lonely cutpurse stalking the

I am grateful for the comments of Brent Fisse, Michael Moore, Stephen Morse, Judi Resnik and Jeff Strand.

241

streets, but rather with an Organization Man, living within the bylaws and furnishings of office. Yet, as Thompson correctly observes, whatever complications these considerations introduce for invocation of the criminal law are not complications peculiar to the criminalization of government conduct; they have to be accounted for in controlling the conduct of bureaucratic organizations generally, be they automobile manufacturers, labor unions, or armies.

On the other hand, government organizations are obviously not just like any other bureaucracies. They are instruments and symbols of politics, operating within their own special aims, traditions, and constraints. As a consequence, the decision how to control them introduces certain special, even specially delicate, considerations: the Special Governmental Considerations that make up the second half of Thompson's analysis. I think we can fairly follow the gist of his paper by analyzing his position on these two considerations in turn, even if it is impossible to do justice to each and every thread of his generally well-developed arguments.

## THE GENERAL BUREAUCRATIC CONSIDERATIONS

Thompson opines that some of the reluctance to criminalize governmental misconduct stems from organizational attributes of the setting in which it typically takes place. Often, if not ordinarily, the wrongdoing will be the joint product of many hands and minds, enjoy the support of institutional resources, occur in furtherance of institutional goals, and be motivated by the informal, if not the formal rules, practices, and customs of the institution. But, as he suggests, these considerations trouble the criminalization of conduct in any large-scale organization.

Thompson begins therefore with a general examination of the sanctioning in a bureaucratic setting, with particular attention to what he calls the "structuralist thesis." This is a position that he associates with two claims: first, that in a bureaucratic setting, criminal conduct may take place for which it is inappropriate[1] to hold any of the organization's agents criminally responsible; and, second, that conduct may occur for which it is appropriate to hold the organization itself criminally responsible.

Thompson's decision to give a central place to structuralism, rather than to "reductionism,"[2] the more familiar term in the literature, deserves some comment. It seems to me that one *could* reach Thompson's two "structuralist" claims through being a nonreductionist, that is, by taking the position (as I do) that statements about the behavior of organizations cannot be translated into a set of statements about the behavior of identifiable persons without remainder; that if we eliminate all reference to the organization and its attributes, we lose something of significance in the translation—of significance both for legal guilt and moral blame. But to be a structuralist in the sense of holding Thompson's two claims, it may not be necessary to reach any position on reductionism at all. A structuralist could favor sanctioning the organization on perfectly plausible practical grounds, unconnected to any metaphysical notion that corporations are independent moral agents. For example, consider a case in which a prosecutor believes that whoever is responsible is buried so deeply in the bureaucratic structure, would be so costly to find and prosecute, and was so tenuously culpable that the likely sanction would not merit the effort of prosecuting him. After all, the prosecutor has the option of prosecuting the organization—a less costly undertaking—and leaving it to the organization to identify and discipline the culprit according to its own devices. Whether such an allocation of prosecution resources is, in any given circumstance, prudent, is one question. But when it is selected, as it commonly is, it implies no special moral ontology, no commitment to "queer entities." Thus, let me stress at the start that one can safely be a structuralist without getting entangled in some of the stumbling blocks that a nonreductionist is often supposed to face.

One might say at the start, too, that most of us who are concerned with what I will follow Thompson in calling structuralism want to speak not only to the liability rules, but also to related questions that commonly and importantly arise in considering whether organizational circumstances may warrant a special justification, excuse, mitigation of sentence, or perhaps even the downgrading of an offense.[3] Assuming, however, that we do well to restrict our focus to liability or nonliability as the two alternatives, the general question, I take it, is this: Respecting misconduct that has occurred in an organizational setting, in what circumstances, if any, is it appropriate to prosecute:

1. the entity but no agent (E but not A);
2. both an agent and the entity (A + E);
3. an agent but not the entity (A but not E); and
4. neither an agent nor the entity (not A and not E).

I will examine these four possibilities in turn.

### The Criminal Liability of the Entity but not of any Agent

I presume that no one, no structuralist of any stripe, claims that under no circumstances ought an agent to be held personally answerable for his conduct in office (particularly if we defer, until the next section, whether immunities might attach to some high governmental offices). If someone adulterates food, his conviction ought not to turn on whether he did it on his own behalf or that of his corporate employer. But the real question comes from the other side: are there circumstances under which it might be appropriate to introduce the law of crimes, but under which it is not appropriate to hold any agent personally responsible? I think the answer is yes.

Consider the following state of affairs. It is a federal offense wilfully to discharge prohibited effluents into a navigable waterway. Each month, corporation Z, which has a plant abutting a river, purchases a certain amount of hydrochloric acid. Some portion of the acid is consumed in the production; some portion not consumed in production is chemically recovered and packaged for recycling to other companies. One agent employed at the plant, the purchasing agent, A, knows the first datum, that is, how many pounds are entering the plant each month. Another employee, the production manager, B, knows the second figure, that is, how many pounds the plant is using in production. It is the job of still another employee, the sales agent, C, to sell the recaptured acid. Hence, C knows how many pounds are being recovered.

In fact, the amount consumed, when added to the amount recaptured for resale, does not equal the amount purchased. The difference, a certain amount of the acid, unknown to A, B, and C, is being discharged into the river. Neither this fact, nor the clues from which he might deduce it, are brought to the attention of D, the plant manager. D might know of the excess, independently, if one of the discharge meters were working correctly, but it is not, having been allowed to fall into disrepair by E, the inadequately trained, understaffed plant manager. As a result, unlawful discharges are spilling out of the plant into a navigable waterway.

Now, my assumption is that, on these facts, none of the agents, not A, B, C, D or E, is *wilfully* committing the offending discharge. If wilfulness is deemed an element of the crime, and if we cannot say that the bits and pieces of knowledge the various agents had, when aggregated, made the *corporation's* actions wilfull, then we face the prospect that, while unlawful discharges (in one sense) are occurring there is no criminal to prosecute: not a victimless crime, but a criminalless one.

Thompson, who is disinclined to drag the corporation into it (for reasons I will turn to), sees at least two ways to make the criminalization of the agents appear more morally palatable. One approach, of which I myself have been a strong advocate, would have the government take a more active hand in the establishment of certain corporate offices and in the definition of their powers and obligations.[4] In terms of our illustration, each plant handling potentially toxic materials could be required to designate one of its employees responsible for monitoring discharges, and for notifying the EPA of any excesses. Failure of this designated employee, F, to carry out his function would not be merely, as at present, a disciplinary matter for the company to handle in accordance with its own internal rules, but a crime, a breach of well-defined duty for which F, clearly forewarned, would be answerable to the outside world. This approach respects the traditional constraints on criminalization, but forces the lawmaking agency to anticipate exactly what might go wrong and exactly what corporate performance might avert it. It also, unfortunately, risks trammelling industry with costs in excess of the social benefits to be realized, if duties are not tailored prudently. And of course it leaves open the question, what are we to do in the great number of circumstances for which no such task-defining rule has been anticipated?

The alternative Thompson favors shifts the burden of foresight from the lawmaking bodies to corporate agents, at their peril. Rather than limit an agent's personal liability to his breaches of clearly defined duties, Thompson proposes resting culpability on, essentially, omissions, via an expansion in the criminalization of negligence and (I gather also, but not so clearly) of vicarious conduct or strict criminal liability. Thompson marshalls several arguments in defense of this technique: the criminalization of negligence is not as radical a departure from tradition as many imagine;[5] the seriousness of the harm that can be done through large-scale organizations warrants some departure in order to "get through" to the agents;[6] we might view people entering the employ of a bureaucracy as "consenting" to strict liability (a particularly nice and I think original point);[7] and at least some of the carelessness that occurs in a bureaucratic setting is so predictable[8] that to criminalize it (or to hold supervisors responsible) does not as sharply conflict with notions of fairness as when we criminalize negligence in the ordinary nonorganizational contexts.

Much can be said for Thompson's argument. We could extend the reach of criminal law by broadening the swath of strict and vicarious liability, and increasing the use of relatively vague negligence-type elements. Doing so in organizational settings might be less offensive than elsewhere. Nonetheless, we cannot blink the fact that to move the law in this direction is, at least by degrees, to loosen the criminal law's moral tethers. Negligence is shadowy. Vicariousness is plastic (who, after all, will appear, after the fact, to have been in "a responsible position?") Neither squares well with fair notice, intent, or real blameworthiness. In fact, I am persuaded that even if the law does go in this direction, the net effect on the agents—on their jeopardy and behavior—will not be considerable. We know that even for deliberate and knowing nonvicarious crimes, courts are loath to come down hard on white-collar offenders except in the most flagrant cases. Where the basis of the crime is nothing but negligent omission or failure to supervise, and where moral responsibility is diluted, nothing more than a light fine is (nor morally ought to be) in store. Everyone will know it and probably act accordingly. Some of the risks of these light fines will be absorbed *ex ante*—that is, the enterprise will be the true bearer of the burden anyway, because it will have to increase the compensation that the agents will demand in return for the hazards of fines they have limited ability to avoid. And what burden the company does not pay up *ex ante,* it may settle *ex post,* through indemnification. Under the state corporations codes, an officer who is fined, particularly in consequence of unintentional criminal conduct, may have a strong case for turning right around and requiring the company to reimburse him or her.[9] In effect, the company will be in much the same position as if it had been the target of the fine originally. The law could be, and should be, amended to restrict these ways of blunting the criminalizing of agents' conduct. But as I have suggested elsewhere, some degree of blunting is uneliminable, particularly where the moral basis of the particular penalty is shaky.[10]

At what point do all these machinations aimed at nailing some officer become pointless—and worse? There is another alternative, to hold that even if no agent is criminally culpable, the corporation might rightly be sanctioned notwithstanding. If Thompson rejects this option, one would expect him to make his case by referring to, and defending, some theory of sanctions, demonstrating how criminalization of the entity (even if not of an agent coincidentally) does not fit. Thompson however, treats the theoretical basis of justifiable punishment fairly summarily (on the view, apparently, that his argument "is compatible with a wide range of theories").[11] My own sense is that one cannot hope to carry through an inquiry such as his without some deeper and more consistent concern for the underlying rationale of the criminal law—the subject, after all, of this volume.

Start with deterrence. Is sanctioning the corporation likely to reduce the incidence of the unwanted conduct (in our illustration, of water pollution)? The answer is clearly yes. Other things being equal, a legal regime in which corporations are criminally liable for water pollution will have less pollution than regimes that hold the corporations immune.[12] Observe that the reductionist's analysis does not undercut the structuralist's position. It may be true that fining the corporation works, because it is the behavior of real flesh and blood people who, one hopes, will be influenced by the threat of the fine. But all the structuralist needs to show is that fining the entity is an efficient and not unfair way to modify the agents' behavior in the right direction, superior, according to some theory of crimes, to pursuing them directly. Rather than beating the bureaucratic under-brush to find a marginally culpable agent, a prosecutor might be warranted *in some cases* (depending upon his resources, among other things) to fine the corporation, turning over to the com-pany's officers the option to identify and discipline anyone they felt required it for their and the company's welfare.

The structuralist's case is certainly no less strong if we con-sider rehabilitation. The criminal sanction is commonly justi-fied as a means to making the wrongdoer mend its ways. But what are the ways in need of mending? One perfectly plausible answer is *the corporation's,* particularly in those circumstances where the misconduct can be traced to omissions to establish procedure and personnel adequate for compliance. It was a failure of corporate rules and practices that no corporate em-ployee was charged with putting together the clues from which the violation might have been deduced: what A knew, what B knew, what C knew, and so on. It is not only the corporation's authority and information network that appear implicated. It might also be the hiring and training practices that put D in a position of monitoring and repairing the discharge meters, a job for which he may not have been prepared or capable. Or the flaw may have lain with the allocation of corporate resources: the maintenance crew having been inadequately staffed to per-form the periodic checkups required. I am not asserting that it lay outside the power of some combination of persons to have altered these things: of stockholders, directors, line managers, supervisors, and so on. But power is simply not coextensive with culpability. It is one thing to claim that someone might have foreseen and averted the wrong; it is a far cry to make from that omission moral, much less criminal, responsibility. In such circumstances, sanctioning the organization may precipitate the necessary changes, "rehabilitating" the company, without dilut-ing the moral force of the law. If the fine by itself seems un-likely to induce the appropriate internal reform, then the crim-inal judgment can serve as the basis of a probation order that mandates institutional improvement directly.[13]

Suppose we conceive, as an independent basis of the criminal law's educative function, the denunciation of wrongful conduct in ceremonies of state. In terms of our illustration, assuming that the effluent discharges were wrongful, and that, without scapegoating, there is no agent to denounce, it hardly seems pointless to underscore the gravity of the conduct by denouncing the corporation. Indeed, to denounce the corporation, whose name is more likely to be recognized than that of any of its employees, is a message calculated to travel.

Granted, retribution against an entity is a more problematical notion.[14] Let us impute to Thompson the position (because it would be the most intelligible one for him to work from) that retribution, somehow conceived, is a limit on the imposition of criminal sanction, and further, that retribution is applicable only to metaphysical persons.[15] This would be a good start. But why should retribution be regarded as a necessary condition? And why cannot corporations be conceived as the sort of "persons" capable of receiving it? Both questions, as well as the nature of retribution, are far too complex to permit us to reject out of hand the possibility that retribution can intelligibly and defensibly apply to corporations.[16] I do not mean just in the loose sense, that prosecuting a corporation may provide a satisfaction of emotions, a blind striking out by the very primitive stuff that vengeance is made of.[17] I mean that if one does carry out an examination of what it means to be a metaphysical person—as Professor Moore does in his contribution to this volume—the basis for excluding corporations (which arguably exhibit their own plans and engage in means-ends analysis over time) is not at all obvious.[18]

The point is that the prima facie case for sanctioning the corporation finds enough support in the traditional bases of the criminal law, that the burden is quite reasonably put on the other side: why *not* criminalize the corporation?[19]

Thompson invokes the traditional appeal to the innocent shareholders, employees, and so on, on whom the brunt of the punishment indirectly falls. What he is saying is that strict or vicarious liability should be viewed with prejudice. Indeed. But the moral and practical difference between extending agent liability (which he advocates) and extending shareholder, etc., liability (which he opposes) is a difference, at best, of degree. Even granting that (most) shareholders have less control over the situation than (most) supervisory officers, the unfairness to the shareholders seems problematical. First, it is not at all clear that the shareholders are entirely innocent; they are the beneficiaries, through elevated share values, of the cost-cutting that results from the substandard pollution monitoring; that is, over the years, they reaped, pro rata, the benefits of the corporation's misconduct. What is unfair about their suffering, pro rata, a diminution of share values when the corporation's misconduct is discovered? Indeed, the notion of "consent," which Thompson invokes on behalf of expanded agent liability, applies with equal if not greater force to the position of the shareholders: having purchased their shares in a regime that allows corporate fines, they in effect consent to their risk that the price that they pay for their shares will be discounted for the hazard that they may suffer consequences of misconduct beyond their control. (It happens when the corporation suffers large awards in torts and contracts cases.)

Second, I find it hard to believe that any stigmatization is involved—that shareholders (who are increasingly pension funds and other institutions, anyway) hang their (institutional) heads in shame when their investment is hauled into court. But even if there were stigma, would it be a more unfair stigma than that which Thompson is prepared to place on corporate agents through the criminalization of their negligence?

In the last analysis, Thompson does not rest his reluctance to criminalize the organization on these grounds. He fears that if we countenance sanctioning organizations, as such, the practice may imply that, at worst, all organizations, and at best, those that we punish, should have their autonomy respected just as ordinary citizens do.[20] In other words, if they are deemed fit to be held responsible, by implication "they should also have the rights that people have."[21]

Where does such an implication come from? I cannot find it in the course of history or the crannies of logic.[22] Look at the record. True, centuries ago, qualms about hauling the corporation into court, not unlike those Thompson invokes, were common.[23] But since then we have come to accept as a matter of course a legal system in which corporations are expected to pay up on their contracts, make good for their torts—even intentional torts—and, more recently, not to discriminate in hiring. Criminalizing their conduct might be regarded as a more morally significant move, and in fact was so viewed. But we hashed that out nearly a century ago, and gradually decided that corporations are the sort of "persons" whose conduct can be criminalized. What have been the dire implications for corporate rights?

Obviously, the imposition of some liabilities raises some questions of rights that would otherwise not have come up. Once we decided that a corporation could be tried, then we had to decide whether it had a right to jury trial. (It was decided that it did.) But while we have conferred some rights on corporations, we have not conferred all; nor have we conferred on them the full moral status of persons, nor is there much clamor that we relent and do so. (Somewhat the same history, I think, could be written of fetuses, animals, species, and even, in some circumstances, the dead.) Corporations do not enjoy the benefit of the privileges and immunities clause. Nor do they have Fifth Amendment rights, nor, as I read the cases, do they have rights equally with a person under the First or Fourth Amendments. They cannot vote. Their participation in political campaigns is restricted.

Moreover, even if we put these differences aside, even if we suppose that there is some slippery slope, that, once we punish corporations as though they were persons, there will be pressure to increase their rights, then the normative basis of Thompson's argument would still need developing: why would a movement in that direction be a bad thing? Some writers—Peter French[24] and I,[25] for example—have suggested both that it is intelligible, and quite defensible, to treat corporations as moral agents in some circumstances.

### Liability of the Agent and the Entity (A + E)

Thus far I have proceeded under the assumption that we are faced with two alternatives, to hold either the agent or the entity liable. This need not be so. In fact, the most common response is to pass a statute that provides the option to coindict. Prosecutors incline to exercise this option, and to indict the entity even in those situations where (as distinct from our illustration) there is a clearly culpable individual they can readily identify. The prosecutors may be persuaded that, while A deserves his sanction, it is equally true that the wrongdoing reflected a pattern of behavior ingrained in the corporation's ways of doing things: its institutional practices in hiring, supervising, monitoring and disciplining employees, gathering and disseminating information, allocating authority and responsibility, and so on. Merely to convict A will not assure reform in these practices. In fact, if these practices are deeply enough entrenched, even the imprisonment—the removal—of A is no assurance that the organization's behavior will be modified; a new A may be placed in the same old work environment and risk the same old criminal tasks. One can put the argument even more strongly. If we adopt the practice that only agents are indictable, the prosecutors, in order to assure the agent's conviction and provide the basis for stiff sentences, will emphasize the individual's responsibility at the cost of distracting attention when it might best be put—on the underlying organizational pathology.[26]

*Liability of the Agent but not the Entity ( A but not E)*

A dyed-in-the-wool structuralist might go even further, and argue that there was no case in which, the agent having committed a crime made possible by dint of corporate office, the entity ought not be liable also—that is, there is no case for which the strategy A but not E is appropriate. This is a tough position to speak for, as illustrated by bank embezzlement, a crime in which the agent acts, not only for his own advantage, but against the interests and orders of E, his employer. Surely, the nonstructuralist will say that here is a case for the prosecution of A but not of E.

But is E's nonresponsibility so clear? Unlike the statutory rape that a bank employee might commit after hours in his own home, this crime took place in the bank, and the opportunity was provided by his position as a bank officer. It is true that A here acted against the bank's clearly implied if not express orders. But the law has taken the position—quite wisely, I think—that an employer may be criminally liable for acts of its agents, notwithstanding their apparent insubordination, as long as the employer had opportunity to control the situation[27] (much on the basis, incidentally, that would support Thompson's criminalization of a supervising agent's omissions). The distinction has got to be that the embezzler is not only acting contrary to the employer's orders, but contrary to its interests, as well. This evaporates our suspicions that the employer (or supervising agent) really did not have its heart in, was perhaps even winking at violations of, its formal enunciations. After all, the nonstructuralist will say, that the employer might itself be a victim already provided it with incentives to prevent the crime.

But we must remember that the crime of embezzlement victimizes more than the bank and its shareholders—which is why it is not merely a tort but a crime against the people, the elimination of which is a public good the public is prepared to pay for. The risk of embezzlement adds to the costs of bank insurance, burdening the entire industry and through it, society. If, as a consequence of the embezzlement, the company should fail, it is not only the shareholders who suffer, but the creditors, depositors, and society as a whole. Therefore, it is not enough to point out that, even absent the specter of criminal liability, the bank's investors and managers have independent incentives to hire and monitor their agents in such a way as to prevent embezzlement. The question remains, might society not have reasons to prevent embezzlement that warrant even more stringent measures than are warranted by the bank's own incentives? Suppose we do not want to bear the expense of figuring out which officers, in which banks, are best put in jeopardy if someone embezzles. Organizational systems, like biological ones, vary in ways that make internal tampering jeopardous to their survival. We might simply threaten to fine the bank, letting the bank's officers work out how best to monitor, to go surety for, its employees' lawful conduct. It is, so far as needs concern us, the entity that hires, compensates (are tellers underpaid?), supervises, and creates the physical and ethical environment in which its agents work. One way to induce the socially optimal level of supervision, etc., is to introduce some further disincentives to animate the corporation to prevent its employees from becoming criminals, knowing that the details of the appropriate response will likely vary from corporation to corporation.

In fact, there seem to be cases going both ways on whether a corporation can be coindicted in comparable circumstances.[28] The courts that have dismissed indictments against corporations have been moved, no doubt, by an intuition that it detaches the law from its moral foundation to penalize the corporation, and through it, its shareholders and others, for action that they not only did not authorize, but was against their interests. To carry this position beyond the intuitive level involves us in very complex questions, none of which has a compelling answer. If the law should firmly establish coindictability in such cases, then the prospect of the corporation being fined for disloyal agent misconduct will be discounted in share values; everyone being on notice of the rule, and paying the right price for the risk, the unfairness argument loses some of its appeal. In those circumstances, the question of indicting E along with A in all cases in which A is indicted would, in the last analysis, be dominated by considerations of efficiency in law enforcement, the force of moral constraints being minimal.

*Neither the Agent nor the Entity (not A and not E)*

Finally, we should at least allude to the range of wrongdoing in which, perhaps, neither the entity nor the agent should be dealt with as criminals. People drawn into institutions get involved in morally knotty situations. As Thompson himself observes (in the government context), many practices that we may wish to regard as criminal must remain the object of only moral and political condemnation. Or, we might add, civil suits. We must remember that, except for wrongs so highly culpable that a prison term is in order, the difference between a criminal suit and, say, a government civil suit, or civil penalty suit, is a thin line, particularly where the defendant is by its nature unimprisonable. I am concerned that many of the considerations Thompson raises as objections to criminalizing conduct could be turned with equal force against ordinary or punitive civil damage suits.[29] What is the difference whether the check a corporate treasurer is forced to write is in satisfaction of a civil judgment or a fine?

Thus, one wonders when the various noncriminal alternatives should supplement the law of crimes, and when supplant it.[30] It is impossible to determine Thompson's response for the same reason it is hard to assess his stand on the other three positions. To decide what sorts of misconduct, if any, suits which of the four alternatives, we need a more developed theory of criminal sanction than Thompson has been able—in the short space allowed him—to provide. Specifically, in the decision to criminalize, what role does he assign to each of the traditional justifications: special and general deterrence, rehabilitation, retribution, denunciation, and so on? I infer that Thompson assigns a key role either to fairness, somehow conceived, or to retribution. But is he regarding one or the other or both as a constraint on the sanctioning power, the prima facie case for which is based on some combination of the traditional justificatory bases? Or do fairness and retribution play, somehow, a more fundamental role, with some of the others—deterrence, for example—serving as boundary conditions?

## The Special Governmental Considerations

In any case, Thompson emerges from the general bureaucratic analysis with, to his satisfaction, a strong presumption in favor of penalizing agents, but not entities. He then focuses on the area of government to consider whether considerations are thereby introduced that require us to alter the general analysis.

This strikes me as a perfectly sensible way to proceed. Ideally, one might review each of the alternatives above, and ask whether anything can be derived from aspects of government that alters how we evaluate that alternative. For example, the possibility that agents might have blanket office-connected (and not merely transactional) immunity seems harder to reject out of hand when it is to a high public office that the immunity would attach. Thompson, I gather, seems unwilling to accept a broad interpretation of *Nixon* v. *Fitzgerald*,[31] which, although a civil suit, could be read to suggest that the United States President is also immune from criminal suits, at least during his term of office. (I presume the President would be liable to impeachment, or— the statute of limitations tolling during his term—to prosecution after office.) One supposes that there is much to be said on both sides of the question.

Moreover, it is not just questions of liability that merit examination, but those of excuse and justification as well. For example, in the *Barker* case,[32] a burglary prosecution that arose out of the Watergate scandal, the majority of the D.C. Court of Appeals took the view that while mistake of law is ordinarily no excuse for a crime, a mistake of law by persons employed by high government officials, who had no reason to doubt the authority of those officials, or to know that their actions were wrongful, might enjoy an exception, a special ignorance-of-law excuse for government employees. Again, to understand how

Thompson would deal with *Barker* would take us a long way toward mapping this conceptually rugged terrain.

Unfortunately, I find it hard to construct or follow Thompson's position on these or the various other prescriptions that the structuralist analysis might be designed to inform. For one thing, the defect of the first part continues to dog us here: the failure to work out any specific and buttressing theory of criminal responsibility. And here, in the second part, that failure is compounded by another omission. Thompson needs to give us a fuller theory of government against which to judge why, or which, government wrongs warrant special treatment. That is to say: by virtue of what special organizational, financial, political accountability, or managerial characteristics are the special considerations derived? Indeed, one misses a theory thick enough even to enable us to decide what, exactly, he identifies as "government" for purposes of his analysis.

Just for a start, Thompson would do well to distinguish between governments at different levels. Some conceivable prosecutions would be *intra*governmental—for example, if the U.S. Department of Justice were to prosecute the CIA or the Public Health Service. In such a case, if the prosecution wins, one could depict the outcome as a mere shuffling of federal funds, an exercise in bookkeeping. To satisfy the fine, the federal government would write itself a check. Similarly, if a federal court, at the instigation of a federal prosecutor, were to decree a probation that reshaped a federal agency, then the separation of powers principle, as Thompson recognizes, would be bruised.[33] But there is a different theoretical tincture in *inter*governmental suits, as where the federal government fines a municipality, or arranges for a state agency—say, the prison system, or the state mental health hospitals—to be put under a sort of trusteeship. These *inter*governmental conflicts raise problems, too, but they are different problems: not those of filmflam bookkeeping, but those of federalism.[34]

Moreover, even if we restrict ourselves to analysis of *intra*governmental prosecutions, the compounded lack of theories—of punishment and of governments—leaves us listless. We are at a loss even to say where, for our purposes, public government leaves off and private begins. The Department of State is clearly government. But what about Comsat or Amtrak or an investor-owned but highly regulated public utility? The problem is pervasive, inasmuch as the line between public and private, never distinct, is becoming increasingly blurry. As governments get involved in many traditionally private lines of business, such as land development, railroading, insurance, and fuels production, are they still to be regarded, for Thompson's analysis, as government? Conversely, services that were traditionally provided by government servants are increasingly being made available from the private sector, sometimes as competitors (private mails, private rent-a-judge) and sometimes under government contract. In such cases, are the the service providers still to be regarded as private?

The answer might depend upon whether we draw the government-private line with reference to the predominant direction of accountability (to investors or to the electorate) or by reference to functions performed. But, again, I doubt that a satisfactory solution can be achieved without reference to *some* theory of punishment. That, I think, is the lesson of the other areas in which a blurring of public-private lines has been the source of major uncertainties in the law. Consider, for example, the question as it arises in the area of sovereign immunity for tort (is a private company under contract to provide governmental services entitled to claim the benefits of sovereign immunity?) and under state action (is a privately owned restaurant that leases space in a public parking structure obligated to abide by the restraints the Constitution places upon governments not to discriminate?).[35] In those cases, we approach a satisfactory solution by identifying the underlying principles—in the torts cases, of torts, and in the constitutional law cases, of the Constitution. So, too, here, where punishment is the question, we need revert to the principles of punishment.

Let me give some specific illustrations of how adrift I think we are, for lack of any theoretical rudder. Imagine a "private" for-profit corporation, chartered under the laws of California, whose entire revenue is derived from government contracts for the manufacture of vital components, on which it owns the patent, for a missile system. The company has fraudulently overbilled the Defense Department. The federal government is considering a criminal suit. We want to know whether, in Thompson's view, the company and its officers are a part of "government." If the dominant consideration is whether a prosecutorial victory would result in mere bookkeeping, a shuffling of tax dollars, there are strong grounds to characterize the defense contractor with the monopoly over the component as a part of government. On the other hand, if investor or electoral control over management is the key, the case is stronger (although still uncertain) that the contractor is private. Which consideration is to control, and why?

Consider, too, the status of public authorities and government corporations. Authorities are established by special act of government. They derive their operating funds not from government, however, but from the bond market in competition with private firms. Their officers are government appointees, but they often are appointed for terms that extend beyond that of the chief executive, and their deliberations are commonly buffered from political winds.[36] Indeed, it may be easier to remove the President of the United States—he can be voted out every four years, or even impeached—than the president of the Synfuels Corporation or of the New York Port Authority.[37] Are we to consider these mixed entities a part of government? If the dominant consideration for distinctive treatment of government derives from the existence of electoral control as an alternative, then the attenuation of electoral control over public authorities and public corporations raises a good argument that they are private—but I do not find this convincing, without more said.

It seems to me that whether we should alter our misconduct strategies when we shift attention to government from nongovernment bureaucracies (from the for-profit corporations, in particular), requires us to examine several possible bases for disparate treatment. These would include the following:[38]

1. The independent (nonliability) rules that prevail in each area. Each sort of corporation, governmental, for-profit, charitable, and so, operates subject to a set of independent rules that exercises strong influence on our choice of liability rule. Consider the implications of limited liability, which prevails among the for-profits but is not available to governments; civil servants often enjoy personal immunity, while their counterparts at for-profit corporations can generally secure indemnification more readily.

2. Since the institution is not imprisonable, threats to the entity are essentially money threats, thereby raising the question, do different sorts of entities (for-profit, governmental entities of various sorts, not-for-profits, and so on) manifest different sensitivities to the prospect of a fine?

3. What sorts of disciplinarian restrictions prevail as we move from area to area? For example, where civil service rules obtain, it is more difficult than it is in the private sector for the entity, however intimidated it may be by the prospect of a fine, to discipline, reprimand, or discharge errant agents, a factor that militates for proceeding directly against civil servant agents more readily than against corporate officers.

4. How are the incentives of the top managers tied to the financial status of the entities they direct? One might suppose that, to the extent managers of for-profit corporations are compensated through stock or stock options, their own welfare is a direct function of the worth of the company, even after they leave the company, assuming that they take a stock interest with them. For this reason, and others, congruence is probably less in the government sector than in the for-profit corporate sector, which would support direct actions against errant agents in the government sector, even where we might substitute anti-entity strategies in the private sector.

I think the reason Thompson feels excused not to carry out any such systematic comparison of organizational features, or, perhaps, why the need does not occur to him, is because, for Thompson, these are details that would not make a difference. He carries forward his predilection against entity liability on the same moral autonomy grounds as dominated his analysis of the general question of bureaucratic sanction, reviewed earlier. By and large, his concern is still largely that if we give these Frankenstein children the rod, next thing you know some writers will want to spoil them with moral autonomy, and then . . . whatever. I don't find the argument any more persuasive the second time through. Thompson himself winds up (or down) by suggesting the issue may be one of nomenclature: he allows that we might have to impose sanctions on government organizations, but says it would be to "misapprehend the moral and political foundations of criminal responsibility" to give it the name "punishment." [39] But this is exactly what we wanted to know.

What are the moral and political foundations of criminal responsibility, and what intelligible distinction is there between a criminal sanction and punishment?

Whatever one makes of Thompson's handling of entity liability in government, I regard the main thrust of his second part to be the treatment of agent liability in government. This I find quite imaginative, at least generally right, and certainly deserving of further attention. His idea is essentially this. First, he points out that government officials can do enormous harm not merely through such crimes as bribery, the prosecution of which presents no real theoretical problems, but from what he calls "supervisory negligence" as well,[40] particularly, I presume, in those activities where the government enjoys a specially significant, even monopoly position, such as in the inspection and certification of mines and potentially dangerous drugs and foodstuffs. Much of the literature concerned with these problems (in particular, Jerry Mashaw's work)[41] has wrestled with the option of civil liability for government employees for harms arising from this sort of official misconduct—from, on the one hand, improper certification, or, on the other, from delays and denials of certification that seem unwarranted, onerous, and unjustified. Thompson wants to go the advocates of extending civil liability one step further: why not criminalize it?

The stock response is that criminalization is too harsh. But Thompson has a comeback, that we ought not to assume that criminal liability is more onerous. Civil liability can expose officials to judgments of enormous, almost unlimited magnitude, while fines can be tailored to a manageable and, it is hoped, ideal level. Further, he points out that one of the defects of civil actions is that the class of people who could institute them (perhaps for harassment) is almost openended: any citizen who can claim injury within the constraints of standing rules. But if the wrongs are criminalized, only authorized prosecutors would be so empowered. The angle from which government employees might have to fend off attack becomes more acute.[42]

A commonly raised argument against civil servant liability of any sort is that it may result in overly cautious behavior—the overdeterrence argument. But Thompson reminds us that we have little empirical evidence to support this worry.[43] I would add in further support of Thompson a comparative point. If overdeterrence of a manager's discretion or authority is a concern for the law, it is a concern when dealing with a private-sector corporate manager no less than with a public official. That is, if we assume that the society is well-ordered in terms of how it has allocated various functions, one might presume that the marginal social product of an hour of the president of General Motors' time is equivalent to an hour of the Secretary of State's, and that therefore, something needs be said why overdeterrence operates, as a constraint, more objectionably in one sector than in the other.

My guess is that something much more than overdeterrence—something in need of a fairly fine-tuned political theory—underlies our readier acceptance of the argument in the public sector (somehow defined). In the for-profit sector, there at least exists a set of clear, positive rewards for the manager who can show an ability for reasonable, competent performance of his duties. The prospect of positive rewards counterbalances the disincentives for negligence and delay. For example, the officer of a pharmaceutical house, faced with the decision whether to subject a new product to additional testing, or to put it on the market at once, weighs the disincentives of lawsuits, should the drug cause harm, against the rewards of profits (and the presumption of social benefit that they carry), should it cure and save. This sets up a crude balancing that may, if doctored appropriately by the law, tend to assure that the pharmaceutical executives' incentives and disincentives play in tune with the social ideal. With highly visible elected officials, the positive rewards are clear enough: reelection, with prestige, power, and so on, exercise their influence. But as we go to lower levels, the civil servant in the Food and Drug Amdinistration is not in exactly the same position as his pharmaceutical company counterpart. One of the problems with achieving good government is that we lack a system of positive incentives that are quite so nicely discriminating. The incentives of the FDA official may already be skewed toward an exercise of excess caution from a social point of view. That is, one may well worry that faced with two alternatives: (1) expediting the processing of the drug application, with a 0.5 probability of saving a thousand lives, and (2) delaying for further testing, with a 0.5 probability of saving only a hundred lives, the official will incline to delay, even if the expected social benefit is less. He knows that if he expedites the license and the drug causes measurable injuries—creates another thalidomide scandal—he or his agency will be dragged before Congressional hearings, denounced in the press, and so on. If we add to the official's environment another downside risk—the prospect of a criminal prosecution—we could tilt the balance even further in the direction of excess caution. Perhaps excess caution is one of the very things Thompson wants criminalized. But is being overcautious really the sort of thing for which a judge can be expected to fine someone? Can such a crime be defined in any way that would not result in officials diverting resources into self-protective activity—covering themselves, making a good record—when they should be processing applications?

Anyone advocating increased criminalization of government servant activity must account for many other factors. For one thing, it is hard for the law to enter this field and not put its appearances of evenhandedness on the line. People in government—at least, in high government positions—are associated with political parties; typically, one of the major parties appoints and appears to have control over the prosecutors, at least in the public eye. The prosecutor prosecuting his own party would be considered too desultory; prosecuting a member of the other party, he may be thought engaged in a political vendetta. Our experience with special prosecutors suggests that it is an unwieldy vehicle, feasible, at best, only in very special situations. (A permanent special prosecutor presents some design anomalies.)

Second, as Thompson says, criminalizing the conduct of government employees would not necessarily discourage good people from serving. They might quite reasonably demand additional compensation to take their post under the hazard of being marked criminals, not merely for their deliberate acts but for acts over which they had minimal personal control. It does not seem unreasonable for citizens, in designing the rules for their agents (as we might conceive our government servants to be), to accept some risks of laxity in exchange for a slightly lower compensation. Ordinary investors do so in establishing their relations with their corporate agents: consider all the defenses shareholders allow directors to erect to charges of their negligence in office. How such a bargain is struck depends upon many factors, including, of course, the relative risk aversity of the parties. I should think that in general, to persuade a prospective public official to shoulder the prospect of a criminal fine for negligence would require higher compensation than it would be worth to the employing society, which is, after all, a spreader of its risks, viz., that the official might be derelict.[44]

None of these considerations undermines what I construe to be Thompson's basic claim: that we need to give more thought to agent criminal responsibility, particularly in government. On the other hand, if I found myself to be a structuralist on picking up Professor Thompson's paper, I might be dubbed an unreconstructed structuralist on putting it down. I like to think, though, that I am—we are all—considerably better prepared to understand the issues, the strengths and weaknesses of both sides, thanks to Professor Thompson's impressive contribution.

## NOTES

1. Thompson puts it, whether "individuals *can be* held criminally responsible" (italics added). I prefer to emphasize the normative aspect.
2. Thompson acknowledges that the nonreductionist position in moral discouse may be correct, but rightly observes that even if so, that does not conclude its status in law.
3. As Thompson need not be reminded. See Dennis F. Thompson, "Moral Responsibility of Public Officials: The Problem of Many Hands," *Amer. Pol. Science Rev.* 74 (1980): 905–916.
4. Thompson's illustrations are of the "inspector general" sort, which I interpret to be tokens of a broad class of measures I have analyzed under the heading of "interventionist" techniques. See Christopher D. Stone, "The Place of Enterprise Liability in the Control of Corporate Conduct," *Yale Law Journal* 90 (1980): 1–77.
5. I think there is in fact considerable concern among criminal law theorists as to the propriety of the sorts of extensions that Thompson urges, many of which, as he indicates, have been proposed for adoption under the proposed Federal Criminal Code. See Note, "Individual Liability of Agents for Corporate Crimes under the Proposed Federal Criminal Code," *Vanderbilt L. Rev.* 31 (1978): 965–1016.
6. Thompson under "The Problem of Moral Responsibility."
7. Brent Fisse has reminded me, however, that forewarning a person

that we will attach certain consequences to his actions is not a justification of our doing so. See Alan H. Goldman, "Towards a Theory of Punishment," *Law and Philosophy* 1 (1982): 57–76.

8. Observe, however, that Thompson also says, in the same breath, that the possibilities for carelessness are "so numerous"—which might make one sympathetic toward *reducing* the agents' liability.

9. See Stone, "Place of Enterprise Liability," pp. 47–56.

10. Ibid.

11. Thompson in introductory section.

12. It is worth observing, too, that in the not uncommon circumstances of the pollution illustration, if we assume no private party to have been recognizably damaged by the pollution, there will be no ordinary civil plaintiff to deter the polluter. As a consequence, the fining mechanism would have to carry the entire burden, unabetted by civil damages, of whatever modification in the corporation's behavior can be achieved through threats to the corporation's treasury.

13. But civil injunctive relief could equally well form the basis for a structural decree. This connects with the question for which I can find no adequate answer in the paper: why criminalize at all?

14. One might consider in this regard the proceedings of the International Military Tribunal (Nuremberg) in which certain Nazi organizations, including the SS, were declared criminal. See *Trial of the Major War Criminals before the International Military Tribunal*, vol. 1 (1947), pp. 255–275. There, however, the principal purpose seems to have been to allow the conviction of individual members of the organization without the defendant's right to question the criminal nature of the group or organization (see p. 255).

15. See Michael S. Moore, "The Moral and Metaphysical Sources of the Criminal Law," in this volume.

16. But see Brent Fisse, "The Social Policy of Corporate Criminal Responsibility," *Adelaide L. Rev.* 6 (1978): 361, 405–408, arguing for corporate punishment on a retribution basis.

17. Loose because this way of regarding retribution can be brought back under utilitarianism.

18. See Moore, "Moral and Metaphysical Sources of the Criminal Law."

19. There are even statutes that have been held to apply only to corporations and not to agents. See *Sherman* v. *United States* 282 U.S. 25 (1930), where the Safety Appliance Act was held to impose penalties only on common carriers, not officers.

20. Thompson under "Organizational Responsibility."

21. Ibid.

22. The logic that underlies Thompson's case is even more complex and perplexing than I indicate in the text. Is it the case that moral

rights pertain if and only if moral responsibilities do likewise? Some people would take the position that animals and fetuses have moral rights, even if they do not have moral responsibilities. Further, is Thompson implying that moral rights and responsibilities pertain (with respect to something) if and only if legal rights and responsibilities do likewise? I doubt that connection could be defended, descriptively or prescriptively.

23. See Frederick Hallis, "Introduction" to *Corporate Personality* (London: Oxford University Press, 1930).

24. Peter French, "The Corporation as a Moral Person," *American Philosophical Quarterly* 16 (1979): 207–15.

25. See Christopher D. Stone, "Corporate Accountability in Law and Morals," in O. Williams and J. Houck, eds., *The Judeo-Christian Vision and the Modern Corporation* (South Bend, Ind.: University of Notre Dame Press, 1982), pp. 264–291.

26. Thompson, in fact, makes a point somewhat like this. The more common point raised against the coindictment option is a more conscious abuse: that prosecutors may clear their docket by dropping the charges against the officers in exchange for their agreement to plead their corporation guilty.

27. See Comment, "The Criminal Responsibility of Corporate Officials for Pollution of the Environment," *Albany L. Rev.* 37 (1972): 61, 79–80, citing, among other cases, *The President Collidge,* 101 F.2d 638 (9th Cir. 1939) in which the defendant was convicted for employees having thrown garbage overboard (onto a habor patrol boatman whose job it was to apprehend refuse dumpers), even though the crew had been specifically ordered not to throw refuse overboard.

28. Compare *Old Monastery Co.* v. *United States,* 147 F.2d 905 (4th Cir. 1945), finding a corporation criminally responsible for its agents' acts, even in the face of evidence that the acts were to the corporation's detriment, if "within scope of agents authority or course of their employment," with *Standard Oil Co. of Texas* v. *United States,* 307 F.2d 120 (5th Cir. 1962), finding the corporation not liable for an employee's violation of a statute requiring "knowingly" as the basis of the offense, where the agents were acting in cooperation with a third person for the third person's benefit in a manner that may have involved some sort of "theft" of the employers' property.

29. For example, in the government discussion, below, much of what worries Thompson about criminal suits that derive from their being under government management applies equally to *civil* suits brought by the government.

30. Consider that statutes often provide for the alternative of civil or

criminal proceedings— the Sherman Antitrust Act, for example. What considerations militate for one route over the other?

31. *Nixon* v. *Fitzgerald,* 102 S.Ct. 2690 (1982), discussed by Thompson.

32. *United States* v. *Barker,* 546 F. 2d 940 (D.C Cir. 1976); compare the accompanying case, *United States* v. *Ehrlichman,* 546 F.29 910 (D.C. Cir. 1976), which rejects the U.S. President's assistant's claim to a national security exemption to Fourth Amendment requirements, at least in the absence of actual authorization by the President.

33. Thompson under "Organizational Responsiblity in Government."

34. My own efforts to examine this issue appear in Christopher D. Stone, "Corporate Vices and Corporate Virtues: Do Public-Private Distinctions Matter?" *U. Penn. L. Rev.* 130 (1982): 1441–1509.

35. See *Burton* v. *Wilmington Parking Association,* 365 U.S. 720 (1961) which holds the restaurant's discrimination to be a "state action" for purposes of the Fourteenth Amendment; see my discussion in Stone, "Corporate Vices and Corporate Virtues," pp. 1499–1500.

36. See Annmarie Walsh, *The Public's Business* (Cambridge, Mass.: M.I.T. Press, 1978).

37. For example, the chairman of the government's Synfuels Corporation serves for seven years, and is removable by the President only for neglect of duty or malfeasance, 42 U.S.C. §8712(b).

38. I have provided a more elaborate treatment of the issues I sketch out in the text in Christopher D. Stone, "Large Organizations and the Law at the Pass: Towards a General Theory of Compliance Strategy," *Wisconsin L. Rev.* 1981: 861–890.

39. Thompson under "Organizational Responsibility in Government."

40. Thompson under "The Problem of Political Responsibility."

41. See Jerry Mashaw, "Civil Liability of Government Officers: Property Rights and Official Accountability," *Law & Contemp. Probs.* 42 (Winter 1978): 8–34; Jerry Mashaw, *Bureaucratic Justice* (New Haven: Yale University Press, 1983).

42. Other considerations, however, such as the need to discipline government misconduct and the distrust of government-driven prosecutors, might lead one to prefer the angle to be more obtuse.

43. Thompson under "The Problem of Political Responsibility."

44. Opportunity costs, the lost production value as officials divert resources into self-protection, must be considered as well.

# 10

# THE LEGAL AND MORAL
RESPONSIBILITY OF ORGANIZATIONS

## SUSAN WOLF

Organizations in our society do many things that we, as members of the society, have both the reason and the right to try to stop. This is true of both public and private organizations, and not only of organizations as wholes but of individuals acting as bearers of specific organizational roles. The question thus arises, How ought we put a stop to these things, and, more particularly, how ought we use the legal system to put a stop to them? The question, though primarily pragmatic, has moral dimensions as well. That is, we want first to know what legal methods would be effective in deterring these activities without undermining significant social goals. But it is possible that an otherwise effective method would be morally impermissible, and it is possible that a method, though not particularly effective, would nonetheless be morally desirable simply as a public expression of severe disapproval.

I restrict my attention here to the moral dimensions of this issue, and particularly to those involved in determining whether

This essay is based upon a comment on Dennis Thompson's paper, "Criminal Responsibility in Government," presented at the twenty-seventh annual meeting of the American Society for Political and Legal Philosophy in Cincinnatti in January, 1983. I profited greatly from the comments of the participants of that conference, and from conversations with David Blumenfeld, Jean Blumenfeld, David Luban, Douglas MacLean, and Larry Thomas.

267

and how to use the criminal law in addition to or instead of the civil law in dealing with organizational acts that we have reason to deter. That moral dimensions are involved results from the fact that the criminal law may be understood to be different from the civil law in certain principled ways. The criminal law may be understood to have a closer, or, at any rate, a different relation to morality than the civil law. In particular, the criminal law may be associated with moral blameworthiness in a way that the civil law may not.

How seriously to take this principled distinction is a matter of some controversy. Indeed, some would deny the distinction altogether, though I shall have nothing to say of their position here. Holders of a more moderate position would point out that the distinction is only useful at a statistical level. Some elements of the criminal law cannot reasonably be associated with judgments of moral blameworthiness, and, much more commonly, elements of the civil law must be understood in moral terms. In this connection, it is often mentioned that most torts are such that one will not have committed them unless one is somehow at fault and that courts not uncommonly award punitive as well as compensatory damages in civil suits.

Although I do not wish to wax over the complications these remarks introduce—indeed, I shall focus explicitly on them later on—their force is not to erase the tendency to associate criminal liability with ascriptions of moral blame. Thus, a moral dimension remains in the choice of whether to use criminal or civil law to deter acts involving organizations in certain important ways. The most obvious and most central question we need to answer is, Are organizations ever morally blameworthy themselves or is the apparent blameworthiness of organizations always more properly regarded as a function of the blameworthiness of some or all the individuals in it? The question could be rephrased as, Are organizations full-fledged, irreducible moral agents?

A negative answer to this question may arise from considering that organizations are, after all, composed of individuals. There would be no Senate if there were no senators; there would be no team if there were no teammates. Moreover, it seems that as organizations are composed of individuals, organizational acts are composed of the acts of individuals. The Senate cannot approve a bill unless a majority of the senators approve it; the team cannot play well unless at least some of its members play well. Since an individual senator might vote against a bill that the Senate as a body approves and an individual player may excel even though the team as a whole plays miserably, it would not do to hold each member of an organization responsible for every organizational act. This takes nothing away from the view that whenever an organization is responsible for an action, one can always trace back the responsibility to *some* of the persons within it.

Let us call this view the Atomic View of Organizational Responsibility. According to this view, just as the actions of an organization are a function of the actions of the individual members, the responsibility of the organization is a function of the responsibility of the members. If an organization has done something for which it deserves blame, then some of its members have done things for which they deserve blame. If an organization has done something for which it deserves praise, then some of its members have done something for which they deserve praise. One may, on this view, speak of the organization as being, in some sense, a morally responsible agent, but one must bear in mind that the responsibility ascribed to the organization is wholly derivative.

One need not, however, be convinced by the considerations put forward in favor of the Atomic View. One may be struck by the fact that though an organization is composed of its members, an organization is not the same as the collection of its members. Senators and teammates may come and go, but the Senate and the Baltimore Orioles continue. Moreover, although an organizational act is composed of the acts of individual members, the organizational act may not be the same as the collection of individual acts. Though individual senators may vote for a law, only the Senate as a whole can pass one. Though individual players can play well on a given day, only the team can win the game. One might draw an analogy between the relation an organization has to its members and the relation a human being has to her muscles and neurons. That my actions are always composed of the actions of my muscles and neurons in no way implies that the responsibility for my actions does not lie fundamentally and irreducibly with me. Why should the fact that an organization's actions are always composed of the actions of its members persuade us that the responsibility for its actions does not rest fundamentally and irreducibly with it?

Let us call the view that organizations can be full-fledged irreducible moral agents the Organic View of Organizational Responsibility. According to this view, the moral responsibility of an organization is not reducible to the moral responsibility of each of its members. Organizations, like individuals, can be wholly or partly responsible for committing objectionable or commendable acts; and organizations, like individuals, can be wholly or partly—but, in any case, irreducibly—to blame or to praise for such acts. On this view, it is at least theoretically possible that an organization do something morally praiseworthy even though none of its members do anything praiseworthy; and it is at least theoretically possible that an organization do something morally blameworthy even though none of its members do anything blameworthy.

The support that has been given for the Organic View so far is weak at best. That an organizational act cannot be identified with the collection of acts that its members perform does not imply that the responsibility for that act cannot be identified with the responsibility of its members. Though it takes the Senate as a whole to enact a law, one or two senators may yet be responsible for its enactment. Though it takes the team as a whole to win the game, one or two players may yet deserve the credit for the win. For that matter, even if it is not one or two players but the whole team that deserves praise, what reason is there for thinking that praising the team as a whole is different from praising each and every player to an equal degree?

If the cases mentioned so far do not speak particularly in favor of the Organic View, however, there seem to be other cases that do. In some cases it seems clear that an organization has done something wrong even though it is not apparent that any of the members of the organization have done anything wrong. In other cases it seems clear that an organization has done something very wrong even though the members of the organization each seem to have done something only slightly wrong at worst. One is tempted to say in these cases that the wrongness of the organizational act is greater than the sum of the wrongness of each of its individually executed parts. It is best, I think, to suppress this temptation, with its intimations that moral wrongness can be quantified. But one can say, somewhat more intelligibly, that organizations as wholes may be responsible for their wrongful acts in ways that are neither reducible nor wholly dependent on the responsibilities their members may have for their contributions to these acts.

If the Organic View is correct, then we have reason to apply the criminal law directly to organizations as well as to individuals. According to the Organic View, organizations can be as guilty of crimes as individuals. Only if we apply the criminal law to organizations, then, do we have a chance of punishing the right parties. If, on the other hand, the Atomic View is correct, then there is reason not to use the criminal law against organizations as wholes. On this view, if any guilty parties are involved in an organizational act, they will be individual members or agents of the organization. They are the ones to be criminally prosecuted, not the organizations themselves.

In choosing between the Organic and the Atomic Views, even more is at stake than an answer to the question of whether to hold organizations criminally responsible. If we accept the Organic View, according organizations the status of full-fledged moral agents, we may be committed to granting organizations a kind of autonomy and a set of corresponding rights that would give organizations a frightening amount of power.[1] If, on the other hand, we accept the Atomic View, denying organizations moral status, then it would seem that we must exclude organizations not only from the scope of the criminal law but also from those portions of the civil law that are generally acknowledged to involve moral judgments. This would seem to imply that organizations not only could not commit crimes, but that they also could not commit many recognized torts, that they could not be legitimately ordered to pay punitive damages, and so forth. If organizations are exempted not only from the criminal law but from large sections of the civil law as well, then our hope of finding a method of stopping organizational crimes or bad acts seems very dim indeed.

Before addressing the problematic consequences of accepting one or the other of these views, however, we should try to choose between them. Perhaps the best way to do this is by examining a case of what seems, on the face of it, to be an obvious instance of organizational crime.

A baby food manufacturer markets a new line of pureed bananas that contains a preservative outlawed by the Food and Drug Administration. As a result, hundreds of babies become violently ill. At first, it may seem an easy matter to trace the responsibility and blame for this back to individual members of the company whose behavior contributed to the result. Someone had to buy the illegal preservative, after all, and someone had to decide to include it in the recipe, so presumably they are responsible and blameworthy for the epidemic. But suppose that at the time the preservative was purchased it was not illegal and that since the preservative was legal at the time of purchase, the label carried no warning to discourage the recipe designer from using it.

Well, one might think, there should have been a warning, or at any rate, the person who concocted the recipe should have known that the ingredient had been found to be dangerous since the time of its purchase. Surely, in a baby food company it is someone's job to see to it that all the ingredients are safe before a new product is released. Or, if not, surely it is someone's responsibility to assure that someone has that job, and so on. In any case, it seems that inquiry into the details of the company's structure will locate at least one and possibly several persons who deserve the ultimate blame.

But maybe not. For maybe, though there is someone whose job is to see that each of the ingredients in each of the recipes is safe, that person had checked the banana recipe before the damaging evidence about the preservative had been released. Or maybe the recipe-checker had learned of the new evidence and had sent a memorandum urging the company to stop production on the puree, but a failure of the information flow prevented its timely receipt by the relevant people. Perhaps there were people occupying various positions in the company about whom it can be said that had they devoted special attention to one or another aspect of this matter, the mistake could have been detected and the unfortunate result avoided. But the people in these positions might themselves have been subject to pressures, which themselves cannot be traced to individuals whose intentions were to produce those pressures, that led them to focus their attention elsewhere, on the vegetable line, for example, or the vitamin A content, or the need to provide better lighting in the labelling and bottling room.

Still, one might feel that the release of an unsafe type of baby food ought to have been prevented. The question of whether baby food meets existing health standards is, after all, so important that the company should have had double, even triple checks to ensure that no product is unsafe. The problem seems to be that though the company ought to have been prevented from putting this product on the market, there is no one in particular who ought to have prevented it.

As the blameworthiness of the individuals directly involved begins to be qualified or obscured, the attraction of the Organic View may seem to increase. The blame that one originally wanted wanted to assign to individual members of the corporate structure cannot, it seems, fairly be allocated to the individuals whose actions were involved. Should the "leftover" blame then be attributed to the organization directly, or should the blame be withdrawn and the case reassessed as an instance of non-moral forces just happening to produce regrettable results?

It speaks strongly in favor of the latter position that, unlike the former, it is at least clearly intelligible; the meaning of the former view is not at all obvious. The former alternative urges that if an organization does something wrong for which we cannot blame the individual members we should assign blame instead to the organization itself. But how can one blame an organization once one has excused all its past and present members? That there is, as the Lord Chancellor says, "no soul to damn, no body to kick"[2] would seem to indicate not just a practical difficulty but a conceptual one. When you have put all the members of an organization to one side, all you have left is a set of abstract relations, a structural scheme, a conceptual flow chart. How can a flow chart be guilty? It seems that either evil lurks in the hearts of men and women, or it lurks nowhere at all.

On the other hand, the suggestion that we simply conclude that no responsibility can be assigned for those bad organizational acts that cannot be attributed to the wrongdoings of morally responsible, and so blameworthy, individuals seems to impugn too quickly the sense of moral indignation we naturally feel. When a corporation puts a defective and dangerous product on the market or a government agency misleads us, there is a sense of moral indignation that needs to be accounted for even after we have convinced ourselves of the relative innocence of the individual agents involved. Of course, it does happen sometimes that things turn out badly even though it is not any responsible being's fault. The rain can spoil a picnic. A puppy can ruin a carpet. An earthquake or a herd of stampeding cattle can bring about disaster. But when an organization does something that leads to bad results, the suggestion that it is just one of those unfortunate things seems to ring false.

Upon reflection, I suspect that a part of the moral indignation we feel in these cases will fade and be replaced by a kind of moral sadness, directed not toward the organization but toward the individuals in it or society or even humanity at large. Part of what is morally disturbing about the cases I have in mind is that, even if none of the individuals directly involved did anything terribly wrong, neither did any of them do anything that was more than minimally right. Though it was no particular individual's responsibility to have taken this precaution or to have spoken out against that, that no one in the group took it upon himself to extend his efforts beyond the minimal limits of what was morally required bespeaks a generally low moral tone, a kind of moral stinginess on the part of the individuals in the group that we are apt to greet less with blame than with a kind of moral despair.

But not all our moral feelings need to be broken down or transformed into sentiments the appropriate objects of which must be individual human agents. Just as it is true of some of the individual members of the organization that they could have taken steps to prevent it from acting badly, it is true of the organization as a whole that it could have taken steps, and in this case succeeded in preventing the bad action. Of course, that the organization could have done otherwise depends on the individuals within it being able to do otherwise. Nonetheless, it is true that the organization could have prevented, or more simply, refrained from performing the bad action that it did perform. Moreover, it could have refrained from the bad action precisely on the grounds that it was a bad action. In other words, the organization could have subjected itself to recognizably moral constraints; it could have incorporated moral considerations and constraints into its decision-making procedure.

Since the organization *could have* chosen, on moral grounds, to do other than what it actually did, it is hard to deny the intelligibility of the claim that the organization *ought to have* so chosen. And since, *ex hypothesi*, what the organization actually did was morally bad, this claim seems not only intelligible but true.

The puzzling nature of this case arises because, on the one hand, the organization's *ability* to do other than what it did depends on the abilities of the individuals within it to do other than what they actually did. But the organization's *responsibility* to do other than what it did does not depend on the individuals' responsibilities to do anything at all. The situation facing us is one in which certain individuals could have taken steps to prevent the organization from doing a bad thing, but were under no obligation to take those steps. Yet the organization as a whole not only was able to prevent the bad thing, but also had an obligation to prevent it.

Are we to conclude then that organizations qua organizations are fully responsible moral agents after all? A moment ago this suggestion seemed incoherent. Ultimately I shall suggest a negative answer to this question, but I think that the implications of this answer are somewhat narrower than they are likely at first to seem. I think that although organizations are not irreducible moral agents, they are agents of another sort, with distinctive features sufficient to make them appropriate bearers of important kinds of *legal* responsibility.

To shed light on this matter, it will be best to turn attention away from organizations for a moment and look instead at the concept of responsibility, or, rather, at the word "responsibility" and at the different concepts to which it may variously refer. At least two senses of responsibility have often been noted, a causal sense and a moral sense. We use the causal sense when we remark that the cat is responsible for the spilt milk or that the weak girder is responsible for the collapse of the bridge. In these cases, we simply name a primary cause of an event or state of affairs. We use the moral sense, on the other hand, when the connection we make between agent and event is not merely causal. Rather, when we claim that an agent is morally responsible for an event or state of affairs, we claim that he or she deserves credit or discredit for what has taken place. Though there is a sense in which we can "blame" the spill on the cat or the bridge's collapse on the girder, there is a recognizable difference between this kind of blame and the kind we might be justified in feeling toward a rowdy teenager or a careless architect if the unfortunate events in question had been attributable to them instead. We may call the first kind of blame superficial, and the second, by contrast, deep. To claim that an agent is morally responsible is to claim that he or she is liable to deep blame or praise, that he or she is capable of being guilty or heroic, that he or she is capable of deserving credit or discredit for what he or she does.

Still a third sense of "responsibility" is of special interest for us. For lack of a better word, we may call it the practical sense of responsibility. We use the practical sense when our claim that an agent is responsible for an action is intended to announce that the agent assumes the risks associated with that action. In other words, the agent is considered the appropriate bearer of damages, should they result from the action, as well as the appropriate reaper of the action's possible benefits.

The practical sense of responsibility is easily confused with the moral sense, since it is easy to confuse damages with punishment and benefits with morally deserved rewards. But we can keep hold of the former distinction if we attend to the latter ones. For example, if while playing softball on a public playing field, I hit a ball that breaks the picture window of the house across the street, I may be regarded as responsible for breaking the window in the practical sense, the sense that implies that I should pay for the window. Still, it would be misleading to say that I am morally responsible for breaking the window, for though I did the damage, I did nothing wrong in playing softball on a public lot designed expressly for that purpose. I deserve no blame whatsoever for my action. Similarly, if I come across a small child who got lost in a crowd and return the child to the parents, it may be appropriate for the parents to reward me on the grounds that I was practically responsible for the child's safe return. But I hardly deserve moral credit for finding a child that I did not actively seek or for subsequently returning the child who, after all, is of no use to me. More dramatic cases in which practical and moral responsibility come apart are to be found by looking at situations in which we regard agents as practically responsible for actions that are not their own. If one's child breaks a neighbor's dish, one feels responsible in the practical sense even if one knows that one cannot reasonably be charged with negligence or the like. If a producer wants to use one's pet in a television commercial, it seems natural to expect the producer to offer to pay even though no performance of one's own takes place.

Even if one recognizes the difference between practical and moral responsibility, though, one might regard it as a relatively superficial distinction. At any rate, one may think that even though one cannot equate an agent's being practically responsible for a particular event with that agent's being morally responsible for that event, one can equate the agent's capacity for practical responsibility with his or her capacity for moral responsibility. One might think, in other words, that the conditions for responsible agency are the same whether one is using "responsibility" in the practical or in the moral sense. If this were so, the conceptual gap between the moral and practical senses of responsibility would be much smaller than the gap between either of these two senses and the causal sense. Clearly, earthquakes and viruses are capable of being causally responsible agents but not capable of being either morally or practically responsible.

Indeed, the assumption that moral and practical responsibility require the same type of agency is quite natural when one takes one's usual survey of causal agents, ranging from inanimate objects to dumb animals to babies to normal adult human beings, in search of the contrast between merely causal agents and agents of a more responsible sort. What the normal adult group has that all the other groups lack is the intellectual or cognitive capacity to be sensitive and responsive to complex reasons for and against various actions. This capacity is clearly a necessary condition of being either a morally or a practically responsible agent. One cannot hold an agent morally responsible for an action if the agent is incapable of recognizing what is morally wrong or right about it, and one cannot hold an agent practically responsible for something if the agent is incapable of seeing what consequences may come of it or of incorporating these expectations and possibilities into the decision procedure that gives rise to it.

Since the cognitive capacity to be sensitive and responsive to complex reasons for and against various actions is a necessary condition of both practical and moral responsibility, and since this capacity is sufficient to mark off one type of agent that is both practically and morally responsible from most other types of agent with which it is usually compared, one might leap to the conclusion that this necessary condition for moral and practical responsibility is a sufficient condition for these types of responsibility as well. If so, the conditions of agency required of a morally responsible being would be identical to the conditions required of a practically responsible one.

A consideration of sociopaths, however, might give one pause. Sociopaths, as I understand them, are fully capable of the same forms of practical reasoning as the rest of us. They are capable of recognizing that if they do things of which society disapproves, they are likely to suffer in various ways ranging from social exclusion or antagonism to fines or imprisonment. What they lack is a sense of inner disapproval that echoes the social disapproval of moral wrongs. That an action will hurt someone else gives them no direct reason not to perform it; that a statement is false gives them no direct reason not to convince others of its truth. Sociopaths, in other words, seem to lack ordinary human sympathy and respect. More generally, they lack whatever motivations most of us have to keep our actions within moral bounds.

It is hard to see how to describe these cases accurately. One might describe them by saying that although sociopaths can achieve an intellectual understanding that cheating, stealing, murdering, etc., are *considered* to be immoral, they cannot understand why they ought not to act in these ways. They cannot achieve an emotional understanding, so to speak, that evokes direct, internal disapproval. They lack consciences.

If this analysis is correct, then it seems inappropriate to regard sociopaths as wholly morally responsible agents. It seems wrong, in particular, to blame them, in the deep sense, for failing to constrain their behavior according to rules they are incapable of being motivated to obey. It does not seem similarly inappropriate, however, to regard these agents as practically responsible—to expect them to pay the consequences or bear the costs of their actions insofar as they can.

That sociopaths have the same intellectual capacities as other human beings, that they can foresee possible consequences of their actions and incorporate their foresight into their practical deliberations, that they therefore are able to assume the risks of their actions, seems sufficient for holding them practically responsible. The considerations above, however, suggest that this is not sufficient for moral responsibility. Moral responsibility seems to require not just intellectual capacities but certain emotional capacities as well.

We may now return to the question of whether organizations as wholes can be considered fully responsible moral agents. Drawing on the conclusions of the previous section, the answer appears to be No. For there it was concluded that a necessary condition of morally responsible agency is the possession of the emotional capacity to be moved by moral concerns. We did not delve into the fascinating question of what this emotional capacity amounts to, whether it can be identified with the capacity for sympathy, or the capacity for respect, whether the objects of the relevant feeling may be persons or the law, and so on. Whatever the relevant emotional capacity should, on analysis, turn out to be, we can be sure in advance that organizations do not have it. Organizations do not have *any* emotional capacities. They lack the unified consciousnesses necessary for feeling. To put it differently, organizations lack souls.

This may seem to fly in the face of the many cases in which it seems quite natural to describe organizations in psychological and moral terms. The various attitudes we have toward the Ku Klux Klan, Amnesty International, and Celestial Seasonings on the basis of their respective "personalities" cannot be simply dismissed as radically inappropriate reactions resulting from an irrational disposition to anthropomorphize. The policies and actions of these organizations to do merely seem to express values and goals, as a tree trunk or an inkblot might seem to represent a human face. Organizational policies and actions typically do express values and goals that are a result of conscious thought and intentional decision. Here, however, one must consider whose thought and decision are involved.

If organizations lack souls, their members, employees, stockholders, and so on, evidently do not. Although organizations as nonreducible wholes are not themselves morally responsible agents, the actions and effects of organizations result from the actions of agents who are. When we blame the Ku Klux Klan for its activities, we blame the members for choosing to band together to perform them. When we praise Amnesty International, we praise the founders, managers, and donors for their well-meaning contributions toward a fine goal. Or, to be more accurate, when we praise or blame an organization, we announce that *some* individuals connected with it deserve praise or blame. We often do not know anything about the internal structure of an organization the external effects of which evoke moral attitudes and sentiments in us. Not knowing who in the organization has contributed to the act that pleases or dismays us, we direct our praise or blame, gratitude, or resentment less precisely toward the organization as a whole.

The point is that if blame, resentment, contempt, or their happier analogues, praise, gratitude, and respect, are to prove ultimately justified, it must be the case that *some* individuals deserve them. If it should turn out, as it did in the baby food case, that no individuals deserve the attitudes that the organizational act or policy called forth, then we should withdraw these attitudes from the organization as well.

So far my position amounts to one more voice supporting the Atomic View of Organizational Responsibility. Organizations, as wholes, are not full-fledged morally responsible agents. Insofar as moral responsibility is legitimately attributed to organizations, the attribution is derivative and reducible to attributions of responsibility to individuals within it. The denial of morally responsible status to organizations, however, need not force us to the conclusion that organizations can be responsible only in a causal sense. For many purposes, we have less reason to care about whether organizations can be morally responsible, and so be appropriate bearers of deep praise and blame, than we have to care about whether they can be practically responsible, and therefore whether they can be held to assume the risks of possible costs.

Can organizations be practically responsible? The case of sociopaths suggests that some agents that are not morally responsible can yet be practically responsible. But organizations are not sociopaths, and it might seem that the same considerations that favored denying moral responsibility to organizations would also favor denying practical responsibility to them. Organizations lack unified consciousnesses, and it is because of this that they lack the emotional capacity necessary for morally responsible agency. One might think that, for the same reason, we must conclude that organizations also lack the intellectual capacity necessary for practically responsible agency. Surely, there is a sense in which just as organizations cannot feel, neither can they think.

But it is not clear that the capacity to think is, strictly speaking, a necessary condition of practical responsibility. What is necessary is the capacity to be sensitive and responsive to complex reasons for and against various actions and the capacity to foresee the possible consequences of one's actions. Although organizations are incapable of thought, they do have the capacity to be sensitive and responsive to all sorts of complex information *by way of* the thoughts and deliberations of the individuals involved in them.

Organizations can have goals, whether established by charter or vote or by some person in authority. Organizations are designed and persons within them trained in ways that are intended to lead to organizational decisions that realize these goals as efficiently and as far as possible. Importantly, organizational goals can be reexamined, rejected, revised, or retained. Such reevaluations can be built into the very structure of an organization, they can be established as a matter of policy, or they can be instigated by collections of individuals either within or without the organization. Moreover, there is no more reason why an organization's goals should be exclusively self-interested than there is for a person's goals to be. An organization's goals need not be restricted to profit or the good of its members or the organization's own self-preservation. An organization can be concerned about the good of the public or the quality of its product or the welfare of its employees. More generally, though also more vaguely, an organization can have as a goal that its actions remain within moral bounds.

It must be remembered that when an organization adopts a goal it is not because it is *moved* to adopt it, and that when an organizational decision is based on the expectation that a certain goal will be achieved, the organization cannot be said to have been motivated by a desire to achieve that goal. Organizational goals are not expressions of the felt concerns of the organization. Organizations, unlike persons, do not have felt concerns. They are not subject to motives or desires. Presumably, organizational goals and decisions usually reflect motives and concerns of persons who have occupied or do occupy organizational roles. But that is not to the point.

The point is that although organizations lack the capacity to be motivated to adopt moral goals and constraints, they have the capacity to be guided by them. Since they have this capacity, there seems no reason not to insist that they exercise it. That is, it is not unreasonable to hold organizations practically responsible, to insist that they act within moral constraints in the sense that they be liable for covering the costs and paying the consequences for the harmful and immoral actions they perform. If it should cross one's mind that it might be unfair to hold organizations practically responsible for harms for which they are not morally responsible, one should recall that an organization's lack of blameworthiness is not a sign of its moral innocence but rather of its exclusion from the dimension along which moral guilt or innocence is marked.

It seems that organizations as wholes are not capable of being morally responsible agents, but they are capable of being practically responsible ones.[3] It makes no sense to credit or blame an organization nonreducibly for good or bad behavior. Depending on the internal constitution of the organization, and its operations, there may be persons deserving of credit or blame or there may not. Often the internal structure and the allocation of credit and blame are of less importance than the external effects of the behavior in question. The more pressing concern is that the damage be paid for or the benefit secured, or that the activity cease or be repeated. Though the absence of emotional capacities excludes organizations from susceptibility to a kind of moral judgment, the presence of cognitive capacities (the capacities to be sensitive and responsive to complex reasons for and against various actions) makes them susceptible to externally imposed moral force.

The most obvious and probably the most effective way to exert moral force on organizations is to make and enforce appropriate laws. The final question to which we turn is whether the curious metaphysical status of organizations gives us any reason to regard certain types of law as more appropriate than others.

Since we began with the acknowledgment that the criminal law differs, by and large, from the civil law in its special and closer connection to the attribution of moral blame, the answer must surely be yes. Since organizations cannot be morally responsible agents, moral blame cannot be appropriately attributed to them, and if negative judgments in the criminal law carry a presumption of moral blame, then there is at least a symbolic reason not to apply the criminal law to organizations. We do not want our legal judgments to express or suggest false moral judgments, and although this is only one reason against which other more pragmatic reasons may be balanced, it is a significant consideration against applying the criminal law to organizations as wholes.

Early on, however, it was also noted that large portions of the civil law are often said to presuppose the morally responsible status of their subjects. If we are to be barred on philosophic grounds from applying not only the criminal law but also these portions of the civil law against organizations as such, then our efforts to keep organizational activity within morally acceptable bounds have almost no chance of success.

When we look again at those portions of the civil law to which we earlier referred, though, it is not obvious that we ought to be barred on philosophic grounds against applying them to organizations. It seems quite appropriate to regard organizations as capable of being at fault in the sense required for torts of negligence and it seems quite appropriate for organizations to be asked to pay not just compensatory but punitive damages in certain kinds of civil suit.

Of course, that they *seem* appropriate may reflect a misguided tendency on our part to anthropomorphize organizations. But a different interpretation is available that reflects less poorly on ourselves—namely, that the alleged moral elements in the civil law are not of a piece with the moral elements in the criminal law. Being at fault in tort law need not be indicative of having done something morally blameworthy, but only of having engaged in an activity for which one has assumed the risk of certain harms. Having to pay punitive damages in a civil suit need not be interpreted as an expression of society's moral condemnation; rather, it may be regarded as a predictable consequence of having committed an act that society has reason to prevent and which cannot be adequately deterred by compensatory damages alone. To be a fit subject of the judgment of fault all it takes is the ability to assume the risk; to be a fit subject of punitive damages all it takes is the ability to respond to the expectation of having to pay a very large fine. To have these abilities involves the exercise of the cognitive capacities of moral agents. But as long as these judgments are not essentially or explicitly associated with pronouncements of moral blameworthiness, being a fit subject of these judgments does not require any emotional capacities at all.

That it should have seemed for so long that the aspects of civil law discussed here were essentially associated with pronouncements of moral blameworthiness—that, at any rate, these aspects of civil law should have seemed as infused with morality as most criminal law, is not, however, wholly surprising. When an agent who possesses the cognitive capacity required to be a fit subject of these laws possesses in addition the emotional capacity that is a condition of liability to moral blame, it may well be that in a large majority of cases the agent who is civilly liable is also morally liable. That is, it may be that if an agent possessing both the relevant cognitive and emotional capacities is justly held to be at fault in the sense required for committing a tort, or if the agent is justly required to pay punitive damages in a civil suit, then, in the large majority of cases, it is likely that the agent has done something deserving of moral blame.

Though there cannot have been a logical connection between these civil law judgments and moral blame, then, there may well have been (and continue to be) an empirical connection. And empirical connections are often hard to distinguish from logical ones until empirical exceptions are brought to light that serve as counterexamples to the logical claim. What was needed in this case was an exception to the law that what has the cognitive capacity necessary to be a practically responsible agent must also have the emotional capacity necessary to be a morally responsible agent. Excluding the difficult and controversial case of sociopaths, and leaving computers aside (which in any case are not yet so advanced as to be able in an irreducible and nonderivative sense to commit torts), organizations are the only type of agent that I know of that can serve as such exceptions. It is not surprising, then, that the logical distinction between being a fit subject for the criminal law and being a fit subject for those parts of the civil law that appear particularly morally tinged should not become evident until the degree to which organizational activity shapes our lives and the danger of organizational crime should have increased to the point of demanding our urgent attention.

Indeed, the empirical connection between the capacity to be practically responsible and the capacity to be morally responsible may also account for the combination of our recognition that organizations are not morally responsible in a nonreducible sense, on the one hand, with the persistent tendency to feel indignation toward organizations as such, on the other. When we learn that an organization has done something dreadful, some coherent and justifiable thoughts apply to the organization directly—e.g., that the organization ought not to have been allowed to have done that or that it would be legitimate to apply force to prevent that sort of behavior. Ordinarily, the legitimacy of applying external moral force to a cognitively competent agent goes hand in hand with the appropriateness of blaming the agent for failing to govern her action appropriately even in the absence of such force. Ordinarily, those features of the unwonted behavior that justify us, from the outside, in constraining the agent's activities are features that should also provide reasons to the agent, on the inside, for constraining her behavior on her own. Organizations are peculiar in being agents with the cognitive capacity to recognize such features but, because they lack the relevant kind of "inside," they cannot be blamed for failing to be moved to respond to these features on their own.

If my analysis is sound, then it will be wholly appropriate to subject organizations to the requirements of civil law, including at least some portions of civil law that generally appear to be infused with moral judgment. It will also be appropriate to subject persons acting within and on behalf of organizations to the requirements of the criminal law, insofar as they knowingly and significantly contribute to acts that violate moral and legal bounds. But it will be inappropriate to apply the criminal law to organizations directly. As long as the criminal law continues to include among its functions the expression of moral blame, the application of criminal law should be restricted to persons and other beings that have, not just cognitive capacities, but souls.


## NOTES

1. For a good discussion of this, see Dennis Thompson, "Criminal Responsibility in Government," in this volume.
2. Edward, first Baron Thurlow (1731–1806), quoted in John C. Coffee, Jr., " 'No Soul to Damn; No Body to Kick': An Unscandalized Inquiry into the Problem of Corporate Punishment," *Michigan Law Review* 79 (1981): 386–433.
3. For an excellent discussion of a view that is in many respects similar to mine, see John Ladd, "Morality and the Ideal of Rationality in Formal Organizations," *The Monist* 54 (1970).

# PART IV

# THE ECONOMIC THEORY
# OF CRIMINAL LAW

# 11

# ON THE ECONOMIC THEORY OF CRIME

## ALVIN K. KLEVORICK

## 1. INTRODUCTION

At the end of his interesting and important article, "Crime and Punishment: An Economic Approach," published in 1968, Gary Becker characterized his efforts at developing an "economic" framework for analyzing illegal behavior "as a resurrection, modernization, and thereby I hope improvement" on the pioneering efforts of Cesare Beccaria and Jeremy Bentham during the eighteenth and nineteenth centuries.[1] Becker hoped, at least implicitly, to give new life and direction to cost-benefit analysis of public policy toward crime. In this effort he surely succeeded, as the fifteen years since his seminal article ap-

This chapter is a revised version of a paper prepared for presentation at the January 1983 meeting of the American Society for Political and Legal Philosophy in Cincinnati. I would like to thank Bruce Ackerman, Guido Calabresi, Owen Fiss, Joseph Goldstein, Geoffrey Hazard, Reinier Kraakman, Rick Levin, George Loewenstein, Jerry Mashaw, A. Mitchell Polinsky, Rob Prichard, Peter Schuck, Stan Wheeler, Kenneth Wolpin, and the Legal Studies Seminar at the University of Pennsylvania Law School for helpful discussions and for their comments on an earlier draft of this chapter. I am also grateful for the helpful research assistance of Jon Pedersen. In revising the paper, I benefited greatly from the discussion at the meeting and especially from the extremely thoughtful comments of the commentators Jules Coleman and Stephen Schulhofer. These people, of course, bear no responsibility for any faults that remain.

peared have seen the development of a substantial literature on the economics of crime and punishment.

Nevertheless, there is a perception, among people in law and economics, that except for the highly controversial empirical work on the deterrent effect of the death penalty, the economists' literature on crime has not entered the mainstream of legal scholarship.[2] This work seems to have remained a literature that is principally of interest to economists rather than to legal scholars, lawyers, and criminologists. In this respect, work on the economics of crime stands in contrast to, for example, the work economists have done on tort law, which has genuinely engaged the interest of torts scholars and teachers.[3]

In this chapter, I wish to suggest that the economists' literature on crime manifests an incompleteness and also a lack of connection among its various strands. Both of these features of the body of work identified as "the economic theory of crime" have restricted the impact that economists' contributions have had in this area. Moreover, these problems reflect an inherent limitation of any economic theory of crime: any such theory must depend on, and simultaneously be confined by, a set of political and legal presuppositions. Furthermore, I believe that an understanding of this intrinsic constraint on the economists' approach to crime will make possible a better appreciation of the kinds of contributions and the scope of the contributions economists can make in this area. Strengths sometimes appear more clearly when inherent limitations are recognized.

## 2. The Structure of the Literature

I shall frame the discussion in a general description of the work that has been done on the economic theory of crime.[4] My intent is to describe the contours of the landscape or the topography of this vast literature rather than to provide a thorough survey or critical review of it. This literature is comprised of three distinguishable strands. I shall discuss each of these strands in turn and draw out the relations among them as I proceed.

### A. *The Individual's Decision About Criminal Activity*

The first branch of this literature applies the microeconomic theory of choice under uncertainty to the decision process of the individual criminal. For the most part, this set of papers views the potential criminal as a rational actor who balances the costs and benefits, uncertain as they are, of his possible actions and allocates his time to legal and illegal activities accordingly.[5] These models analyze the choice of whether or not to commit a criminal act with its potential gain and its potential cost in the form of punishment, where the probability of winning or losing the gamble is determined by law-enforcement agencies' success in catching, convicting, and punishing criminal actors. The literature also models the potential criminal's "labor allocation" between legitimate and illegitimate activities. The kinds of results that emerge take the standard form of the economist's comparative static conclusions about how changes in one or more parameters—for example, the probability and severity of punishment—affect the actor's choice. The perspective emphasized by the models is that the potential criminal responds, as others do, in a rational way to the incentives provided by the environment in which he operates.

In some analytical studies of individual criminal behavior the authors are attentive to the (perhaps) problematic nature of the assumptions about rationality and information concerning the risks presented by the criminal justice system. For example, Philip Cook suggests bringing to bear the literature on bounded rationality[6] and rules of thumb or "standing decisions" in analyses of criminal behavior. Cook also treats in greater detail how the threats that the criminal justice system poses for the criminal are communicated to the actor through the media, the visible presence of enforcers (for example, police), and personal experience and observation.[7] Other analyses of the criminal's choice process[8] emphasize the importance of nonpecuniary aspects of the criminal's decision. They show, for example, the problems with postulating that monetary equivalents of some forms of punishment exist and the assumptions that one must make in deriving such equivalents. They also note that because illegal activity is time-consuming, the criminal's decision must take into account effects on things other than wealth. These considerations lead these authors to focus on labor allocation models that take account of both pecuniary and nonpecuniary characteristics of the potential outcomes that the criminal faces. Finally, some students of individual participation in criminal activity are attentive to the organizational or market environment within which individual decisions are made. Particular examples include Susan Rose-Ackerman's work on corruption[9] and Peter Reuter's work on organized crime.[10]

## B. Criminal Justice Policy

While some of the literature on the economic t..eory of crime focuses on cost-benefit calculations of individuals—the potential criminals—a second strand is concerned with cost-benefit analysis at the social level. Research on the latter, with Becker's 1968 article being the first formal treatment and still the most prominent example, views "optimal policies to combat illegal behavior [as] part of an optimal allocation of resources."[11] Here the tools of economic analysis are applied to derive results about the socially optimal ways to enforce the criminal law. The principal focus of such policy analysis has been on the choice of the optimal probability of punishment and the optimal type and severity of punishment.[12] It is assumed, in these models, that the type and severity of punishment can be set directly while the probability of punishment is determined indirectly by society's expenditures on police, courts, and other law enforcement resources.[13]

Of course, characterization of an optimal set of policies presupposes a function to be optimized. In his 1968 article, Becker introduced as the minimand a general social loss function whose arguments were the damages from offenses, the costs of apprehending and convicting offenders, and the social cost of punishments. For the most part, however, his analysis proceeded with a less general formulation of society's objective function. Specifically, Becker took the social goal to be minimization of the total social loss in real income from offenses, convictions, and punishments. At some points in the analysis, though, he did introduce generalizations—for example, an additional term in the loss function to recognize the social loss due to "*ex post* 'price discrimination' between offenses that are not and those that are cleared by punishment."[14] That is, he recognized explicitly that society may incur an additional loss if two individuals who commit the same crime are, in the end, treated differently, with one being punished while the other is not.

Other writers have generalized the social loss function in a variety of ways. John Harris[15] introduced a term for the social loss from wrongful punishment. Then in their 1977 contribution, Roy Carr-Hill and Nicholas Stern[16] suggested incorporating retributive considerations—specifically, departures from the "retributionist target" punishment—in the term measuring the net social cost of punishment in Becker's social loss function. But in his 1978 paper, "On the Economic Theory of Policy Towards Crime," Stern withdrew the suggestion. He continued to argue for the importance of retribution as a determinant of punishment levels but indicated that it would not be "particularly helpful" to "amalgamate different criteria on modes of conduct into a grand social loss function."[17] Mitchell Polinsky and Steven Shavell in specifying the social loss function in their 1979 article took explicit account of the attitudes toward risk of those who engaged in activities for which they might be apprehended and fined.[18] Finally, Isaac Ehrlich[19] examined the implications of introducing three alternative elements into Becker's social loss function. They were terms representing equality under the law, avoidance of legal error, and retribution. These features correspond to suggestions that others had previously made—including Becker himself, Harris, and Carr-Hill and Stern—but Ehrlich's analysis of the consequences of introducing them is more thorough and complete.

All of these variants of the social loss function share one striking feature. The term representing the net cost or damage to society is, in each case, taken to be the difference between the harm to society *and* the social value of the gain to offenders. That is, the utility of the offender is counted in the social welfare function. Indeed, in two of the more elegant and sophisticated analyses in this literature, by Polinsky and Shavell,[20] the social welfare function to be maximized is the sum of the expected utilities of the individual members of the society. This seems plausible in their 1979 article where the analysis focuses on fines—both civil and criminal—and the heuristic example is double parking. The aggregation seems more questionable in their latest contribution, "The Optimal Use of Fines and Imprisonment," where the harms involved are obviously severe enough for imprisonment to be contemplated as a punishment.

To be sure, this apparent anomaly in the social loss function has been noted before. George Stigler, in a paper stimulated by Becker's "Crime and Punishment: An Economic Approach," and following closely in time upon the publication of that work, made the same observation. He wrote that:

> Becker introduces . . . the "social value of the gain to offenders" from the offense. The determination of this social value is not explained, and one is entitled to doubt its usefulness as an explanatory concept: what evidence is there that society sets a positive value upon the utility derived from a murder, rape, or arson? In fact the society has branded the utility derived from such activities as illicit.[21]

The subsequent literature has never taken serious account of this point. It is an issue to which I shall return below, though I will not resolve the question of exactly whose gains and losses or whose preferences should be counted in the social welfare function that is optimized.

The nexus between the first two strands of the economic analysis of crime is a close one. The models of individual behavior yield predictions about the supply of offenses by individuals. These individual supply functions are aggregated to derive a market supply function—also known as a deterrence function—that relates the total number of offenses to the probability and severity of punishment. This deterrence function is at the heart of the policy model that is used to obtain conclusions about optimal strategies to combat illegal behavior.

Moreover, Becker's model and the theoretical work that followed it have emphasized the two-way interaction between criminal activity and the policies adopted by law enforcement authorities. The latter affect the number of offenses at the same time as the level and effects of criminal activity affect the choice of values for the policy instruments—the probability and severity of punishment. In technical terms, criminal activity and criminal justice system activity are simultaneously determined. This has clear implications for empirical efforts to estimate the deterrence function, that is, the responsiveness of offenses to policy variables. Because of the interdependence between crime and punishment, simultaneous-equations estimating techniques ought to be used if one hopes to unravel the deterrence effects.

## C. *The Existence of the Criminal Category*

The close ties and mutual enrichment that exist between the work on economic theories of individual criminal behavior and the research on economic theories of the criminal justice system stand in sharp contrast to the lack of communication between the social cost-benefit analysis and the third strand in the economics literature on crime. This last enterprise, to which little effort has been devoted, draws upon economic analysis to explain the existence of the criminal category. It maintains that economic analysis can help to explain why we distinguish a set of acts that we call crimes—why we have the criminal law at all. The two principal (perhaps only) contributions to this part of the literature on the economic theory of crime are by Guido Calabresi and Douglas Melamed in "Property Rules, Liability Rules, and Inalienability: One View of the Cathedral"[22] and by Richard Posner in *Economic Analysis of Law*.[23]

Calabresi and Melamed use the framework developed in their article to consider the use of criminal sanctions in cases of theft and violations of bodily integrity. They do not believe that problems of detection and apprehension, which render the probability of apprehension less than one, explain fully why we "charge"[24] people who commit these acts more than the value of what they take. They argue instead that even if every such offender were caught, "the penalty we would wish to impose would be greater than the objective damages."[25] The explanation, Calabresi and Melamed suggest, "lies in a consideration of the difference between property entitlements and liability entitlements. For us to charge the thief with a penalty equal to an objectively determined value of the property stolen would be to convert all property rule entitlements into liability rule entitlements."[26] But they demonstrated earlier in their paper that economic efficiency considerations, distributional goals, and "other justice reasons" would lead a collectivity not to employ only liability rules to protect entitlements. Instead, as Calabresi and Melamed persuasively argue, the state will employ a mixture of property rules, liability rules, and inalienability rules.[27] Consequently, from the perspective of their analysis,

> The thief not only harms the victim, he undermines rules and distinctions of significance beyond the specific case. . . . Since in the majority of cases we cannot be sure of the economic efficiency of the transfer by theft, we must add to each case an undefinable kicker which represents society's need to keep all property rules from being changed at will into liability rules.[28]

Of course, the need for the "undefinable kicker" applies as well to each violation of bodily integrity.

The basic distinction that Calabresi and Melamed draw between the criminal who robs or violates another person's bodily integrity *and* the injurer in an automobile accident or a polluter in a nuisance case is that the criminal resorts to nonmarket transactions when the costs of market transactions are low, while the driver and the polluter find themselves engaged in nonmarket rather than market transactions when the latter are too costly. Posner's analysis is similar except for the singularly important fact that, within his scheme, the sole reason for preferring one form of transaction to another—in Calabresi-Melamed terms, one mode of entitlement protection to another—is economic efficiency, as Posner defines it. For Posner, the only desideratum in social policy is value maximization: the distributional goals that form an integral part of the Calabresi-Melamed framework, and the "other justice" reasons they discuss, receive no weight in his analysis.

For Posner, "A 'crime' is simply an act that subjects the perpetrator to a distinctive form of punishment that is meted out in a distinctive kind of proceeding," where the unlawfulness of the act derives from "the policy of some other body of law—the tort law, in the case of 'the common law crimes' . . . and various laws regulating business and personal behavior, in the case of . . . statutory crimes."[29] Under this approach, "the criminal sanction is simply a method of pricing conduct"[30] and "The function of the criminal law—is to impose additional costs on unlawful conduct where the conventional damages remedy alone would be insufficient to limit that conduct to the efficient level."[31]

Posner, like Calabresi and Melamed, shows how a probability of punishment that is less than one should lead to a punishment that exceeds the damages caused by the criminal. But he also makes the stronger point that although a sanction in which the expected punishment cost is equal to the damage to the victim is "adequate where the crime in question is simply the violation of a regulatory statute,"[32] a heavier penalty is required in other situations. Specifically, "if the law's purpose in prohibiting the act in question was to channel activity into the market, i.e. the arena of voluntary transacting,"[33] then an expected punishment in excess of the damage inflicted is needed to induce the perpetrator to substitute a voluntary transaction for a coercive one. When market alternatives are available, the expected punishment for a violation would be set equal to "the sum of (1) the social costs of the violation and (2) the additional costs to the legal system of substituting coercive transactions for market transactions."[34]

Although Posner is not explicit on this point, it is consistent with his argument that the "additional costs" under item 2 would include the Calabresi-Melamed "kicker." Of course, where there is no market alternative—Posner offers the example of "a driver who violates the speed limit because the opportunity costs of his time are very high"[35]—the penalty should be large enough to reflect the hazards the criminal creates, subsumed in his item 1, but there would be no add-on designed to induce substitution of a market for a legal transaction.

3. IMPLICATIONS OF ECONOMIC EXPLANATIONS OF THE CRIMINAL CATEGORY FOR THE ECONOMIC THEORY OF CRIMINAL JUSTICE POLICY

This third, relatively undeveloped, strand of work on the economic theory of crime has several important implications for research on the economic theory of policy toward crime. First, it suggests that economists' theoretical work on cost-benefit analysis of public policy toward criminal activity is best viewed as a partial equilibrium approach. The insights offered by economic theories of the criminal justice system are conditional, for those theories take as given the set of acts or activities that are designated as crimes. The results in what I have labelled the second strand of the literature on the economic theory of crime tell us how to allocate resources to apprehension and conviction, on the one hand, and to punishment, on the other, *once* the crimes have been identified. A full, unconditional theory of the criminal justice system—a general equilibrium approach, if you will—would take a more global perspective. It might have Posner's wealth measure, or an appropriate amalgam of the Calabresi-Melamed desiderata, or yet another measure as the criterion to be optimized. The full "solution" would then yield the set of actions that are optimally to be designated as crimes *as well as* the optimal probability and severity of punishment for each crime.

For example, suppose one accepted Becker's measure of the total social loss in real income as the relevant quantity of concern (and the economic theory of the criminal category speaks to this issue as well). Then one can imagine solving the problem that Becker posed for each of the possible configurations of the criminal/noncriminal division of activities. What I have referred to as the full or general equilibrium solution would then be the categorization of activities and the associated set of probability of punishment/severity of punishment values that yielded the minimum minimorum of the Beckerian social loss function.

Of course, to observe that Becker and those who followed him in developing economic models of policy toward crime delimited the scope of the problem they analyzed is not to diminish their contribution. Nor is it to say that they claimed more for their analyses than they ought to have. In particular, Becker himself was quite clear about the confines of his model. But the partial character of these models does suggest difficulties for one who would seek to develop a complete economic theory of crime. Suppose that the objective function of the broader problem, in which one determines the optimal partition of acts into criminal and noncriminal categories as well as the optimal severity and probability of punishment for each of the criminal acts, is not confined to economic values—as, for instance, Posner would seemingly restrict it, but Calabresi and Melamed would not. Then the explanation of, or the derivation of results about, the criminal justice system could not be fully economic in character.

A second important point of contact between the Calabresi-Melamed and Posner contributions, which explain the use of the criminal sanction, and the resource allocation problem that Becker and others have addressed, concerns the function that relates the net cost or damage to society to the number of offenses. This function, which is central to the overall objective function in Becker's and others' analyses of public policy toward crime, is intended to measure the damage or net cost that society sustains as the result of the offenses that occur. But it is difficult to see how one can assess the social damages from offenses unless one has a theory of the criminal category. The thrust of the Calabresi-Melamed and Posner analyses is that an act is classified as criminal precisely because the harm it does to society exceeds the conventional measure of damages. To specify the social loss function in a Beckerian analysis, one must assess the costs of these additional harms and be sure that they are appropriately reckoned in the analysis.

In particular, the socially disapproved nature of the criminal's act, as Calabresi-Melamed and Posner explain its disfavored status, raises serious questions about the appropriateness of subtracting the criminal's gain from the harm that his act does to the rest of society. A theory or an explanation of why certain acts are labelled criminal that provides reasons for objecting to the particular action may also provide reasons for discounting the criminal's gain. Alternatively, since Becker was careful, though others have not been, to say that what ought to be subtracted is the "social value of the gain to offenders," the explanation of the criminal category provides a means to—indeed the explanation is required to—assess that "social value."

Once again, I do not wish to suggest that Becker was not clear about the scope of his analysis; on the contrary, he was precise in drawing the lines around what he did. As he wrote,

> Reasonable men will often differ on the amount of damages or benefits caused by different activities. . . . These differences are basic to the development and implementation of public policy but have been excluded from my inquiry. I assume consensus on damages and benefits and simply try to work out rules for an optimal implementation of this consensus.[36]

His analysis is fine, then, as far as it goes.

The difficulty, however, is that by setting aside issues of how social losses are assessed and by not having a theory of the criminal category to inform that reckoning, Becker's analysis is subject to characterizations that make it unattractive and seemingly unhelpful to legal scholars concerned with criminal law. And the characterization is one that Becker himself uses, not one that is provided as a caricature by a critic. Specifically, he writes, "criminal activities are an important subset of the class of activities that cause diseconomies, with the level of criminal activities measured by the number of offenses."[37] In further characterizing his analysis, he says

> Our analysis of crime is a generalization of the economist's analysis of external harm or diseconomies. Analytically, the generalization consists in introducing costs of apprehension and conviction, which make the probability of apprehension and conviction an important decision variable, and in treating punishment by imprisonment and other methods as well as by monetary payments. A crime is apparently not so different analytically from any other activity that produces external harm and when crimes are punishable by fines, the analytical differences virtually vanish.[38]

The criminal's actions surely have "external effects." But it is difficult to see a student of criminal law vigorously pursuing an approach to crime and punishment that self-consciously characterizes itself as a branch of the theory of external diseconomies, albeit one that extends that theory by introducing costs of apprehension and conviction and by taking account of nonmonetary penalties. Legal scholars will find such an approach even less inviting if they recall the fundamental contribution of Ronald Coase in clarifying the *reciprocal* nature of externalities and his criticism of the view that one party *causes* the harm in an externality situation.[39]

The absence of explicit concern for the origin of the criminal category affects other analyses of public policy toward crime as well. For example, in Polinsky and Shavell's 1982 article, implications for the use of fines and imprisonment are drawn from a truly classical model of external diseconomies. The basic activity that "causes" external harm is socially beneficial and the social welfare function, which is at the heart of the analysis, is the sum of the expected utilities of all the members of the community.[40] The results that Polinsky and Shavell derive are interesting and important for policy settings where both monetary and nonmonetary penalties can be used to control an activity that yields social benefits but also results in harm to others. One can think of many such examples—analyses of public policy toward automobile accidents or pollution are two instances—but the economic literature on the existence of the criminal category suggests that policy about criminal activity is not among them.

## 4. THE INHERENT LIMITATION OF ANY ECONOMIC THEORY OF CRIME

The efforts to use economic analysis to explain why some acts are distinguished as crimes have yet another and more fundamental implication about the kinds of insights economists, or the use of economic analysis, can provide about criminal law. The implication might be viewed by some as negative because it points to an inherent limitation of the economist's approach. But it seems, to me at least, that recognizing this boundary is not in any way depreciatory. Rather, it is to recognize that although economics *can* indeed contribute to our understanding of criminal behavior and optimal enforcement policy, it cannot provide a full or complete economic theory of crime. The work of economists in this area must be informed by work in other disciplines.

What, then, is this implication? It is that although an explanation of the criminal category can be *stated* in economic terms, that vocabulary and mode of analysis does not, in fact, provide the substantive understanding we seek. To see this, it is helpful to frame more generally the answers offered by Calabresi and Melamed and by Posner.

Society (or the collectivity or the state) establishes a "transaction structure" that stipulates the terms on which particular transactions or exchanges are to take place under different circumstances. For example, society might determine that if you and I are walking down the street, having no contact with one another, and you desire my watch, then you are permitted to have it if, but only if, we agree to a voluntary exchange of my watch for something you have (or promise to deliver, etc.). Society might also say that if the circumstances are different—for example, as you pedal your motorized bicycle down the sidewalk you knock me over and my watch is destroyed—you are permitted to "have" my watch but you must pay a collectively set value for it. In Calabresi-Melamed terminology, the first situation corresponds to protecting my entitlement to my watch by a property rule, while in the second setting it is protected only by a liability rule. In Posner's terms, the former exchange, if consummated, would be a market transaction while the latter would be a nonmarket transaction.

As to some possible exchanges, society might impose an absolute bar. In many societies (it is at least stated that) you cannot buy my vote in the sense that you cannot pay me a certain amount of money in exchange for the capacity to cast my ballot in my place. In many societies, an individual cannot sell himself into bondage. This last form of regulating transactions corresponds to what Calabresi and Melamed refer to as protecting my entitlement to my vote and my freedom from bondage with an inalienability rule.

The reason I introduce yet another layer of economics vocabulary, with the term "transaction structure," is to help us to move beyond the Calabresi-Melamed and Posner characterizations of crime. For Calabresi and Melamed, the imposition of the criminal sanction and the characterization of particular acts as crimes derives from a need to keep property rules and inalienability rules from being "changed at will" into liability rules; for Posner, it derives from a desire to induce individuals to substitute voluntary transactions with one another for coercive ones when the former are possible at low enough cost.

Note, however, that a society that imposes the criminal sanction on individuals who engage in the selling and buying of votes makes it a crime to change an inalienability rule into a property rule or in Posner's terms, to substitute a market for a nonmarket transaction. One can also imagine a society in which it is determined that all decisions about pollution should be made in a collective setting, that is, in which all entitlements to be free from pollution are protected by liability rules. Such a society might well apply the criminal sanction to parties who engage in a market transaction in which the polluter "buys off" the pollutees. Similarly, a criminal sanction might be applied to an employer who hires workers at a (mutually agreeable) wage below the legislatively mandated minimum or to a seller who sells goods (to willing consumers) for more than or less than a legislatively set price. A society that would make each of these last two actions a crime would do so because a liability-rule protection had been converted into a property-rule protection.

In each instance, the act that is characterized as a crime involves the actor(s) forcing society to deal with a transaction in a way in which society did not want to treat it. What makes the act a crime is that the individual assaults the transaction structure that has been established by society.[41] One could say, alternatively, that the individual coerces *society* into considering and coping with an exchange or transaction in a way that differs from the mode society had chosen. Finally, one might characterize the criminal as arrogating to himself the power or the authority to determine at least a part of the societal transaction structure, that is, appropriating to himself a power or right that society had reserved to itself. The criminal sanction is then a sanction to enforce the transaction structure that society has chosen as well as to compensate for the harms to individuals within the society.[42]

But, then, an explanation of the criminal category—even an explanation stated in economic terms—requires answers to questions and elaboration of concepts that economic analysis is not particularly well-suited to provide.[43] The point is not that the language describing the grounds for invoking the criminal sanction—for calling an act a crime—is not drawn from economics. One can, after all, describe the reasons in terms that are much less evocative and less clearly located in another discipline than are the terms "assault," "coercion," and "arrogation of power." For example, one could simply say that the criminal acts contrary to the transaction structure society has established.[44] But the critical observation is that the explication of why some acts are crimes while other are not requires an inquiry into the legitimation of the transaction structure. It forces one to confront questions like: Why does the collectivity have the right to decide the terms on which particular transactions will take place under different circumstances? Why do some rights reside in the individual while others rest with the state?

To be sure, one can propose a unified, and unitary, economic basis for determining what acts are categorized as crimes and what probability and severity of punishment is associated with each criminal act. If one posits that wealth maximization[45] is the sole criterion by which social arrangements are to be evaluated, the objective function in Becker's partial equilibrium approach to criminal justice policy, which sets only the probabilities of punishment and the penalties, will be consistent with the global problem in which the categorization of acts is determined as well. Indeed, determination of the optimal probability and severity of punishment will be a subordinated part of the larger problem. In the solution to the global problem, it will emerge that inefficient substitutions of nonmarket transactions for market exchanges are subjected to the criminal sanction, and that probabilities and severities of punishment are chosen to minimize the reduction in society's wealth. But even such a theory necessarily invokes certain political presuppositions—to wit, that society has a right to choose a structure that strives to maximize wealth and that individuals do not have the right to resist that choice. Such a theory does not answer the question: Why is the chosen transaction structure legitimate? And an answer to that question is a necessary component of an explanation of why some acts are treated as crimes.

In sum, to give a coherent explanation of the criminal category, as I have couched it in economic terms, one needs at least a political theory of rights. Undertaking a microeconomic analysis of crime requires as a precondition a certain minimum of political and legal structure.

## NOTES

1. Gary S. Becker, "Crime and Punishment: An Economic Approach," *J. Pol. Econ.* 76 (1968): 169, 209.
2. See, for example, the survey by Henry Hansmann, "The Current State of Law-and-Economics Scholarship," *J.L.E.* 33 (1983): 217.
3. This is not to say that economists' writings on crime have had no influence on the way criminal law scholars think about their subject. It would have been difficult, after all, for the outpouring of economists' work on the subject to have been ignored. But the insights about crime that lawyers have drawn from the work of economists have been specialized and fragmented. The economic theory of crime has not taken on anything like the salience of the economic approach to torts, which has been accepted as one of the

competing paradigms that torts scholars use in analyzing their subject. In torts, a scholar may reject the economic approach but must reckon with it. This is not the case with the economic theory of crime.

4. In keeping with the focus of this volume on theories of criminal justice, I restrict my discussion to economists' theoretical work on crime. The vast body of empirical work that has been informed by that theory and that has, in turn, influenced theoretical developments lies outside the purview of this chapter. An interesting set of empirical papers on the economics of crime is collected in J.M. Heineke, ed., *Economic Models of Criminal Behavior* (Amsterdam: North-Holland, 1978), and a useful assessment of empirical work on the subject is provided by Philip J. Cook, "Research in Criminal Deterrence: Laying the Groundwork for the Second Decade," in Norval Morris and Michael Tonry, eds., *Crime and Justice: An Annual Review of Research,* vol. 2 (Chicago: The University of Chicago Press, 1980) p. 211.

5. See Becker, "Crime and Punishment," Michael K. Block and John M. Heineke, "A Labor Theoretic Analysis of the Criminal Choice," *Am. Econ. Rev.* 65 (1975): 314; Isaac Ehrlich, "Participation in Illegitimate Activities: A Theoretical and Empirical Investigation," *J. Pol. Econ.* 81 (1973): 68; John M. Heineke, "Economic Models of Criminal Behavior: An Overview," in *Economic Models of Criminal Behavior,* volume 1.

6. See Cook, "Research in Criminal Deterrence," p. 220. For the classic discussion of bounded rationality, see Herbert A. Simon, *Models of Man* (New York: John Wiley, 1957).

7. Philip J. Cook, "A Unified Treatment of Deterrence, Incapacitation, and Rehabilitation: A Simulation Study" (Durham, N.C.: Institute of Policy Sciences and Public Affairs, Duke University, 1979).

8. See Block and Heineke, "Labor Theoretic Analysis of the Criminal Choice;" Michael K. Block and Robert C. Lind, "Crime and Punishment Reconsidered," *J. L. Stud.* 4 (1975): 241; Michael K. Block and Robert C. Lind, "An Economic Analysis of Crimes Punishable by Imprisonment," *J. L. Stud.* 4 (1975): 479; Heineke, "Economic Models of Criminal Behavior."

9. Susan Rose-Ackerman, *Corruption: A Study in Political Economy* (New York: Academic Press, 1978).

10. Peter Reuter, *Disorganized Crime: The Economics of the Visible Hand* (Cambridge: MIT Press, 1983).

11. Becker, "Crime and Punishment," p. 209.

12. A related interesting literature, which can be viewed as an outgrowth of the early social cost-benefit analysis of public policy toward crime, concerns the comparative advantages of private ver-

sus public enforcement of the law. The principal works are Gary S. Becker and George J. Stigler, "Law Enforcement, Malfeasance, and Compensation of Enforcers," *J. L. Stud.* 3 (1974): 1; William M. Landes and Richard A. Posner, "The Private Enforcement of Law," *J. L. Stud.* 4 (1975): 1; and A. Mitchell Polinsky, "Private versus Public Enforcement of Fines," *J. L. Stud.* 9 (1980): 105. Their analyses rely heavily on Becker's seminal article and its progeny, in particular, on the results concerning the optimal probability and optimal severity of punishment. These analyses of the relative efficacy of private and public enforcement apply to legal commands generally and not to criminal law alone.

13. In reality, the type and severity of punishment are also set only indirectly. There may be legislative directives about sentences or fines, for example, but there is usually at least a residual element of judicial discretion in setting punishments.

14. Becker, "Crime and Punishment," p. 184.

15. John R. Harris, "On the Economics of Law and Order," *J. Pol Econ.* 78 (1970): 165.

16. Roy A. Carr-Hill and Nicholas H. Stern, "Theory and Estimation in Models of Crime and Its Social Control and Their Relations to Concepts of Social Output," in Martin S. Feldstein and Robert P. Inman, eds., *The Economics of Public Services* 116 (London: Macmillan, 1977).

17. Nicholas H. Stern, "On the Economic Theory of Policy Towards Crime," in Heineke, ed., *Economic Models of Criminal Behavior* 123, p. 148.

18. A. Mitchell Polinsky and Steven Shavell, "The Optimal Tradeoff Between the Probability and Magnitude of Fines," *Am. Econ. Rev.* 69 (1979): 880.

19. Isaac Ehrlich, "The Optimum Enforcement of Law and the Concept of Justice: A Positive Analysis," *Int. R. L. & Econ.* 2 (1982): 3.

20. Polinsky and Shavell, "The Optimal Tradeoff," and A. Mitchell Polinsky and Steven Shavell, "The Optimal Use of Fines and Imprisonment," *J. Pub. Econ.* (forthcoming).

21. George J. Stigler, "The Optimum Enforcement of Laws," *J. Pol. Econ.* 78 (1970): 526, 527.

22. Guido Calabresi and A. Douglas Melamed, "Property Rules, Liability Rules, and Inalienability: One View of the Cathedral," *Harv. L. Rev.* 88 (1972): 1089, 1124–1127.

23. Richard A. Posner, *Economic Analysis of Law*, 2d ed. (Boston: Little, Brown, 1977), pp. 163–172.

24. The "charge" to which Calabresi and Melamed refer includes whatever monetary and nonmonetary penalties are imposed on the

criminal. There is no assumption that the payment, if it is a fine, is used to make restitution to the victim.

25. Calabresi and Melamed, "Property Rules, Liability Rules, and Inalienability," p. 1125.

26. Ibid.

27. I will discuss the substance of each of these rules in greater detail below.

28. Calabresi and Melamed, "Property Rules, Liability Rules, and Inalienability," p. 1126.

29. Posner, *Economic Analysis of Law,* p. 163.

30. Ibid., p. 172.

31. Ibid., pp. 163–4.

32. Ibid., p. 165.

33. Ibid.

34. Ibid., p. 166.

35. Ibid.

36. Becker, "Crime and Punishment," p. 209.

37. Ibid., p. 173.

38. Ibid., p. 201.

39. In his classic article about externalities, "The Problem of Social Cost," *J. L. & Econ.* 3 (1960): 1, Ronald Coase considers, in particular, "those actions of business firms which have harmful effects on others . . . [as] a factory the smoke from which has harmful effects on those occupying neighbouring properties" (p. 1). He begins the body of his argument as follows:

### The Reciprocal Nature of the Problem

The traditional approach has tended to obscure the nature of the choice that has to be made. The question is commonly thought of as one in which A inflicts harm on B and what has to be decided is: how should we restrain A? But this is wrong. We are dealing with a problem of a reciprocal nature. To avoid the harm to B would inflict harm on A. The real question that has to be decided is: should A be allowed to harm B or should B be allowed to harm A? The problem is to avoid the more serious harm . . . (p. 2).

40. Polinsky and Shavell, "The Optimal Tradeoff," p. 21. In addition, "it is assumed that each individual is equally likely to be the victim of someone else's harm" (ibid.). This latter assumption, which is made for reasons of analytical tractability, is common in other areas of law and economics, too, for example, the analysis of alternative

liability rules in torts. Whether or not the assumption is plausible in the accident context, it calls for careful scrutiny in a model analyzing law enforcement policy. It is clear that all the results in the Polinsky and Shavell contribution are robust to some relaxation of the assumption as, for example, if different individuals can have different exogenously given probabilities of suffering harm. How the results would be altered if one went further and had the probability of suffering harm depend on whether or not one engaged in the harm-engendering activity is another matter. The conclusions about (1) the optimal punishment—be it a fine or imprisonment—when only one type of punishment is used and when there is only one wealth class and (2) the desirability of using fines to the maximum feasible extent before imposing nonmonetary penalties, do not depend on the exogeneity of the probability of being harmed. But when the likelihood of being harmed is endogenously determined, some of Polinsky and Shavell's statements about underdeterrence and overdeterrence and some of their results for the two-class model may require modification.

41. In the case of theft, the criminal not only challenges the way in which society has chosen to protect an entitlement but also overturns the placement of the entitlement itself.

42. Those harms include the damages due to violation of what Calabresi and Melamed call moralisms. See Calabresi and Melamed, "Property Rules, Liability Rules, and Inalienability," pp. 1111–2. The compensation is "paid" to society. As noted before (see note 24), there is no assumption that monetary payments, if there are any, are used to make restitution to victims.

43. Economists have, for example, never shed much light on the concept of coercion, despite the fact that the term is often invoked. Some speak of the coercion involved in governmental intervention in the market while others speak of the coercion of the market itself.

44. An interesting issue, but one that I do not address here, is whether all crimes can be usefully described as acts that are contrary to the chosen transaction structure. For example, can one, without straining language, describe the act of perjury by saying that the perjuror forces society to deal with a transaction in a way that society did not want to treat it? If all acts that we characterize as criminal cannot be described in this language—or, more generally, using the vocabulary of economics—then it is clear that the scope of an economic theory of crime is necessarily limited. My discussion applies only to those crimes that the economic theory of the criminal category purports to explain.

45. For the purpose of this discussion, I assume *arguendo* that wealth

maximization can be given a clear, substantive, and commonly agreed upon definition. That providing such a definition is not a straightforward task is attested to by the pages of controversy about it in the law-and-economics literature. The point that follows applies if, for example, one takes as the criterion the maximization of the total value of all goods and services the society produces where quantities are valued at the equilibrium prices, or if one substitutes utilitarianism for wealth maximization.

# 12

## COMMENT ON "ON THE ECONOMIC THEORY OF CRIME"

### RICHARD A. POSNER

The question Professor Klevorick poses at the outset of his paper is why the economic analysis of crime,[1] unlike the economic analysis of torts, has not entered into the mainstream of lawyers' thinking. The question is a somewhat surprising one for an economist to put, as it is a question about the sociology of legal education and practice rather than about economic analysis. But Professor Klevorick's answer is more surprising. It is that the economic analysis of crime is incomplete; it presupposes a political theory that (by implication) is not yet in place. This is a surprising answer, because most people think the economic analysis of tort law is also incomplete and in just the same sense—that it presupposes a political theory that has not yet been developed. If tort law decides that the farmer shall have to bear the costs of damage from locomotive sparks—that he has no "right" to prevent the railroad from causing such damage—it is making the same kind of judgment that it makes when it says that a woman does have a property right in her body, i.e., that rape is a crime.

While it would be very nice to have a complete economic theory of any field of law, it is hardly a prerequisite for entering the mainstream of legal theory. There is a much simpler answer to Professor Klevorick's question. It is that there has been very little applied work on the economics of criminal law—very little attempt, that is to say, to apply the theory to the specific legal doctrines taught in a criminal law class or deployed in a judicial opinion in a criminal appeal. You are not entitled to expect economic originality from judges or practicing lawyers. The lead must be taken by Professor Klevorick and his law school colleagues.

I should add that I think the incompleteness that Professor Klevorick observes in the economic analysis of criminal law is of a rather peripheral character. The crime of buying votes or slaves is not likely to be in the forefront of attention either in a course on criminal law or in the practice of criminal law. While the prohibitions against paying workers less than the minimum wage are important, I believe they are rarely enforced by criminal sanctions. Some victimless crimes that Professor Klevorick does not mention, notably trafficking in narcotics, are very important, and raise questions for an economist because what is being punished are voluntary, and hence presumptively welfare-enhancing, transactions. But most such crimes are made so by legislation rather than by the common law; few economists believe any more that the characteristic product of legislation is welfare-enhancing in an economic sense. Most of the common law crimes are, as the economic analysts claim, attempts to bypass the market in settings of low transaction costs—theft in its myriad forms being the best example. Though in principle, as Professor Klevorick points out, the victim rather than the aggressor might be the "cheaper cost avoider," in Calabresi's terminology, it appears that the market-bypassing acts that have been made criminal are primarily those where the victim is never (or very rarely) the cheapest cost avoider. Other harmful acts are more likely to be governed by tort law, with its concepts of assumption of risk and contributory negligence that facilitate comparing the costs to potential injurer and to potential victim of avoiding injury.[2]

The problem with the economic analysis of criminal law is not that it is incomplete or lacks rigorous philosophical foundations, though it is and does, but that the economic analysts have yet to tackle the principal concepts that trouble legal analysts of the field—such concepts as attempt, conspiracy, diminished responsibility, provocation, insanity, strict criminal liability, recklessness, compulsion or necessity, and premeditation. Moreover, although I do not know whether Professor Klevorick would regard criminal procedure as a separate field (his citation of the Harris article and Isaac Ehrlich's work on capital punishment suggests he would not), the procedural aspects of criminal law are much more important in the practice of law than the substantive aspects. Yet apart from the debate over the deterrent effect of capital punishment, there has been very little economic analysis of criminal procedure, though a recent article by Professor Frank Easterbrook suggests that there are many promising applications of economics to criminal procedure.[3]

The economic analysis of criminal law is indeed full of promise. It offers exciting research opportunities for academic economists interested in law and academic lawyers interested in economics. It would be a shame to defer this research pending the development of a political theory of rights that commands wide agreement.

## NOTES

1. For a brief and already rather outdated summary, see Richard A. Posner, *Economic Analysis of Law,* 2d ed., (Boston: Little, Brown, 1977), chap. 7. For an up-to-date bibliography see C.G. Veljanovski, *The New Law-and-Economics: A Research Review* (1982), pp. 83–87. Veljanovski mingles substantive criminal law and criminal procedure; I shall hold them separate till the end of this comment.
2. Professor William Landes and I have discussed this distinction in the context of intentional torts (many of which are also crimes). See William M. Landes and Richard A. Posner, "An Economic Theory of Intentional Torts," *Int 'l. Rev. L. & Econ.,* (1981): 127.
3. Frank H. Easterbrook, "Criminal Procedure as a Market System," *J. Legal Stud.* 12 (1983): 289. See also Posner, Economic Analysis of Law, chap. 21.

# 13

# CRIME, KICKERS, AND TRANSACTION STRUCTURES

## JULES L. COLEMAN

These remarks are occasioned by Alvin Klevorick's very thoughtful chapter "On the Economic Theory of Crime" in this volume.[1] The economic approach to law, Klevorick notes, has had a far wider and deeper impact on areas of the private law—especially torts, contracts, and property—than it has on the criminal law. The reason: economic analysis simply fails (or has failed so far) to elucidate central features of the criminal law. In some ways, Klevorick's chapter attempts to identify the weak link in the chain of economic reasoning about crime. Klevorick does not stop at identifying what he takes to be the problem; he offers a tentative solution to it. In the end, however, he finds even aspects of his solution wanting and gives an all too brief, but provocative, explanation of why *all* economic theories of the criminal law are likely to prove unsatisfying.

Just where is the weakness in the economic theory of crime? We can begin by considering where the economic analysis of crime has proven most fruitful. In general, economists have done well at setting optimal penalties for criminal conduct and at determining how much of a community's resources ought to be spent on enforcing criminal prohibitions. In both endeavors, the economist takes as given that a certain aspect or category of conduct has been designated criminal. In the first instance he

313

wants to determine just how much punishment is necessary to reduce to an efficient level conduct that has been independently identified as criminal. In doing so, the economist relies on basic models of individual rational choice, usually under conditions of uncertainty. The criminal is a rational utility maximizer deciding, among other things, whether or not to engage in criminal activity. The economist's concern: given that the probability of apprehension is less than one, just what penalty is necessary to induce the rational criminal to a life beyond reproach—or at least to one more or less in confromity with the dictates of the criminal law.

It would be nice if we could impose sanctions on criminal mischief such that the actor's expected marginal cost of engaging in criminality was set equal to his expected marginal gain so that each criminal would have no good reason for preferring criminal activity to a noncriminal alternative. The problem is that most communities cannot afford the expenditures necessary to eliminate crime entirely. So a community must determine just how much of its resources to devote to the criminal justice system. To the economist, this concern translates into the question: what is the optimal use of resources in controlling crime? The answer depends on a number of variables. For example, suppose a community wanted to put a virtual end to jaywalking but did not want overly to tax its resource base to do so. Instead of employing resources to increase the rate of detection, it might simply impose a very heavy sanction on jaywalking. If we assume that potential jaywalkers are risk-neutral, then they have just as much reason to avoid a $1,000 fine they are unlikely to incur as they have to avoid a $10 fine they are 100 times more likely to get.[2] The likelihood of being apprehended and sentenced is a partial function of the amount of money the community is prepared to spend on detecting and convicting jaywalkers. So a reduction in expenditures may call for an increase in the weight of the sanction. But then sanctions for those apprehended and sentenced are unlikely to "fit" the offence, and thereby to depart from the requirement that the penalty fit the crime. This departure from the ideal is for the economist a "cost"—the cost of injustice—which, however, is *not* to say that it ought not be reckoned with. Moreover, as the "price" of an offence increases, the social cost of a mistake in judgment increases. It is one thing to impose a $5 fine mistakenly, another to impose a life sentence. And as the level of expenditure drops, the likelihood of mistakes increases, thus further increasing the expected social costs of punishment. Economists concerned about the allocation of resources to the criminal justice system are concerned primarily with determining the costs and benefits of various allocation decisions in the light of the kinds of factors I have just mentioned. Again, however, part of the fruitfulness of these efforts is due to the fact that the allocation decision—the decision about how much crime is permissible—presupposes an independently defined category of criminal conduct.

According to Klevorick—and he is surely right—economic analysis has proven least fruitful in explaining the very existence of a criminal category. What economic reasons, if any, do we have for making certain conduct criminal? Put another way: there is an economic theory of undesirable actions—acts whose costs (however conceived) outweigh their benefits (however conceived). These are actions economists think ought to be curtailed, limited, or, in some cases, if the costs of doing so are not too high, eliminated entirely. Any number of mechanisms for reducing the incidence of socially undesirable activity are worth exploring. We might counsel against mischief; or we might implore, cajole, persuade, plead with, even beg doers of dastardly deeds to forebear. We can ostracize and morally brandish. Or we can tax, impose tort liability, or criminalize. Why do we ever criminalize? Why do we set out a category of conduct, designate it as criminal, and thereby subject violators to a particular kind of sanction? Is there a particularly economic argument for our doing so?

Here is one way in which economists have thought about the need for a criminal prohibition against certain activities. Suppose A harms B. Now what? Should we prevent future As from harming future Bs, by giving B the right not to be harmed; or should we put future Bs on notice that the losses shall lie where they have fallen by giving A the right to harm B. To the economist this is a perfectly serious question that is not easily answered. Suppose in harming B, A causes B $10 worth of damage, but by doing so he secures $1,000 gain. Were we to prohibit A from harming B, B would gain $10 and A would lose $1,000.

This seems hardly the rational thing to do, for few of us would forego a $1,000 gain to avoid a $10 loss. This suggests we should not prevent A from harming B. But it seems equally wrong to give A license to harm B whenever it is to his, A's, advantage to do so. At this point perhaps you are inclined to say the difference between the original example and the rationality of an individual's decision not to forego a large gain to avoid a small loss is that in the former case we are dealing with two persons, not one, each of whom's autonomy must be respected. In that case, the economist has a suggestion that should satisfy you. Why not give B the right not to be harmed by A, but permit A to buy from B the right to harm him. Then A will harm B, but will do so at a mutually agreed upon price. In effect, what we have done is decide both that B has a right not to be harmed by A, and that A has a right to harm B as long as he secures B's consent. In terminology that has been widely accepted by economists since the publication of the famous Calabresi-Melamed paper,[3] we have assigned the right to B not to be harmed and protected it by a *property rule*.

We could have assigned B the right not to be harmed by A and secured it in a different way, that is, by a *liability rule*. In that case, B would have a right that A not harm him, but A would nevertheless be free to harm B anyway, provided he paid B compensation *ex post* for whatever damage his harmful conduct occasioned. Under the property rule scheme, A and B must reach an agreement *ex ante* before A can harm B (act contrary to B's right). Under the liability rule scheme, A need secure no agreement with B. He may act as he deems fit provided he is prepared to render B compensation *ex post*.[4]

In the traditional economic analysis, the point of assigning and protecting rights according to various options is to encourage individuals to engage in activities at their efficient levels. For example, suppose B has a right protected by a property rule that A not harm him. In our example, it would be inefficient for A not to harm B, since by not harming B there is a net loss of $990 (a foregone opportunity cost of $1,000 minus a savings of $10). The efficient result of A harming B is secured through a market transaction required by the property rule at B's disposal. Sometimes efficient outcomes cannot be secured if rights are protected by property rules. There are two straightforward cases to consider. In one, the costs of negotiations are high. If the costs of negotiations exceeds the difference in the value of the right to A and B, then no transfer will occur. So if it costs A and B $991 to reach agreement *ex ante,* A would have to incur $1001 in cost for something he values at $1000. Where negotiations are costly, it is sometimes necessary to substitute liability rules for property rules, since the former do not require *ex ante* agreements. The standard example is automobile accident law. Think how difficult it would be to track down all the individuals you might put at risk by your driving, let alone to negotiate with them.

The second sort of inefficiency in property rules arises from strategic behavior. If B knows that the value to A of harming him is $1,000, then he is unlikely to settle for $10. If A knows that the value of B's damages is $10, he is likely to press for an agreement that gives B not much more than that. We have in these negotiations a bargaining game: a mixed game—mixed because it involves a redistributive and a productive element. A possible $990 of surplus exists to distribute provided agreement can be reached. Agreement to *distribute* the surplus (the redistributive element) is necessary and sufficient to *produce* it (the productive element). If A or B holds out for a share of the gains from trade that is unacceptable to the other, no transfer will occur and the outcome will be inefficient. Once again, to avoid the pitfalls of negotiations, liability rules may be substituted for property rules.

We can follow a slightly different, but no less standard line of economic argument to reach the same point in the overall argument. Most behavior has external effects, called "externalities." The cost of externalities can either lie where they have fallen—on victims—or be shifted to those whose conduct occasions them—injurers. Economists believe that shifting of losses provides a powerful mechanism for inducing efficient behavior. For example, one way of inducing efficiency by shifting losses is to impose liability on the party whose conduct causes the externality. This process is called "internalizing externalities;" its effect is to force the injurer to take the social costs of his conduct into account. Ronald Coase's important article, "The Problem of Social Cost,"[5] may be read as demonstrating that certain conditions support a market solution to the problem of externalities. In other words, externalities may be internalized by private negotiations as well as by the imposition of liability. Roughly, the Coasian approach corresponds to the Calabresi-Melamed property rule approach. In both cases inefficiencies are eliminated in standard market ways. When the market approach is unavailable because transaction costs are high or the threat of strategic behavior is substantial, the liability rule approach is appropriately substituted. The purpose of the liability rule is to "mimic" the market solution, that is, produce the efficient result the costless market would have.

Now what does all this have to do with crime? Why criminalize when a perfectly good property rule/liability rule structure for responding to right violations or to other wrongful conduct is available? In the classical economic theory, the criminal law is seen as a way to induce individuals to comply with the relevant rules of transfer, that is, to adhere to the property rule/liability rule distinction, or to pursue market solutions to externality problems where they are available and feasible.

In order to explore one way in which economic analysis tries to tie the criminal law to the property rule/liability rule distinction, consider the situation where no market solution to an externality exists. Then the liability rule method seems in order. It differs from the property rule approach not only in terms of *ex ante* vs. *ex post* perspectives, but also because liability rules raise the problem of detection. If someone has to buy B's right from him, he reveals his identity to us through negotiations. But it anyone, including A, can simply injure B at will, then he has an incentive to avoid detection, since whether or not he has to render B compensation depends on his being "caught." The probability of detection is less than 1.0. Therefore, in order to induce efficiency, the penalty imposed upon the injurer must exceed the actual damages he causes. The actual damages he pays represents the tort or liability rule remedy. The additional penalty necessary to induce compliance (because detection is imperfect) is what we think of as the criminal sanction.

In this view, the criminal law is parasitic upon tort law: crimes are defined in terms primarily of torts. Criminal sanctions are "kickers" imposed in addition to tort liability to foster compliance. But if this is the basis of the criminal law, notice that it would become otiose if detection rates approached 1.0. This seems an implausible basis for the criminal law—even to economists.

Let us try something more sophisticated. Either there is a market (property rule) solution to such a problem or there is not. If there is a market solution to an externality problem, then one reason for imposing a criminal sanction is to induce individuals to opt for the market solution when it is available to them. So we criminalize theft, for example, because theft involves a coercive transfer of resources when a noncoercive one—exchange—is available. This is basically Richard Posner's explanation of the criminal category. The criminal is someone who chooses a nonmarket solution to a problem when the market solution is available, and the penal sanction is intended to encourage him to opt for the market solution.

The Calabresi-Melamed analysis differs only slightly from Posner's. The difference is that in Posner's view liability rules and property rules are used to promote efficiency only. On the Calabresi-Melamed theory, the rules promote a mix of social goals, including efficiency and justice. With this difference in mind, the two views proceed in almost exactly the same way. For Calabresi and Melamed the criminal sanction is necessary because tort liability by itself would in effect allow pertetrators to change property rules into liability rules at will. So we penalize theft not just because there is a market alternative—exchange—but because if we required only that the thief pay damages, we, in effect, give thieves the option of not taking property rules seriously. If a society wishes individuals to pursue market solutions to problems, then it cannot allow individuals the option of ignoring the property rule/liability rule distinction. The criminal sanction is the "kicker" added to keep individuals from changing property rules into liability rules at will, not a "kicker" added to the tort remedy to compensate for imperfect detection rates.

As Klevorick points out, however, neither Posner's nor the Calabresi-Melamed analyses handle the cases. A rule against selling oneself into slavery, in effect, prevents individuals from turning inalienability rules into property rules. Similarly, a rule against blackmail, by preventing an individual who owns information from exchanging it, might be aimed at preventing that individual from turning an inalienability rule into a property rule. A society might impose tort liability for pollution and not permit private agreements between the parties to circumvent the liability decision. In effect, criminalizing "buy-offs" would prevent the relevant parties from turning liabilities rules into property rules. What these examples show is that both the Posner and Calabresi-Melamed suggestions are too narrow. Posner's is too narrow because he sees the criminal law as directing actors to market solutions when their costs are acceptably low, whereas some criminal statutes may be aimed at prohibiting market transactions. Calabresi and Melamed go astray by over-emphasizing the role of the criminal law in inducing individuals not to turn property rules into liability rules, whereas at least sometimes the criminal law is aimed at inducing individuals not to turn liability rules into property rules.

The moral Klevorick draws from all this is that the proper economic analysis would emphasize the criminal law's role in enforcing a general transaction structure rather than particular elements of it. As Klevorick puts it:

> In each instance, the act that is characterized as a crime involves the actor(s) forcing society to deal with a transaction in a way in which society did not want to treat it. What makes the act a crime is that the individual assaults the transaction structure that has been established by society. One could say, alternatively, that the individual coerces society into considering and coping with an exchange or transaction in a way that differs from the mode society had chosen. Finally, one might characterize the criminal as arrogating to himself the power or the authority to determine at least a part of the societal transaction structure, that is, appropriating to himself a power or right that society had reserved to itself. The criminal sanction is then a sanction to enforce the transaction structure that society has chosen as well as to compensate for the harms to individuals within the society.[6]

These are very suggestive remarks indeed. Notice, however, that Klevorick takes the basic insight of Posner and Calabresi and Melamed to be correct: namely, that the criminal law is de-

fined in terms of offences independently characterized elsewhere in the law, that it serves to redirect conduct to comply
with requirements set forth elsewhere in the law (the property
rule/liability rule distinction), and that the criminal law is concerned largely with the transfer of resources among individuals
in a society. Klevorick's contribution is to generalize from particular inducements within a given transaction structure to the
transaction structure itself. Next, what Klevorick adds to the
traditional accounts is a "moral" vocabulary of "assault," "coercion," and "arrogation of power" that he claims is essential to
the characterization of criminal conduct, but which is in fact
nowhere implied or even suggested by the discussion to that
point. In my oral commentary, I suggested that we might describe what the criminal does as acting "contrary to the transaction structure," thus removing the essentially moral features
of the characterization of criminality. Klevorick appears to accept my point, but underestimates it, for there is all the difference in the world between characterizing criminal behavior as
action contrary to a prevailing transaction structure and as an
assault against it or as involving an arrogation of powers.

Klevorick's claim is that the economic analysis of crime is essentially unsatisfying to the extent it does not adequately explain the criminal category itself. His particular objections to the
Posner and Calabresi-Melamed accounts are of two sorts. The
first is that the previous work emphasizes the role of the criminal law in providing particular inducements—usually to market behavior or to respecting property rules—whereas the proper
account would see the criminal law as a mechanism for securing an entire transaction structure. To the extent that this is
Klevorick's view, it is an essentially economic one.

Klevorick's other objection, the one I believe he takes to be
the more important, is that an account of the criminal category
involves an essentially noneconomic normative vocabulary: that
of assault, coercion, arrogation of power; that while it may be
possible to give an economic analysis of these concepts, such an
account is likely to be artifical, uninformative, and ultimately
unconvincing. Klevorick's argument rests on describing the
criminal's behavior in these morally charged terms, and there
is nothing in the argument that supports such a characterization. Can anyone seriously believe that a jaywalker, auto thief,

rapist, or embezzler is essentially involved in a struggle over fundamental political power and authority—taking upon himself a power that is legitimately the state's—or that it is necessary to our characterizing his conduct as a crime that we describe it as such? For one reason or another—usually personal gain—individuals sometimes act contrary to the rules of the game. It's as simple as that.

Klevorick tacitly recognizes that he builds too much into his characterization of criminal conduct, because he shifts his objection to the economic analysis from the morality of the actor's assault against the transaction structure to questions of the legitimacy of the transaction structure itself:

> . . . one could simply say that the criminal acts contrary to the transaction structure society had established. But the critical observation is that the explication of why some acts are crimes while others are not requires an inquiry into the legitimation of the transaction structure. If forces one to confront questions like: why does the collectivity have the right to decide the terms on which particular transactions will take place under different circumstances? Why do some rights reside in the individual while others rest with the state?[7]

No doubt these are good questions, but they do not bear on the explanation of the existence of a criminal category. Rather, they are questions about the legitimacy of the rules society lays down to govern transactions. They are essentially normative, not analytic. Presumably a society could decide to criminalize conduct even if the rules it sets forth to govern transactions were not ultimately defensible. In such a case we would be inclined to say that the criminal law was being unjustly or wrongly used, and that punishment for violations of its prohibitions would not be justified. But we might nevertheless have no difficulty in explaining in purely economic terms (of the transaction-structure sort) why that society found it necessary to have a criminal law. In short, Klevorick's argument, though thoughtful and provocative, does not move the economic analysis much beyond its previous frontier.

As an economist, Klevorick is taken by the transaction structure analysis. His efforts to explain the missing ingredient in the economic account take the transaction structure model as basically correct and seek to augment it either by explaining the criminal category in terms of the moral or political nature of the criminal's conduct ("assault," "coercion," or "arrogation of power"), or in terms of the legitimacy of the transaction structure itself. Efforts of the first sort involve a leap not warranted by the evidence. Those of the second sort confuse the problem of explaining the criminal category with the problem of justifying particular instances of it.

For all that, I agree with Klevorick that the economic analysis of crime gives a less than convincing account of the criminal category. The real problem, however, is that it is simply a mistake to think of the criminal law as an enforcer of resource transfers. Moreover, the key moral notions of criminal responsibility—of guilt and fault—are simply absent from the economic infrastructure. Let me close by saying something brief and sketchy on behalf of both of these points.

First, the economic theory goes wrong by seeing the criminal law primarily as a mechanism for securing a transaction structure. A good deal of the criminal law has nothing to do with transactions or the transfer of resources. What, for example, do murder, rape, and treason have to do with the exchange or the transfer of resources? Consider two cases. In one case, B and A reach an agreement *ex ante* whereby A will kill B in exchange for which A will pay a substantial sum to B's family. It is "plausible" in this case to describe the prohibition against such agreements as a refusal to permit individuals to turn inalienability rules into property rules. One's right not to be murdered cannot be bargained away; it is inalienable. In the other case, A simply murders B. Presumably, what A did constitutes a crime. Now it cannot possibly be the explanation of the crime of murder that were murder not a crime we would be allowing individuals to turn property rules into liability rules, since the previous case demonstrates that the right not to be murdered is not protected by a property rule, but by an inalienability rule instead. Nor can we describe it as an effort to prevent offenders from turning inalienability rules into liability rules at their discretion, since the point of inalienability rules is that they limit the free-

dom of those who possess rights from bargaining them away
either *ex ante* or *ex post,* i.e., whether by contract or by compensation *ex post.*[8]

Consider rape. Can anyone seriously argue that rape is criminal because otherwise individuals have the option of changing
property rules into liability rules? What could possibly be the
market (or property rule) equivalent of rape? Sex? Sex plus
dominance? If it is either, then how do we make sense of the
prohibition against prostitution, that is, a prohibition against
placing certain exchanges in the marketplace? Is it plausible,
therefore, to think of it as an effort to induce people not to turn
inalienability rules into property rules? What is the right that is
said to be protected by an inalienability rule: the right to one's
sexual organs? Presumably that right entails control over one's
organs and their use. It may be that one cannot relinquish ultimate control of one's sex organs—though even that may be
false—but one can surely negotiate their use in all sorts of contexts. The criminal law is a set of prohibitions—mandatory legal requirements. And it is a very impoverished view of the range
of human interaction that analyzes all such constraints on behavior in terms of directives based exclusively on exchange relations.

Second, the criminal law states legal requirements and prohibitions, not prices. The economist misses important features
of the criminal law by conceiving of it as a pricing mechanism.
The criminal law sets out prohibitions that are themselves perfectly intelligible, and meant to serve as guides to behavior quite
apart from sanctions for noncompliance being attached to them.
The sanction is of secondary importance and comes into effect
only when the criminal law fails sufficiently to deter behavior.
It is wrong to murder, to rape, or to assault, and society is right
to prohibit such conduct, whether or not the prohibition is
backed by a threat of sanction. So it is fundamentally mistaken
to try to understand the criminal category by trying to explain
the uses to which one can put the criminal sanction.

Klevorick is in fact neither alone nor first among economists
in trying to explain the criminal category by a mixture of economic and moral terms. Even Posner's analysis has an essential
moral dimension. His view is that the main reason we punish is
to induce criminals to substitute, where they are available, vol-

untary market transactions for coercive transfers. Since it is an empirical question whether voluntary transfers are more efficient than involuntary ones, the grounds for preferring market to nonmarket transfers is the moral one—the value of voluntary over coercive transfer.

Posner is closer to the way we ordinarily think about crime when he puts the argument in terms of criminal conduct (usually) being coercive: one party imposing his or her will on another. Of course, not all crime involves a person acting contrary to the will of another. In some cases there are no victims in this sense; in others, an activity may be criminal even if the "victim" consents. Where criminal law is concerned with coercion, it is concerned with an individual's coercion against others, not the sort of coercion against an institutional arrangement of the sort Klevorick has in mind.

Striking in both Posner and Klevorick's analyses is the absence of a discussion of the conditions of responsibility as a requirement of criminal liability. If the criminal law is simply a mechanism for inducing compliance with a transaction structure, why the enormous emphasis on guilt as a condition for imposing the sanction? Indeed, why the criminal sanction as we know it? Why, in other words, do incarceration and the deprivation of liberty seem appropriate responses to criminal misconduct, if the purpose of the criminal law is to encourage respect for a transaction structure? Perhaps a course in economics would be a more suitable "punishment."

The criminal sanction is not imposed unless fairly rigid standards of personal responsibility or culpability are met. With few exceptions involving strict liability, these standards are more rigid than those required to impose tort liability. This emphasis on individual culpability cannot be explained in terms of the "inducement" function of the criminal law. If a body of law cannot serve its inducement or deterrent function unless individuals have available to them a wide range of possible excusing conditions, then tort law, as well as the law of crimes, should be replete with discussions of excusing conditions. As we know, tort law does not recognize a wide range of excuses, but the law of crimes does. Moreover, strict liability is rare in criminal law, and a general theory of strict criminal liability has never been seriously advanced. In contrast, in torts strict liability is on the increase, and even the rule of fault liability has several dimensions of strict liability embedded in it. For example, in negligence law, an individual may be at fault for the harm his conduct occasions even if his failure to comply with standard of due care is not his fault: even if he did the best he could. Negligence (in torts), as the jurisprude Terry pointed out seventy years ago, is "conduct, not a state of mind." Indeed, it is the essentially nonmoral character of negligence in torts that has led economists like Posner to develop a plausible economic analysis of torts based on Learned Hand's famous characterization of negligence in *U.S.* v. *Carrol Towing.* It is precisely the essentially moral aspect of the conditions of responsibility in the criminal law that makes an economic analysis of it so fundamentally implausible.

Put another way: in crimes the question is whether the state has the right to deprive a particular person of his liberty by incarcerating him. In torts, it is whether the state has sufficient grounds for shifting a loss from the party upon whom it has initially fallen to another individual, when the loss must fall on one or the other of them. In the first case, the state must be satisfied that the individual *deserves* to be punished. In the second, it must feel that there are good reasons as between two parties (one of whom is bound to be made worse off) to have one rather than the other shoulder the costs. No equivalent situation exists in the criminal law. There is no individual who must be punished—whose liberty must be constrained; there is no loss or cost that must be born by somebody. So, in order for the state to take the extraordinary step of imposing this burden on someone, it must show that in some sense he deserves it. That argument requires an inquiry not only into what a person does, but his responsibility and guilt in having done it. These are essential features of the criminal law and it is not surprising that an economic analysis of crimes that focuses on the inducement aspect of the criminal law in terms of securing compliance with transfer mechanism should miss it entirely. Such a theory has no place for the moral sentiments and virtues appropriate to matters of crime and punishment: guilt, shame, remorse, forgiveness, and mercy, to name a few. A purely economic theory of crime can only impoverish rather than enrich our understanding of the nature of crime.[9]

## NOTES

1. See chapter 11 in this volume.
2. Risk neutral actors are concerned only with expected outcomes and are indifferent among outcomes with the same expected value, regardless of the likelihood of the outcomes's occurence.
3. Guido Calabresi and Douglas Melamed, "Property Rules, Liability Rules and Inalienability: One View of the Cathedral" *Harv. L. Rev.* 85 (1972).
4. One reason I have always been troubled by the Calabresi-Melamed approach is that if a right is secured by a property rule, then when one negotiates successfully with the right bearer for it there is no sense in which the bargainer acts *contrary* to the right bearer's entitlement; whereas under a liability rule the action is contrary to the right bearer's entitlement *period,* and it makes no matter that the intruder renders compensation *ex post.*

   It strikes me as simply confused to see liability rules as entitling injurers to purchase at their will "parts" of (another very peculiar notion) the rights of others. It is hard to conceive of an individual as having a freedom that consists of nothing other than his acting contrary to the rights of others. Normally we would think of such action as prima facie wrong and in need of justification. The root of the problem is that advocates of the Calabresi-Melamed dichotomy ask the notion of a liability rule to do too much work, much of it internally inconsistent: how can we conceive of a liability rule as a protector of one's rights to the security of one's holding and at the same time as a vehicle that enables others to act contrary to the duties those rights are presumed to entail?
5. Ronald Coase, "The Problem of Social Cost," *J. Law and Economics,* 3 (1960).
6. Klevorick, under "The Inherent Limitation of Any Economic Theory of Crime."
7. Ibid.
8. In other words, the very idea of turning an inalienability rule into a liability rule may be incoherent. Inalienability rules are aimed at restricting the freedom of those who have rights, not those whose conduct interferes with rights. So there is a sense in which it is impossible for an offender to act contrary to an inalienability rule; only one whose rights are protected by an inalienability rule can do that by, for example, trading one's rights—that is, by trying to turn an inalienability rule into a property rule.
9. Let me summarize what I take to be the differences among Posner, Calabresi-Melamed, and Klevorick. Posner sees the criminal sanction as a device to induce market behavior when it is available. The

Calabresi-Melamed approach would seem to be the same in so far as the criminal sanction is seen as appropriate to prevent people from turning property rules into liability rules: i.e., criminal sanctions induce compliance with market alternatives. However, Posner and Calabresi-Melamed do differ. The latter emphasize not only the inducement to market alternatives, but the need for individuals to respect the importance of the distinction between liability rules and property rules. It is not so much a commitment to the market—as it is in Posner—that warrants a criminal category, as much as it is commitment to the importance of a distinction drawn by the public power among the rules of transfer. Klevorick builds on both elements of the Calabresi-Melamed approach: the framework of transaction and the importance of public power. For the Calabresi-Melamed distinction between liability and property rules Klevorick substitutes a "transaction structure;" for the argument that the criminal sanction is warranted to support that structure, Klevorick substitutes the claim that it is warranted because otherwise individual perpetrators *arrogate* authority that is not their's to exercise.

# 14

# IS THERE AN ECONOMIC THEORY OF CRIME?

## STEPHEN J. SCHULHOFER

Professor Klevorick's interesting and instructive chapter directs our attention to two important questions. First, is the vast economic literature on criminal justice matters grounded in a coherent economic theory of crime? Second, does its value depend on its being so grounded? Klevorick concludes that an economic theory of crime is inherently incomplete. Such a theory must draw upon political concepts that in the nature of things cannot be derived from an economic source.[1] Klevorick goes on to suggest that economists should enlarge their models to allow for a noneconomic concept of the social loss from crime.

Klevorick's suggestion may save the economists from what is, by their own criteria, a mistake, but will it suffice to render their work more interesting or more helpful to criminal justice scholars who are not economists? His analysis seems to imply that although an economic analysis of crime can be helpful in certain ways, that kind of analysis cannot in the very nature of things speak to the most fundamental concerns of students of criminal

This paper was presented at the January 1983 meeting of the American Society for Political and Legal Philosophy as commentary on Alvin Klevorick's paper. I am grateful for the comments of participants at the meeting, especially Jules Coleman and Alvin Klevorick, for the research assistance and substantive comments of John Summers, and for support in revising the paper from the Institute for Law and Economics at the University of Pennsylvania.

justice. Can this really be so? Or can economic analysis be of genuine interest to criminal justice scholars?

The first point to be made is that in wondering about the failure of economists to engage the main interests of criminal law scholars, Klevorick has devoted nearly all of his attention to only one side of the potential intellectual exchange. As perhaps befits an economist who is both rigorous and tactful, Klevorick has carefully probed the work of his own colleagues in economics, but has abstained from questioning whether the fundamental concerns of criminal justice scholars ought to be defined and confined in the way that they are. Criminal law scholarship is, of course, very much preoccupied with working out notions of culpability and fairness (I will have more to say about this later), but this body of scholarship is by and large not particularly concerned with questions of optimal resource allocation. Very few law teachers, I am sure, spend any time in their criminal law course talking about the relative effectiveness of automobile patrol versus foot patrol or of one officer in the car versus two. Precisely because this is perceived as "only" a question of resource allocation,[2] it is not on their agenda. For the same reason, the relative effectiveness of increasing the certainty or increasing the severity of punishment would not normally be considered an "interesting" question;[3] it would become interesting to the mainstream criminal justice scholar only when it involved questions of proportionality, distributive justice, and the like.

But is the criminal law scholar really justified in his or her disinterest in matters of resource allocation as such? I cannot help but think that the myopia of many criminal law teachers is at least partially responsible for the failure of communication that Klevorick describes. Without ignoring the grand issues of moral culpability, legal scholars must also accept that the problem of protecting society from crime while protecting offenders from unnecessarily stringent sanctions, that is, the problem of optimal resource allocation, is central to the work they should be doing. Thus, the work and interests of many criminal justice scholars is seriously incomplete. Though I will not try to pursue this point any further here, this incompleteness needs to be borne in mind if Klevorick's criticisms of the economists are to be kept in perspective.

For now I will return to the incompleteness that Klevorick finds on the economists' side and attempt to assess to what extent it impairs the value of the economic approach. This question will lead me to others because of its implication that criminal justice may differ from other areas of law, where economic analysis has engaged the interests of many legal scholars. In concluding that there *cannot* be a purely economic theory of crime, Klevorick has left us with a dilemma that I will formulate as I proceed.

## THE EXISTENCE OF THE CRIMINAL CATEGORY

Where, if anywhere, can economic analysis be illuminating or useful? Klevorick identifies three themes in the literature. The one that he sees as most fundamental (and most fundamentally flawed) draws upon economic analysis to explain the existence of the criminal category. Richard Posner pursues this theme. It is not clear, however, that Posner is attempting a comprehensive account of the existence of the criminal category. He is uncharacteristically vague on this point.[4] But Posner does imply that the category of unlawful behavior ordinarily will include the resort to nonmarket transactions where efficient market transactions are feasible, and he also attempts to show that efficient "pricing" of such behavior ordinarily will require a penal sanction in addition to other remedies. Klevorick offers several examples to show that this will not do—society might and sometimes does choose to prohibit the resort to market transactions (e.g., the selling of votes and human slavery). Posner might have an economic explanation for some of these prohibitions, but Klevorick is surely right in saying that many crimes are not readily explained in Posner's terms, or in those of Calebresi-Melamed (cited and discussed below).

I find it at least equally instructive to test the Posner and Calabresi-Melamed explanations of the criminal category from the other direction—that is, by asking whether they call for criminal punishment of behavior that society in fact chooses to treat as noncriminal. A right to contractual performance ordinarily is protected only by a liability rule (that is, a right to collect damages). Yet in this situation a market transaction for modification or recission is quite feasible,[5] and thus the Posner and Calabresi-Melamed criteria seem to require granting the promisee the protection of a property rule (that is, a right to specific performance).[6] Those criteria also appear to require backing up that property rule with the added "kicker" of penal sanctions. In other words, this kind of economic analysis leads to the conclusion that deliberate breach of contract is (or should be) treated as a crime. Of course, society does not and should not do any such thing.[7]

Klevorick tries to avoid these problems by modifying the Posner and Calabresi-Melamed explanations of crime. Criminal sanctions, Klevorick suggests, are not designed to channel transactions into the market where feasible (or efficient), but rather serve to enforce whatever transactions structure society has chosen—market or nonmarket. Of course, this move is unattractive to Posner, because the determining factors become noneconomic. But the terminology at least remains economic, and this approach could therefore preserve for the economist a useful, though more humble role.

I have two sets of concerns about economic explanations of the criminal category, and my concerns may extend even to Klevorick's intriguing reformulation. The first concern is that too often, the law fails to stipulate a single, well-defined transactions structure for particular exchange situations. The second concern is that even where the transactions structure is well-specified, one too often fails to observe the predicted reliance on penal law to enforce that structure.

Let me elaborate on these two concerns, starting with the first. Klevorick's approach requires that analysis begin by identifying the particular socially approved transactions structure "that stipulates the terms on which particular transactions or exchanges are to take place under different circumstances."[8] Social and legal rules sometimes do generate a single, well-specified transaction structure for sufficiently particularized exchange situations, but very often, in the cases that interest us, no single "transactions structure" is uniquely specified. While I am driving on the highway, is my entitlement to bodily integrity protected by an inalienability rule, a property rule, or a liability rule? One might want to say that the answer depends on the nature of the interference. If another motorist deliberately collides with my car, this is an intentional interference, and in this case I am protected by an inalienability rule: *intentional* interference is absolutely prohibited, a crime even if done with my consent. Reckless interference arguably could be placed in the same category. But merely negligent interference, one wants to say, is protected only by a liability rule—I can recover only a socially determined value as damages. The difficulty here is that in fact even the negligent interference is absolutely prohibited; society still treats it as a crime.[9] Indeed, since the act remains a crime even if done with my consent or voluntary assumption of the risk,[10] we would have to say that the transaction is structured by an inalienability rule, even though the civil courts would grant only a damages remedy at most.

If we introduce further changes into the "terms" of the exchange situation, we can find circumstances in which the civil courts would not grant even a right to damages. Suppose that the interference occurs despite the exercise of due care, or that there is a negligent interference to which I contribute by my own negligence. In both cases I cannot recover damages; in a sense I do not have a protected entitlement at all. Nonetheless, in both cases the interference could be a crime.[11] Thus, from the perspective of penal law an exchange transaction can be structured by an inalienability rule (or at least a property rule), while the same highly particularized transaction can, from the perspective of civil law, be structured by a liability rule or indeed by a rule of no entitlement at all. Too often, there appears to be no uniquely specified transactions structure.

My second concern relates to the Posner and Calabresi-Melamed notion that where we do have a coherent transactions structure, the penal law can be seen as a device for efficiently enforcing compliance with that structure. To test this notion we must consider cases in which society does protect the entitlement by an unambiguous right to specific performance. A real estate sales contract provides one common example; my right to withhold my watch from a would-be thief is another. The Posner and Calabresi-Melamed criteria seem to require backing up these property rules with a criminal sanction. Otherwise, the argument runs, the property rule could be "changed at will into [a] liability rule."[12] The argument seems plausible, but its logic is not tight. How does the defaulting promisor (or thief) convert a property rule into a liability rule? The courts in a civil action will not simply award damages but will grant specific performance (or replevin, in the case of stolen goods). Thus, whatever the penal law may provide, the property rule remains a property rule, and the civil courts are not limited to mere liability-rule protection.

According for uncertainties of apprehension does not alter this criticism of the economic approach. The Posner and Calabresi-Melamed critieria call for the added "kicker" of penal sanctions even when the probability of apprehension approaches one (as it ordinarily does in the real estate case).[13] But in fact, the criminal sanction is much more sparingly used; in such cases society usually chooses to preserve the integrity of its property rules simply by permitting them to be enforced in civil actions. Conversely, where probabilities of apprehension are low, the danger is not that property rules will be converted into liability rules but rather that the uncaught thief will elude both the replevin remedy *and* a damage judgment.[14] Thus, penal sanctions are used to punish some violations of the transactions structure, but they are not used consistently enough, in the ways that the Posner and Calabresi-Melamed analysis would predict.

One has to wonder, of course, whether the two kinds of anomalies I have mentioned suggest incoherence in the transactions structure approach or whether instead they suggest incoherence in the law itself. An economist certainly might regard much of the law of remedies as inconsistent, inefficient, and even irrational. The seeming incoherence of the remedial structure may, nonetheless, reflect nothing more than rational adaptations to the complexities of administration in different contexts, together with the divergence between the dominant goals of civil and criminal justice. Given these possibilities, I prefer not to dismiss Klevorick's way of conceptualizing the transactions structure problem. His approach should instead challenge the economists to see whether the combined structure of civil and criminal remedies will yield to an analysis in economic terms. But we surely do not yet have a satisfactory explanatory model. It is too soon to say that the transactions structure approach can provide even a vocabulary for talking about what behavior is or should be criminal.

Does all this leave any role for economics, in connection with efforts to study the scope of the criminal category? At most, we seem to have only the possibility of using economic tools and economic ways of thinking, many layers below the level of grand theory, to provide a comparative cost-effectiveness analysis, with the crucial judgments about moral and political rights taken as given. Ironically, legal scholars concerned with the criminalization decision have tended to treat this seemingly limited kind of analysis as their central preoccupation and have argued for relegating the ostensibly fundamental political and moral issues to the background. These scholars, such as Sanford Kadish and Louis Schwartz,[15] have never been mistaken for Posnerians, but they show us how economists can be helpful in a modest, instrumental way. The more comprehensive claim—for a general descriptive model—has a long way to go.

## CRIMINAL JUSTICE POLICY

The second theme in the literature attempts a cost-benefit analysis of the optimal allocation of resources to sanctioning and law enforcement. Professor Gary Becker's pathbreaking analysis[16] seems useful in its treatment of certainty-severity trade-offs and the cost-effectiveness of alternative allocations of resources. But the attempt to establish a general model to guide the punishment decision in particular, concrete cases strikes the criminal justice scholar as hopelessly myopic or naive.

Posner's work tries to avoid this problem by applying economic analysis to sanctioning issues as they actually arise in the context of particular legal doctrines. He elaborates a concept of criminal punishment as a "price" of engaging in prohibited behavior and argues that the legal system attempts to set this price at a level appropriate to deter inefficient transfers.

As an example, Posner mentions the provocation defense, which mitigates the punishment for homicide. Posner explains the lower penalty as a consequence of the higher probability of apprehension in heat-of-passion killings; the killer who premeditates will likely be more successful in covering his traces, the probability of apprehension is lower, and therefore the severity of punishment must be increased.[17] Very few criminal lawyers will find this explanation plausible, even on its face. An economist could just as well argue that because there is greater temptation in a provocation situation (and future penalties would be discounted at a higher rate), a *higher* penalty should be imposed. In any case, when the lawyer thinks about the rules on legally adequate provocation, cooling time, and the rejection of subjective standards, he or she knows that probabilities of apprehension are simply not involved in these doctrines regulating the severity of punishment for homicide. The lawyer may have been confused or perplexed about these doctrines before, but he is not likely to think that a Posnerian deterrence analysis helps him understand them. Obviously something relevant has been left out—the concept of fault, which explains these legal doctrines in a more-or-less straightforward way, even though its implications in this context run directly contrary to notions of efficiency, social loss minimization, and the like.

The other major theme for Becker and Posner is that society *wants* some crimes to occur, and that it adjusts the punishment price so that potential offenders will be willing to commit crimes and pay that price when their behavior is value-maximizing. To illustrate this, Posner gives the example of a lost hiker who chooses to steal food to avoid starvation. The price of theft, Posner says, must be set low enough so that this efficient transfer will take place.[18] The difficulty is that in the case Posner puts, the behavior, precisely because it *is* value maximizing, would not be a crime at all, and the actor would not be charged any price. The lawyer's notion of the necessity defense involves a straightforward cost-benefit analysis.[19] An economist with limited ambitions might be happy to help elucidate the legal standard. But Posner and Becker want to make more sweeping claims—that crime as such is neither good nor bad and that criminal sanctions are simply prices used to prevent inefficient transactions while encouraging efficient ones. On their terms, it should be deemed inefficient to displace market incentives and to rely on a court to conduct a particularized cost-benefit calculation case by case.[20] But that particularity is by and large what the criminal law method is all about. Socially value-maximizing behavior is not punished at all. An analysis restricted to efficiency suppresses something too important to be left out—once again, the notion of fault.

Finally, as to the second theme, let me turn to the literature on sanctioning methods. The capital punishment studies are well known and the issue deservedly commands attention, but overall the death penalty accounts only for a very small part of the sanctioning machinery—it is imposed in only a tiny fraction of all cases.

Next, there are the many studies on the use of fines. These studies recognize that fines are rarely used and most of them seek to change that, but it is important to see where we are starting from. Fines without imprisonment are imposed in only 13 percent of all federal convictions.[21] In state cases, fines are very unusual; in one large urban jurisdiction fines without imprisonment were imposed in only 20 percent of the misdemeanor convictions and only 0.4 percent of serious felony convictions.[22]

That leaves imprisonment, which the economic literature has treated on its own terms and as a problem of the trade-off between this sanction and fines. Cases involving imprisonment or imprisonment plus fine are estimated to represent only about 23 percent of all convictions.[23]

I have so far accounted for only 20 to 50 percent of all convictions. Again, something has been left out. According to best estimates, more than 50 percent and in one careful sample 77 percent of all convicted defendants received only a sentence of probation.[24]

There appear to be very few economic studies on the use of probation. In one,[25] Professor Kenneth Wolpin used regression analysis to estimate the impact of three different sanctions—imprisonment, probation, and fine—upon the rate of crime in England.[26] He found the expected negative relation between changes in the sanctioning rate and changes in the crime rate, and found this negative relation not only for the rate of fine and imprisonment but also for the probation rate. Wolpin found that the impact on the crime rate was strongest for imprisonment (as expected) and, interestingly, he also found that the impact on the crime rate was stronger for probation than for fines.[27] Wolpin's paper does not offer, however, any account of the *mechanism* by which probationary sanctions generate a deterrent effect, and within the time-allocation model that he takes as his framework, the nature of that mechanism is not obvious.[28] Indeed, within the traditional economic framework of utility maximization, it seems particularly perplexing that probation should have a stronger deterrent effect than fines do.[29] What seems to be missing, then, is a *theory* of probation, and probation is, after all, the most common criminal sanction.

Of course, it is easy to guess why the economists have not leaped at the opportunity to analyze a sanction that takes neither time nor money from the offender. But what does Becker's analysis imply about a society that invests so much in a process that more often than not imposes only a probationary sentence? I do not mean this question to suggest, rhetorically, that Becker's analysis is wholly empty. On the contrary, what Becker's own analysis implies is that society itself attributes great importance to the imposition of a sanction the consequences of which are difficult to understand in economic terms.

What is missing from the economists' account is, once again, the concept of fault. I have said that this notion is central to the criminal law method in making decisions about criminalization, excuses, and the grading of offenses. To understand the sanctioning structure, one must see that having identified fault, the criminal law responds first and foremost simply by condemning. In the majority of cases this is the only response.

Even in what I previously called the fine cases, the fine is generally much lower than efficiency considerations warrant, as the economists themselves have shown us. Their policy recommendations are interesting here, but they may be overlooking the implications of their work for a satisfactory descriptive model. What society is actually doing in these low-fine cases is not, in any significant sense, taking money, but in most cases condemning.[30] The importance of that act can be measured in economic terms—by the resources society devotes to achieving it and, at least in some cases, the resources that defendants devote to resisting it.[31] But the concept of condemnation, and the mechanism by which it yields its deterrent, retributive, and educative effects, probably will not yield to a comprehensive and satisfying economic analysis. Becker himself may have been trying to tell us this when he made the otherwise incomprehensible statement that "when crimes are punishable by fines, the analytical differences [from tort law] virtually vanish."[32] Because the analytical differences, in strictly economic terms, do virtually vanish, we know not that torts and crimes are the same but instead that the economic analysis is fundamentally incomplete.

I wish to repeat that policy studies can be useful for many purposes. They can help us to estimate, for example, the relative effectiveness of devoting more resources to police, to prosecutors, or to prisons. The point, however, is that these economic studies probably cannot, in the nature of things, illuminate much of what has to be important to optimum law enforcement policy.

## THE INDIVIDUAL'S DECISION ABOUT CRIMINAL ACTIVITY

The first theme that Klevorick identifies in the literature analyzes in economic terms an individual's decision whether or not to commit a crime. What is new and striking about this literarure is not its claim that individuals are influenced by the certainty and severity of punishment, but rather its more comprehensive claim that the entire decision calculus can be usefully modeled in economic terms. Of course, the model abstracts from reality and thus deliberately leaves out some things that influence some people. The limited, but still momentous, claim is that one can usefully describe a significant segment of reality, that one can better understand it, by postulating that the decision-maker is a rational utility maximizer, allocating his time and labor among various activities. Becker, for example, writes that his approach "assumes that a person commits an offense if the expected utility to him exceeds the utility he could get by using his time and other resources at other activities. . . . [C]riminal behavior becomes part of a much more general theory and does not require ad hoc concepts of differential association, anomie and the like. . . ."[33]

The lawyer or criminologist is not likely to find this explanatory model very satisfactory, even when buttressed by regression analysis and very impressive $R^2$ figures. The problem is not that the economic explanation is totally implausible, because the criminal justice scholar would not want to deny the existence of rational, utility-maximizing behavior. The problem, rather, is that in postulating such behavior the economist assumes away the very question in which the noneconomist is most interested. Justice Thurgood Marshall reflected the lawyer's frame of mind very well in this regard when he responded to claims advanced on behalf of the medical model in *Powell* v. *Texas:* "The doctrines of actus reus, mens rea, insanity, mistake, justification and duress have historically provided the tools for a constantly shifting adjustment of the tension between the evolving aims of the criminal law and changing religious, moral, philosophical, and medical views of the nature of man."[34]

In this area the criminal justice scholar sees himself as struggling with an eternal problem: what is man? The Posner-Becker answer—man is a rational maximizer of utility—is simply beside the point, even to the extent that it may be true. The lawyer or philosopher wants to learn about economic rationality and its implications, much as he wants to learn about the disease concept of alcoholism, but the intellectual problem is to sort out the appropriate contributions of these diverse perspectives, and thus to locate, for our own time, the domain of human autonomy and the accountability of an individual for his acts.

I am aware, of course, that a science like economics can use its results to turn back on itself and measure the validity of its assumptions. The kind of hypothesis-testing required here, however, lies far beyond the capability of the econometric models with which I am familiar.[35]

So my conclusion is that the first strand, like the others, can be put to a limited use by criminal justice scholars. It sheds light on one piece of their puzzle. But it cannot, in the nature of things, illuminate their most fundamental concerns.

## The Limitations of Economic Theory

With respect to all three strands of the economic literature, I have suggested that, perhaps surprisingly, the policy-oriented dimensions of this literature can be put to good use by criminal justice scholars and are not likely to strike them as problematical. The policy role is not really controversial. It is the descriptive claims that are ambitious, unconventional, and likely to be highly controversial, except that those descriptive claims are often so implausible that no one will bother to consider them at all.

So we have something of a paradox, in that in most fields of law, the normative claims of economic analysis have evoked intense controversy, while the descriptive analysis has been widely conceded to have a good measure of validity and considerable power as an explanatory tool. The application of economic analysis to criminal justice appears to have produced the opposite situation, with the policy analysis useful and the descriptive claims very wide of the mark.

This paradox has some troubling implications. I said earlier that Klevorick's conclusion—to the effect that there *cannot*, in the very nature of things, be a purely economic theory of crime— has left us with a dilemma. Does the body of law and human experience relating to crime differ so radically from all other areas of law and experience? Or do the profound limitations that Klevorick demonstrates in the economic theory of crime point to latent but fundamental shortcomings in the general economic analysis of law? If Klevorick is right, then it seems likely that at least one of these questions will have to be answered affirmatively. In that event we will then, all of us, have to start quite a bit of rethinking.

## NOTES

1. Alvin K. Klevorick, "On the Economic Theory of Crime," in this volume.
2. Much more, of course, is involved, including the proper definition of the police role and the effect of that role on community attitudes, community coherence, and like matters that may have an importance independent of their relation to crime rates.
3. But see Stephen Schulhofer, "Harm and Punishment: A Critique of Emphasis on the Results of Conduct in the Criminal Law," *U. Pa. L. Rev.* 122 (1974): 1497, 1544–57.
4. See Richard Posner, *Economic Analysis of Law,* 2d ed. (Boston: Little Brown, 1977), p. 163. Posner seems to suggest that conduct is a crime when it is unlawful (e.g., tortious), a notion that is either inaccurate or deliberately incomplete.
5. See Ian Macneil, "Efficient Breach of Contract: Circles in the Sky," *Va. L. Rev.* 68 (1982): 947.
6. See Anthony Kronman, "Specific Performance," *U. Chi. L. Rev.* 45 (1978): 351; Alan Schwartz, "The Case for Specific Performance," *Yale L. J.* 89 (1979): 271.
7. From the strictly economic perspective, it becomes difficult to see any distinction between deliberate breach of contract and ordinary theft. For some of the problems faced by lawyers in sorting out the distinction in close cases, see generally S. Kadish, S. Schul-

hofer, and M. Paulsen, eds., *Criminal Law and Its Processes*, 2d ed (Boston: Little, Brown, 1983) pp. 935–42.

8. Klevorick, under "The Inherent Limitation of Any Economic Theory of Crime."

9. In a vehicle homicide prosecution, some states impose penal liability only when the defendant's negligence can be characterized as "wanton" or "gross," but in other states responsibility for homicide can be based on ordinary negligence. See generally Kadish, *Criminal Law and Its Processes*, pp. 411, 441–47.

10. E.g., *Commonwealth v. Atencio*, 345 Mass. 627, 189 N.E.2d 223 (1963); *Jacobs v. State*, 184 So.2d 711 (Fla. 1966). But cf. *Commonwealth v. Root*, 403 Pa. 571, 170 A.2d 310 (1961). Even in the Root case, where the court set aside an involuntary manslaughter conviction, finding an absence of proximate cause, the court still emphasized that the defendant was guilty of criminal conduct: "This evidence would of course amply support a conviction of the defendant for speeding, reckless driving and, perhaps, other violations of The Vehicle Code" (ibid.).

11. See generally Kadish, *Criminal Law and Its Processes*, pp. 443–44, 470–74.

12. Calabresi and Melamed, "Property Rules, Liability Rules, and Inalienability: One View of the Cathedral," *Harv. L. Rev.* 85 (1972): 1089, 1126.

13. Ibid., p. 1125.

14. Cf. Klevorick, under "The Existence of the Criminal Category," at n.26.

15. See, e.g., Sanford Kadish, "The Crisis of Overcriminalization," *Annals* 374 (1967): 157; Louis Schwartz, "The Proposed Federal Criminal Code," in Kadish, *Criminal Law and Its Processes*, p. 231.

16. Gary Becker, "Crime and Punishment: An Economic Approach," *J. Pol. Econ.* 76 (1968): 169.

17. Posner, *Economic Analysis of Law*, p. 174; cf. Becker, "Crime and Punishment," pp. 189–90.

18. Posner, *Economic Analysis of Law*, pp. 166, 175.

19. See Model Penal Code §3.02(1) (a) (Proposed Official Draft, 1962).

20. See Posner, *Economic Analysis of Law*, p. 175:

> [S]uppose the thief would be excused from criminal liability for stealing the food in the cabin if he could show . . . that the benefit to him from stealing the food exceeded the cost to the owner. . . . This would require the court to balance the gains to the thief against the costs to the owner of the cabin. But it is preferable to make the thief strike the balance himself, by forcing him to pay whatever costs his act imposed on

the cabin owner. The analogy to the requirement of paying compensation in eminent domain cases should be evident.

It is not clear how Posner's analysis here is to be reconciled with his rejection of strict liability in tort; in that context he endorses judicial balancing of costs and benefits (under a negligence standard) as the efficient solution. For a fuller discussion, see Steven Shavell, "Strict Liability versus Negligence," *J. Legal Studies* 11 (1980): 1.

21. M. Hindelang, M. Gottfredson, and T. Flanagan, eds., *Sourcebook of Criminal Justice Statistics* (Washington, D.C.: U.S. Government Printing Office, 1981), pp. 428–29.

22. Office of Court Administrator, *Statistical Report of the Common Pleas and Municipal Courts of Philadelphia,* December Term 1981, pp. 18, 38. The misdemeanor cases referred to in the text include those cases falling within the jurisdiction of the Municipal Court (those involving authorized imprisonment of five years or less). The "serious felony" cases are those within the jurisdiction of the Common Pleas Court (authorized punishment in excess of five years).

23. See Kadish, *Criminal Law and Its Processes,* pp. 6, 219. In Philadelphia, imprisonment was imposed in 50 percent of the Common Pleas (serious felony) convictions but only in 19 percent of the Municipal Court (less serious) convictions. See Office of Court Administrator, *Statistical Report,* pp. 18, 38. Becker appears to assume a sharply different distribution of penalties. See Becker, "Crime and Punishment," pp. 169, 179.

24. See Kadish, *Criminal Law and Its Processes,* p. 219.

25. Called to my attention at the Society's meeting by George Priest.

26. Kenneth Wolpin, "An Economic Analysis of Crime and Punishment in England and Wales, 1894–1967," *J. Pol. Econ.* 86 (1978):815.

27. This relation was observed across all the crime categories studied, with the exception of auto theft, for which (curiously) the crime rate appeared to be more strongly affected by the probation rate than by the imprisonment rate. Ibid., p. 826.

28. Isaac Ehrlich has argued that probationary sanctions involve enough stigma to interfere with employment prospects and thus to reduce the offender's expected stream of future earnings. Ehrlich, "The Deterrent Effect of Criminal Law Enforcement," *J. Legal Studies* 1 (1972): 259, 262. As an empirical claim, this hypothesis is, for many reasons, quite problematic, and in any event it fails to explain why probation should prove a more effective deterrent than fines, which *ceteris paribus* involve the same stigma of criminality upon conviction. Within a strictly economic framework, one could argue that

probation takes more of the offender's time than a fine does, because of reporting requirements. This difference seems too slight to be consequential, but further research from this perspective might be worthwhile.

29. Part of the difficulty here may stem from the way in which Wolpin was forced to define his variables. Due to data limitations, he was able to measure only the frequency with which fines and probation were imposed and could not control for length of probation or amount of fine. With respect to imprisonment, Wolpin used data on the average court-imposed term, but recognized that this figure is only imperfectly correlated with average time actually served. Wolpin, "Economic Analysis of Crime and Punishment," p. 824.

30. For recognition of this point in an economic analysis, see R.A. Carr-Hill and N.H. Stern, "Theory and Estimation in Models of Crime and its Social Control and their Relations to Concepts of Social Output," in M. Feldstein and R. Inman, eds., *The Economics of Public Services* (London: Macmillan, 1977), pp. 116, 127–131.

31. Two striking examples are *United States* v. *Park*, 421 U.S. 658 (1975), in which the defendant took appeals all the way to the U.S. Supreme Court in an unsuccessful effort to resist a $250 fine; and the Ford Pinto prosecution, in which $1 million was spent resisting a maximum possible sentence of a $10,000 fine. See Kadish, *Criminal Law and Its Processes,* pp. 995–96. Some of these expenditures may have been motivated by concern about the civil liability consequences of a criminal conviction. But even that motivation may have been an insignificant factor in *Park,* where no major injuries had occurred and where the conviction, on a strict liability theory, would have had no clear implications for civil liability.

32. Becker, "Crime and Punishment," p. 201.

33. Ibid., p. 176.

34. 392 U.S. 514, 536 (1968) (opinion of Marshall, J.).

35. Compare Posner, *Economic Analysis of Law,* pp. 164–65.

# BIBLIOGRAPHY

## ANDREW C. BLANAR

The following list of books and articles does not attempt to be comprehensive and exhaustive. The listed bibliographies can be supplemented by the bibliographies in many more recent volumes, including Bedau, Hugo A. ed. *The Death Penalty in America,* 3rd ed. New York: Oxford University Press, 1982 and Gross, Hymn. *A Theory of Criminal Justice.* New York: Oxford University Press, 1979.

### BIBLIOGRAPHIES

*Index to Legal Periodicals*
Oxbridge Communications. *Legal and Law Enforcement Periodicals.* New York: Facts on File, 1981.
Radzinowicz, Sir Leon and Hood, Roger, eds. *Criminology and the Administration of Criminal Justice: A Bibliography.* Westport, Conn.: Greenwood Press, 1976.
Wright, Martin, ed. *Use of Criminology Literature.* Hamden, Conn.: Shoe String Press, 1974.

### CRIMINAL JUSTICE AND CRIMINOLOGY JOURNALS

*American Journal of Corrections*
*British Journal of Criminology.*
*Crime and Delinquency.*
*Criminal Law Journal.*
*Criminology.*

*Journal of Criminal Justice.*

*Journal of Criminal Law and Criminology.* Besides many other specialized journals in the fields of criminal justice and criminology, articles in these areas can be found in most law reviews and in sociological, psychological, and public police journals. Of special interest is a yearly journal edited by Norval Morris and Michael Terry, *Crime and Justice: An Annual Review of Research,* (four volumes to date), and *Criminal Justice History* (1980–83, four volumes to date) from Meckler Publishing.


CRIMINAL LAW AND THE ADMINISTRATION OF CRIMINAL JUSTICE

Auerbach, Gerald. *Unequal Justice.* New York: Oxford University Press, 1976.

Baker, Keith, and Robert J. Rubel, eds. *Violence and Crime in the Schools.* Lexington: Lexington Books, 1981.

Balbus, Isaac D. *The Dialectics of Legal Repression: Black Rebels Before the American Criminal Courts.* New Brunswick, N.J.: Transaction Books, 1977.

Baldwin, John, and Michael McConville. *Jury Trials.* Oxford University, Press, 1979.

Baldwin, John, and Michael McConville, *Negotiated Justice Pressures on Defendants to Plead Guilty.* Oxford: Martin Robertson, 1979.

Becker, Gary and Stigler, George. "Law Enforcement, Malfeasance, and Compensation of Enforcers," *Journal of Legal Studies* 3 (January 1974): 1–19.

Becker, H.K. and E.O. Hjellemo. *Justice in Modern Sweden: A Description of the Components of the Swedish Criminal Justice System.* New York: Thomas, 1979.

Bennett, W. Lance, and Martha S. Feldman. *Reconstructing Reality in the Courtroom.* London: Tavistock, 1981.

Blumberg, Abraham. *Criminal Justice.* 2d ed. New York: New Viewpoints, 1979.

Burger, Warren. "The Perspective of the Chief Justice of the U.S. Surpreme Court." *Crime and Social Justice* (Summer 1981): 43.

Center for Research on Criminal Justice. *The Iron Fist and the Velvet Glove.* Berkeley: University of California Press, 1975.

Chambliss, William J. *On the Take: From Petty Crooks to Presidents.* Bloomington: Indiana University Press, 1982.

Cohen, S.A. *Due Process of Law: The Canadian System of Criminal Justice.* Agincourt, Ontario: Carswell, 1977.

Cole, George R. et al. *Major Criminal Justice Systems.* Beverly Hills: Sage, 1981.

Cole, George R., ed. *Criminal Justice: Law & Politics.* 4th ed. Monterey: Brooks/Cole, 1974.

Comaroff, John, and Simon Roberts. *Rules and Processes: The Cultural Logic of Dispute in an African Context.* Chicago: University of Chicago Press, 1981.

Crime and Social Justice Collective. *Crime and Social Justice.* San Francisco: Macmillan, 1980.

Cronin, Thomas E. et al. *U.S. v. Crime in the Streets.* Bloomington: Indiana University Press, 1981.

Dershowitz, Alan M. *The Best Defense.* New York: Random House, 1982.

Devlin, Partick. *The Judge.* Oxford: Oxford University Press, 1979.

Dressler, Joshua. "Substantive Criminal Law Through the Looking Glass of *Rummel* v. *Estelle:* Proportionality and Justice as Endangered Doctrines." *Southwestern Law Review* 34 (1981): 1063–1130.

Dufee, D. et al. *Criminal Justice: Organization, Structure, and Analysis.* Englewood Cliffs: Prentice-Hall, 1978.

Ericson, Richard V., and Patricia M. Baranek. *The Ordering of Justice: A Study of Accused Persons as Dependents in the Criminal Process.* Toronto: University of Toronto Press, 1982.

Feely, Malcolm M., and Austin D. Sarat. *The Policy Dilemma: Federal Crime Policy and the Law Enforcement Assistance Administration.* Minneapolis: University of Minnesota Press, 1980.

Feinberg, Stephen E., and Albert J. Reiss, eds. *Indicators of Crime and Criminal Justice.* New York: Social Science Research Council, 1980.

Floud, Jean, and Warren Young. *Dangerousness and Criminal Justice.* Totowa, N.J.: Barnes & Noble, 1982.

Frankowski, Stanislaw. *Major Criminal Justice Systems: Criminal Law in Western Europe.* Forthcoming.

French, Laurence, ed. *Indians and Criminal Justice.* Totowa, N.J.: Allanheld, Osmun, 1982.

Foust, C.H., and D.R. Webster, eds. *An Anatomy of Criminal Justice: A System Overview.* Lexington: Lexington Books, 1980.

Graham, Michael H. *Tightening the Reins of Justice in America: A Comparative Analysis of the Criminal Jury Trial in England and the United States.* Westport, Conn.: Greenwood Press, 1983.

Gray, Virginia, and Bruce Williams. *The Organizational Politics of Criminal Justice: Policy in Context.* Lexington: Lexington Books, 1980.

Gurr, T.R. *Rogues, Rebels, and Reformers: A Political History of Urban Crime and Conflict.* Beverly Hills: Sage, 1976.

Gurr, Ted Robert et al. *The Politics of Crime and Conflict: A Comparative Study of Four Cities.* Beverly Hills: Sage, 1977.

Heumann, Milton. *Plea Bargaining: The Experiences of Prosecutors, Judges and Defense Attorneys.* Chicago: University of Chicago Press, 1978.

Holten, Gary, and Melvin E. Jones. *The System of Criminal Justice.* 2nd ed. Boston: Little, Brown, 1982.

Inciardi, J.A., and C.E. Faupel, eds. *History and Crime: Implications for Criminal Justice Policy.* Beverly Hills: Sage, 1983.

Jacoby, Joan E. *The American Prosecutor: A Search for Identity.* Lexington: Lexington Books, 1980.

Jones, David A. *Crime and Criminal Responsibility.* Chicago: Nelson-Hall, 1978.

Jones, David A. *The Law of Criminal Procedure.* Boston: Little, Brown, 1981.

Kalmanoff, Alan. *Criminal Justice.* Boston: Little, Brown, 1976.

Kalven, Harry, Jr., and Hans Zeisel. *The American Jury.* Chicago: University of Chicago Press, 1971.

Kamisar, Yale. *Police Interrogation and Confessions: Essays in Law and Policy.* Ann Arbor: University of Michigan Press, 1980.

King, Michael. *The Framework of Criminal Justice.* London: Croom Helm, 1981.

La Fave, Walter, and Austin W. Scott, Jr. *Handbook of Criminal Law.* St. Paul: West, 1972.

Levin, Martin A. *Urban Politics and the Criminal Courts.* Chicago: University of Chicago Press, 1977.

Littrell, W. Boyd. *Bureaucratic Justice: Police, Prosecutors and the Construction of Crime.* Beverly Hills: Sage, 1979.

McConville, Michael, and John Baldwin. *Courts, Prosecution, and Conviction.* Oxford: Oxford University Press, 1981.

McDonald, William F., ed. *Criminal Justice and the Victim*. Beverly Hills: Sage, 1976.

McGuigan, Patrick B. and Randall R. Roder, eds. *Criminal Justice Reform*. Chicago: Regency/Gateway, 1983.

McNeely, R. L., and Carl E. Pope, eds. *Race, Crime, and Criminal Justice*. Beverly Hills: Sage, 1981.

Michalos, Alex C. *Crime, Justice, and Politics*. Hingman, Mass.: D. Reidel, 1980.

Morash, Merry. *Implementing Criminal Justice Policies: Common Problems and Their Sources*. Beverly Hills: Sage, 1982.

Pattenden, Rosemary. *The Judge, Discretion, and the Criminal Trial*. Oxford: Oxford University Press, 1982.

Pepinsky, Harold E. *Crime Control Strategies: An Introduction to the Study of Crime*. New York: Oxford University Press, 1980.

Perkins, Rolln M., and Ronald N. Boyce. *Criminal Law*. 3rd Ed., Mineola, N.Y.: Foundation Press, 1982.

Phillips, Llad, and Harold L. Votey, Jr. *The Economics of Crime Control*. Beverly Hills: Sage, 1981.

Puttkamer, Ernst W. *Administration of Criminal Law*. Chicago: University of Chicago Press, 1953.

Radzinowicz, Sir Leon. *A History of English Criminal Law and Its Administration from 1750*. 4 vols. London: Stevens, 1948, 1956, 1956, and 1968.

Radzinowicz, Sir Leon and M.E. Wolfgang, eds. *Crime and Justice*. 2nd ed. 3 vols. New York: Basic Books, 1977.

Robbins, I.P. *Comparative Post-conviction Remedies*. Lexington: Lexington Books, 1980.

Roesch, Ronald, and Raymond R. Corrado, eds. *Evaluation and Criminal Justice Policy*. Beverly Hills: Sage, 1981.

Sigler, Jay. *Understanding Criminal Law*. Boston: Little, Brown, 1981.

Silberman, Charles E. *Criminal Violence, Criminal Justice*. New York: Random House, 1978.

Swigert, Victoria L., ed. *Law and the Legal Process*. Beverly Hills: Sage, 1982.

Vidich, Arthur J., and Ronald M. Glassman, eds. *Conflict and Control: Challenge to Legitimacy of Modern Governments*. Beverly Hills: Sage, 1979.

Von Bar, Carl L. et al. *A History of Continental Criminal Law*. New York: A.M. Kelley, 1916.

Walker, Samuel E. *Popular Justice: A History of American Criminal Justice*. New York: Oxford, 1980.

Weinreb, L.L. *Denial of Justice: Criminal Process in the United States*. New York: The Free Press, 1977.

Williams, Glanville. *Textbook of Criminal Law*. London: Stevens, 1979.

Wilson, James Q., ed. *The Politics of Crime*. San Francisco: ICS Press, 1983.

Wilson, James Q. *Thinking About Crime*. 2nd ed. New York: Basic Books, 1984.

Wolfgang, Marvin E., and Neil Alan Weiner, eds. *Criminal Violence*. Beverly Hills: Sage, 1982.

Wright, Kevin N. and Myer, Peter B. "A Systems Analysis of Crime and Control Strategies." *Criminology* 18 (1981): 531.

## CRIMINOLOGY

Abrahamsen, David. *The Psychology of Crime*. New York: Columbia University Press, 1960.

Allen, Francis A. *The Borderland of Criminal Justice: Essays in Law and Criminology*. Chicago: University of Chicago Press, 1964.

Barak-Glantz, Israel L., and Elmer H. Johnson, eds. *Comparative Criminology*. Beverly Hills: Sage, 1983.

Barlow, Hugh D. *Introduction to Criminology*. 2nd ed. Boston: Little, Brown, 1981.

Beccaria, Cesare, *On Crimes and Punishment*. Henry Paolucci, tr. (Originally published in 1764 and first translated into English in 1767.) Indianapolis: Bobbs-Merrill, 1963.

Brantingham, Paul J., and Patricia Brantingham, eds. *Environmental Criminology*. Beverly Hills: Sage, 1981.

Carlen, Pat, and Mike Collison, eds. *Radical Issues in Criminology*. Totowa, N.J.: Barnes & Noble, 1980.

Clinard, Marshall B., ed. *Anomie and Deviant Behavior*. New York: The Free Press, 1964.

Conklin, John E. *Criminology*. New York: Collier-Macmillan, 1981.

Cullen, Francis T., Jr. *Theories of Crime and Deviance: Accounting for Form and Content*. Totowa, N.J.: Allenheld, Osmun, 1983.

Davidson, R.N. *Crime and Environment*. London: Croom Helm, 1981.

Doleschal, Eugene, and Nora Klopmuts. "Toward a New Criminology." *Crime and Delinguency Literature* 5(4) (Dec. 1973): 607–626.

Downes, David, and Paul Rock. *Understanding Deviance.* Oxford: Oxford University Press, 1982.

Eckland, Bruce K. "Genetics and Sociology: A Reconsideration." *American Sociological Review* 32(3) (April 1967): 173–94.

Eysenck, H.J. *Crime and Personality.* Boston: Houghton-Mifflin, 1964.

Ferri, Enrico. *Criminal Sociology.* Boston: Little, Brown, 1917.

Ferri, Enrico. *The Positive School of Criminology.* Edited with an introduction by Stanley E. Grupp. Pittsburgh: University of Pittsburgh Press, 1968.

Fitzgerald, M. et al., eds. *Crime and Society: Readings in History and Theory.* London: Routledge and Kegan Paul, 1981.

Fletcher, G.T. *Rethinking Criminal Law.* Boston: Little, Brown, 1978.

Glasser, Daniel, ed. *Handbook of Criminology.* Chicago: Rand-McNally, 1974.

Gorecki, J. *A Theory of Criminal Justice.* New York: Columbia University Press, 1979.

Green, Gary S. "A Test of the Ortega Hypothesis in Criminology." *Criminology* 19 (1981): 45.

Gross, Hyman. *A Theory of Criminal Justice.* New York: Oxford University Press, 1979.

Hagan, John, ed. *Deterrence Reconsidered: Methodological Innovations.* Beverly Hills: Sage, 1982.

Hagan, John, ed. *Quantitative Criminology: Innovations and Applications.* Beverly Hills: Sage, 1982.

Hall, Jerome. *Law, Social Science and Criminal Theory.* New York: Rothman, 1982.

Halleck, Seymour L. *Psychiatry and the Dilemmas of Crime.* New York: Harper & Row, 1967.

Hart, H.L.A. *Punishment and Responsibility: Essays in the Philosophy of Law.* Oxford: Oxford University Press, 1968.

Hirschi, Travis, and Michael Gottfredson, eds. *Understanding Crime: Current Theory and Research.* Beverly Hills: Sage, 1980.

Hirschi, Travis, and David Rudsill. "The Great American Search: Causes of Crime 1876–1976." *Annals of the American Association of Political and Social Sciences* 423 (Jan. 1976): 14–22.

Hood, R., ed. *Crime, Criminology and Public Policy: Essays in Honour of Sir Leon Radzinowicz.* New York: Heineman, 1974.

Hooten, Ernest A. *Crime and the Man.* Cambridge: Harvard University Press, 1939. Reprint. Westport, Conn.: Greewood Press, 1968.

Hurwitz, Stephan, and Karl O. Christiansen. *Criminology.* 2nd ed. London: Allen & Unwin, 1979.

Jacoby, Joseph E., ed. *Classics of Criminology.* Oak Park, Ill.: Moore Publishing, 1979.

Jeffery, Clarence R. "The Structure of American Criminological Thinking." *Journal of Criminal Law, Criminology and Police Science* 46 (Jan.–Feb. 1956): 658–72.

Inciardi, James A., ed. *Radical Criminology: The Coming Crises.* Beverly Hills: Sage, 1980.

Kairys, David, ed. *The Politics of Law: A Progressive Critique.* New York: Pantheon, 1982.

Krisberg, Barry. *Crime and Privilege: Toward a New Criminology.* Englewood Cliffs: Prentice-Hall, 1975.

Lombroso, Cesare. *Crime: Its Causes and Remedies.* Montclair: Patterson-Smith, 1912 (1968).

Maestro, Marcello. *Voltaire and Beccaria as Reformers of Criminal Law.* New York: Columbia University Press, 1943. Reprint. New York: Octagon, 1972.

Mannheim, Hermann. *Comparative Criminology.* Boston: Houghton-Mifflin, 1965.

Mannheim, Hermann, ed. *Pioneers in Criminology.* 2nd ed. Montclair: Patterson-Smith, 1972.

McDonald, Lynn. *The Sociology of Law and Order.* Boulder: Westview Press, 1976.

Mednick, Sarnoff, and Karl O. Christianson, eds. *Biosocial Bases of Criminal Behavior.* New York: Gardner Press, 1977.

Morris, Terrence. *The Criminal Area: A Study in Social Ecology.* London: Routledge and Kegan Paul, 1957.

Pepinsky, Harold D., ed. *Rethinking Criminology: Breaking the Criminological Mould.* Beverly Hills: Sage, 1982.

Phillipson, Coleman. *Three Criminal Law Reformers: Beccaria, Bentham and Romily.* New York: Dutton, 1923. Reprint. Montclair: Patterson-Smith, 1970.

Radzinowicz, Sir Leon. *Ideology and Crime.* New York: Columbia University Press, 1966.

Rees, W.L.L. "Constitutional Psychology." In *International En-*

*cyclopedia of the Social Sciences.* New York: Macmillan and The Free Press, 1968.

Schafer, Stephen. *Theories in Criminology.* New York: Random House, 1969.

Schafer, Stephen. *The Political Criminal.* New York: The Free Press, 1974.

Sagarin, Edward. *Deviants and Deviance.* New York: Praeger, 1975.

Schuessler, Karl, ed. *Edwin H. Sutherland on Analyzing Crime.* Chicago: University of Chicago Press, 1973.

Shelley, Louise I. *Readings on Comparative Criminology.* Carbondale: Southern Illinois University Press, 1981.

Sherman, Lawrence, W. *Ethics in Criminal Justice Education.* Hastings-on-Hudson: The Hastings Center, 1982.

Struchkov, Nikolai. *Correction of the Convicted: Law, Theory, Practice.* Moscow: Progress Publishers, 1982.

Sutherland, Edwin. *White Collar Crime.* New York: Dryden Press, 1949.

Taylor, Ian et al. *The New Criminology.* London: Routledge & Kegan Paul, 1973.

Toch, Hans, ed. *Psychology of Crime and Criminal Justice.* New York: Holt, Rinehart & Winston, 1979.

Wilson, Edward O. *Sociobiology.* Cambridge: Harvard University Press, 1975.

Wolfgang, Marvin E., and Franco Ferracuti. *The Subculture of Violence: Toward an Integrated Theory in Criminology.* Beverly Hills: Sage, 1982.

Young, Jock et al. *Critical Criminology.* London: Routledge & Kegan Paul, 1975.

PUNISHMENT

*Theoretical and Ethical (Including Criminal Responsibility)*

Action, H.B., ed. *The Philosophy of Punishment.* New York: St. Martin's Press, 1969.

Allen, Francis A. *The Decline of the Rehabilitative Ideal: Penal Policy and Social Purpose.* New Haven: Yale University Press, 1981.

Andenas, J. "The Morality of Deterrence." *University of Pennsylvania Law Review* 114 (1970): 649.

Aristotle. *Nicomachean Ethics.* Book V.

Aristotle. *Rhetoric.* Chaps. 11 and 12.

Bayles, Michael D. "Character, Purpose and Criminal Responsibility." *Law and Philosophy* 1 (April 1982): 5–20.

Bean, Philip. *Punishment: A Philosophical and Criminological Inquiry.* London: Martin Robertson, 1981.

Becker, Gary. "Crime and Punishment: An Economic Approach." *Journal of Political Economy* 1976 (January–February 1969): 169–217.

Bedau, Hugo A. "Book review of Walter Berns, *For Capital Punishment: Crime and the Morality of the Death Penalty.*" *Ethics* 90: 450–52.

Bedau, Hugo A. "Retribution and the Theory of Punishment." *Journal of Philosophy* 75 (1978): 601–22.

Bedau, Hugo A., ed. *The Death Penalty in America.* 3rd ed. New York: Oxford University Press, 1982.

Bedau, Hugo A. *Retribution and the Theory of Punishment.* Totowa, N.J.: Rowman & Littlefield, 1982.

Benn, Stanley, I. "An Approach to the Problem of Punishment." *Philosophy* 33 (1958): 334–37.

Berns, Walter. *For Capital Punishment: Crime and the Morality of the Death Penalty.* New York: Basic Books 1979.

Bentham, Jeremy. *An Introduction to the Principles of Morals and Legislation.* Edited by J.H. Burns and H.L.A. Hart. London: Macmillan, 1982.

Black, Charles. *Capital Punishment: The Inevitability of Caprice and Mistake.* 2 ed. New York: W.W. Norton, 1981.

Bodenheimer, Edgar. "Is Punishment Obsolete?" In Carl J. Friedrich, ed. *Responsibility (NOMOS III).* New York: Lieber Atherton, 1960.

Brandt, Richard B. "The Conditions of Criminal Responsibility." In Carl J. Friedrich, ed. *Responsibility (NOMOS III).* New York: Lieber Atherton, 1960.

Davis, Michael. "Sentencing: Must Justice be Evenhanded?" *Law and Philosophy* 1 (April 1982): 77–118.

Davis, Michael. "How to Make the Punishment Fit the Crime." *Ethics* 93 (July 1983).

Davitt, Thomas E. "Criminal Responsibility and Punishment." In Carl J. Friedrich, ed. *Responsibility (NOMOS III).* New York: Lieber Atherton, 1960.

Donnelly, S.J.M. "A Theory of Justice, Judicial Methodology and the Constitutionality of Capital Punishment: Rawls, Dworkin and a Theory of Criminal Responsibility." *Syracuse Law Review* 29 (1978): 1109–1174.

Feinberg, Joel. On Justifying Legal Punishment. In Carl J. Friedrich, ed. *Responsibility (NOMOS III)*. New York: Lieber Atherton, 1960.

Fletcher, George. "Punishment and Compensation." *Creighton Law Review* 14 (1981): 691–705.

Gardner, R.L. "Capital Punishment: The Philosophers and the Court." *Syracuse Law Review.* 29 (1978): 1175–1216.

Goldberg, S. "On Capital Punishment." *Ethics.* 85 (1974): 67–74.

Goldman, Alan H. "Toward a New Theory of Punishment." *Law and Philosophy* 1 (April 1982): 57–76.

Goldstein, Abraham S. *The Insanity Defense.* New Haven: Yale University Press, 1967.

Lehtinen, M.W. "The Value of Life—An Argument for the Death Peanlty." *Crime and Delinquency* 23 (1977): 237–252.

Lempert, Richard. "Desert and Deterrence: An Assessment of the Moral Bases of the Case for Capitol Punishment." *University of Michigan Law Review* 49 (1981): 1171–1231.

Mackenzie, Mary Margaret. *Plato on Punishment.* Berkeley: University of California Press, 1982.

Moran, Richard. *Knowing Right From Wrong: The Insanity Defense of Daniel MacNaughtan.* New York: The Free Press, 1982.

Morris, Herbert. "Persons and Punishments." *Monist* 52 (1968): 475–501.

Morris, Norval. *Madness and the Criminal Law.* Chicago: University of Chicago Press, 1982.

Murphy, Jeffrey G. "Morrison and Retribution." *Philosophy and Public Affairs* 2 (1973): 217–243.

Murphy, Jeffrey G. *Retribution, Justice, and Therapy: Essays in the Philosophy of Law.* Hingman, Mass.: D. Reidel, 1979.

Pincoffs, E. *The Rationale of Legal Punishment.* New York: Humanities Press, 1966.

Plamenatz, John. "Responsibility, Blame and Punishment." In Peter Laslett and W.G. Runciman, eds. *Philosophy, Politics and Society: Third Series.* Oxford: Basil Blackwell, 1967.

Quinney, Richard. *Critique of Legal Order: Crime Control in Capitalist Society.* Boston: Little, Brown, 1974.

Quinney, Richard. *The Social Reality of Crime*. Boston: Little, Brown, 1970.

Quinton, Anthony. "On Punishment." In Peter Laslett, ed. *Philosophy, Politics and Society*. London: Macmillan, 1956.

Richards, David A.J. "Human Rights and the Moral Foundations of the Substantive Criminal Law." *Georgia Law Review* 13 (1979): 1395–1446.

Ross, A. *On Guilt, Responsibility, and Punishment*. London: Stevens, 1975.

Smith, G.W. "The Value of Life—Arguments Against the Death Penalty: A Reply to Professor Lehtinen." *Crime and Delinquency* 23 (1977): 253–259.

Smith, Roger. *Trial by Medicine: The Insanity Defense in Victorian England*. New York: Columbia University Press, 1981.

Stone, Lawrence. "Madness." *The New York Review of Books* (December 1982).

Symposium. "Punishment: Critiques and Justifications." *Rutgers Law Review* 33 (1981): 607–864.

Szasz, Thomas S. *The Myth of Mental Illness: Foundations of a Theory of Personal Conduct*. New York: Hoeber-Harper, 1961.

Szasz, Thomas S. *Psychiatric Justice*. New York: Macmillan, 1965.

Szasz, Thomas S. "The Insanity Plea and the Verdict." *Temple Law Quarterly* 40 (Spring–Summer 1967): 271–282.

Vatz, Richard E., and Lee S. Weinberg, eds. *Thomas Szasz: Primary Values and Major Contentions*. Buffalo: Prometheus, 1983.

Van den Haag, E. *Punishing Criminals: Concerning a Very Old and Painful Question*. New York: Basic Books, 1975.

Walker, Nigel. *Punishment, Danger and Stigma: The Morality of Criminal Justice*. Totowa, N.J.: Barnes & Noble, 1981.

Weihofen, Henry. "Retribution Is Obsolete." In Carl J. Friedrich, ed. *Responsibility (NOMOS III)*. New York: Lieber Atherton, 1960.

Wertheimer, A. "Should Punishment Fit the Crime." *Social Theory and Practice* 3 (1975): 403–423.

Wilcox, William. "Taking a Good Look at the Bad Man's Point of View." *Cornell Law Review* 66 (1981): 1058–1073.

Wolfe, Nancy Travis. "Mala In Se: A Disappearing Doctrine?" *Criminology* 19 (1981).

Not included in this bibliography are any statistical articles on the deterrent effect of capital punishment on the commission of criminal homocide. Hugo Adam Bedau, ed., *The Death Penalty In America,* 3rd ed., 1982, contains a good discussion of the issue, pp. 95–185, as well as an extensive bibliography.


*Corrections*

Anttila, Inkeri. "Punishment Versus Treatment—Is There a Third Alternative?" *Abstracts on Criminology and Penology* 12 (1972): 287–90.

Argow, Claire. "Corrections in the Community: Multnomach County, Oregon." *Corrections Today* 1980 (Jan.–Feb.): 28.

Austin, James, and Barry Krisberg, "The Unmet Promise of Alternatives to Incarceration." *Crime & Delinquency* 28 (1982): 374.

Barnes, Harry Elmer. *The Story of Punishment: A Record of Man's Inhumanity to Man.* 2nd rev. ed. Montclair: Patterson-Smith, 1972.

Bayer, Ronald. "Crime, Punishment and the Decline of Liberal Optimism." *Crime & Delinquency* (1981): 169.

Bowher, Lee E. "Crime and the Use of Prisons in the United States: A Time Series Analysis." 1981, *Crime & Delinquency* (1981): 206.

Box, Steven, and Chris Hale. "Economic Crisis and the Rising Prison Population in England and Wales." *Crime & Social Justice* (Summer 1982): 20.

Carlson, Eric N. "ACA Policy on Community Based Corrections." *Corrections Today* (Jan.–Feb. 1980):18.

Carlson, Eric N. "Field Testing Pre-release Centers." *Corrections Today* (Jan.–Feb. 1980): 18.

Christoph, James B. *Punishment and British Politics.* Chicago: University of Chicago Press, 1962.

Clements, Carl B. "The Relationship of Offender Classification to the Problems of Prison Overcrowding." *Crime & Delinquency* 28 (1982): 72.

Coontz, Phyllis. "Women on Death Row." *The Prison Journal* vol. LXIII, no. 2 Autumn–Winter, 1983.

David, Marjorie. "Canadian Correctional Industries: The Total Perspective." *Corrections Today* (Nov.–Dec. 1981): 73.

Fine, Bob. "The Birth of Bourgeoise Punishment." *Crime & Social Justice* (Summer 1980): 19.

Fitzgerald, Mike, and Joe Sim. *British Prisons*. Oxford: Blackwell, 1979.

Fogel, David. *We Are The Living Proof of The Justice Model for Corrections*. Cincinnati: Anderson, 1975.

Forer, Lois G. *Criminals and Victims: A Trial Judge Reflects on Crime and Punishment*. New York: W.W. Norton, 1980.

Foucault, Michel. *Discipline and Punish: The Birth of the Prison*. Tranlated by Alan Sheridan. New York: Pantheon, 1977.

Fowler, Lorraine. "Managing Correctional Change." *Corrections Today* (May–June 1981): 10.

Friedman, Lawrence M., and Robert V. Percival. *The Roots of Justice: Crime and Punishment in Alameda County, California, 1870–1910*. Chapel Hill: Univeristy of North Carolina Press, 1981.

Goetting, Ann. "Conjugal Association in Prison: Issues and Perspectives." *Crime & Delinquency* 28 (1982): 52.

Goldfarb, Ronald L., and Linda R. Singer. *After Conviction: A Review of the American Correction System*. New York: Simon & Schuster, 1973.

Grisson, Grant R., and Coran N. Louis. "The Evolution of Prison Industries." *Corrections Today* (Nov.–Dec. 1981): 42.

Hawkins, Gordon. *The Prison: Policy and Practice*. Chicago: University of Chicago Press, 1976.

Hylton, John H. "Rhetoric and Reality: A Critical Appraisal of Community Correctional Programs." *Crime & Delinquency* 28 (1982): 341.

Hylton, John H. "The Growth of Punishment: Imprisonment and Community Corrections in Canada." *Crime & Social Justice* (Summer 1981): 18.

Ignatieff, M. *A Just Measure of Pain: Penitentiary in the Industrial Revolution: 1750–1850*. London: Macmillan, 1978.

Jacobs, James. B. *Stateville: The Penitentiary in Mass Society*. Chicago: University of Chicago Press, 1977.

Jones, David A. *The Health Risks of Imprisonment*. Lexington: Lexington Books, 1976.

Jones, David A. *Crime Without Punishment*. Lexington: Lexington Books, 1979.

Koontz, John F., Jr. "Pragmatic Conditions of Probation." *Corrections Today* (Jan.–Feb. 1980): 14.

McDonald, Douglas. *The Price of Punishment: Public Spending for Corrections in New York*. Boulder: Westview, 1980.

McKelvey, Blake. *American Prisons: A History of Good Intentions.* Montclair: Patterson-Smith, 1977.

Martinson, Robert. "What Works? Questions and Answers About Prison Reform." *The Public Interest* (Spring 1974): 22–54.

Mawly, R.I. "Women in Prison: A British Study." *Crime & Delinquency* 28 (1982): 24.

Melossi, Dario, and Massimo Pavarini. *The Prison and the Factory: Origins of the Penitentiary System.* Translated by Glynis Cousin. Totowa, N.J.: Barnes & Noble, 1981.

Miller, Martin B. "Sinking Gradually into the Proletariat: The Emergence of the Penitentiary in the United States." *Crime & Social Justice* (Winter 1980): 37.

Moberly, Sir Walter. *The Ethics of Punishment.* Hamden, Conn.: Archon Books, 1968.

Morris, Norval. *The Future of Imprisonment.* Chicago: University of Chicago Press, 1974.

Murton, Thomas O. *The Dilemma of Prison Reform.* New York: Holt, Rinehart & Winston, 1976.

Nemerson, Steven. "Coercive Sentencing." *Minnesota Law Review* 64 (1980): 669–750.

O'Brien, Patricia. *The Promise of Punishment: Prisons in Nineteenth-Century France.* Princeton: Princeton University Press, 1981.

Petersilia, Joan. "The Career Criminal and Prison Management." *Corrections Today* (May–June 1981): 42.

Platt, Tony. "Crime and Punishment in the United States: Immediate and Long Term Reforms From a Marxist Perspective." *Crime & Social Justice* (Winter 1982): 38.

Poole, Eric D., and Robert M. Reyoli. "Alienation in Prison: An Exmaination of the Work Relations of Prison Guards." *Criminology* 19 (1981): 251.

Poole, Eric D., and Robert M. Reyoli. "Periodical Prestige in Criminology and Criminal Justice: A Comment." *Criminology* 19 (1981): 470.

Pugh, R.G. *Imprisonment in Medieval England.* Chicago: University of Chicago Press, 1968.

Ross, R.R., and P. Gendreau. *Effective Correctional Treatment.* London: Butterworth, 1980.

Rusche, George. "Prison Revolts or Social Policy: Lessons From America." *Crime & Social Justice* (Summer 1980): 41.

Schechor, David, Robert M. O'Brien, and David L. Decher.

"Prestige in Journals in Criminology and Criminal Justice." *Criminology* 19 (1981): 461.

Sellin, Thurston. *The Penalty of Death.* Beverly Hills: Sage, 1980.

Sharpe, J.A. *Crime in Seventeenth-Century England.* Cambridge: Cambridge University Press, 1983.

Sherman, Michael, and Gordon Hawkins. *Imprisonment In America: Choosing the Future.* San Francisco: Jossey-Bass, 1983.

Stinchcombe, Arthur L. et al. *Crime and Punishment: Changing Attitudes in America.* San Francisco: Jossey-Bass, 1980.

Tefft, Larry. "Capitol Punishment Research, Policy, and Ethics: Defining Murder and Placing Murderers." *Crime & Social Justice* (Summer 1982): 61.

Telaroyan, Timothy J. "Correctional Policy and the Long-Term Prisoner." *Crime & Delinquency* 28 (1982): 82.

Toby, Jackson. "Deterrence Without Punishment." *Criminology* 19 (1981): 195.

Weisser, M.R. *Crime and Punishment in Early Modern Europe.* London: Harvester, 1981.

Wooten, Barbara. *Crime and Penal Policy: Reflections on Five Years' Experience.* London: Allen & Unwin, 1978.

Wright, Martin. *Prisons, Punishment and Beyond.* New York: Humanities Press, 1982.

Zehr, H. *Crime and the Development of Modern Society.* London: Croom Helm, 1976.

Zimmerman, Sherwood E., and Harold D. Miller, eds. *Corrections at the Crossroads: Designing Policy.* Beverly Hills: Sage, 1981.

Zimring, Franklin E., and Gordon J. Hawkins. *Deterrence: The Legal Threat in Crime Control.* Chicago: University of Chicago Press, 1973.

## WHITE COLLAR, POLITICAL, AND ORGANIZED CRIME

Albanese, Jay S. "What Lockheed and La Cosa Nostra Have in Common: The Effect of Ideology on Criminal Justice Policy." *Crime & Delinquency* 28 (1982): 211.

Anderson, Annelise, G. *The Business of Organized Crime: A Cosa Nostra Family.* Stanford: Hoover Institution Press, 1979.

Aronson, Harvey. *The Killing of Joey Gallo.* New York: New American Library, 1973.

Bacon, Seldon D. "Review of Sutherland, *White Collar Crime*." *American Sociological Review* 15 (April 1950): 309–310.

Barnett, Harold C. "Corporate Capitalism, Corporate Crime." *Crime & Delinquency* (1981): 4.

Bequai, A. *Computer Crime*. Lexington: Lexington Books, 1978.

Bickel, Alexander M. "Watergate and the Legal Order." *Commentary* 57 (January 1974): 19–25.

Braithwaite, John, and Gilbert Geis. "On Theory and Action for Corporate Crime Control." *Crime & Delinquency* 28 (1982): 292.

Brill, Harry. "Auto Theft and the Role of Big Business." *Crime & Social Justice* (Winter 1982): 62.

Chambliss, William J. "Vice, Corruption, Bureaucracy, and Power." *Wisconsin Law Review* 4 (1971): 1150–73.

Clinard, Marshall B. *Corporate Ethics and Crime: The Role of Middle Management*. Beverly Hills: Sage, 1983.

Conklin, John E. *Illegal But Not Criminal*. Englewood Cliffs: Prentice-Hall, 1977.

Cressey, Donald R. *Criminal Organization: Its Elementary Forms*. New York: Harper & Row, 1972.

Cressey, Donald R. *Other People's Money: The Social Psychology of Embezzlement*. New York: The Free Press. 1953.

Cressey, Donald R. *Theft of a Nation*. New York: Harper & Row, 1969.

Dershowitz, Alan M. "Increasing Community Control over Corporate Crime: A Problem in the Law of Sanctions." *Yale Law Journal* 71 (September 1961): 289–306.

"Economic Crimes—The Proposed New Federal Criminal Code." *Business Lawyer* 27 (November 1971): 177–193.

Edelhertz, Herbert. *The Nature, Impact and Prosecution of White-Collar Crime*. Washington, D.C.: Government Printing Office, 1970.

Edelhertz, Herbert, and Charles Rogovin, eds. *A National Strategy for Containing White-Collar Crime*. Lexington: Lexington Books, 1980.

Emerson, Thomas I. "Review of Sutherland, *White Collar Crime*." *Yale Law Journal* 59 (January 1950): 581–585.

Ermann, M. David, and Richard J. Lundman, eds. *Corporate and Governmental Deviance*. New York: Oxford University Press, 1978.

Fein, C.C. "Corporate Responsibility Under Criminal Law: A

Study of the Mens Rea." *Manitoba Law Review* 5 (1973): 422–439.

Geis, Gilbert, and Ezra Stotland, eds. *White Collar Crime: Theory and Research.* Beverly Hills: Sage, 1980.

Geis, Gilbert, and Robert F. Meier, eds. *White Collar Crime:* Offenses in Business, Politics, and the Professions. Rev. ed. New York: The Free Press, 1977.

Horozowski, Pawel. *Economic Special Opportunity Conduct and Crime.* Lexington: Lexington Books, 1980.

Ianni, Francis A.J. *Black Mafia: Ethnic Succession in Organized Crime.* New York: Simon & Schuster, 1974.

Ianni, Francis A.J., and Elizabeth Reuss-Ianni. *A Family Business: Kinship and Social Control of Organized Crime.* New York: Russell Sage, 1972.

Inciardi, James A. "Vocational Crime." In Daniel Glaser, ed. *Handbook of Criminology.* Chicago: Rand-McNally, 1974.

Jacoby, Neil H., Peter Nehemkis, and Richard Eells. *Bribery and Extortion in World Business: A Study of Corporate Political Payments Abroad.* New York: Macmillan, 1977.

Jones, Kelvin. *Law and Economy: The Legal Regulation of Corporate Capitalism.* New York: Academic Press, 1983.

Kelly, Robert, ed. *Organized Crime: A Global Perspective.* Totowa, N.J.: Allenheld, Osmun, 1983.

Klockars, Carl B. "White Collar Crime." In Edward Sagarin and Fred Montanino, eds., *Deviants: Voluntary Actors in a Hostile World.* Morristown N.J.: General Learning Press, 1977.

Kuehn, Lowell L. "Syndicated Crime in America." In Edward Sagarin and Fred Montanino, eds. *Deviants: Voluntary Actors in a Hostile World.* Morristown N.J.: General Learning Press, 1977.

Kurland, Phillip. *Watergate and the Constitution.* Chicago: University of Chicago Press, 1978.

Leigh, L.H., ed. *Economic Crime in Europe.* New York: St. Martin's Press, 1981.

Leigh, Leonard H. *The Criminal Liability of Corporations in English Law.* London: Weidenfeld & Nicolson, 1969.

Maas, Peter. *The Valachi Papers.* New York: Putnam, 1968.

Mueller, Gerhard O.W. "Mens Rea and the Corporation: A Study of the Model Penal Code Position on Corporate Criminal Liability." *University of Pittsburgh Law Review* 19 (Fall 1957): 21–50.

National Chamber of Commerce. *A Handbook on White Collar Crime.* Washington, D.C.: Chamber of Commerce of the United States, 1974.

Newman, Donald J. "The Agnew Plea Bargain." *Criminal Law Bulletin* 10 (January–February 1974): 85–90.

Ogren, Robert W. "The Ineffectiveness of the Criminal Sanction in Fraud and Corruption Cases: Losing the Battle Against White-Collar Crime." *American Criminal Law Review* 11 (Summer 1973): 959–988.

Packer, Herbert L. *The Limits of the Criminal Sanction.* Stanford: Stanford University Press, 1968.

Parker, Donn D. *Crime by Computer.* New York: Scribners, 1982.

President's Commission on Law Enforcement and Administration of Justice. *Task Force Report: Organized Crime.* Washington, D.C.: U.S. Government Printing Office, 1967.

Rossi, Peter, H., Emily Waite, Christine E. Rose, and Richard E. Berk. "The Seriousness of Crimes: Normative Structure and Individual Differences." *American Sociological Review* 39 (April 1974): 224–237.

Schwenk, Edmund H. "The Administrative Crime, Its Creation and Punishment by Administrative Agencies." *Michigan Law Review* 42 (August 1943): 51–86.

Sherwin, Robert. "White Collar Crime, Conventional Crime and Merton's Deviant Behavior Theory." *Wisconsin Sociologist* 2 (Spring 1963): 7–10.

Scott, James C. *Comparative Political Corruption.* Englewood Cliffs: Prentice-Hall, 1972.

Simis, Konstantin. "The Machinery of Corruption in the Soviet Union." *Survey* (1979): 36–55.

Sobel, Lester A., ed. *Corruption in Business.* New York: Facts on File, 1977.

Sorenson, Robert C. "Review of Sutherland, *White Collar Crime.*" *Journal of Criminal Law, Criminology and Police Science* 41 (May–June 1950): 80–82.

Sutherland, Edwin H. *White Collar Crime.* New York: Holt, Rinehart & Winston, 1961.

Tompkins, Dorothy C. *White Collar Crime—A Bibliography.*

Berkeley: Berkeley Institute of Governmental Studies, University of California, 1967.

Turk, Austin E. *Political Criminality: The Defiance and Defense of Authority.* Beverly Hills: Sage, 1982.


POLICE AND POLICING

Bennett, Richard R., ed. *Police at Work: Policy Issues and Analysis.* Beverly Hills: Sage, 1983.

Berkely, George E. *The Democratic Policeman.* Boston: Beacon Press, 1969.

Biegel, Herbert. "The Investigation and Prosecution of Police Corruption." *Journal of Criminal Law and Criminology* 65 (1974): 135–156.

Binder, Arnold. "Deadly Force in Law Enforcement." *Crime & Delinquency* 28 (1982): 1.

Bordua, David J., ed. *The Police: Six Sociological Essays.* New York: John Wiley, 1967.

Blalock, Joyce. *Civil Liability of Law Enforcement Officers.* Springfield, Ill.: Charles C. Thomas, 1974.

Broadaway, Fred M. "Police Misconduct: Positive Alternatives." *Journal of Police Science and Administration* 2 (1974): 210–218.

Burger, Warren E. "Who Will Watch the Watchman?" *American University Law Review* 14 (1964): 1–23.

Caplan, Gerald M. "The Police Legal Advisor." *Journal of Criminal Law, Criminology and Police Science* 58 (1967): 303–309.

Colley, J.W. "Police Discretion." *Abstracts on Police Science* 2 (1974): 131–137.

Cumming, Elaine, Ian Cumming, and Laura Edell. "Policeman as Philospher, Guide and Friend." *Social Problems* 12 (1965): 276–286.

Davis, Kenneth Culp. "An Approach to Legal Control of the Police." *Texas Law Review* 52 (1974): 703–725.

Davis, Kenneth Culp. *Police Discretion.* St. Paul: West, 1975.

Givelber, Nathan. *The Differential Selection of Juvenile Offenders for Court Appearance.* New York: National Council on Crime and Delinquency, 1963.

Goldstein, Herman. "Administrative Problems in Controlling the Exercise of Police Authority." *Journal of Criminal Law, Criminology and Police Science* 58 (1967): 160–172.

Goldstein, Herman. *Policing in a Free Society.* Cambridge: Ballinger, 1977.

Elliston, Frederick, and Michael Feldberg, eds. *Moral Issues in Policing.* Totowa, N.J.: Rowman & Littlefield, 1983.

Ehrlich, Isaac. "Participation in Illegitimate Activities: A Theoretical and Empirical Investigation." *Journal of Political Economy* 81 (1973): 531–565.

Hall, Jerome. "Police and Law in a Democratic Society." *Indiana Law Journal* 28 (1953): 133–177.

Hart, J.M. *The British Police.* London: Allen & Unwin, 1951.

Holdaway, Simon, ed. *The British Police.* Beverly Hills: Sage, 1980.

Jones, David. *Crime, Protest, Community and Police in Nineteenth-Century Britain.* London: Routledge & Kegan Paul, 1982.

Knapp Commission (Commission to Investigate Allegations of Police Corruption and the City's Anti-corruption Procedures). *Commission Report.* New York, 1974.

LaFave, Wayne R. "Improving Police Performance Through the Exclusionary Rule." *Missouri Law Review* 30 (1965): 391–458, 566–610.

Liberman, Ronald. "Police as a Community Mental Health Resource." *Community Mental Health Journal* 5 (1969): 111–120.

Lundman, Richard J. *Police Behavior: A Sociological Perspective.* Oxford: Oxford University Press: 1980.

McConville, Sean. *A History of English Prison Administration. Volume I: 1750–1877.* London: Routledge & Kegan Paul, 1981.

McGee, R.A. *Prisons and Politics.* Lexington: Lexington Books, 1981.

Manning, Peter K. *Police Work: The Social Organization of Policing.* Cambridge: Massachusetts Institute of Technology, 1977.

Marx, Gary T. "Who Really Gets Stung? Some Issues Raised by the New Police Undercover Work." *Crime & Delinquency* 28 (1982): 165.

Mawly, R.I. "Overcoming the Barriers of Privacy: Police Strategies Against Nonvisible Crime." *Criminology* 18 (1981): 501.

Miller, Wilbur R. *Cops and Bobbies: Police Authority in New York and London, 1830–1870.* Chicago: University of Chicago Press, 1977.

Monkkonen, Eric H. *Police in Urban America: 1860–1920.* Cambridge: Cambridge University Press, 1981.

Murphy, Patrick V. "A Decade of Urban Police Problems." Six-

teenth Annual Wherett Lecture on Local Government. Pittsburgh: Institute for Urban Policy and Administration, Graduate School of Public and International Affairs, University of
Pittsburgh, 1974.

National Advisory Commission on Civil Disorders. *Report of the
National Advisory Commission on Civil Disorders.* Washington,
D.C.: Government Printing Office, 1968.

Pennsylvania Crime Commission. *Report on Police Corruption and
the Quality of Law Enforcement in Philadelphia.* Saint Davids, Pa.:
The Commission, 1974.

Pope, David, and Norman Weiner, eds. *Modern Policing.* London: Croom Helm, 1981.

Price, Barbara R. "Police Corruption: An Analysis." *Criminology*
10 (1972): 161–176.

Reuss-Ianni, Elizabeth. *Two Cultures of Policing: Street Cops and
Management Officers.* New York: Transaction Books, 1982.

Sherman, Lawrence W., ed. *Police Corruption: A Sociological Perspective.* Garden City, N.Y.: Anchor Press, 1974.

Skolnick, Jerome H. *Justice Without Trial: Law Enforcement in
Democratic Society.* New York: John Wiley, 1966.

"The Scarman Report and the Police." *The Political Quarterly* 53
(April–June 1982).

Tobias, J. J. *Crime and Police in England: 1700–1900.* New York:
St. Martin's Press, 1979.

Toch, Hans, J. Douglas Grant, and Raymond T. Galvin. *Agents
of Change: A Study in Police Reform.* New York: John Wiley,
1975.

Weiner, Norman L. "The Effect of Education of Police Attitudes." *Journal of Criminal Justice* 2 (1974): 317–328.

Wilson, James Q. "The Police and Their Problems: A Theory."
*Public Policy* 12 (1963): 189–216.

Wilson, James Q. *Varieties of Police Behavior: The Management of
Law and Order in Eight Communities.* Cambridge: Harvard
University Press, 1969.

Wilson, Jerry V., and Geoffrey Alprin. "Controlling Police
Conduct: Alternatives to the Exclusionary Rule." *Law and
Contemporary Problems* 36 (1971): 488–499.

# INDEX